5-

The Lovers who exchanged Fans.
(See page 245*)*

MYTHS AND LEGENDS OF JAPAN

F. HADLAND DAVIS

Illustrated by Evelyn Paul

DOVER PUBLICATIONS, INC., NEW YORK

DEDICATED TO
MY WIFE

Published in Canada by General Publishing Company, Ltd., 30 Lesmill Road, Don Mills, Toronto, Ontario.

Published in the United Kingdom by Constable and Company, Ltd., 3 The Lanchesters, 162–164 Fulham Palace Road, London W6 9ER.

This Dover edition, first published in 1992, is an unabridged republication of the work originally published by George G. Harrap & Company, London, 1913. The 32 plates, originally in color, are reproduced here in black and white, and the position of many of the plates has been altered.

Manufactured in the United States of America
Dover Publications, Inc., 31 East 2nd Street, Mineola, N.Y. 11501

Library of Congress Cataloging-in-Publication Data

Davis, F. Hadland (Frederick Hadland)
    [Myths & legends of Japan]
    Myths and legends of Japan / F. Hadland Davis.
        p.   cm.
    Originally published: Myths & legends of Japan. London : G.G. Harrap & Co., 1913.
    Includes bibliographical references and indexes.
    ISBN 0-486-27045-9 (pbk.)
    1. Folklore—Japan. 2. Legends—Japan. 3. Mythology, Japanese.
I. Title.
GR340.D3   1992
398'.0952—dc20   91-37288
                                                              CIP

PREFACE

IN writing *Myths and Legends of Japan* I have been much indebted to numerous authorities on Japanese subjects, and most especially to Lafcadio Hearn, who first revealed to me the Land of the Gods. It is impossible to enumerate all the writers who have assisted me in preparing this volume. I have borrowed from their work as persistently as Japan has borrowed from other countries, and I sincerely hope that, like Japan herself, I have made good use of the material I have obtained from so many sources.

I am indebted to Professor Basil Hall Chamberlain for placing his work at my disposal, and I have found his encyclopædic volume, *Things Japanese*, his translation of the *Kojiki*, his *Murray's Hand-book for Japan* (in collaboration with W. B. Mason), and his *Japanese Poetry*, of great value. I thank the Executors of the late Dr. W. G. Aston for permission to quote from this learned authority's work. I have made use of his translation of the *Nihongi* (*Transactions of the Japan Society*, 1896) and have gathered much useful material from *A History of Japanese Literature*. I am indebted to Mr. F. Victor Dickins for allowing me to make use of his translation of the *Taketori Monogatari* and the *Hō-jō-ki*. My friend Mrs. C. M. Salwey has taken a sympathetic interest in my work, which has been invaluable to me. Her book, *Fans of Japan*, has supplied me with an exquisite legend, and many of her articles have yielded a rich harvest. I warmly thank Mr. Yone Noguchi for allowing me to quote from his poetry, and also Miss Clara A. Walsh for so kindly putting at my disposal her fascinating volume, *The Master-Singers of Japan*, published by Mr. John Murray in the " Wisdom of the East " series. My thanks are due to Messrs. Houghton, Mifflin Company, for allowing me to quote from Lafcadio Hearn's *Glimpses of Unfamiliar Japan* and *The Japanese Letters of Lafcadio Hearn*; to Messrs. George Allen & Sons, for giving me permission to quote from Sir F. T. Piggott's *Garden of Japan*; to the Editor of the *Academy*, for permitting me to reprint my article on "Japanese Poetry," and to Messrs. Cassell and Co. Ltd., for allowing me to reproduce "The Garden of Japan," which I originally contributed to *Cassell's Magazine*. The works of Dr. William Anderson, Sir Ernest Satow, Lord Redesdale, Madame Ozaki, Mr. R. Gordon Smith, Captain F. Brinkley, the late Rev. Arthur Lloyd, Mr. Henri L. Joly, Mr. K. Okakura, the Rev. W. E. Griffis, and others, have been of immense value to me, and in addition I very warmly thank all those writers I have left unnamed, through want of space, whose works have assisted me in the preparation of this volume.

CONTENTS

CONTENTS

LIST OF ILLUSTRATIONS

INTRODUCTION

PIERRE LOTI in *Madame Chrysanthème*, Gilbert and Sullivan in *The Mikado*, and Sir Edwin Arnold in *Seas and Lands*, gave us the impression that Japan was a real fairyland in the Far East. We were delighted with the prettiness and quaintness of that country, and still more with the prettiness and quaintness of the Japanese people. We laughed at their topsyturvy ways, regarded the Japanese woman, in her rich-coloured *kimono*, as altogether charming and fascinating, and had a vague notion that the principal features of Nippon were the tea-houses, cherry-blossom, and *geisha*. Twenty years ago we did not take Japan very seriously. We still listen to the melodious music of *The Mikado*, but now we no longer regard Japan as a sort of glorified willow-pattern plate. The Land of the Rising Sun has become the Land of the Risen Sun, for we have learnt that her quaintness and prettiness, her fairy-like manners and customs, were but the outer signs of a great and progressive nation. To-day we recognise Japan as a power in the East, and her victory over the Russian has made her army and navy famous throughout the world.

The Japanese have always been an imitative nation, quick to absorb and utilise the religion, art, and social life of China, and, having set their own national seal upon what they have borrowed from the Celestial Kingdom, to look elsewhere for material that should strengthen and advance their position. This imitative quality is one of Japan's most marked characteristics. She has ever been loath to impart information to others, but ready at all times to gain access to any form of knowledge likely to make for her advancement. In the fourteenth century Kenkō wrote in his *Tsure-dzure-*

INTRODUCTION

gusa : " Nothing opens one's eyes so much as travel, no matter where," and the twentieth-century Japanese has put this excellent advice into practice. He has travelled far and wide, and has made good use of his varied observations. Japan's power of imitation amounts to genius. East and West have contributed to her greatness, and it is a matter of surprise to many of us that a country so long isolated and for so many years bound by feudalism should, within a comparatively short space of time, master our Western system of warfare, as well as many of our ethical and social ideas, and become a great world-power. But Japan's success has not been due entirely to clever imitation, neither has her place among the foremost nations been accomplished with such meteor-like rapidity as some would have us suppose.

We hear a good deal about the New Japan to-day, and are too prone to forget the significance of the Old upon which the present *régime* has been founded. Japan learnt from England, Germany and America all the tactics of modern warfare. She established an efficient army and navy on Western lines ; but it must be remembered that Japan's great heroes of to-day, Togo and Oyama, still have in their veins something of the old *samurai* spirit, still reflect through their modernity something of the meaning of *Bushido*. The Japanese character is still Japanese and not Western. Her greatness is to be found in her patriotism, in her loyalty and whole-hearted love of her country. Shintōism has taught her to revere the mighty dead ; Buddhism, besides adding to her religious ideals, has contributed to her literature and art, and Christianity has had its effect in introducing all manner of beneficent social reforms.

There are many conflicting theories in regard to the racial origin of the Japanese people, and we have no definite knowledge on the subject. The first inhabitants of Japan were probably the Ainu, an Aryan people who possibly came from North-Eastern Asia at a time when the distance separating the Islands from the mainland was not so great as it is to-day. The Ainu were followed by two distinct Mongol invasions, and these invaders had no difficulty in subduing their predecessors ; but in course of time the Mongols were driven northward by Malays from the Philippines. "By the year A.D. 500 the Ainu, the Mongol, and the Malay elements in the population had become one nation by much the same process as took place in England after the Norman Conquest. To the national characteristics it may be inferred that the Ainu contributed the power of resistance, the Mongol the intellectual qualities, and the Malay that handiness and adaptability which are the heritage of sailor-men."[1] Such authorities as Baelz and Rein are of the opinion that the Japanese are Mongols, and although they have intermarried with the Ainu, "the two nations," writes Professor B. H. Chamberlain, "are as distinct as the whites and reds in North America." In spite of the fact that the Ainu is looked down upon in Japan, and regarded as a hairy aboriginal of interest to the anthropologist and the showman, a poor despised creature, who worships the bear as the emblem of strength and fierceness, he has, nevertheless, left his mark upon Japan. Fuji was possibly a corruption of Huchi, or Fuchi, the Ainu Goddess of Fire, and there is no doubt that these aborigines originated a vast number of geographical names, particularly in the north of the main island, that are recognisable to this day. We can also trace Ainu influence in regard to certain Japanese superstitions, such as the belief in the *Kappa*, or river monster.

[1] *The Full Recognition of Japan*, by Robert P. Porter.

INTRODUCTION

The Chinese called Japan Jih-pén, "the place the sun comes from," because the archipelago was situated on the east of their own kingdom, and our word Japan and Nippon are corruptions of Jih-pén. Marco Polo called the country Zipangu, and one ancient name describes it as "The-Luxuriant-Reed-Plains-the-land-of-Fresh-Rice-Ears-of-a-Thousand-Autumns-of-Long-Five-Hundred-Autumns." We are not surprised to find that such a very lengthy and descriptive title is not used by the Japanese to-day; but it is of interest to know that the old word for Japan, Yamato, is still frequently employed, Yamato Damashii signifying "The Spirit of Unconquerable Japan." Then, again, we still hear Japan referred to as The Island of the Dragon-fly. We are told in the old Japanese *Chronicles* that the Emperor, in 630 B.C., ascended a hill called Waki Kamu no Hatsuma, from which he was able to view the land on all sides. He was much impressed by the beauty of the country, and said that it resembled "a dragon-fly licking its hinder parts," and the Island received the name of Akitsu-Shima ("Island of the Dragon-fly").

The *Kojiki*, or "Records of Ancient Matters," completed A.D. 712, deals with the early traditions of the Japanese race, commencing with the myths, the basis of Shintōism, and gradually becoming more historical until it terminates in A.D. 628. Dr. W. G. Aston writes in *A History of Japanese Literature* : "The *Kojiki*, however valuable it may be for research into the mythology, the manners, the language, and the legends of early Japan, is a very poor production, whether we consider it as literature or as a record of facts. As history it cannot be compared with the *Nihongi*,[1] a contemporary work

---

[1] *Chronicles of Japan*, completed A.D. 720, deals, in an interesting manner, with the myths, legends, poetry and history from the earliest times down to A.D. 697.

in Chinese ; while the language is a strange mixture of Chinese and Japanese, which there has been little attempt to endue with artistic quality. The circumstances under which it was composed are a partial explanation of the very curious style in which it is written. We are told that a man named Yasumaro, learned in Chinese, took it down from the lips of a certain Hiyeda no Are, who had such a wonderful memory that he 'could repeat with his mouth whatever was placed before his eyes, and record in his heart whatever struck his ears.'" It is possible that Hiyeda no Are was one of the Kataribe or " Reciters," whose duty it was to recite " ancient words " before the Mikado at the Court of Nara on certain State occasions.

The *Kojiki* and the *Nihongi* are the sources from which we learn the early myths and legends of Japan. In their pages we are introduced to Izanagi and Izanami, Ama-terasu, Susa-no-o, and numerous other divinities, and these august beings provide us with stories that are quaint, beautiful, quasi-humorous, and sometimes a little horrible. What could be more naïve than the love-making of Izanagi and Izanami, who conceived the idea of marrying each other after seeing the mating of two wagtails ? In this ancient myth we trace the ascendency of the male over the female, an ascendency maintained in Japan until recent times, fostered, no doubt, by Kaibara's *Onna Daigaku*, " The Greater Learning for Women." But in the protracted quarrel between the Sun Goddess and her brother, the Impetuous Male, the old chroniclers lay emphasis upon the villainy of Susa-no-o ; and Ama-terasu, a curious mingling of the divine and the feminine, is portrayed as an ideal type of Goddess. She is revealed preparing for warfare, making fortifications by stamping upon the ground, and she is also depicted peeping out of her rock-cavern and gazing in the Sacred Mirror. Ama-terasu is the central figure in Japanese mythology, for it is from the Sun Goddess that the Mikados are descended. In the cycle of legends known as the Period of the Gods, we are introduced to the Sacred Treasures, we discover the origin of the Japanese dance, and in imagination wander through the High Plain of Heaven, set foot upon the Floating Bridge, enter the Central Land of Reed-Plains, peep into the Land of Yomi, and follow Prince Fire-Fade into the Palace of the Sea King.

Early heroes and warriors are always regarded as minor divinities, and the very nature of Shintōism, associated with ancestor worship, has enriched those of Japan with many a fascinating legend. For strength, skill, endurance, and a happy knack of overcoming all manner of difficulties by a subtle form of quick-witted enterprise, the Japanese hero must necessarily take a high position among the famous warriors of other countries. There is something eminently chivalrous about the heroes of Japan that calls for special notice. The most valiant men are those who champion the cause of the weak or redress evil and tyranny of every kind, and we trace in the Japanese hero, who is very far from being a crude swashbuckler, these most excellent qualities. He is not always above criticism, and sometimes we find in him a touch of cunning, but such a characteristic is extremely rare, and very far from being a national trait. An innate love of poetry and the beautiful has had its refining influence upon the Japanese hero, with the result that his strength is combined with gentleness.

Benkei is one of the most lovable of Japanese heroes. He possessed the strength of many men, his tact amounted to genius, his sense of humour was strongly developed, and the most loving of Japanese mothers could not have shown more gentleness when his master's wife gave birth to a child. When Yoshitsune and Benkei, at the head of the Minamoto host, had finally vanquished the Taira at the sea-fight of Dan-no-ura, their success awakened the jealousy of the Shōgun, and the two great warriors were forced to fly the country. We follow them across the sea, over mountains, outwitting again and again their numerous enemies. At Matsue a great army was sent out against these unfortunate warriors. Camp-fires stretched in a glittering line about the last resting-place of Yoshitsune and Benkei. In an apartment were Yoshitsune with his wife and little child. Death stood in the room, too, and it was better that Death should come at the order of Yoshitsune than at the command of the enemy without the gate. His child was killed by an attendant, and, holding his beloved wife's head under his left arm, he plunged his sword deep into her throat. Having accomplished these things, Yoshitsune committed *hara-kiri*. Benkei, however, faced the enemy. He stood with his great legs apart, his back pressed against a rock. When the dawn came he was still standing with his legs apart, a thousand arrows in that brave body of his. Benkei was dead, but his was a death too strong to fall. The sun shone on a man who was a true hero, who had ever made good his words : " Where my lord goes, to victory or to death, I shall follow him."

Japan is a mountainous country, and in such countries we expect to find a race of hardy, brave men, and certainly the Land of the Rising Sun has given us many a warrior worthy to rank with the Knights of King Arthur. More than one legend deals with the destruction of devils and goblins, and of the rescue of maidens who had the misfortune to be their captives. One hero slays a great monster that crouched upon the roof of the Emperor's palace, another despatches the Goblin of Oyeyama, another thrusts his sword through a gigantic spider, and another slays a serpent. All the Japanese heroes, whatever enterprise they may be engaged in, reveal the spirit of high adventure, and that loyalty of purpose, that cool disregard for danger and death which are still characteristic of the Japanese people to-day.

"The Bamboo-Cutter and the Moon-Maiden" (Chapter III) is adapted from a tenth-century story called *Taketori Monogatari*, and is the earliest example of the Japanese romance. The author is unknown, but he must have had an intimate knowledge of court life in Kyōto. All the characters in this very charming legend are Japanese, but most of the incidents have been borrowed from China, a country so rich in picturesque fairy-lore. Mr. F. V. Dickins writes concerning the *Taketori Monogatari* : "The art and grace of the story of the Lady Kaguya are native, its unstrained pathos, its natural sweetness, are its own, and in simple charm and purity of thought and language it has no rival in the fiction of either the Middle Kingdom or of the Dragon-fly Land."

In studying Japanese legend one is particularly struck by its universality and also by its very sharp contrasts. Most nations have deified the sun and moon, the stars and mountains, and all the greatest works of Nature ; but the Japanese have described the red blossoms of azaleas as the fires of the Gods, and the white snow of Fuji as the garments of Divine Beings. Their legend, on the one hand at any rate, is essentially poetical, and those who worshipped Mount Fuji also had ghostly tales to tell about the smallest insect. Too much stress cannot be laid upon Japan's love of Nature. The early myths recorded in the *Kojiki* and *Nihongi* are of considerable interest, but they cannot be compared with the later legends that have given souls to trees and flowers and butterflies, or with those pious traditions that have revealed so tenderly and yet so forcibly the divine significance of Nature. The Festival of the Dead could only have originated among a people to whom the beautiful is the mainstay and joy of life, for that festival is nothing less than a call to the departed dead to return to their old earthly haunts in the summertime, to cross green hills dotted with pine-trees, to wander down winding ways, by lake and seashore, to linger in old, well-loved gardens, and to pass into homes where, without being seen, they see so much. To the Japanese mind, to those who still preserve the spirit of Old Yamato, the most glowing account of a Buddhist Paradise is not so fair as Japan in the summertime.

Perhaps it is as well that Japanese myth, legend, fairy tale, and folk-lore are not exclusively poetical, or we should be in danger of becoming satiated with too much sweetness. It may be that we admire the arches of a Gothic cathedral none the less for having gazed upon the hideous gargoyles on the outside of the sacred edifice, and in the legends of Japan we find many grotesques in sharp contrast with the traditions associated with the gentle and loving Jizō. There is plenty of crude realism in Japanese legend. We are repelled by the Thunder God's favourite repast, amazed by the magical power of foxes and cats; and the story of "Hōïchi-the-Earless" and of the corpse-eating priest afford striking examples of the combination of the weird and the horrible. In one story we laugh over the antics of a performing kettle, and in another we are almost moved to tears when we read about a little Japanese quilt that murmured : " Elder Brother probably is cold ? Nay, thou probably art cold ? "

We have had numerous volumes of Japanese fairy tales, but hitherto no book has appeared giving a comprehensive study of the myths and legends of a country so rich in quaint and beautiful traditions, and it is hoped that the present volume, the result of much pleasant labour, will be a real contribution to the subject. I have made no attempt to make a complete collection of Japanese myths and legends because their number is legion ; but I have endeavoured to make a judicious selection that shall at any rate be representative, and many of the stories contained in this volume will be new to the general reader.

Lafcadio Hearn wrote in one of his letters : " The fairy world seized my soul again, very softly and sweetly—as a child might a butterfly," and if we too would adopt a similar spirit, we shall journey to the Land of the Gods, where the great Kōbō Daishi will write upon the sky and running water, upon our very hearts, something of the glamour and magic of Old Japan. With Kōbō Daishi for guide we shall witness the coming of Mount Fuji, wander in the Palace of the Sea King and in the Land of Perpetual Youth, watch the combats of mighty heroes, listen to the wisdom of saints, cross the Celestial River on a bridge of birds, and when we are weary nestle in the long sleeve of the ever-smiling Jizō.

F. HADLAND DAVIS

CHAPTER I: THE PERIOD OF THE GODS

In the Beginning

WE are told that in the very beginning "Heaven and Earth were not yet separated, and the *In* and *Yo* not yet divided." This reminds us of other cosmogony stories. The *In* and *Yo*, corresponding to the Chinese *Yang* and *Yin*, were the male and female principles. It was more convenient for the old Japanese writers to imagine the coming into being of creation in terms not very remote from their own manner of birth. In Polynesian mythology we find pretty much the same conception, where Rangi and Papa represented Heaven and Earth, and further parallels may be found in Egyptian and other cosmogony stories. In nearly all we find the male and female principles taking a prominent, and after all very rational, place. We are told in the *Nihongi* that these male and female principles "formed a chaotic mass like an egg which was of obscurely defined limits and contained germs." Eventually this egg was quickened into life, and the purer and clearer part was drawn out and formed Heaven, while the heavier element settled down and became Earth, which was "compared to the floating of a fish sporting on the surface of the water." A mysterious form resembling a reed-shoot suddenly appeared between Heaven and Earth, and as suddenly became transformed into a God called Kuni-toko-tachi, ("Land-eternal-stand-of-august-thing"). We may pass over the other divine births until we come to the important deities known as Izanagi and Izanami ("Male-who-invites" and "Female-who-invites"). About these beings has been woven an entrancing myth.

Izanagi and Izanami

Izanagi and Izanami stood on the Floating Bridge of Heaven and looked down into the abyss. They inquired of each other if there were a country far, far below the great Floating Bridge. They were determined to find out. In order to do so they thrust down a jewel-spear, and found the ocean. Raising the spear a little, water dripped from it, coagulated, and became the island of Onogoro-jima (" Spontaneously-congeal-island ").

Upon this island the two deities descended. Shortly afterwards they desired to become husband and wife, though as a matter of fact they were brother and sister ; but such a relationship in the East has never precluded marriage. These deities accordingly set up a pillar on the island. Izanagi walked round one way, and Izanami the other. When they met, Izanami said : " How delightful ! I have met with a lovely youth." One would have thought that this naïve remark would have pleased Izanagi ; but it made him extremely angry, and he retorted : " I am a man, and by that right should have spoken first. How is it that on the contrary thou, a woman, shouldst have been the first to speak ? This is unlucky. Let us go round again." So it happened that the two deities started afresh. Once again they met, and this time Izanagi remarked : " How delightful ! I have met a lovely maiden." Shortly after this very ingenuous proposal Izanagi and Izanami were married.

When Izanami had given birth to islands, seas, rivers, herbs, and trees, she and her lord consulted together, saying : " We have now produced the Great-Eight-Island country, with the mountains, rivers, herbs, and trees. Why should we not produce some one who shall be the Lord of the Universe ? "

IZANAGI AND IZANAMI

The wish of these deities was fulfilled, for in due season Ama-terasu, the Sun Goddess, was born. She was known as "Heaven-Illumine-of-Great-Deity," and was so extremely beautiful that her parents determined to send her up the Ladder of Heaven, and in the high sky above to cast for ever her glorious sunshine upon the earth.

Their next child was the Moon God, Tsuki-yumi. His silver radiance was not so fair as the golden effulgence of his sister, the Sun Goddess, but he was, nevertheless, deemed worthy to be her consort. So up the Ladder of Heaven climbed the Moon God. They soon quarrelled, and Ama-terasu said: "Thou art a wicked deity. I must not see thee face to face." They were therefore separated by a day and night, and dwelt apart.

The next child of Izanagi and Izanami was Susa-no-o ("The Impetuous Male"). We shall return to Susa-no-o and his doings later on, and content ourselves for the present with confining our attention to his parents.

Izanami gave birth to the Fire God, Kagu-tsuchi. The birth of this child made her extremely ill. Izanagi knelt on the ground, bitterly weeping and lamenting. But his sorrow availed nothing, and Izanami crept away into the Land of Yomi (Hades).

Her lord, however, could not live without her, and he too went into the Land of Yomi. When he discovered her, she said regretfully: "My lord and husband, why is thy coming so late? I have already eaten of the cooking-furnace of Yomi. Nevertheless, I am about to lie down to rest. I pray thee do not look at me."

Izanagi, moved by curiosity, refused to fulfil her wish. It was dark in the Land of Yomi, so he secretly took out his many-toothed comb, broke off a piece, and lighted it. The sight that greeted him was ghastly and horrible in the extreme. His once beautiful wife had now become a swollen and festering creature. Eight varieties of Thunder Gods rested upon her. The Thunder of the Fire, Earth, and Mountain were all there leering upon him, and roaring with their great voices.

Izanagi grew frightened and disgusted, saying : " I have come unawares to a hideous and polluted land." His wife retorted : " Why didst thou not observe that which I charged thee ? Now am I put to shame."

Izanami was so angry with her lord for ignoring her wish and breaking in upon her privacy that she sent the Eight Ugly Females of Yomi to pursue him. Izanagi drew his sword and fled down the dark regions of the Underworld. As he ran he took off his head-dress, and flung it to the ground. It immediately became a bunch of grapes. When the Ugly Females saw it, they bent down and ate the luscious fruit. Izanami saw them pause, and deemed it wise to pursue her lord herself.

By this time Izanagi had reached the Even Pass of Yomi. Here he placed a huge rock, and eventually came face to face with Izanami. One would scarcely have thought that amid such exciting adventures Izanagi would have solemnly declared a divorce. But this is just what he did do. To this proposal his wife replied : " My dear lord and husband, if thou sayest so, I will strangle to death the people in one day." This plaintive and threatening speech in no way influenced Izanagi, who readily replied that he would cause to be born in one day no less than fifteen hundred.

The above remark must have proved conclusive, for when we next hear of Izanagi he had escaped from the

Land of Yomi, from an angry wife, and from the Eight
Ugly Females. After his escape he was engaged in
copious ablutions, by way of purification, from which
numerous deities were born. We read in the *Nihongi* :
"After this, Izanagi, his divine task having been accomplished, and his spirit-career about to suffer a change,
built himself an abode of gloom in the island of Ahaji,
where he dwelt for ever in silence and concealment."

Ama-terasu and Susa-no-o

Susa-no-o, or "The Impetuous Male," was the brother
of Ama-terasu, the Sun Goddess. Now Susa-no-o was a
very undesirable deity indeed, and he figured in the Realm
of the Japanese Gods as a decidedly disturbing element.
His character has been clearly drawn in the *Nihongi*, more
clearly perhaps than that of any other deity mentioned in
these ancient records. Susa-no-o had a very bad temper,
which often resulted in many cruel and ungenerous acts.
Moreover, in spite of his long beard, he had a habit of
continually weeping and wailing. Where a child in a
tantrum would crush a toy to pieces, the Impetuous Male,
when in a towering rage, and without a moment's warning,
would wither the once fair greenery of mountains, and in
addition bring many people to an untimely end.

His parents, Izanagi and Izanami, were much troubled
by his doings, and, after consulting together, they decided
to banish their unruly son to the Land of Yomi.
Susa, however, had a word to say in the matter. He
made the following petition, saying : "I will now obey
thy instructions and proceed to the Nether-Land
(Yomi). Therefore I wish for a short time to go
to the Plain of High Heaven and meet with my
elder sister (Ama-terasu), after which I will go away for
ever." This apparently harmless request was granted,
and Susa-no-o ascended to Heaven. His departure

occasioned a great commotion of the sea, and the hills and mountains groaned aloud.

Now Ama-terasu heard these noises, and perceiving that they denoted the near approach of her wicked brother Susa-no-o, she said to herself : " Is my younger brother coming with good intentions ? I think it must be his purpose to rob me of my kingdom. By the charge which our parents gave to their children, each of us has his own allotted limits. Why, therefore, does he reject the kingdom to which he should proceed, and make bold to come spying here ? "

Ama-terasu then prepared for warfare. She tied her hair into knots and hung jewels upon it, and round her wrists "an august string of five hundred Yasaka jewels." She presented a very formidable appearance when in addition she slung over her back "a thousand-arrow quiver and a five-hundred-arrow quiver," and protected her arms with pads to deaden the recoil of the bowstring. Having arrayed herself for deadly combat, she brandished her bow, grasped her sword-hilt, and stamped on the ground till she had made a hole sufficiently large to serve as a fortification.

All this elaborate and ingenious preparation was in vain. The Impetuous Male adopted the manner of a penitent. "From the beginning," he said, "my heart has not been black. But as, in obedience to the stern behest of our parents, I am about to depart for ever to the Nether-Land, how could I bear to depart without having seen face to face thee my elder sister ? It is for this reason that I have traversed on foot the clouds and mists and have come hither from afar. I am surprised that my elder sister should, on the contrary, put on so stern a countenance."

Ama-terasu regarded these remarks with a certain

amount of suspicion.   Susa-no-o's filial piety and
Susa-no-o's cruelty were not easily to be reconciled.   She
thereupon resolved to test his sincerity by a remarkable
proceeding we need not describe.   Suffice it to say that
for the time being the test proved the Impetuous Male's
purity of heart and general sincerity towards his sister.

But Susa-no-o's good behaviour was a very short-lived
affair indeed.   It happened that Ama-terasu had made
a number of excellent rice-fields in Heaven.   Some were
narrow and some were long, and Ama-terasu was justly
proud of these rice-fields.   No sooner had she sown
the seed in the spring than Susa-no-o broke down the
divisions between the plots, and in the autumn let
loose a number of piebald colts.

One day when he saw his sister in the sacred
Weaving Hall, weaving the garments of the Gods, he
made a hole through the roof and flung down a flayed
horse.   Ama-terasu was so frightened that she accidentally wounded herself with the shuttle.   Extremely
angry, she determined to leave her abode ; so, gathering
her shining robes about her, she crept down the blue
sky, entered a cave, fastened it securely, and there
dwelt in seclusion.

Now the world was in darkness, and the alternation
of night and day was unknown.   When this dreadful
catastrophe had taken place the Eighty Myriads of
Gods assembled together on the bank of the River of
Heaven and discussed how they might best persuade
Ama-terasu to grace Heaven once more with her
shining glory.   No less a God than " Thought-com-
bining," after much profound reasoning, gathered
together a number of singing-birds from the Eternal
Land.   After sundry divinations with a deer's leg-bone,
over a fire of cherry-bark, the Gods made a number of
tools, bellows, and forges.   Stars were welded together

to form a mirror, and jewellery and musical instruments were eventually fashioned.

When all these things had been duly accomplished the Eighty Myriads of Gods came down to the rock-cavern where the Sun Goddess lay concealed, and gave an elaborate entertainment. On the upper branches of the True Sakaki Tree they hung the precious jewels, and on the middle branches the mirror. From every side there was a great singing of birds, which was only the prelude to what followed. Now Uzume ("Heavenly-alarming-female") took in her hand a spear wreathed with Eulalia grass, and made a head-dress of the True Sakaki Tree. Then she placed a tub upside down, and proceeded to dance in a very immodest manner, till the Eighty Myriad Gods began to roar with laughter.

Such extraordinary proceedings naturally awakened the curiosity of Ama-terasu, and she peeped forth. Once more the world became golden with her presence. Once more she dwelt in the Plain of High Heaven, and Susa-no-o was duly chastised and banished to the Yomi Land.

Susa-no-o and the Serpent

With the usual inconsistency of myths and legends, we are not surprised to find that all reference to Susa dwelling in the Land of Yomi is entirely omitted. When we next see him it is apart from his usual mischievous disposition. Indeed, we find him in a *rôle* worthy of one of the Knights of the Round Table. Whether the sudden display of knight-errantry was a cunning move on his part for some ulterior motive, or whether his sister's sudden withdrawal from Heaven had made him permanently reform his ways, we are left in entire ignorance.

Uzume awakens the Curiosity of Ama-terasu.

(See page 28)

Susa-no-o and Kushi-nada-hime.

(See page 29*)*

SUSA-NO-O AND THE SERPENT

Susa-no-o, having descended from Heaven, arrived at the river Hi, in the province of Idzumo. Here he was disturbed by a sound of weeping. It was so unusual to hear any other than himself weep that he went in search of the cause of the sorrow. He discovered an old man and an old woman. Between them was a young girl, whom they fondly caressed and gazed at with pitiful eyes, as if they were reluctantly bidding her a last farewell. When Susa-no-o asked the old couple who they were and why they lamented, the old man replied: " I am an Earthly Deity, and my name is Ashi-nadzuchi (" Foot-stroke-elder "). My wife's name is Te-nadzuchi (" Hand-stroke-elder "). This girl is our daughter, and her name is Kushi-nada-hime (" Wondrous-Inada-Princess "). The reason of our weeping is that formerly we had eight children, daughters ; but they have been devoured year by year by an eight-forked serpent, and now the time approaches for this girl to be devoured. There is no means of escape for her, and therefore do we grieve exceedingly."

The Impetuous Male listened to this painful recital with profound attention, and, perceiving that the maiden was extremely beautiful, he offered to slay the eight-forked serpent if her parents would give her to him in marriage as a fitting reward for his services. This request was readily granted.

Susa-no-o now changed Kushi-nada-hime into a many-toothed comb and stuck it in his hair. Then he bade the old couple brew a quantity of *saké*. When the *saké* was ready, he poured it into eight tubs, and awaited the coming of the dreadful monster.

Eventually the serpent came. It had eight heads, and the eyes were red, " like winter-cherry." Moreover it had eight tails, and firs and cypress-trees grew on its back. It was in length the space of eight hills

29

and eight valleys. Its lumbering progress was necessarily slow, but finding the *saké*, each head eagerly drank the tempting beverage till the serpent became extremely drunk, and fell asleep. Then Susa-no-o, having little to fear, drew his ten-span sword and chopped the great monster into little pieces. When he struck one of the tails his weapon became notched, and bending down he discovered a sword called the Murakumo-no-Tsurugi. Perceiving it to be a divine sword, he gave it to the Gods of Heaven.

Having successfully accomplished his task, Susa-no-o converted the many-toothed comb into Kushi-nada-hime again, and at length came to Suga, in the province of Idzumo, in order that he might celebrate his marriage. Here he composed the following verse:

> "Many clouds arise,
> On all sides a manifold fence,
> To receive within it the spouses,
> They form a manifold fence—
> Ah! that manifold fence!"
>
> *Nihongi*, trans. by W. G. ASTON.

The Divine Messengers

Now at that time the Gods assembled in the High Plain of Heaven were aware of continual disturbances in the Central Land of Reed-Plains (Idzumo). We are told that " Plains, the rocks, tree-stems, and herbage have still the power of speech. At night they make a clamour like that of flames of fire; in the day-time they swarm up like flies in the fifth month." In addition certain deities made themselves objectionable. The Gods determined to put an end to these disturbances, and after a consultation Taka-mi-musubi decided to send his grandchild Ninigi to govern the Central Land of Reed-Plains, to wipe out insurrection, and to bring peace and prosperity to the country. It was deemed necessary to send messengers to prepare the way in advance. The first envoy was Ama-no-ho ; but as he spent three years in the country without reporting to the Gods, his son was sent in his place. He adopted the same course as his father, and defied the orders of the Heavenly Ones. The third messenger was Ame-waka (" Heaven-young-Prince "). He, too, was disloyal, in spite of his noble weapons, and instead of going about his duties he fell in love and took to wife Shita-teru-hime (" Lower-shine-Princess ").

Now the assembled Gods grew angry at the long delay, and sent a pheasant down to ascertain what was going on in Idzumo. The pheasant perched on the top of a cassia-tree before Ame-waka's gate. When Ame-waka saw the bird he immediately shot it. The arrow went through the bird, rose into the Place of Gods, and was hurled back again, so that it killed the disloyal and idle Ame-waka.

The weeping of Lower-shine-Princess reached Heaven, for she loved her lord and failed to recognise in his sudden death the just vengeance of the Gods. She wept so loud and so pitifully that the Heavenly Ones heard her. A swift wind descended, and the body of Ame-waka floated up into the High Plain of Heaven. A mortuary house was made, in which the deceased was laid. Mr. Frank Rinder writes : " For eight days and eight nights there was wailing and lamentation. The wild goose of the river, the heron, the kingfisher, the sparrow, and the pheasant mourned with a great mourning."

Now it happened that a friend of Ame-waka, Aji-shi-ki by name, heard the sad dirges proceeding from Heaven. He therefore offered his condolence. He so resembled the deceased that when Ame-waka's parents, relations, wife, and children saw him, they

exclaimed : "Our lord is still alive!" This greatly
angered Aji-shi-ki, and he drew his sword and cut
down the mortuary house, so that it fell to the Earth
and became the mountain of Moyama.

We are told that the glory of Aji-shi-ki was so
effulgent that it illuminated the space of two hills and
two valleys. Those assembled for the mourning cele-
brations uttered the following song :

> "Like the string of jewels
> Worn on the neck
> Of the Weaving-maiden,
> That dwells in Heaven—
> Oh! the lustre of the jewels
> Flung across two valleys
> From Aji-suki-taka-hiko-ne!

> "To the side-pool—
> The side-pool
> Of the rocky stream
> Whose narrows are crossed
> By the country wenches
> Afar from Heaven,
> Come hither, come hither!
> (The women are fair)
> And spread across thy net
> In the side-pool
> Of the rocky stream."
>
> *Nihongi*, trans. by W. G. ASTON.

Two more Gods were sent to the Central Land of
Reed-Plains, and these Gods were successful in their
mission. They returned to Heaven with a favourable
report, saying that all was now ready for the coming of
the August Grandchild.

The Coming of the August Grandchild

Ama-terasu presented her grandson Ninigi, or Prince
Rice-Ear-Ruddy-Plenty, with many gifts. She gave
him precious stones from the mountain-steps of Heaven,

white crystal balls, and, most valuable gift of all, the divine sword that Susa-no-o had discovered in the serpent. She also gave him the star-mirror into which she had gazed when peeping out of her cave. Several deities accompanied Ninigi, including that lively maiden of mirth and dance Uzume, whose dancing, it will be remembered, so amused the Gods.

Ninigi and his companions had hardly broken through the clouds and arrived at the eight-forked road of Heaven, when they discovered, much to their alarm, a gigantic creature with large and brightly shining eyes. So formidable was his aspect that Ninigi and all his companions, except the merry and bewitching Uzume, started to turn back with intent to abandon their mission. But Uzume went up to the giant and demanded who it was that dared to impede their progress. The giant replied : "I am the Deity of the Field-paths. I come to pay my homage to Ninigi, and beg to have the honour to be his guide. Return to your master, O fair Uzume, and give him this message."

So Uzume returned and gave her message to the Gods, who had so ignominiously retreated. When they heard the good news they greatly rejoiced, burst once more through the clouds, rested on the Floating Bridge of Heaven, and finally reached the summit of Takachihi.

The August Grandchild, with the Deity of the Field-paths for guide, travelled from end to end of the kingdom over which he was to rule. When he had reached a particularly charming spot, he built a palace.

Ninigi was so pleased with the service the Deity of the Field-paths had rendered him that he gave that giant the merry Uzume to wife.

Ninigi, after having romantically rewarded his faithful guide, began to feel the stirring of love himself, when one day, while walking along the shore, he saw an extremely lovely maiden. "Who are you, most beautiful lady?" inquired Ninigi. She replied: "I am the daughter of the Great-Mountain-Possessor. My name is Ko-no-Hana, the Princess who makes the Flowers of the Trees to Blossom."

Ninigi fell in love with Ko-no-Hana. He went with all haste to her father, Oho-yama, and begged that he would favour him with his daughter's hand.

Oho-yama had an elder daughter, Iha-naga, Princess Long-as-the-Rocks. As her name implies, she was not at all beautiful; but her father desired that Ninigi's children should have life as eternal as the life of rocks. He therefore presented both his daughters to Ninigi, expressing the hope that the suitor's choice would fall upon Iha-naga. Just as Cinderella, and not her ugly sisters, is dear to children of our own country, so did Ninigi remain true to his choice, and would not even look upon Iha-naga. This neglect made Princess Long-as-the-Rocks extremely angry. She cried out, with more vehemence than modesty: "Had you chosen me, you and your children would have lived long in the land. Now that you have chosen my sister, you and yours will perish as quickly as the blossom of trees, as quickly as the bloom on my sister's cheek."

However, Ninigi and Ko-no-Hana lived happily together for some time; but one day jealousy came to Ninigi and robbed him of his peace of mind. He had no cause to be jealous, and Ko-no-Hana much resented his treatment. She retired to a little wooden hut, and set it on fire. From the flames came three baby boys. We need only concern ourselves with two of them— Hoderi ("Fire-shine") and Hoori ("Fire-fade"). Hoori, as we shall see later on, was the grandfather of the first Mikado of Japan.

34

IN THE PALACE OF THE SEA GOD

In the Palace of the Sea God

Hoderi was a great fisherman, while his younger brother, Hoori, was an accomplished hunter. One day they exclaimed : "Let us for a trial exchange gifts." This they did, but the elder brother, who could catch fish to some purpose, came home without any spoil when he went a-hunting. He therefore returned the bow and arrows, and asked his younger brother for the fish-hook. Now it so happened that Hoori had lost his brother's fish-hook. The generous offer of a new hook to take the place of the old one was scornfully refused. He also refused to accept a heaped-up tray of fish-hooks. To this offer the elder brother replied : "These are not my old fish-hook : though they are many, I will not take them."

Now Hoori was sore troubled by his brother's harshness, so he went down to the sea-shore and there gave way to his grief. A kind old man by the name of Shiko-tsutsu no Oji ("Salt-sea-elder") said : "Why dost thou grieve here ?" When the sad tale was told, the old man replied : "Grieve no more. I will arrange this matter for thee."

True to his word, the old man made a basket, set Hoori in it, and then sank it in the sea. After descending deep down in the water Hoori came to a pleasant strand rich with all manner of fantastic seaweed. Here he abandoned the basket and eventually arrived at the Palace of the Sea God.

Now this palace was extremely imposing. It had battlements and turrets and stately towers. A well stood at the gate, and over the well there was a cassia-tree. Here Hoori loitered in the pleasant shade. He had not stood there long before a beautiful woman appeared. As she was about to draw water, she raised her eyes, saw the stranger, and immediately returned, with much alarm, to tell her mother and father what she had seen.

The God of the Sea, when he had heard the news, "prepared an eightfold cushion" and led the stranger in, asking his visitor why he had been honoured by his presence. When Hoori explained the sad loss of his brother's fish-hook the Sea God assembled all the fishes of his kingdom, "broad of fin and narrow of fin." And when the thousands upon thousands of fishes were assembled, the Sea God asked them if they knew anything about the missing fish-hook. "We know not," answered the fishes. "Only the Red-woman (the *tai*) has had a sore mouth for some time past, and has not come." She was accordingly summoned, and on her mouth being opened the lost fish-hook was discovered.

Hoori then took to wife the Sea God's daughter, Toyo-tama ("Rich-jewel"), and they dwelt together in the palace under the sea. For three years all went well, but after a time Hoori hungered for a sight of his own country, and possibly he may have remembered that he had yet to restore the fish-hook to his elder brother. These not unnatural feelings troubled the heart of the loving Toyo-tama, and she went to her father and told him of her sorrow. But the Sea God, who was always urbane and courteous, in no way resented his son-in-law's behaviour. On the contrary he gave him the fish-hook, saying : "When thou givest this fish-hook to thy elder brother, before giving it to him, call to it secretly, and say, 'A poor hook!'" He also presented Hoori with the Jewel of the Flowing Tide and the Jewel of the Ebbing Tide, saying : "If thou dost dip the Tide-flowing Jewel, the tide will suddenly flow, and therewithal thou shalt drown thine

Hoori and the Sea God's Daughter.

(See page 35*)*

Yorimasa slays the Monster.

(See page 39)

elder brother. But in case thy elder brother should repent and beg forgiveness, if, on the contrary, thou dip the Tide-ebbing Jewel, the tide will spontaneously ebb, and therewithal thou shalt save him. If thou harass him in this way thy elder brother will of his own accord render submission."

Just before Hoori was about to depart his wife came to him and told him that she was soon to give him a child. Said she: "On a day when the winds and waves are raging I will surely come forth to the sea-shore. Build for me a house, and await me there."

Hoderi and Hoori Reconciled

When Hoori reached his own home he found his elder brother, who admitted his offence and begged for forgiveness, which was readily granted.

Toyo-tama and her younger sister bravely confronted the winds and waves, and came to the sea-shore. There Hoori had built a hut roofed with cormorant feathers, and there in due season she gave birth to a son. When Toyo-tama had blessed her lord with offspring, she turned into a dragon and slipped back into the sea. Hoori's son married his aunt, and was the father of four children, one of whom was Kamu-Yamato-Iware-Biko, who is said to have been the first human Emperor of Japan, and is now known as Jimmu Tennō.

CHAPTER II : HEROES AND WARRIORS

Yorimasa

A LONG time ago a certain Emperor became
seriously ill. He was unable to sleep at night
owing to a most horrible and unaccountable
noise he heard proceeding from the roof of the palace,
called the Purple Hall of the North Star. A number
of his courtiers decided to lie in wait for this strange
nocturnal visitor. As soon as the sun set they noticed
that a dark cloud crept from the eastern horizon, and
alighted on the roof of the august palace. Those who
waited in the imperial bed-chamber heard extraordinary
scratching sounds, as if what had at first appeared to be
a cloud had suddenly changed into a beast with gigantic
and powerful claws.

Night after night this terrible visitant came, and
night after night the Emperor grew worse. He at last
became so ill that it was obvious to all those in
attendance upon him that unless something could be
done to destroy this monster the Emperor would
certainly die.

At last it was decided that Yorimasa was the one
knight in the kingdom valiant enough to relieve his
Majesty of these terrible hauntings. Yorimasa accordingly made elaborate preparations for the fray.
He took his best bow and steel-headed arrows, donned
his armour, over which he wore a hunting-dress, and a
ceremonial cap instead of his usual helmet.

At sunset he lay in concealment outside the palace.
While he thus waited thunder crashed overhead, lightning blazed in the sky, and the wind shrieked like a
pack of wild demons. But Yorimasa was a brave man,
and the fury of the elements in no way daunted him.
When midnight came he saw a black cloud rush through

the sky and rest upon the roof of the palace. At the north-east corner it stopped. Once more the lightning flashed in the sky, and this time he saw the gleaming eyes of a large animal. Noting the exact position of this strange monster, he pulled at his bow till it became as round as the full moon. In another moment his steel-headed arrow hit its mark. There was an awful roar of anger, and then a heavy thud as the huge monster rolled from the palace roof to the ground.

Yorimasa and his retainer ran forward and despatched the fearful creature they saw before them. This evil monster of the night was as large as a horse. It had the head of an ape, and the body and claws were like those of a tiger, with a serpent's tail, wings of a bird, and the scales of a dragon.

It was no wonder that the Emperor gave orders that the skin of this monster should be kept for all time as a curiosity in the Imperial treasure-house. From the very moment the creature died the Emperor's health rapidly improved, and Yorimasa was rewarded for his services by being presented with a sword called Shishi-wo, which means "the King of Lions." He was also promoted at Court, and finally married the Lady Ayame, the most beautiful of ladies-in-waiting at the Imperial Court.

Yoshitsune and Benkei

We may compare Yoshitsune with the Black Prince or Henry V., and Benkei with "Little John, Will Scarlet, and Friar Tuck rolled in one." Yoshitsune would have seemed a very remarkable hero had not his faithful henchman, Benkei, also figured in Japanese history and legend. As it is we are forced to admit that Benkei was far and away the greater man. He not only towered in stature above his companions, but he rose above his brethren in courage, wit, resource, and a wonderful tenderness. Here was a man who could slay a hundred men with absolute ease, and with the same quiet assurance expound the Buddhist Scriptures. He could weep over Yoshitsune when, by way of strategy, he found it necessary to severely beat him, and with infinite gentleness render assistance when his lord's wife gave birth to a son. There was yet another side to Benkei's versatile character—his love of a practical joke. The bell incident, referred to elsewhere, is a case in point, and his enormous feast at the expense of a number of priests another; but if he had his joke he never failed to pay for the laugh to the full. Benkei remarked on one occasion: "When there is an unlucky lot to draw my lord sees to it that I am the one to get it." This was certainly true. Benkei always made a point of doing the dirty work, and when his master asked him to do anything Benkei's only complaint was that the task was not sufficiently difficult, though as a matter of fact it was often so dangerous that it would have frightened a dozen less gifted heroes.

We are told that when Benkei was born he had long hair, a complete set of teeth, and, moreover, that he could run as swiftly as the wind. Benkei was too big for a modest Japanese home. When he struck Jinsaku's anvil that useful object sank deep into the earth, and for firewood he would bring a great pine-tree. When Benkei was seventeen years old he became a priest in a Buddhist temple; but that did not prevent him from having a thrilling escapade with a beautiful young girl called Tamamushi. We soon find our hero breaking away from love and priestcraft, and entirely devoting his attention to the exciting adventures of a

lawless warrior. Here, for the moment, we must leave
him, and give the story of Yoshitsune, and how he had
the good fortune to meet and retain the service and
friendship of Benkei till his dying day.

Yoshitsune and the Taira

Yoshitsune's father, Yoshitomo, had been killed in
a great battle with the Taira. At that time the Taira
clan was all-powerful, and its cruel leader, Kiyomori,
did all he could to destroy Yoshitomo's children. But
the mother of these children, Tokiwa, fled into hiding,
taking her little ones with her. With characteristic
Japanese fortitude, she finally consented to become the
wife of the hated Kiyomori. She did so because it was
the only way to save the lives of her children. She
was allowed to keep Yoshitsune with her, and she
daily whispered to him : " Remember thy father,
Minamoto Yoshitomo ! Grow strong and avenge his
death, for he died at the hands of the Taira ! "

When Yoshitsune was seven years of age he was sent
to a monastery to be brought up as a monk. Though
diligent in his studies, the young boy ever treasured in
his heart the dauntless words of his brave, self-sacrificing
mother. They stirred and quickened him to action. He
used to go to a certain valley, where he would flourish
his little wooden sword, and, singing fragments of war-
songs, hit out at rocks and stones, desiring that he might
one day become a great warrior, and right the wrongs
so heavily heaped upon his family by the Taira clan.

One night, while thus engaged, he was startled by a
great thunderstorm, and saw before him a mighty giant
with a long red nose and enormous glaring eyes, bird-
like claws, and feathered wings. Bravely standing his
ground, Yoshitsune inquired who this giant might be,
and was informed that he was King of the Tengu—that

is, King of the elves of the mountains, sprightly little beings who were frequently engaged in all manner of fantastic tricks.

The King of the Tengu was very kindly disposed towards Yoshitsune. He explained that he admired his perseverance, and told him that he had appeared upon the scene with the meritorious intention of teaching him all that was to be learnt in the art of swordsmanship. The lessons progressed in a most satisfactory manner, and it was not long before Yoshitsune could vanquish as many as twenty small *tengu*, and this extreme agility stood Yoshitsune in very good stead, as we shall see later on in the story.

Now when Yoshitsune was fifteen years old he heard that there lived on Mount Hiei a very wild *bonze* (priest) by the name of Benkei. Benkei had for some time waylaid knights who happened to cross the Gojo Bridge of Kyōto. His idea was to obtain a thousand swords, and he was so brave, although such a rascal, that he had won from knights no less than nine hundred and ninety-nine swords by his lawless behaviour. When the news of these doings reached the ears of Yoshitsune he determined to put the teaching of the King of the Tengu to good use and slay this Benkei, and so put an end to one who had become a terror in the land.

One evening Yoshitsune started out, and, in order to establish the manner and bearing of absolute indifference, he played upon his flute till he came to the Gojo Bridge. Presently he saw coming towards him a gigantic man clad in black armour, who was none other than Benkei. When Benkei saw the youth he considered it to be beneath his dignity to attack what appeared to him to be a mere weakling, a dreamer who could play excellently, and no doubt write a pretty poem about the moon, which was then shining in the sky, but one who was in no way a warrior. This affront naturally angered Yoshitsune, and he suddenly kicked Benkei's halberd out of his hand.

Yoshitsune and Benkei Fight

Benkei gave a growl of rage, and cut about indiscriminately with his weapon. But the sprightliness of the *tengu* teaching favoured Yoshitsune. He jumped from side to side, from the front to the rear, and from the rear to the front again, mocking the giant with many a jest and many a peal of ringing laughter. Round and round went Benkei's weapon, always striking either the air or the ground, and ever missing its adversary.

At last Benkei grew weary, and once again Yoshitsune knocked the halberd out of the giant's hand. In trying to regain his weapon Yoshitsune tripped him up, so that he stumbled upon his hands and knees, and the hero, with a cry of triumph, mounted upon the now four-legged Benkei. The giant was utterly amazed at his defeat, and when he was told that the victor was none other than the son of Lord Yoshitomo he not only took his defeat in a manly fashion, but begged that he might henceforth become a retainer of the young conqueror.

From this time we find the names of Yoshitsune and Benkei linked together, and in all the stories of warriors, whether in Japan or elsewhere, never was there a more valiant and harmonious union of strength and friendship. We hear of them winning numerous victories over the Taira, finally driving them to the sea, where they perished at Dan-no-ura.

We get one more glimpse of Dan-no-ura from a legendary point of view. Yoshitsune and his faithful henchman arranged to cross in a ship from the province

43

of Settsu to Saikoku. When they reached Dan-no-ura a great storm arose. Mysterious noises came from the towering waves, a far-away echo of the din of battle, or the rushing of ships and the whirling of arrows, of the footfall of a thousand men. Louder and louder the noise grew, and from the lashing crests of the waves there arose a ghostly company of the Taira clan. Their armour was torn and blood-stained, and they thrust out their vaporous arms and tried to stop the boat in which Yoshitsune and Benkei sailed. It was a ghostly reminiscence of the battle of Dan-no-ura, when the Taira had suffered a terrible and permanent defeat. Yoshitsune, when he saw this great phantom host, cried out for revenge even upon the ghosts of the Taira dead ; but Benkei, always shrewd and circumspect, bade his master lay aside the sword, and took out a rosary and recited a number of Buddhist prayers. Peace came to the great company of ghosts, the wailing ceased, and gradually they faded into the sea which now became calm.

Legend tells us that fishermen still see from time to time ghostly armies come out of the sea and wail and shake their long arms. They explain that the crabs with dorsal markings are the wraiths of the Taira warriors. Later on we shall introduce another legend relating to these unfortunate ghosts, who seem never to tire of haunting the scene of their defeat.

The Goblin of Oyeyama

In the reign of the Emperor Ichijo many dreadful stories were current in Kyōto in regard to a demon that lived on Mount Oye. This demon could assume many forms. Sometimes appearing as a human being, he would steal into Kyōto, and leave many a home destitute of well-loved sons and daughters. These young men and women he took back to his mountain

Yoshitsune and Benkei attacked by a ghostly company
of the Taira Clan.

(See page 44*)*

Raiko and the Enchanted Maiden.

(See page 46)

stronghold, and, sad to narrate, after making sport of them, he and his goblin companions made a great feast and devoured these poor young people. Even the sacred Court was not exempt from these awful happenings, and one day Kimitaka lost his beautiful daughter. She had been snatched away by the Goblin King, Shutendoji.

When this sad news reached the ears of the Emperor he called his council together and consulted how they might slay this dreadful creature. His ministers informed his Majesty that Raiko was a doughty knight, and advised that he should be sent with certain companions on this perilous but worthy adventure.

Raiko accordingly chose five companions and told them what had been ordained, and how they were to set out upon an adventurous journey, and finally to slay the King of the Goblins. He explained that subtlety of action was most essential if they wished for success in their enterprise, and that it would be well to go disguised as mountain priests, and to carry their armour and weapons on their backs, carefully concealed in unsuspicious-looking knapsacks. Before starting upon their journey two of the knights went to pray at the temple of Hachiman, the God of War, two at the shrine of Kwannon, the Goddess of Mercy, and two at the temple of Gongen.

When these knights had prayed for a blessing upon their undertaking they set out upon their journey, and in due time reached the province of Tamba, and saw immediately in front of them Mount Oye. The Goblin had certainly chosen the most formidable or mountains. Mighty rocks and great dark forests obstructed their path in every direction, while almost bottomless chasms appeared when least expected.

Just when these brave knights were beginning to

feel just a little disheartened, three old men suddenly appeared before them. At first these newcomers were regarded with suspicion, but later on with the utmost friendliness and thankfulness. These old men were none other than the deities to whom the knights had prayed before setting out upon their journey. The old men presented Raiko with a jar of magical *saké* called Shimben-Kidoku-Shu ("a cordial for men, but poison for goblins"), advising him that he should by strategy get Shutendoji to drink it, whereupon he would immediately become paralysed and prove an easy victim for the final despatch. No sooner had these old men given the magical *saké* and proffered their valuable advice than a miraculous light shone round them, and they vanished into the clouds.

Once again Raiko and his knights, much cheered by what had happened, continued to ascend the mountain. Coming to a stream, they noticed a beautiful woman washing a blood-stained garment in the running water. She was weeping bitterly, and wiped away her tears with the long sleeve of her *kimono*. Upon Raiko asking who she was, she informed him that she was a princess, and one of the miserable captives of the Goblin King. When she was told that it was none other than the great Raiko who stood before her, and that he and his knights had come to kill the vile creature of that mountain, she was overcome with joy, and finally led the little band to a great palace of black iron, satisfying the sentinels by telling them that her followers were poor mountain priests who sought temporary shelter.

After passing through long corridors Raiko and his knights found themselves in a mighty hall. At one end sat the awful Goblin King. He was of gigantic stature, with bright red skin and a mass of white hair. When Raiko meekly informed him who they were, the Goblin King, concealing his mirth, bade them be seated and join the feast that was about to be set before them. Thereupon he clapped his red hands together, and immediately many beautiful damsels came running in with an abundance of food and drink, and as Raiko watched these women he knew that they had once lived in happy homes in Kyōto.

When the feast was in full progress Raiko took out the jar of magic *saké*, and politely begged the Goblin King to try it. The monster, without demur or suspicion, drank some of the *saké*, and found it so good that he asked for a second cup. All the goblins partook of the magic wine, and while they were drinking Raiko and his companions danced.

The power of this magical drink soon began to work. The Goblin King became drowsy, till finally he and his fellow goblins fell fast asleep. Then Raiko sprang to his feet, and he and his knights rapidly donned their armour and prepared for war. Once more the three deities appeared before them, and said to Raiko : "We have tied the hands and feet of the Demon fast, so you have nothing to fear. While your knights cut off his limbs do you cut off his head : then kill the rest of the *oni* (evil spirits) and your work will be done." Then these divine beings suddenly disappeared.

Raiko Slays the Goblin

Raiko and his knights, with their swords drawn, cautiously approached the sleeping Goblin King. With a mighty sweep Raiko's weapon came crashing down on the Goblin's neck. No sooner was the head severed than it shot up into the air, and smoke and fire poured out from the nostrils, scorching the valiant Raiko. Once more he struck out with his sword, and this time the horrible head fell to the floor, and never moved again. It was not long before these brave knights despatched the Demon's followers also.

There was a joyful exit from the great iron palace. Raiko's five knights carried the monster head of the Goblin King, and this grim spectacle was followed by a company of happy maidens released at last from their horrible confinement, and eager to walk once again in the streets of Kyōto.

The Goblin Spider

Some time after the incident mentioned in the previous legend had taken place the brave Raiko became seriously ill, and was obliged to keep to his room. At about midnight a little boy always brought him some medicine. This boy was unknown to Raiko, but as he kept so many servants it did not at first awaken suspicion. Raiko grew worse instead of better, and always worse immediately after he had taken the medicine, so he began to think that some supernatural force was the cause of his illness.

At last Raiko asked his head servant if he knew anything about the boy who came to him at midnight. Neither the head servant nor any one else seemed to know anything about him. By this time Raiko's suspicions were fully awakened, and he determined to go carefully into the matter.

When the small boy came again at midnight, instead of taking the medicine, Raiko threw the cup at his head, and drawing his sword attempted to kill him. A sharp cry of pain rang through the room, but as the boy was flying from the apartment he threw something at Raiko. It spread outward into a huge white sticky web, which clung so tightly to Raiko that he could hardly move. No sooner had he cut the web through with his sword than another enveloped him. Raiko

48

Raiko slays the Goblin of Oyeyama.

(See page 47*)*

Prince Yamato and Takeru.

(See page 52)

then called for assistance, and his chief retainer met the miscreant in one of the corridors and stopped his further progress with extended sword. The Goblin threw a web over him too. When he at last managed to extricate himself and was able to run into his master's room, he saw that Raiko had also been the victim of the Goblin Spider.

The Goblin Spider was eventually discovered in a cave writhing with pain, blood flowing from a sword-cut on the head. He was instantly killed, and with his death there passed away the evil influence that had caused Raiko's serious illness. From that hour the hero regained his health and strength, and a sumptuous banquet was prepared in honour of the happy event.

Another Version

There is another version of this legend, written by Kenkō Hōshi, which differs so widely in many of its details from the one we have already given that it almost amounts to a new story altogether. To dispense with this version would be to rob the legend of its most sinister aspect, which has not hitherto been accessible to the general reader.[1]

On one occasion Raiko left Kyōto with Tsuna, the most worthy of his retainers. As they were crossing the plain of Rendai they saw a skull rise in the air, and fly before them as if driven by the wind, until it finally disappeared at a place called Kagura ga Oka.

Raiko and his retainer had no sooner noticed the disappearance of the skull than they perceived before them a mansion in ruins. Raiko entered this dilapidated building, and saw an old woman of strange aspect.

[1] This version appears in the *Catalogue of Japanese and Chinese Paintings in the British Museum*, by Dr. William Anderson.

" She was dressed in white, and had white hair; she opened her eyes with a small stick, and the upper eyelids fell back over her head like a hat; then she used the rod to open her mouth, and let her breast fall forward upon her knees." Thus she addressed the astonished Raiko :

"I am two hundred and ninety years old. I serve nine masters, and the house in which you stand is haunted by demons."

Having listened to these words, Raiko walked into the kitchen, and, catching a glimpse of the sky, he perceived that a great storm was brewing. As he stood watching the dark clouds gather he heard a sound of ghostly footsteps, and there crowded into the room a great company of goblins. Nor were these the only supernatural creatures which Raiko encountered, for presently he saw a being dressed like a nun. Her very small body was naked to the waist, her face was two feet in length, and her arms "were white as snow and thin as threads." For a moment this dreadful creature laughed, and then vanished like a mist.

Raiko heard the welcome sound of a cock crowing, and imagined that the ghostly visitors would trouble him no more; but once again he heard footsteps, and this time he saw no hideous hag, but a lovely woman, " more graceful than the willow branches as they wave in the breeze." As he gazed upon this lovely maiden his eyes became blinded for a moment on account of her radiant beauty. Before he could recover his sight he found himself enveloped in countless cobwebs. He struck at her with his sword, when she disappeared, and he found that he had but cut through the planks of the floor, and broken the foundation-stone beneath.

At this moment Tsuna joined his master, and they perceived that the sword was covered with *white* blood, and that the point had been broken in the conflict.

After much search Raiko and his retainer discovered a den in which they saw a monster with many legs and a head of enormous size covered with downy hair. Its mighty eyes shone like the sun and moon, as it groaned aloud : "I am sick and in pain ! "

As Raiko and Tsuna drew near they recognised the broken sword-point projecting from the monster. The heroes then dragged the creature out of its den and cut off its head. Out of the deep wound in the creature's stomach gushed nineteen hundred and ninety skulls, and in addition many spiders as large as children. Raiko and his follower realised that the monster before them was none other than the Mountain Spider. When they cut open the great carcass they discovered, within the entrails, the ghostly remains of many human corpses.

The Adventures of Prince Yamato Take

King Keiko bade his youngest son, Prince Yamato, go forth and slay a number of brigands. Before his departure the Prince prayed at the shrines of Ise, and begged that Ama-terasu, the Sun Goddess, would bless his enterprise. Prince Yamato's aunt was high-priestess of one of the Ise temples, and he told her about the task his father had entrusted to him. This good lady was much pleased to hear the news, and presented her nephew with a rich silk robe, saying that it would bring him luck, and perhaps be of service to him later on.

When Prince Yamato had returned to the palace and taken leave of his father, he left the court accompanied by his wife, the Princess Ototachibana, and a number of staunch followers, and proceeded to the Southern

Island of Kiushiu, which was infested by brigands. The country was so rough and impassable that Prince Yamato saw at once that he must devise some cunning scheme by which he might take the enemy unawares.

Having come to this conclusion, he bade the Princess Ototachibana bring him the rich silk robe his aunt had given him. This he put on under the direction, no doubt, of his wife. He let down his hair, stuck a comb in it, and adorned himself with jewels. When he looked into a mirror he saw that the disguise was perfect, and that he made quite a handsome woman.

Thus gorgeously apparelled, he entered the enemy's tent, where Kumaso and Takeru were sitting. It happened that they were discussing the King's son and his efforts to exterminate their band. When they chanced to look up they saw a fair woman coming towards them.

Kumaso was so delighted that he beckoned to the disguised Prince and bade him serve wine as quickly as possible. Yamato was only too delighted to do so. He affected feminine shyness. He walked with very minute steps, and glanced out of the corner of his eyes with all the timidity of a bashful maiden.

Kumaso drank far more wine than was good for him. He still went on drinking just to have the pleasure of seeing this lovely creature pouring it out for him.

When Kumaso became drunk Prince Yamato flung down the wine-jar, whipped out his dagger, and stabbed him to death.

Takeru, when he saw what had happened to his brother, attempted to escape, but Prince Yamato leapt upon him. Once more his dagger gleamed in the air, and Takeru fell to the earth.

"Stay your hand a moment," gasped the dying

brigand. "I would fain know who you are and whence you have come. Hitherto I thought that my brother and I were the strongest men in the kingdom. I am indeed mistaken."

"I am Yamato," said the Prince, "and son of the King who bade me kill such rebels as you!"

"Permit me to give you a new name," said the brigand politely. "From henceforth you shall be called Yamato Take, because you are the bravest man in the land."

Having thus spoken Takeru fell back dead.

The Wooden Sword

When the Prince was on his way to the capital he encountered another outlaw named Idzumo Takeru. Again resorting to strategy, he professed to be extremely friendly with this fellow. He cut a sword of wood and rammed it tightly into the sheath of his own steel weapon. He wore this whenever he expected to meet Takeru.

On one occasion Prince Yamato invited Takeru to swim with him in the river Hinokawa. While the brigand was swimming down-stream the Prince secretly landed, and, going to Takeru's clothes, lying on the bank, he managed to change swords, putting his wooden one in place of the keen steel sword of Takeru.

When Takeru came out of the water and put on his clothes the Prince asked him to show his skill with the sword. "We will prove," said he, "which is the better swordsman of the two."

Nothing loath, Takeru tried to unsheath his sword. It stuck fast, and as it happened to be of wood it was, of course, useless in any case. While the brigand was thus struggling Yamato cut off his head. Once again cunning had served him, and when he had returned to the palace he was feasted, and received many costly gifts from the King his father.

The "Grass-Cleaving-Sword"

Prince Yamato did not long remain idle in the palace, for his father commanded him to go forth and quell an Ainu rising in the eastern provinces.

When the Prince was ready to depart the King gave him a spear made from a holly-tree called the "Eight-Arms-Length-Spear." With this precious gift Prince Yamato visited the temples of Ise. His aunt, the high-priestess, again greeted him. She listened with interest to all her nephew told her, and was especially delighted to know how well the robe she had given him had served in his adventures.

When she had listened to his story she went into the temple and brought forth a sword and a bag containing flints. These she gave to Yamato as a parting gift.

The sword was the sword of Murakumo, belonging to the insignia of the Imperial House of Japan. The Prince could not have received a more auspicious gift. This sword, it will be remembered, once belonged to the Gods, and was discovered by Susa-no-o.

After a long march Prince Yamato and his men found themselves in the province of Suruga. The governor hospitably received him, and by way of entertainment organised a deer-hunt. Our hero for once in a way was utterly deceived, and joined the hunt without the least misgiving.

The Prince was taken to a great and wild plain covered with high grass. While he was engaged in hunting down the deer he suddenly became aware of fire. In another moment he saw flames and clouds of smoke shooting up in every direction. He was surrounded by fire, from which there was, apparently, no escape. Too late the guileless warrior realised that he had fallen into a trap, and a very warm trap too !

Our hero opened the bag his aunt had given him, set fire to the grass near him, and with the sword of Murakumo he cut down the tall green blades on either side as quickly as possible. No sooner had he done so than the wind suddenly changed and blew the flames away from him, so that eventually the Prince made good his escape without the slightest burn of any kind. And thus it was that the sword of Murakumo came to be known as the "Grass-Cleaving-Sword."

The Sacrifice of Ototachibana

In all these adventures the Prince had been followed by his faithful wife, the Princess Ototachibana. Sad to say, our hero, so praiseworthy in battle, was not nearly so estimable in his love. He looked down on his wife and treated her with indifference. She, poor loyal soul, had lost her beauty in serving her lord. Her skin was burnt with the sun, and her garments were soiled and torn. Yet she never complained, and though her face became sad she made a brave effort to maintain her usual sweetness of manner.

Now Prince Yamato happened to meet the fascinating Princess Miyadzu. Her robes were charming, her skin delicate as cherry-blossom. It was not long before he fell desperately in love with her. When the time came for him to depart he swore that he would return again and make the beautiful Princess Miyadzu his wife. He had scarcely made this promise when he looked up and saw Ototachibana, and on her face was a look of intense sadness. But Prince Yamato hardened his heart, and rode away, secretly determined to keep his promise.

When Prince Yamato, his wife and men, reached the sea-shore of Idzu, his followers desired to secure a number of boats in order that they might cross the Straits of Kadzusa.

The Prince cried haughtily : " Bah ! this is only a brook ! Why so many boats ? I could jump across it ! "

When they had all embarked and started on their journey a great storm arose. The waves turned into water-mountains, the wind shrieked, the lightning blazed in the dark clouds, and the thunder roared. It seemed that the boat that carried the Prince and his wife must needs sink, for this storm was the work of Rin-Jin, King of the Sea, who was angry with the proud and foolish words of Prince Yamato.

When the crew had taken down the sails in the hope of steadying the vessel the storm grew worse instead of better. At last Ototachibana arose, and, forgiving all the sorrow her lord had caused her, she resolved to sacrifice her life in order to save her much-loved husband.

Thus spoke the loyal Ototachibana : " Oh, Rin-Jin, the Prince, my husband, has angered you with his boasting. I, Ototachibana, give you my poor life in the place of Yamato Take. I now cast myself into your great surging kingdom, and do you in return bring my lord safely to the shore."

Having uttered these words, Ototachibana leapt into the seething waves, and in a moment they dragged that brave woman out of sight. No sooner had this sacrifice been made than the storm abated and the sun shone forth in a cloudless sky.

Yamato Take safely reached his destination, and succeeded in quelling the Ainu rising.

Our hero had certainly erred in his treatment of his faithful wife. Too late he learnt to appreciate her goodness ; but let it be said to his credit that she remained a loving memory till his death, while the Princess Miyadzu was entirely forgotten.

The Slaying of the Serpent

Now that Yamato Take had carried out his father's instructions, he passed through the province of Owari until he came to the province of Omi.

The province of Omi was afflicted with a great trouble. Many were in mourning, and many wept and cried aloud in their sorrow. The Prince, on making inquiries, was informed that a great serpent every day came down from the mountains and entered the villages, making a meal of many of the unfortunate inhabitants.

Prince Yamato at once started to climb up Mount Ibaki, where the great serpent was said to live. About half-way up he encountered the awful creature. The Prince was so strong that he killed the serpent by twisting his bare arms about it. He had no sooner done so than sudden darkness came over the land, and rain fell heavily. However, eventually the weather improved, and our hero was able to climb down the mountain.

When he reached home he found that his feet burned with a strange pain, and, moreover, that he felt very ill. He realised that the serpent had stung him, and, as he was too ill to move, he was carried to a famous mineral spring. Here he finally regained his accustomed health and strength, and for these blessings gave thanks to Ama-terasu, the Sun Goddess.

The Adventures of Momotaro

One day, while an old woman stood by a stream washing her clothes, she chanced to see an enormous peach floating on the water. It was quite the largest she had ever seen, and as this old woman and her

husband were extremely poor she immediately thought
what an excellent meal this extraordinary peach would
make. As she could find no stick with which to draw
the fruit to the bank, she suddenly remembered the
following verse :

> " Distant water is bitter,
> The near water is sweet ;
> Pass by the distant water
> And come into the sweet."

This little song had the desired effect. The peach
came nearer and nearer till it stopped at the old woman's
feet. She stooped down and picked it up. So delighted
was she with her discovery that she could not stay to
do any more washing, but hurried home as quickly as
possible.

When her husband arrived in the evening, with a
bundle of grass upon his back, the old woman excitedly
took the peach out of a cupboard and showed it to him.

The old man, who was tired and hungry, was equally
delighted at the thought of so delicious a meal. He
speedily brought a knife and was about to cut the
fruit open, when it suddenly opened of its own accord,
and the prettiest child imaginable tumbled out with a
merry laugh.

"Don't be afraid," said the little fellow. "The
Gods have heard how much you desired a child, and
have sent me to be a solace and a comfort in your old
age."

The old couple were so overcome with joy that they
scarcely knew what to do with themselves. Each in
turn nursed the child, caressed him, and murmured
many sweet and affectionate words. They called him
Momotaro, or "Son of a Peach."

When Momotaro was fifteen years old he was a lad
far taller and stronger than boys of his own age. The

making of a great hero stirred in his veins, and it was a knightly heroism that desired to right the wrong.

One day Momotaro came to his foster-father and asked him if he would allow him to take a long journey to a certain island in the North-Eastern Sea where dwelt a number of devils, who had captured a great company of innocent people, many of whom they ate. Their wickedness was beyond description, and Momotaro desired to kill them, rescue the unfortunate captives, and bring back the plunder of the island that he might share it with his foster-parents.

The old man was not a little surprised to hear this daring scheme. He knew that Momotaro was no common child. He had been sent from heaven, and he believed that all the devils in the world could not harm him. So at length the old man gave his consent, saying : "Go, Momotaro, slay the devils and bring peace to the land."

When the old woman had given Momotaro a number of rice-cakes the youth bade his foster-parents farewell, and started out upon his journey.

The Triumph of Momotaro

While Momotaro was resting under a hedge eating one of the rice-cakes, a great dog came up to him, growled, and showed his teeth. The dog, moreover, could speak, and threateningly begged that Momotaro would give him a cake. "Either you give me a cake," said he, "or I will kill you ! "

When, however, the dog heard that the famous Momotaro stood before him, his tail dropped between his legs and he bowed with his head to the ground, requesting that he might follow "Son of a Peach," and render to him all the service that lay in his power.

Momotaro readily accepted the offer, and after

throwing the dog half a cake they proceeded on their way.

They had not gone far when they encountered a monkey, who also begged to be admitted to Momotaro's service. This was granted, but it was some time before the dog and the monkey ceased snapping at each other and became good friends.

Proceeding upon their journey, they came across a pheasant. Now the innate jealousy of the dog was again awakened, and he ran forward and tried to kill the bright-plumed creature. Momotaro separated the combatants, and in the end the pheasant was also admitted to the little band, walking decorously in the rear.

At length Momotaro and his followers reached the shore of the North-Eastern Sea. Here our hero discovered a boat, and after a good deal of timidity on the part of the dog, monkey, and pheasant, they all got aboard, and soon the little vessel was spinning away over the blue sea.

After many days upon the ocean they sighted an island. Momotaro bade the bird fly off, a winged herald to announce his coming, and bid the devils surrender.

The pheasant flew over the sea and alighted on the roof of a great castle and shouted his stirring message, adding that the devils, as a sign of submission, should break their horns.

The devils only laughed and shook their horns and shaggy red hair. Then they brought forth iron bars and hurled them furiously at the bird. The pheasant cleverly evaded the missiles, and flew at the heads of many devils.

In the meantime Momotaro had landed with his two companions. He had no sooner done so than he saw

Momotaro and the Pheasant.

(See page 60*)*

Hidesato and the Centipede.

(See page 63)

two beautiful damsels weeping by a stream, as they wrung out blood-soaked garments.

"Oh!" said they pitifully, "we are daughters of *daimyōs*, and are now the captives of the Demon King of this dreadful island. Soon he will kill us, and alas! there is no one to come to our aid." Having made these remarks the women wept anew.

"Ladies," said Momotaro, "I have come for the purpose of slaying your wicked enemies. Show me a way into yonder castle."

So Momotaro, the dog, and the monkey entered through a small door in the castle. Once inside this fortification they fought tenaciously. Many of the devils were so frightened that they fell off the parapets and were dashed to pieces, while others were speedily killed by Momotaro and his companions. All were destroyed except the Demon King himself, and he wisely resolved to surrender, and begged that his life might be spared.

"No," said Momotaro fiercely. "I will not spare your wicked life. You have tortured many innocent people and robbed the country for many years."

Having said these words he gave the Demon King into the monkey's keeping, and then proceeded through all the rooms of the castle, and set free the numerous prisoners he found there. He also gathered together much treasure.

The return journey was a very joyous affair indeed. The dog and the pheasant carried the treasure between them, while Momotaro led the Demon King.

Momotaro restored the two daughters of *daimyōs* to their homes, and many others who had been made captives in the island. The whole country rejoiced in his victory, but no one more than Momotaro's foster-parents, who ended their days in peace and plenty, thanks to the great treasure of the devils which Momotaro bestowed upon them.

"My Lord Bag of Rice"

One day the great Hidesato came to a bridge that spanned the beautiful Lake Biwa. He was about to cross it when he noticed a great serpent-dragon fast asleep obstructing his progress. Hidesato, without a moment's hesitation, climbed over the monster and proceeded on his way.

He had not gone far when he heard some one calling to him. He looked back and saw that in the place of the dragon a man stood bowing to him with much ceremony. He was a strange-looking fellow with a dragon-shaped crown resting upon his red hair.

"I am the Dragon King of Lake Biwa," explained the red-haired man. "A moment ago I took the form of a horrible monster in the hope of finding a mortal who would not be afraid of me. You, my lord, showed no fear, and I rejoice exceedingly. A great centipede comes down from yonder mountain, enters my palace, and destroys my children and grandchildren. One by one they have become food for this dread creature, and I fear soon that unless something can be done to slay this centipede I myself shall become a victim. I have waited long for a brave mortal. All men who have hitherto seen me in my dragon-shape have run away. You are a brave man, and I beg that you will kill my bitter enemy."

Hidesato, who always welcomed an adventure, the more so when it was a perilous one, readily consented to see what he could do for the Dragon King.

When Hidesato reached the Dragon King's palace he found it to be a very magnificent building indeed, scarcely less beautiful than the Sea King's palace itself.

He was feasted with crystallised lotus leaves and flowers, and ate the delicacies spread before him with choice ebony chopsticks. While he feasted ten little goldfish danced, and just behind the goldfish ten carp made sweet music on the *koto* and *samisen*. Hidesato was just thinking how excellently he had been entertained, and how particularly good was the wine, when they all heard an awful noise like a dozen thunderclaps roaring together.

Hidesato and the Dragon King hastily rose and ran to the balcony. They saw that Mount Mikami was scarcely recognisable, for it was covered from top to bottom with the great coils of the centipede. In its head glowed two balls of fire, and its hundred feet were like a long winding chain of lanterns.

Hidesato fitted an arrow to his bowstring and pulled it back with all his might. The arrow sped forth into the night and struck the centipede in the middle of the head, but glanced off immediately without inflicting any wound. Again Hidesato sent an arrow whirling into the air, and again it struck the monster and fell harmlessly to the ground. Hidesato had only one arrow left. Suddenly remembering the magical effect of human saliva, he put the remaining arrow-head into his mouth for a moment, and then hastily adjusted it to his bow and took careful aim.

The last arrow struck its mark and pierced the centipede's brain. The creature stopped moving ; the light in its eyes and legs darkened and then went out, and Lake Biwa, with its palace beneath, was shrouded in awful darkness. Thunder rolled, lightning flashed, and it seemed for the moment that the Dragon King's palace would topple to the ground.

The next day, however, all sign of storm had vanished. The sky was clear. The sun shone brightly.

In the sparkling blue lake lay the body of the great centipede.

The Dragon King and those about him were over-joyed when they knew that their dread enemy had been destroyed. Hidesato was again feasted, even more royally than before. When he finally departed he did so with a retinue of fishes suddenly converted into men. The Dragon King bestowed upon our hero five precious gifts—two bells, a bag of rice, a roll of silk, and a cooking-pot.

The Dragon King accompanied Hidesato as far as the bridge, and then he reluctantly allowed the hero and the procession of servants carrying the presents to proceed on their way.

When Hidesato reached his home the Dragon King's servants put down the presents and suddenly disappeared.

The presents were no ordinary gifts. The rice-bag was inexhaustible, there was no end to the roll of silk, and the cooking-pot would cook without fire of any kind. Only the bells were without magical pro-perties, and these were presented to a temple in the vicinity. Hidesato grew rich, and his fame spread far and wide. People now no longer called him Hidesato, but Tawara Toda, or " My Lord Bag of Rice."

CHAPTER III : THE BAMBOO-CUTTER AND THE MOON-MAIDEN

The Coming of the Lady Kaguya

LONG ago there lived an old bamboo-cutter by the name of Sanugi no Miyakko. One day, while he was busy with his hatchet in a grove of bamboos, he suddenly perceived a miraculous light, and on closer inspection discovered in the heart of a reed a very small creature of exquisite beauty. He gently picked up the tiny girl, only about four inches in height, and carried her home to his wife. So delicate was this little maiden that she had to be reared in a basket.

Now it happened that the Bamboo-cutter continued to set about his business, and night and day, as he cut down the reeds, he found gold, and, once poor, he now amassed a considerable fortune.

The child, after she had been but three months with these simple country folk, suddenly grew in stature to that of a full-grown maid ; and in order that she should be in keeping with such a pleasing, if surprising, event, her hair, hitherto allowed to flow in long tresses about her shoulders, was now fastened in a knot on her head. In due season the Bamboo-cutter named the girl the Lady Kaguya, or "Precious-Slender-Bamboo-of-the-Field-of-Autumn." When she had been named a great feast was held, in which all the neighbours participated.

The Wooing of the "Precious-Slender-Bamboo-of-the-Field-of-Autumn"

> "When a woman is somewhat fairer than the crowd of women how greatly do men long to gaze upon her beauty !"—*Taketori.*

Now the Lady Kaguya was of all women the most beautiful, and immediately after the feast the fame of her beauty spread throughout the land. Would-be lovers gathered around the fence and lingered in the porch with the hope of at least getting a glimpse of this lovely maiden. Night and day these forlorn suitors waited, but in vain. Those who were of humble origin gradually began to recognise that their love-making was useless. But five wealthy suitors still persisted, and would not relax their efforts. They were Prince Ishizukuri and Prince Kuramochi, the Sadaijin Dainagon Abe no Miushi, the Chiunagon Otomo no Miyuki, and Morotada, the Lord of Iso. These ardent lovers bore "the ice and snow of winter and the thunderous heats of midsummer with equal fortitude." When these lords finally asked the Bamboo-cutter to bestow his daughter upon one of them, the old man politely explained that the maiden was not really his daughter, and as that was so she could not be compelled to obey his own wishes in the matter.

At last the lords returned to their mansions, but still continued to make their supplications more persistently than ever. Even the kindly Bamboo-cutter began to remonstrate with the Lady Kaguya, and to point out that it was becoming for so handsome a maid to marry, and that among the five noble suitors she could surely make a very good match. To this the wise Kaguya replied : "Not so fair am I that I may be certain of a man's faith, and were I to mate with one whose heart proved fickle what a miserable fate were mine ! Noble lords, without doubt, are these of whom thou speakest, but I would not wed a man whose heart should be all untried and unknown."

It was finally arranged that Kaguya should marry the suitor who proved himself the most worthy. This news brought momentary hope to the five great lords, and when night came they assembled before the house where the maiden dwelt "with flute music and with singing, with chanting to accompaniments and piping, with cadenced tap and clap of fan." Only the Bamboo-cutter went out to thank the lords for their serenading. When he had come into the house again, Kaguya thus set forth her plan to test the suitors :

"In Tenjiku (Northern India) is a beggar's bowl of stone, which of old the Buddha himself bore, in quest whereof let Prince Ishizukuri depart and bring me the same. And on the mountain Horai, that towers over the Eastern ocean, grows a tree with roots of silver and trunk of gold and fruitage of pure white jade, and I bid Prince Kuramochi fare thither and break off and bring me a branch thereof. Again, in the land of Morokoshi men fashion fur-robes of the pelt of the Flame-proof Rat, and I pray the Dainagon to find me one such. Then of the Chiunagon I require the rainbow-hued jewel that hides its sparkle deep in the dragon's head ; and from the hands of the Lord Iso would I fain receive the cowry-shell that the swallow brings hither over the broad sea-plain."

The Begging-bowl of the Lord Buddha

The Prince Ishizukuri, after pondering over the matter of going to distant Tenjiku in search of the Lord Buddha's begging-bowl, came to the conclusion that such a proceeding would be futile. He decided, therefore, to counterfeit the bowl in question. He laid his plans cunningly, and took good care that the Lady Kaguya was informed that he had actually undertaken the journey. As a matter of fact this artful suitor hid in Yamato for three years, and after that time discovered in a hill-monastery in Tochi a bowl of extreme age resting upon an altar of Binzuru (the Succourer in Sickness). This bowl he took away with him, and wrapped it in brocade, and attached to the gift an artificial branch of blossom.

When the Lady Kaguya looked upon the bowl she found inside a scroll containing the following:

> " Over seas, over hills
> hath thy servant fared, and weary
> and wayworn he perisheth :
> O what tears hath cost this bowl of
> stone,
> what floods of streaming tears ! "

But when the Lady Kaguya perceived that no light shone from the vessel she at once knew that it had never belonged to the Lord Buddha. She accordingly sent back the bowl with the following verse :

> " Of the hanging dewdrop
> not even the passing sheen
> dwells herein :
> On the Hill of Darkness, the Hill
> of Ogura,
> what couldest thou hope to find ? "

The Prince, having thrown away the bowl, sought to turn the above remonstrance into a compliment to the lady who wrote it.

> " Nay, on the Hill of Brightness
> what splendour
> will not pale ?
> Would that away from the light
> of thy beauty
> the sheen of yonder Bowl might
> prove me true ! "

It was a prettily turned compliment by a suitor who was an utter humbug. This latest poetical sally availed nothing, and the Prince sadly departed.

JEWEL-BEARING BRANCH OF MOUNT HORAI

The Jewel-bearing Branch of Mount Horai

Prince Kuramochi, like his predecessor, was equally wily, and made it generally known that he was setting out on a journey to the land of Tsukushi in quest of the Jewel-bearing Branch. What he actually did was to employ six men of the Uchimaro family, celebrated craftsmen, and secure for them a dwelling hidden from the haunts of men, where he himself abode, for the purpose of instructing the craftsmen as to how they were to make a Jewel-bearing Branch identical with the one described by the Lady Kaguya.

When the Jewel-bearing Branch was finished, he set out to wait upon the Lady Kaguya, who read the following verse attached to the gift:

> " Though it were at the peril
> of my very life,
> without the Jewel-laden Branch
> in my hands never again
> would I have dared to return ! "

The Lady Kaguya looked sadly upon this glittering branch, and listened without interest to the Prince's purely imaginative story of his adventures. The Prince dwelt upon the terrors of the sea, of strange monsters, of acute hunger, of disease, which were their trials upon the ocean. Then this incorrigible story-teller went on to describe how they came to a high mountain rising out of the sea, where they were greeted by a woman bearing a silver vessel which she filled with water. On the mountain were wonderful flowers and trees, and a stream "rainbow-hued, yellow as gold, white as silver, blue as precious *ruri* (lapis lazuli) ; and the stream was spanned by bridges built up of divers gems, and by it grew trees laden with dazzling jewels, and from one of these I broke off the branch which I venture now to offer to the Lady Kaguya."

No doubt the Lady Kaguya would have been forced to believe this ingenious tale had not at that very moment the six craftsmen appeared on the scene, and by loudly demanding payment for the ready-made Jewel-Branch, exposed the treachery of the Prince, who made a hasty retreat. The Lady Kaguya herself rewarded the craftsmen, happy, no doubt, to escape so easily.

The Flame-proof Fur-Robe

The Sadaijin (Left Great Minister) Abe no Miushi commissioned a merchant, by the name of Wokei, to obtain for him a fur-robe made from the Flame-proof Rat, and when the merchant's ship had returned from the land of Morokoshi it bore a fur-robe, which the sanguine Sadaijin imagined to be the very object of his desire. The Fur-Robe rested in a casket, and the Sadaijin, believing in the honesty of the merchant, described it as being " of a sea-green colour, the hairs tipped with shining gold, a treasure indeed of incomparable loveliness, more to be admired for its pure excellence than even for its virtue in resisting the flame of fire."

The Sadaijin, assured of success in his wooing, gaily set out to present his gift to the Lady Kaguya, offering in addition the following verse :

> " Endless are the fires of love
> that consume me, yet unconsumed
> is the Robe of Fur :
> dry at last are my sleeves,
> for shall I not see her face this day ! "

At last the Sadaijin was able to present his gift to the Lady Kaguya. Thus she addressed the Bamboo-cutter, who always seems to have been conveniently on the scene at such times : "If this Robe be thrown amid the flames and be not burnt up, I shall know it is in very truth the Flame-proof Robe, and may no longer refuse this lord's suit." A fire was lighted, and the Robe thrown into the flames, where it perished immediately. "When the Sadaijin saw this his face grew green as grass, and he stood there astonished." But the Lady Kaguya discreetly rejoiced, and returned the casket with the following verse :

> "Without a vestige even left
> thus to burn utterly away,
> had I dreamt it of this Robe of Fur.
> Alas the pretty thing ! far otherwise
> would I have dealt with it."

The Jewel in the Dragon's Head

The Chiunagon Otomo no Miyuki assembled his household and informed his retainers that he desired them to bring him the Jewel in the Dragon's head.

Aften some demur they pretended to set off on this quest. In the meantime the Chiunagon was so sure of his servants' success that he had his house lavishly adorned throughout with exquisite lacquer-work, in gold and silver. Every room was hung with brocade, the panels rich with pictures, and over the roof were silken cloths.

Weary of waiting, the Chiunagon after a time journeyed to Naniwa and questioned the inhabitants if any of his servants had taken boat in quest of the Dragon. The Chiunagon learnt that none of his men had come to Naniwa, and, considerably displeased at the news, he himself embarked with a helmsman.

Now it happened that the Thunder God was angry and the sea ran high. After many days the storm grew so severe and the boat was so near sinking that the helmsman ventured to remark : "The howling of the wind and the raging of the waves and the mighty roar of the thunder are signs of the wrath of the God whom my lord offends, who would slay the Dragon of the deep, for through the Dragon is the storm raised, and well it were if my lord offered a prayer."

As the Chiunagon had been seized with "a terrible sickness," it is not surprising to find that he readily took the helmsman's advice. He prayed no less than a thousand times, enlarging on his folly in attempting to slay the Dragon, and solemnly vowed that he would leave the Ruler of the deep in peace.

The thunder ceased and the clouds dispersed, but the wind was as fierce and strong as ever. The helmsman, however, told his master that it was a fair wind and blew towards their own land.

At last they reached the strand of Akashi, in Harima. But the Chiunagon, still ill and mightily frightened, vowed that they had been driven upon a savage shore, and lay full length in the boat, panting heavily, and refusing to rise when the governor of the district presented himself.

When the Chiunagon at last realised that they had not been blown upon some savage shore he consented to land. No wonder the governor smiled when he saw "the wretched appearance of the discomfited lord, chilled to the very bone, with swollen belly and eyes lustreless as sloes."

At length the Chiunagon was carried in a litter to his own home. When he had arrived his cunning servants humbly told their master how they had failed in the quest. Thus the Chiunagon greeted them : "Ye have done well to return empty-handed. Yonder Dragon, assuredly, has kinship with the Thunder God, and whoever shall lay hands on him to take the jewel that gleams in his head shall find himself in peril. Myself am sore spent with toil and hardship, and no guerdon have I won. A thief of men's souls and a destroyer of their bodies is the Lady Kaguya, nor ever will I seek her abode again, nor ever bend ye your steps thitherward."

We are told, in conclusion, that when the women of his household heard of their lord's adventure "they laughed till their sides were sore, while the silken cloths he had caused to be drawn over the roof of his mansion were carried away, thread by thread, by the crows to line their nests with."

The Royal Hunt[1]

Now the fame of the Lady Kaguya's beauty reached the court, and the Mikado, anxious to gaze upon her, sent one of his palace ladies, Fusago, to go and see the Bamboo-cutter's daughter, and to report to his Majesty of her excellences.

However, when Fusago reached the Bamboo-cutter's house the Lady Kaguya refused to see her. So the palace lady returned to court and reported the matter to the Mikado. His Majesty, not a little displeased, sent for the Bamboo-cutter, and made him bring the Lady Kaguya to court that he might see her, adding: "A hat of nobility, perchance, shall be her father's reward."

The old Bamboo-cutter was an admirable soul, and mildly discountenanced his daughter's extraordinary behaviour. Although he loved court favours and

---

[1] The Fifth Quest, that of Lord Iso, is omitted. The story is trivial and of no particular interest. Suffice it to say that Lord Iso's search for the cowry-shell was in vain.

probably hankered after so distinguished a hat, it must be said of him that he was first of all true to his duty as a father.

When, on returning to his home, he discussed the matter with the Lady Kaguya, she informed the old man that if she were compelled to go to court it would certainly cause her death, adding : "The price of my father's hat of nobility will be the destruction of his child."

The Bamboo-cutter was deeply affected by these words, and once more set out on a journey to the court, where he humbly made known his daughter's decision.

The Mikado, not to be denied even by an extraordinarily beautiful woman, hit on the ingenious plan of ordering a Royal Hunt, so arranged that he might unexpectedly arrive at the Bamboo-cutter's dwelling, and perchance see the lady who could set at defiance the desires of an emperor.

On the day appointed for the Royal Hunt, therefore, the Mikado entered the Bamboo-cutter's house. He had no sooner done so than he was surprised to see in the room in which he stood a wonderful light, and in the light none other than the Lady Kaguya.

His Majesty advanced and touched the maiden's sleeve, whereupon she hid her face, but not before the Mikado had caught a glimpse of her beauty. Amazed by her extreme loveliness, and taking no notice of her protests, he ordered a palace litter to be brought ; but on its arrival the Lady Kaguya suddenly vanished. The Emperor, perceiving that he was dealing with no mortal maid, exclaimed: "It shall be as thou desirest, maiden ; but 'tis prayed that thou resume thy form, that once more thy beauty may be seen."

So the Lady Kaguya resumed her fair form again.

THE CELESTIAL ROBE OF FEATHERS

As his Majesty was about to be borne away he composed the following verse :

> " Mournful the return
> of the Royal Hunt,
> and full of sorrow the brooding
> heart ;
> for she resists and stays behind,
> the Lady Kaguya ! "

The Lady Kaguya thus made answer :

> " Under the roof o'ergrown with
> hopbine
> long were the years
> she passed.
> How may she dare to look upon
> The Palace of Precious Jade ? "

The Celestial Robe of Feathers

In the third year after the Royal Hunt, and in the spring-time, the Lady Kaguya continually gazed at the moon. On the seventh month, when the moon was full, the Lady Kaguya's sorrow increased so that her weeping distressed the maidens who served her. At last they came to the Bamboo-cutter, and said : " Long has the Lady Kaguya watched the moon, waxing in melancholy with the waxing thereof, and her woe now passes all measure, and sorely she weeps and wails ; wherefore we counsel thee to speak with her."

When the Bamboo-cutter communed with his daughter, he requested that she should tell him the cause of her sorrow, and was informed that the sight of the moon caused her to reflect upon the wretchedness of the world.

During the eighth month the Lady Kaguya explained to her maids that she was no ordinary mortal, but that her birthplace was the Capital of Moonland, and that the time was now at hand when she was destined to leave the world and return to her old home.

Not only was the Bamboo-cutter heart-broken at this sorrowful news, but the Mikado also was considerably troubled when he heard of the proposed departure of the Lady Kaguya. His Majesty was informed that at the next full moon a company would be sent down from that shining orb to take this beautiful lady away, whereupon he determined to put a check upon this celestial invasion. He ordered that a guard of soldiers should be stationed about the Bamboo-cutter's house, armed and prepared, if need be, to shoot their arrows upon those Moonfolk, who would fain take the beautiful Lady Kaguya away.

The old Bamboo-cutter naturally thought that with such a guard to protect his daughter the invasion from the moon would prove utterly futile. The Lady Kaguya attempted to correct the old man's ideas on the subject, saying : " Ye cannot prevail over the folk of yonder land, nor will your artillery harm them nor your defences avail against them, for every door will fly open at their approach, nor may your valour help, for be ye never so stout-hearted, when the Moonfolk come vain will be your struggle with them." These remarks made the Bamboo-cutter exceedingly angry. He asserted that his nails would turn into talons—in short, that he would completely annihilate such impudent visitors from the moon.

Now while the royal guard was stationed about the Bamboo-cutter's house, on the roof and in every direction, the night wore away. At the hour of the Rat[1] a great glory, exceeding the splendour of the moon and stars,

[1] Midnight until two in the morning. "Years, days, and hours," writes Professor B. H. Chamberlain, "were all accounted as belonging to one of the signs of the zodiac."

shone around. While the light still continued a strange cloud approached, bearing upon it a company of Moon-folk. The cloud slowly descended until it came near to the ground, and the Moonfolk assembled themselves in order. When the royal guard perceived them every soldier grew afraid at the strange spectacle ; but at length some of their number summoned up sufficient courage to bend their bows and send their arrows flying ; but all their shafts went astray.

On the cloud there rested a canopied car, resplendent with curtains of finest woollen fabric, and from out the car a mighty voice sounded, saying : "Come thou forth, Miyakko Maro ! "

The Bamboo-cutter tottered forth to obey the summons, and received for his pains an address from the chief of the Moonfolk commencing with, " Thou fool," and ending up with a command that the Lady Kaguya should be given up without further delay.

The car floated upward upon the cloud till it hovered over the roof. Once again the same mighty voice shouted : "Ho there, Kaguya ! How long wouldst thou tarry in this sorry place ? "

Immediately the outer door of the storehouse and the inner lattice-work were opened by the power of the Moonfolk, and revealed the Lady Kaguya and her women gathered about her.

The Lady Kaguya, before taking her departure, greeted the prostrate Bamboo-cutter and gave him a scroll bearing these words : " Had I been born in this land, never should I have quitted it until the time came for my father to suffer no sorrow for his child ; but now, on the contrary, must I pass beyond the boundaries of this world, though sorely against my will. My silken mantle I leave behind me as a memorial, and when the moon lights up the night let my father gaze upon it.

77

Now my eyes must take their last look and I must mount to yonder sky, whence I fain would fall, meteorwise, to earth."

Now the Moonfolk had brought with them, in a coffer, a Celestial Feather Robe and a few drops of the Elixir of Life. One of them said to the Lady Kaguya : "Taste, I pray you, of this Elixir, for soiled has your spirit become with the grossnesses of this filthy world."

The Lady Kaguya, after tasting the Elixir, was about to wrap up some in the mantle she was leaving behind for the benefit of the old Bamboo-cutter, who had loved her so well, when one of the Moonfolk prevented her, and attempted to throw over her shoulders the Celestial Robe, when the Lady Kaguya exclaimed : "Have patience yet awhile ; who dons yonder robe changes his heart, and I have still somewhat to say ere I depart." Then she proceeded to write the following to the Mikado :

"Your Majesty deigned to send a host to protect your servant, but it was not to be, and now is the misery at hand of departing with those who have come to bear her away with them. Not permitted was it to her to serve your Majesty, and despite her will was it that she yielded not obedience to the Royal command, and wrung with grief is her heart thereat, and perchance your Majesty may have thought the Royal will was not understood, and was opposed by her, and so will she appear to your Majesty lacking in good manners, which she would not your Majesty deemed her to be, and therefore humbly she lays this writing at the Royal Feet. And now must she don the Feather Robe and mournfully bid her lord farewell."

Having delivered this scroll into the hands of the captain of the host, together with a bamboo joint con-

The Moonfolk demand the Lady Kaguya.
(See page 77)

Buddha and the Dragon.

(See page 80)

taining the Elixir, the Feather Robe was thrown over her, and in a moment all memory of her earthly existence departed.

Then the Lady Kaguya entered the car, surrounded by the company of Moonfolk, and the cloud rapidly rose skyward till it was lost to sight.

The sorrow of the Bamboo-cutter and of the Mikado knew no bounds. The latter held a Grand Council, and inquired which was the highest mountain in the land. One of the councillors answered : " In Suruga stands a mountain, not remote from the capital, that towers highest towards heaven among all the mountains of the land." Whereupon his Majesty composed the following verse :

> " Never more to see her !
> Tears of grief overwhelm me,
> and as for me,
> with the Elixir of Life
> what have I to do ? "

Then the scroll, which the Lady Kaguya had written, together with the Elixir, was given to Tsuki no Iwakasa. These he was commanded to take to the summit of the highest mountain in Suruga, and, standing upon the highest peak, to burn the scroll and the Elixir of Life.

" So Tsuki no Iwakasa heard humbly the Royal command, and took with him a company of warriors, and climbed the mountain and did as he was bidden. And it was from that time forth that the name of Fuji (*Fuji-yama*, 'Never Dying') was given to yonder mountain, and men say that the smoke of that burning still curls from its high peak to mingle with the clouds of heaven."

CHAPTER IV : BUDDHA LEGENDS

The Legend of the Golden Lotus

THE following legend is obviously not of Japanese origin. The priests of Buddhism in Japan knew that the success of their religion lay, not in sweeping out the old gods of Shintō, but in adapting them with infinite cleverness to the needs of their own teaching. In this case Japan has borrowed from India and in a minor degree from China, if we may look upon the dragon as originally belonging to the Celestial Kingdom. We have followed closely Mr. Edward Greey's version, and insert it here because it often enters into a Nippon priest's discourse, and has a decidedly Japanese setting. We might duplicate legends of this kind, but one will be sufficient for our purpose. The other two legends given in this chapter are strictly Japanese.

The Lord Buddha, having concluded his holy meditations upon Mount Dan-doku, slowly walked along a rocky pathway on his way to the city. The dark shadows of night crept over the country, and there was profound stillness everywhere.

On nearing his destination the Lord Buddha heard some one shout : "*Shio-giyo mu-jiyo !*" ("The outward manner is not always an index to the natural disposition.")

The Lord Buddha was delighted at these words, and desired to learn who had spoken so wisely. Over and over again he heard the same words, and, drawing to the edge of a precipice, he looked down into the valley beneath, and perceived an extremely ugly dragon gazing up at him with angry eyes.

The Holy One then seated himself upon a rock, and inquired of the dragon how he had come to learn one

80

of the highest mysteries of Buddhism. Such profound wisdom suggested a store of spiritual truths yet to be revealed, and the Lord Buddha, therefore, requested that the dragon should give utterance to other wise sayings.

Then the dragon, having coiled himself round the rock, shouted with a great voice : "*Ze-shio metsu-po !*" ("All living things are antagonistic to the law of Buddha !")

After uttering these words the dragon was silent for some time. Then the Lord Buddha begged to hear yet another sentence.

"*Shio-metsu metsu-i !*" ("All living things must die !") shouted the dragon.

At these words the dragon looked up at the Lord Buddha, and upon his dreadful countenance there was an expression of extreme hunger.

The dragon then informed the Lord Buddha that the next truth was the last, and so precious that he could not reveal it until his hunger had been appeased.

At this the Holy One remarked that he would deny the dragon nothing so long as he heard the fourth truth revealed, and inquired of the dragon what he demanded. When the Lord Buddha heard that human flesh was what the dragon required in exchange for his last precious fragment of wisdom, the Master informed the dragon that his religion forbade the destruction of life, but that he would, for the welfare of his people, sacrifice his own body.

The dragon opened his great mouth and said : "*Jaku-metsu I-raku !*" ("The greatest happiness is experienced after the soul has left the body !")

The Lord Buddha bowed, and then sprang into the gaping mouth of the dragon.

No sooner had the Holy One touched the jaws of

the monster than they suddenly divided into eight
parts, and in a moment changed into the eight petals
of the Golden Lotus.

The Bronze Buddha of Kamakura and the Whale[1]

"Above the old songs turned to ashes and pain,
  Under which Death enshrouds the idols and trees with mist of sigh,
  (Where are Kamakura's rising days and life of old ?)
  With heart heightened to hush, the Daibutsu forever sits."
                                        Yone Noguchi.

The great bronze Buddha of Kamakura, or the
Daibutsu, is undoubtedly one of the most remarkable
sights in Japan. At one time Kamakura was the capital
of Nippon. It was a great city of nearly a million inhabitants, and was the seat of the Shōguns and of the
Regents of the Hōjō family during the troublous
period of the Middle Ages. But Kamakura, for all its
devout worshippers of the Lord Buddha, was destroyed
by storm on two occasions, until it finally lost its importance. To-day rice-fields and woods are to be seen
in place of the glory of old. Storm and fire, however,
have left untouched the temple of Hachiman (the God
of War) and the bronze image of Buddha. At one
time this gigantic figure reposed in a temple, but now
it stands high above the trees, with an inscrutable smile
upon its great face, with eyes full of a peace that cannot
be shaken by the petty storms of the world.

Legend is nearly always elemental. Divinities,
irrespective of their austerity, are brought down to a
very human level. It is a far cry from the complex
teaching of the Lord Buddha to the story of Amida
Butsu and the whale. One can trace in the following
legend an almost pathetic desire to veil the greatness of
Buddha. The gigantic size of the Daibutsu is not

[1] Adapted from *Fairy Tales of Old Japan*, by W. E. Griffis.

really in keeping with that curious love of little things which is so characteristic of the Japanese people. There is a playful irony in this story, a desire to take down the great Teacher a peg or two—if only to take him down in stature a paltry two inches!

So many things appear to us to be done in a topsy-turvy way in Japan that we are not surprised to find that in measuring metal and soft goods the feet on the yard-stick are not alike. For soft goods a whale measure is used, for any hard material a metal foot. There are two inches of difference in these measures, and the following legend may possibly give us the reason for this apparently rather confusing discrepancy.

The Bronze Buddha, in its sitting posture, is fifty feet high, ninety-seven feet in circumference, the length of its face eight feet, and as for its thumbs they are three feet round. It is probably the tallest piece of bronze in the world. Such an enormous image naturally created a considerable sensation in the days when Kamakura was a flourishing city, laid out by the great General Yoritomo. The roads in and about the city were densely packed with pilgrims, anxious to gaze upon the latest marvel, and all agreed that this bronze image was the biggest thing in the world.

Now it may be that certain sailors who had seen this marvel chatted about it as they plied their nets. Whether this was so or not, a mighty whale, who lived in the Northern Sea, happened to hear about the Bronze Buddha of Kamakura, and as he regarded himself as being far bigger than anything on land, the idea of a possible rival did not meet with his approval. He deemed it impossible that little men could construct anything that could vie with his enormous bulk, and laughed heartily at the very absurdity of such a conception.

His laughter, however, did not last long. He was

83

inordinately jealous, and when he heard about the numerous pilgrimages to Kamakura and the incessant praise evoked from those who had seen the image he grew exceedingly angry, lashed the sea into foam, and blew down his nose with so much violence that the other creatures of the deep gave him a very wide berth. His loneliness only aggravated his trouble, and he was unable to eat or sleep, and in consequence grew thin. He at last decided to chat the matter over with a kindly shark.

The shark answered the whale's heated questions with quiet solicitude, and consented to go to the Southern Sea in order that he might take the measurement of the image, and bring back the result of his labour to his agitated friend.

The shark set off upon his journey, until he came to the shore, where he could see the image towering above him, about half a mile inland. As he could not walk on dry land he was about to renounce his quest, when he had the good fortune to discover a rat enjoying a scamper along a junk. He explained his mission to the rat, and requested that much-flattered little creature to take the measurement of the Bronze Buddha.

So the rat climbed down the junk, swam ashore, and entered the dark temple where the Great Buddha stood. At first he was so overcome by the magnificence he saw about him that he was uncertain as to how to proceed in carrying out the shark's request. He eventually decided to walk round the image, counting his footsteps as he went. He discovered after he had performed this task that he had walked exactly five thousand paces, and on his return to the junk he told the shark the measurement of the base of the Bronze Buddha.

The shark, with profuse thanks to the rat, returned

to the Northern Sea, and informed the whale that the reports concerning the size of this exasperating image were only too true.

" A little knowledge is a dangerous thing " evidently applies equally well to whales, for the whale of this legend, after receiving the information, grew more furious than ever. As in a story familiar to English children, he put on magic boots in order to travel on land as well as he had always done in the sea.

The whale reached the Kamakura temple at night. He discovered that the priests had gone to bed, and were apparently fast asleep. He knocked at the door. Instead of the dismal murmur of a half-awake priest he heard the Lord Buddha say, in a voice that rang like the sound of a great bell : "Come in !"

" I cannot," replied the whale, " because I am too big. Will you please come out and see me ?"

When Buddha found out who his visitor was, and what he wanted at so unearthly an hour, he condescendingly stepped down from his pedestal and came outside the temple. There was utter amazement on both sides. Had the whale possessed knees they would assuredly have knocked together. He knocked his head on the ground instead. For his part, Buddha was surprised to find a creature of such gigantic proportions.

We can imagine the consternation of the chief priest when he found that the pedestal did not bear the image of his Master. Hearing a strange conversation going on outside the temple, he went out to see what was taking place. The much-frightened priest was invited to join in the discussion, and was requested to take the measurement of the image and the whale, and accordingly began to measure with his rosary. During this proceeding the image and the whale awaited the result with bated breath. When the measurements had been taken the whale was found to be two inches longer and taller than the image.

The whale went back to the Northern Sea more utterly vain than ever, while the image returned to its temple and sat down again, and there it has remained to this day, none the worse, perhaps, for finding that it was not quite so big as it imagined. Dealers in dry goods and dealers in wood and iron agreed from that day to this to differ as to what was a foot—and the difference was a matter of two inches.

The Crystal of Buddha[1]

In ancient days there lived in Japan a great State Minister named Kamatari. Now Kamatari's only daughter, Kohaku Jo, was extremely beautiful, and as good as she was beautiful. She was the delight of her father's heart, and he resolved that, if she married, no one of less account than a king should be her husband. With this idea continually in his mind, he steadfastly refused the offers for her hand.

One day there was a great tumult in the palace courtyard. Through the open gates streamed a number of men bearing a banner on which was worked a silken dragon on a yellow background. Kamatari learnt that these men had come from the court of China with a message from the Emperor Koso. The Emperor had heard of the exceeding beauty and exquisite charm of Kohaku Jo, and desired to marry her. As is usual in the East on such occasions, the Emperor's offer was accompanied with the promise that if Kohaku Jo should become his bride he would allow her to choose from his store of treasures whatever she liked to send to her own country.

[1] Adapted from *Buddha's Crystal*, by Madame Yei Ozaki.

THE CRYSTAL OF BUDDHA

After Kamatari had received the envoys with due pomp and ceremony, and put at their disposal a whole wing of the palace, he returned to his own room and bade his servant bring his daughter into his presence.

When Kohaku had entered her father's room she bowed before him and sat patiently on the white mats waiting for her august parent to speak to her.

Kamatari told her that he had chosen the Emperor of China to be her husband, and the little maid wept on hearing the news. She had been so happy in her own home, and China seemed such a long way off. When, however, her father foretold more happiness in the future than she had ever had in the past, she dried her eyes and listened to her parent's words, a little amazed to hear, perhaps, that all China's treasures were to be laid at her own small feet. She was glad when her father told her that she would be able to send three of these treasures to the temple of Kofukuji, where she had received a blessing when a little babe.

So Kohaku obeyed her father with not a little misgiving, not a little heartache. Her girl companions wept when they heard the news, but they were comforted when Kohaku's mother told them that some of their number would be chosen to go with their mistress.

Before Kohaku sailed for China she wended her way to the beloved temple of Kofukuji, and, arriving at the sacred shrine, she prayed for protection in her journey, vowing that if her prayers were answered she would search China for its three most precious treasures, and send them to the temple as a thank-offering.

Kohaku reached China in safety and was received by the Emperor Koso with great magnificence. Her childish fears were soon dispelled by the Emperor's kindness. Indeed, he showed her considerably more than kindness. He spoke to her in the language of a lover : "After long, long days of weary waiting I have gathered the 'azalea of the distant mountain,' and now I plant it in my garden, and great is the gladness of my heart ! "[1]

The Emperor Koso led her from palace to palace, and she knew not which was the most beautiful, but her royal husband was aware that she was far more lovely than any of them. Because of her great loveliness he desired that it should be ever remembered throughout the length and breadth of China, even beyond the bounds of his kingdom. "So he called together his goldsmiths and gardeners," as Madame Ozaki writes in describing this story, "and commanded them to fashion a path for the Empress such as had never been heard of in the wide world. The stepping-stones of this path were to be lotus-flowers, carved out of silver and gold, for her to walk on whenever she strolled forth under the trees or by the lake, so that it might be said that her beautiful feet were never soiled by touching the earth ; and ever since then, in China and Japan, poet-lovers and lover-poets in song and sonnet and sweet conversation have called the feet of the women they love 'lotus feet.'"

But in spite of all the magnificence that surrounded Kohaku she did not forget her native land or the vow she had made in the temple of Kofukuji. One day she timidly informed the Emperor of her promise, and he, only too glad to have another opportunity of pleasing her, set before her such a store of beautiful and precious things that it seemed as if an exquisite phantom world of gay colour and perfect form had suddenly come into being at her very feet. There was such a wealth of beautiful things that she found it very

[1] Madame Ozaki.

difficult to make a choice. She finally decided upon the following magical treasures : a musical instrument, which if one struck would continue to play for ever, an ink-stone box, which, on opening the lid, was found to contain an inexhaustible supply of Indian ink, and, last of all, "a beautiful Crystal, in whose clear depths was to be seen, from whichever side you looked, an image of Buddha riding on a white elephant. The jewel was of transcendent glory and shone like a star, and whoever gazed into its liquid depths and saw the blessed vision of Buddha had peace of heart for evermore." [1]

After Kohaku had gazed for some time upon these treasures she sent for Admiral Banko and bade him safely convey them to the temple of Kofukuji.

Everything went well with Admiral Banko and his ship until they were in Japanese waters, sailing into the Bay of Shido-no-ura, when a mighty tempest whirled the vessel hither and thither. The waves rolled up with the fierceness of wild beasts, and lightning continually blazed across the sky, to light up for a moment a rolling ship, now flung high upon a mountain of water, now swept into a green valley from which it seemed it could never rise again.

Suddenly the storm abated with the same unexpectedness with which it had arisen. Some fairy hand had brushed up all the clouds and laid a blue and sparkling carpet across the sea. The admiral's first thought was for the safety of the treasures entrusted to him, and on going below he discovered the musical instrument and ink-stone box just as he had left them, but that the most precious of the treasures, Buddha's Crystal, was missing. He contemplated taking his life, so grieved was he at the loss ; but on reflection he

[1] Madame Ozaki.

saw that it would be wiser to live so long as there was anything he could do to find the jewel. He accordingly hastened to land, and informed Kamatari of his dreadful misfortune.

No sooner had Kamatari been told about the loss of Buddha's Crystal than this wise minister perceived that the Dragon King of the Sea had stolen it, and for that purpose had caused the storm, which had enabled him to steal the treasure unperceived.

Kamatari offered a large reward to a number of fishermen he saw upon the shore of Shido-no-ura if any of their number would venture into the sea and bring back the Crystal. All the fishermen volunteered, but after many attempts the precious jewel still remained in the keeping of the Sea King.

Kamatari, much distressed, suddenly became aware of a poor woman carrying an infant in her arms. She begged the great minister that she might enter the sea and search for the Crystal, and in spite of her frailty she spoke with conviction. Her mother-heart seemed to lend her courage. She made her request because, if she succeeded in bringing back the Crystal, she desired that as a reward Kamatari should bring up her little son as a *samurai* in order that he might be something in life other than a humble fisherman.

It will be remembered that Kamatari in his day had been ambitious for his daughter's welfare. He readily understood the poor woman's request, and solemnly promised that if she carried out her part faithfully he would gladly do his.

The woman withdrew, and taking off her upper garments, and tying a rope round her waist, into which she stuck a knife, she was prepared for her perilous journey. Giving the end of the rope to a number of fishermen, she plunged into the water.

THE CRYSTAL OF BUDDHA

At first the woman saw the dim outline of rocks, the dart of a frightened fish, and the faint gold of the sand beneath her. Then she suddenly became aware of the roofs of the palace of the Sea King, a great and gorgeous building of coral, relieved here and there with clusters of many-coloured seaweed. The palace was like a huge pagoda, rising tier upon tier. The woman swam nearer in order to inspect it more closely, and she perceived a bright light, more brilliant than the light of many moons, so bright that it dazzled her eyes. It was the light of Buddha's Crystal, placed on the pinnacle of this vast abode, and on every side of the shining jewel were guardian dragons fast asleep, appearing to watch even in their slumber!

Up swam the woman, praying in her brave heart that the dragons might sleep till she was out of harm's way and in possession of the treasure. No sooner had she snatched the Crystal from its resting-place than the guardians awoke; their great claws extended and their tails furiously lashed the water, and in another moment they were in hot pursuit. Rather than lose the Crystal, which she had won at so much peril, the woman cut a wound in her left breast and forced the jewel into the bleeding cavity, pressing her hand, without a murmur of pain, upon the poor torn flesh. When the dragons perceived that the water was murky with the woman's blood they turned back, for sea-dragons are afraid of the very sight of blood.

Now the woman sharply pulled the rope, and the fishermen, sitting upon the rocks far above, drew her to land with ever-quickening speed. They gently laid her upon the shore, and found that her eyes were closed and her breast bleeding profusely. Kamatari at first thought that the woman had risked her life in vain; but bending over her he noticed the wound in her breast.

At that moment she opened her eyes, and, taking the jewel from its place of concealment, she murmured a few words about Kamatari's promise, then fell back dead with a smile of peace upon her face.

Kamatari took the woman's child home and looked after him with all the loving care of a father. In due time the boy grew to manhood and became a brave *samurai*, and at Kamatari's death he, too, became a great State minister. When in later years he learnt the story of his mother's act of self-sacrifice he built a temple in the Bay of Shido-no-ura, in memory of one who was so brave and true. It is called Shidoji, and pilgrims visit this temple and remember the nobility of a poor shell-gatherer to this day.

CHAPTER V : FOX LEGENDS

Inari, the Fox God

THE fox takes an important place in Japanese legend, and the subject is of a far-reaching and complex kind.[1] Inari was originally the God of Rice, but in the eleventh century he became associated with the Fox God, with attributes for good and evil, mostly for evil, so profuse and so manifold in their application that they cause no little confusion to the English reader. All foxes possess supernatural powers to an almost limitless degree. They have the power of infinite vision ; they can hear everything and understand the secret thoughts of mankind generally, and in addition they possess the power of transformation and of transmutation. The chief attribute of the bad fox is the power to delude human beings, and for this purpose it will take the form of a beautiful woman, and many are the legends told in this connection.[2] If the shadow of a fox-woman chance to fall upon water, only the fox, and not the fair woman, is revealed. It is said that if a dog sees a fox-woman the feminine form vanishes immediately, and the fox alone remains.

Though the legends connected with the fox in Japan are usually associated with evil, Inari sometimes poses as a beneficent being, a being who can cure coughs and colds, bring wealth to the needy, and answer a woman's prayer for a child. Another kindly act on the part of

[1] The strange supernatural powers of the fox do not belong exclusively to Japan. Numerous examples of this animal's magical attainments may be found in Chinese legend. See *Strange Tales from a Chinese Studio*, by Professor H. A. Giles.

[2] See my *Land of the Yellow Spring, and other Japanese Stories*, p. 113.

Inari, which we might well have associated with Jizō, is to enable little boys and girls to bear with fortitude the troublesome performance of being shaved with a none too perfect razor, and also to help the little ones to go through the painful process of a hot bath, never less in Japan than 110° F. !

Inari not infrequently rewards human beings for any act of kindness to a fox. Only a part of his reward, however, is real ; at least one tempting coin is bound to turn very quickly into grass ! The little good done by Inari—and we have tried to do him justice—is altogether weighed down by his countless evil actions, often of an extremely cruel nature, as will be seen later on. The subject of the fox in Japan has been aptly described by Lafcadio Hearn as "ghostly zoology," and this cunning and malignant animal is certainly ghostly with a completeness far more horribly subtle than our own stock-in-trade ghost with luminous garment and clanking chain !

Demoniacal Possession

Demoniacal possession is frequently said to be due to the evil influence of foxes. This form of possession is known as *kitsune-tsuki*. The sufferer is usually a woman of the poorer classes, one who is highly sensitive and open to believe in all manner of superstitions. The question of demoniacal possession is still an unsolved problem, and the studies of Dr. Baelz, of the Imperial University of Japan, seem to point to the fact that animal possession in human beings is a very real and terrible truth after all.[1] He remarks that a fox usually enters a woman either through the breast or between the finger-nails, and that the fox lives a separate life of its own, frequently speaking in a voice totally different from the human.

[1] See *Pastor Shi, one of China's Questions*, by Mrs. Taylor.

The Death-Stone [1]

> " The Death-Stone stands on Nasu's moor
> Through winter snows and summer heat ;
> The moss grows grey upon its sides,
> But the foul demon haunts it yet.

> " Chill blows the blast : the owl's sad choir
> Hoots hoarsely through the moaning pines ;
> Among the low chrysanthemums
> The skulking fox, the jackal whines,
> As o'er the moor the autumn light declines."
>
> Translated by B. H. CHAMBERLAIN.

The Buddhist priest Genno, after much weary travel, came to the moor of Nasu, and was about to rest under the shadow of a great stone, when a spirit suddenly appeared, and said : " Rest not under this stone. This is the Death-Stone. Men, birds, and beasts have perished by merely touching it ! "

These mysterious and warning remarks naturally awakened Genno's curiosity, and he begged that the spirit would favour him with the story of the Death-Stone.

Thus the spirit began : " Long ago there was a fair girl living at the Japanese Court. She was so charming that she was called the Jewel Maiden. Her wisdom equalled her beauty, for she understood Buddhist lore and the Confucian classics, science, and the poetry of China."

> " So sweetly decked by nature and by art,
> The monarch's self soon clasp'd her to his heart."
>
> Translated by B. H. CHAMBERLAIN.

"One night," went on the spirit, " the Mikado gave

1 " The Death-Stone " is certainly one of the most remarkable of fox legends. It illustrates a malignant fox taking the form of a seductive woman in more than one life. She is a coming and vanishing creature of alluring but destructive power, a sort of Japanese version of Fata Morgana. The legend has been adapted from a *No*, or lyrical drama, translated by Professor B. H. Chamberlain.

a great feast in the Summer Palace, and there he assembled the wit, wisdom, and beauty of the land. It was a brilliant gathering; but while the company ate and drank, accompanied by the strains of sweet music, darkness crept over the great apartment. Black clouds raced across the sky, and there was not a star to be seen. While the guests sat rigid with fear a mysterious wind arose. It howled through the Summer Palace and blew out all the lanterns. The complete darkness produced a state of panic, and during the uproar some one cried out, 'A light! A light!'"

> "And lo! from out the Jewel Maiden's frame
> There's seen to dart a weirdly lustrous flame!
> It grows, it spreads, it fills th' imperial halls;
> The painted screens, the costly panell'd walls,
> Erst the pale viewless damask of the night
> Sparkling stand forth as in the moon's full light."
> Translated by B. H. CHAMBERLAIN.

"From that very hour the Mikado sickened," continued the spirit. "He grew so ill that the Court Magician was sent for, and this worthy soul speedily ascertained the cause of his Majesty's decline. He stated, with much warmth of language, that the Jewel Maiden was a harlot and a fiend, 'who, with insidious art, the State to ravage, captivates thy heart!'

"The Magician's words turned the Mikado's heart against the Jewel Maiden. When this sorceress was spurned she resumed her original shape, that of a fox, and ran away to this very stone on Nasu moor."

The priest looked at the spirit critically. "Who are you?" he said at length.

"I am the demon that once dwelt in the breast of the Jewel Maiden! Now I inhabit the Death-Stone for evermore!"

The good Genno was much horrified by this dreadful

The Mikado and the Jewel Maiden.
(See page 96)

Jizō.

(See page 104*)*

confession, but, remembering his duty as a priest, he said : " Though you have sunk low in wickedness, you shall rise to virtue again. Take this priestly robe and begging-bowl, and reveal to me your fox form."

Then this wicked spirit cried pitifully :

> " In the garish light of day
> I hide myself away,
> Like pale Asama's fires :
> With the night I'll come again,
> Confess my guilt with pain
> And new-born pure desires."
>
> Translated by B. H. CHAMBERLAIN.

With these words the spirit suddenly vanished.

Genno did not relinquish his good intentions. He strove more ardently than ever for this erring soul's salvation. In order that she might attain Nirvana, he offered flowers, burnt incense, and recited the sacred Scriptures in front of the stone.

When Genno had performed these religious duties, he said : " Spirit of the Death-Stone, I conjure thee ! what was it in a former world that did cause thee to assume in this so foul a shape ?"

Suddenly the Death-Stone was rent and the spirit once more appeared, crying :

> " In stones there are spirits,
> In the waters is a voice heard :
> The winds sweep across the firmament ! "
>
> Translated by B. H. CHAMBERLAIN.

Genno saw a lurid glare about him and, in the shining light, a fox that suddenly turned into a beautiful maiden.

Thus spoke the spirit of the Death-Stone : " I am she who first, in Ind, was the demon to whom Prince Hazoku paid homage. . . . In Great Cathay I took the form of Hōji, consort of the Emperor Iuwao ; and at

97

the Court of the Rising Sun I became the Flawless Jewel Maiden, concubine to the Emperor Toba."

The spirit confessed to Genno that in the form of the Jewel Maiden she had desired to bring destruction to the Imperial line. "Already," said the spirit, "I was making my plans, already I was gloating over the thought of the Mikado's death, and had it not been for the power of the Court Magician I should have succeeded in my scheme. As I have told you, I was driven from the Court. I was pursued by dogs and arrows, and finally sank exhausted into the Death-Stone. From time to time I haunted the moor. Now the Lord Buddha has had compassion upon me, and he has sent his priest to point out the way of true religion and to bring peace."

The legend concludes with the following pious utterances poured forth by the now contrite spirit :

> "' I swear, O man of God ! I swear,' she cries,
> ' To thee whose blessing wafts me to the skies,
> I swear a solemn oath, that shall endure
> Firm as the Death-Stone standing on the moor,
> That from this hour I'm virtue's child alone ! '
> Thus spake the ghoul, and vanished 'neath the Stone."
>
> Translated by B. H. CHAMBERLAIN.

How Tokutaro was Deluded by Foxes

Tokutaro was a complete sceptic in regard to the magical power of foxes. His scepticism exasperated a number of his companions, who challenged him to go to Maki moor. If nothing happened to him, Tokutaro was to receive, writes A. B. Mitford (Lord Redesdale) in *Tales of Old Japan*, "five measures of wine and a thousand copper cash [1] worth of fish." If, on the other

---

[1] The *cash*, now no longer in use, was roughly equivalent to one penny.

hand, Tokutaro should suffer through the power of the foxes, he was to present a similar gift to his companions. Tokutaro jeeringly accepted the bet, and when night had come he set out for the Maki moor.

Tokutaro was determined to be very cute and very wary. On reaching his destination he happened to meet a fox running through a bamboo grove. Immediately afterwards he perceived the daughter of the headman of Upper Horikané. On telling the woman that he was going to this village, she explained that as she was going there too they might journey together.

Tokutaro's suspicions were fully aroused. He walked behind the woman, vainly searching for a fox's tail. When they reached Upper Horikané the girl's parents came out, and were much surprised to see their daughter, who had married, and was living in another village.

Tokutaro, with a smile of superior wisdom, explained that the maid before them was not really their daughter, but a fox in disguise. The old people were at first indignant, and refused to believe what Tokutaro had told them. Eventually, however, he persuaded them to leave the girl in his hands while they waited for the result in the store-closet.

Tokutaro then seized the girl, and brutally knocked her down, pouring abuse upon her. He stamped upon her, and tortured her in every possible way, expecting every moment to see the woman turn into a fox. But she only wept and cried piteously for her parents to come to her rescue.

This whole-hearted sceptic, finding his efforts so far fruitless, piled wood upon the floor and burnt her to death. At this juncture her parents came running in and bound Tokutaro to a pillar, fiercely accusing him of murder.

Now a priest happened to pass that way, and, hearing the noise, requested an explanation. When the girl's parents had told him all, and after he had listened to Tokutaro's pleadings, he begged the old couple to spare the man's life in order that he might become in time a good and devout priest. This extraordinary request, after some demur, was agreed to, and Tokutaro knelt down to have his head shaved, happy, no doubt, to be released from his predicament so easily.

No sooner had Tokutaro's wicked head been shaved than he heard a loud peal of laughter, and he awoke to find himself sitting on a large moor. He instinctively raised his hand to his head, to discover that foxes had shaved him and he had lost his bet !

A Fox's Gratitude

After the preceding gruesome legend describing the evil propensities of the fox, it is refreshing to come across one that was capable of considerable self-sacrifice.

Now it happened, on a certain spring day, that two little boys were caught in the act of trying to catch a baby fox. The man who witnessed the performance possessed a kind heart, and, on hearing that the boys were anxious to sell the cub, gave them half a *bu*.[1]

When the children had joyfully departed with the money the man discovered that the little creature was wounded in the foot. He immediately applied a certain herb, and the pain speedily subsided. Perceiving at a short distance a number of old foxes watching him, he generously let the cub go, and it sprang with a bound to its parents and licked them profusely.

Now this kind-hearted man had a son, who was afflicted with a strange disease. A great physician at last prescribed the liver of a live fox as being the only

[1] About 8*d*.

remedy likely to effect a cure. When the boy's parents heard this they were much distressed, and would only consent to accept a fox's liver from one who made it his business to hunt foxes. They finally commissioned a neighbour to obtain the liver, for which they promised to pay liberally.

The following night the fox's liver was brought by a strange man totally unknown to the good people of the house. The visitor professed to be a messenger sent by the neighbour whom they had commissioned. When, however, the neighbour himself arrived he confessed that though he had tried his utmost to obtain a fox's liver he had failed to do so, and had come to make his apologies. He was utterly amazed to hear the story the parents of the suffering boy told him.

The next day the fox's liver was made into a concoction by the great physician, and immediately restored the little boy to his usual health again.

In the evening a beautiful young woman appeared at the bedside of the happy parents. She explained that she was the mother of the cub the master had saved, and that in gratitude for his kindness she had killed her offspring, and that her husband, in the guise of the mysterious messenger, had brought the desired liver.[1]

Inari Answers a Woman's Prayer

Inari, as we have already found, is often extremely benevolent. One legend informs us that a woman who had been married many years and had not been blessed with a child prayed at Inari's shrine. At the conclusion of her supplication the stone foxes wagged their tails, and snow began to fall. She regarded these phenomena as favourable omens.

[1] The liver, both animal and human, frequently figures in Japanese legend as a remedy for various ailments.

When the woman reached her home a *yeta* (beggar) accosted her, and begged for something to eat. The woman good-naturedly gave this unfortunate wayfarer some red bean rice, the only food she had in the house, and presented it to him in a dish.

The next day her husband discovered this dish lying in front of the shrine where she had prayed. The beggar was none other than Inari himself, and the woman's generosity was rewarded in due season by the birth of a child.

The Meanness of Raiko

Raiko was a wealthy man living in a certain village. In spite of his enormous wealth, which he carried in his *obi* (girdle), he was extremely mean. As he grew older his meanness increased till at last he contemplated dismissing his faithful servants who had served him so well.

One day Raiko became very ill, so ill that he almost wasted away, on account of a terrible fever. On the tenth night of his illness a poorly dressed *bozu* (priest) appeared by his pillow, inquired how he fared, and added that he had expected the *oni* to carry him off long ago.

These home truths, none too delicately expressed, made Raiko very angry, and he indignantly demanded that the priest should take his departure. But the *bozu*, instead of departing, told him that there was only one remedy for his illness. The remedy was that Raiko should loosen his *obi* and distribute his money to the poor.

Raiko became still more angry at what he considered the gross impertinence of the priest. He snatched a dagger from his robe and tried to kill the kindly *bozu*. The priest, without the least fear, informed Raiko that he had heard of his mean intention to dismiss his worthy servants, and had nightly come to the old man to drain his life-blood. "Now," said the priest, "my object is attained!" and with these words he blew out the light.

The now thoroughly frightened Raiko felt a ghostly creature advance towards him. The old man struck out blindly with his dagger, and made such a commotion that his loyal servants ran into the room with lanterns, and the light revealed the horrible claw of a monster lying by the side of the old man's mat.

Carefully following the little spots of blood, Raiko's servants came to a miniature mountain at the extreme end of the garden, and in the mountain was a large hole, from whence protruded the upper part of an enormous spider. This creature begged the servants to try to persuade their master not to attack the Gods, and in future to refrain from meanness.

When Raiko heard these words from his servants he repented, and gave large sums of money to the poor. Inari had assumed the shape of a spider and priest in order to teach the once mean old man a lesson.

CHAPTER VI : JIZŌ, THE GOD OF CHILDREN

The Significance of Jizō

JIZŌ, the God of little children and the God who makes calm the troubled sea, is certainly the most lovable of the Buddhist divinities, though Kwannon, the Goddess of Mercy, has somewhat similar attributes. The most popular Gods, be they of the East or West, are those Gods with the most human qualities. Jizō, though of Buddhist origin, is essentially Japanese, and we may best describe him as being the creation of innumerable Japanese women who have longed to project into the Infinite, into the shrouded Beyond, a deity who should be a divine Father and Mother to the souls of their little ones. And this is just what Jizō is, a God essentially of the feminine heart, and not a being to be tossed about in the hair-splitting debates of hoary theologians. A study of the nature and characteristics of Jizō will reveal all that is best in the Japanese woman, for he assuredly reveals her love, her sense of the beautiful, and her infinite compassion. Jizō has all the wisdom of the Lord Buddha himself, with this important difference, namely, that Jizō has waived aside Nirvana, and does not sit upon the Golden Lotus, but has become, through an exquisitely beautiful self-sacrifice, the divine playmate and protector of Japanese children. He is the God of smiles and long sleeves, the enemy of evil spirits, and the one being who can heal the wound of a mother who has lost her child in death. We have a saying that all rivers find their way to the sea. To the Japanese woman who has laid her little one in the cemetery all rivers wind their silver courses into the place where the ever-waiting and ever-gentle

JIZŌ AND LAFCADIO HEARN

Jizō is. That is why mothers who have lost their children in death write prayers on little slips of paper, and watch them float down the rivers on their way to the great spiritual Father and Mother who will answer all their petitions with a loving smile.

At Jizō's Shrine

> "Fronting the kindly Jizō's shrine
> The cherry-blooms are blowing now,
> Pink cloud of flower on slender bough,
> And hidden tracery of line.

> "Rose-dawn against moss-mellowed grey,
> Through which the wind-tost sprays allow
> Glimpse of calm smile and placid brow,
> Of carven face where sunbeams play.

> "Dawn-time, I pluck a branch, and swift
> Flutters a flight of petals fair ;
> Through the fresh-scented morning air
> Down to the waving grass they drift.

> "Noon-tide my idle fingers stray,
> Through the fair maze of bud and flower,
> Sending a sudden blossom-shower
> From the sweet fragance-haunted spray.

> "Low in the west the red fire dies,
> Vaguely I lift my hand, but now
> Jizō is not—nor cherry bough—
> Only the dark of starless skies ! "

CLARA A. WALSH.

Jizō and Lafcadio Hearn

Lafcadio Hearn, in one of his letters,[1] writes : "There is a queer custom in Izumo which may interest you. When a wedding takes place in the house of an

---

[1] *The Japanese Letters of Lafcadio Hearn*, edited by Elizabeth Bisland.

unpopular man in the country the young men of the village carry a roadside statue of Jizō into the Zashiki, and announce the coming of the God. (This is especially done with an avaricious farmer, or a stingy family.) Food and wine are demanded by the God. The members of the family must come in, salute the deity, and give all the *sakè* and food demanded while any remains in the house. It is dangerous to refuse ; the young peasants would probably wreck the house. After this the statue is carried back again to its place. The visit of Jizō is much dreaded. It is never made to persons who are liked."

On one occasion Lafcadio Hearn, who had a very warm admiration for this God, desired to restore the head and arms of a broken Jizō image. His wife remonstrated with him, and we quote his quaint reply because it reminds us not a little of the last legend mentioned in this chapter : "*Gomen, gomen !* ["Forgive me !"] I thought only to give a little joy as I hoped. The Jizō I wrote you about is not the thing you will find in the graveyards ; but it is Jizō who shall guard and pacify the seas. It is not a sad kind, but you do not like my idea, so I have given up my project. It was only papa's foolish thought. However, poor Jizō-sama wept bitterly when it heard of your answer to me. I said to it, 'I cannot help it, as Mamma San doubted your real nature, and thinks that you are a graveyard-keeper. I know that you are the saviour of seas and sailors.' The Jizō is crying even now."

"The Dry Bed of the River of Souls"

Under the earth there is the Sai-no-Kawara, or "the Dry Bed of the River of Souls." This is the place where all children go after death, children and those who have never married. Here the little ones play with the smiling Jizō, and here it is that they build small towers of stones, for there are many in this river-bed. The mothers of these children, in the world above them, also pile up stones around the images of Jizō, for these little towers represent prayers ; they are charms against the *oni*, or wicked spirits. Sometimes in the Dry Bed of the River of Souls the *oni* for a moment gain a temporary victory, and knock down the little towers which the ghosts of children have built with so much laughter. When such a misfortune takes place the laughter ceases, and the little ones fly to Jizō for protection. He hides them in his long sleeves, and with his sacred staff drives away the red-eyed *oni*.

The place where the souls of children dwell is a shadowy and grey world of dim hills and vales through which the Sai-no-Kawara winds its way. All the children are clad in short white garments, and if occasionally the evil spirits frighten them there is always Jizō to dry their tears, always one who sends them back to their ghostly games again.

The following hymn of Jizō, known as " The Legend of the Humming of the Sai-no-Kawara," gives us a beautiful and vivid conception of Jizō and this ghostly land where children play :

The Legend of the Humming of the Sai-no-Kawara

"Not of this world is the story of sorrow.
The story of the Sai-no-Kawara,
At the roots of the Mountain of Shide ;—
Not of this world is the tale ; yet 'tis most pitiful to hear.
For together in the Sai-no-Kawara are assembled
Children of tender age in multitude,—
Infants but two or three years old,
Infants of four or five, infants of less than ten :
In the Sai-no-Kawara are they gathered together.
And the voice of their longing for their parents,

The voice of their crying for their mothers and their fathers—
Is never as the voice of the crying of children in this world,
But a crying so pitiful to hear
That the sound of it would pierce through flesh and bone.
And sorrowful indeed the task which they perform,—
Gathering the stones of the bed of the river,
Therewith to heap the tower of prayers.
Saying prayers for the happiness of father, they heap the first tower;
Saying prayers for the happiness of mother, they heap the second tower;
Saying prayers for their brothers, their sisters, and all whom they loved at home, they heap the third tower.
Such, by day, are their pitiful diversions.
But ever as the sun begins to sink below the horizon,
Then do the *Oni*, the demons of the hells, appear,
And say to them,—' What is this that you do here ?
Lo ! your parents still living in the Shaba-world
Take no thought of pious offering or holy work :
They do nought but mourn for you from the morning unto the evening.
Oh ! how pitiful ! alas ! how unmerciful !
Verily the cause of the pains that you suffer
Is only the mourning, the lamentation of your parents.'
And saying also, ' Blame never us ! '
The demons cast down the heaped-up towers,
They dash their stones down with their clubs of iron.
But lo ! the teacher Jizō appears.
All gently he comes, and says to the weeping infants :—
' Be not afraid, dears ! be never fearful !
Poor little souls, your lives vere brief indeed !
Too soon you were forced to make the weary journey to the Meido,
The long journey to the region of the dead !
Trust to me ! I am your father and mother in the Meido,
Father of all children in the region of the dead.'
And he folds the skirt of his shining robe about them ;
So graciously takes he pity on the infants.
To those who cannot walk he stretches forth his strong *shakujō*,[1]
And he pets the little ones, caresses them, takes them to his loving bosom.
So graciously he takes pity on the infants.
        Namu Amida Butsu ! " [2]
                                    Lafcadio Hearn.

---

[1] Sacred staff.   [2] " Hail, omnipotent Buddha !"

THE CAVE OF THE CHILDREN'S GHOSTS

This abode of the souls of children is certainly not an ideal land.   It is Jizō, and not his country, who has sprung from the hearts of Japanese women.   The stern Buddhist teaching of cause and effect, of birth and re-birth, applies to even gentle infants.   But if the great Wheel of Existence revolves with unerring force, and only fails to move when the desire for not-being is finally attained in Nirvana, Jizō lovingly stands at the foot of Destiny and makes easy the way where the feet of little children so softly patter.

The Cave of the Children's Ghosts

There is a cave in Japan known as Kyu-Kukedo-San, or Ancient Cavern, and far within its recess there is to be found an image of Jizō, with his mystic jewel and sacred staff.   Before Jizō there is a little *torii*[1] and a pair of *gohei*,[2] both symbols of the Shintō faith ; but, as Lafcadio Hearn observes, "this gentle divinity has no enemies ; at the feet of the lover of children's ghosts both creeds unite in tender homage."   Here it is that the ghosts of little children meet, softly whispering together as they stoop hither and thither in order to build their towers of stones.   At night they creep over the sea from their Dry Bed of the River of Souls, and cover the sand in the cavern with their ghostly footsteps, building, ever building those prayers of stone, while Jizō smiles down upon their loving labour.   They depart before the rising of the sun, for it is said that the dead fear to gaze upon the Sun Goddess, and most especially are these infants afraid of her bright gold eyes.

[1] A gateway.

[2] " A wand from which depend strips of white paper cut into little angular bunches (*gohei*), intended to represent the offerings of cloth which were anciently tied to branches of the sacred cleyera tree at festival time."—B. H. Chamberlain.

The Fountain of Jizō

Another beautiful sea-cave contains the Fountain of Jizō. It is a fountain of flowing milk, at which the souls of children quench their thirst. Mothers suffering from want of milk come to this fountain and pray to Jizō, and mothers having more milk than their infants require pray to the same God that he may take some of their milk and give it to the souls of children in his great shadowy kingdom. And Jizō is said to answer their prayers.

How Jizō Remembered

A woman named Soga Sadayoshi lived by feeding silkworms and gathering their silk. One day, on a visit to the temple of Ken-cho-ji, she thought that an image of Jizō looked cold, and went home, made a cap, returned with it, and set it upon Jizō's head, saying : " Would I were rich enough to give thee a warm covering for all thine august body ; but, alas ! I am poor, and even this which I offer thee is unworthy of thy divine acceptance."

In her fiftieth year the woman died, and as her body remained warm for three days her relatives would not consent to her burial. On the evening of the third day, however, much to the surprise and joy of those about her, she came to life once more.

Shortly after the woman had resumed her work again she narrated how her soul had appeared before the great and terrible Emma-Ō, Lord and Judge of the dead, and how that dread being had been angry with her because, contrary to Buddha's teaching, she had killed innumerable silkworms. Emma-Ō was so angry that he ordered her to be thrown into a pot filled with molten metal. While she cried out in intense agony Jizō came and stood beside her, and immediately the metal ceased to burn. After Jizō had spoken kindly to the woman he led her to Emma-Ō, and requested that she who had once kept warm one of his images should receive pardon. And Emma-Ō granted the request of the ever-loving and compassionate God, and the woman returned to the sunny world of Japan again.

CHAPTER VII : LEGEND IN JAPANESE ART

The Significance of Japanese Art

SIR ALFRED EAST, in lecturing on the subject of Japanese art, described it as "great in small things, but small in great things," and this, generally speaking, is very true. The Japanese artist excels in depicting flowers and insects and birds. He is triumphant in portraying the curl of a wave, a branch of cherry-blossom against a full moon, a flight of heron, a group of pine-trees, and carp swimming in a stream; but that genius for minute and accurate detail seems to have prevented him from depicting what we understand as a great subject-picture, an historical scene crowded with many figures. This zest to portray various fragments from Nature was no narrow and academic affair. Art was not intended solely for the *kakemono*, or hanging scroll, to be suspended in the alcove of a Japanese home, to be admired for a time, and then to be replaced by another. Art in Japan was universal to an extent not to be found in any other country, where a cheap towel had a pleasing design upon it, and where the playing cards, unlike our own, were works of art.

It has been said that the woman in Japanese art is wooden. This is not really so, if by wooden we mean entirely without expression ; but it is necessary first of all to know something about the Japanese woman in actual life before we can understand her representation in art. There is a wealth of old tradition behind that apparently immobile face. It is a curious fact that until we get accustomed to the various Japanese types one face so closely resembles another that discrimination is out of the question, and we are apt to run away with the idea that Nature in Japan has been content to repeat the same physiognomy over and over again, forgetting that we in turn present no diversity of type to the Japanese on first acquaintance. The Japanese face in art is not without expression, only it happens to be an expression rather different from that with which we are familiar, and this is particularly true in regard to the portrayal of Japanese women. Most of us have seen a number of colour-prints devoted to this subject in which we find no shading in the face. We are apt to exclaim that this omission gives an extremely flat effect to the face, and to observe in consequence that the work before us must be very bad art. But it is not bad art, for the Japanese face *is* flat, and the artists of that country never fail to reflect this characteristic. Colour-prints depicting Nipponese women do not reveal emotion—a smile, a gesture of yearning, are absent; but because we find so much negation we should be very far from the truth to suppose that a colour-print of this kind expresses no feeling, that the general effect is doll-like and uninteresting. We must take into consideration the long period of suppression through which the Japanese woman had to pass. A superficial study of that extraordinary treatise by Kaibara known as *Onna Daigaku*, or " The Greater Learning for Women," will help us to realise that it was the duty of every Japanese woman to be sweet, amiable, virtuous ; to obey those in authority without demur, and above all to suppress her feelings. When we have taken these points into consideration we shall very slowly perceive that there is strength and not weakness in a portrait of a Japanese woman ; a quiet and dignified beauty in which impulse is held in check, veiled, as it were, behind a cloud of rigid tradition. The Japanese woman, though she has been surrounded at every turn by severe discipline, has, nevertheless,

given us a type of womanhood supreme in her true
sweetness of disposition, and the Japanese artist has
caught the glamour of her charm. In the curve of her
form he suggests the grace of a wind-blown willow,
in the designs upon her robe the promise of spring,
and behind the small red mouth a wealth of infinite
possibilities.

Japan owed her art to Buddhism, and it was quickened and sustained by Chinese influence. Buddhism
gave Nippon her pictorial art, her mural decoration
and exquisite carving. Shintō temples were severe
and plain, those of Buddhism were replete with all
that art could give them; and last, out not least, it
was Buddha's teaching that brought into Japan the
art of gardening, with all its elaborate and beautiful
symbolism.

A Japanese art critic wrote : "If in the midst of a
stroke a sword-cut had severed the brush it would have
bled." From this we may gather that the Japanese
artist put his whole heart into his work ; it was a part
of him, something vital, something akin to religion
itself. With this great force behind his brush it is
no wonder that he was able to give that extraordinary
life and movement to his work, so strikingly depicted
in portraits of actors.

Though we have so far only shown the Japanese
artist as a master of little things, he has, nevertheless,
faithfully and effectively represented the Gods and
Goddesses of his country, and many of the myths and
legends connected with them. If he excelled in the
beautiful, he no less excelled in depicting the horrible,
for no artists, excepting those of China, have succeeded
in portraying the supernatural to more effect. What a
contrast there is between an exquisite picture of Jizō or
Buddha or Kwannon and the pictorial representation

of a Japanese goblin ! Extreme beauty and extreme ugliness are to be found in Japanese art, and those who love the many pictures of Mount Fuji and the moth-like colouring of Utamaru's women will turn in horror from the ghastly representations of supernatural beings.

The Gods of Good Fortune

Many of the legendary stories given in this volume have been portrayed by Japanese artists, and in the present chapter we propose to deal with the legends in Japanese art not hitherto mentioned. The favourite theme of the Japanese artist is undoubtedly that of the Seven Gods of Good Fortune, nearly always treated with rollicking good-humour. There was Fukurokuju, with a very long head, and attended by a crane, deer, or tortoise ; Daikoku, who stood upon rice-bales and was accompanied by a rat ; Ebisu, carrying a fish ; Hotei, the merry God of Laughter, the very embodiment of our phrase "Laugh and grow fat." There was Bishamon, resplendent in armour, and bearing a spear and toy pagoda ; Benten, the Goddess of Beauty, Wealth, Ferti- lity, and Offspring ; while Jurōjin was very similar to Fukurokuju. These Seven Gods of Good Fortune, or, to be more accurate, six Gods and one Goddess, seem to have sprung from Shintōism, Taoism, Buddhism, and Brahmanism, and apparently date from the seventeenth century.

The Treasure Ship

In connection with this theme the Japanese artist is fond of portraying the Gods of Good Fortune as jovial passengers on the *Takara-bune,* or Treasure Ship, which is said to come to port on New Year's Eve, with no less a cargo than the Hat of Invisibility, the Lucky Raincoat, the Sacred Key, the Inexhaustible Purse, and other curious and magical treasures. At this time of the year pictures of the Treasure Ship are placed under children's wooden pillows, and the practice is said to bring a lucky dream.

> " Sleep, my own, till the bell of dusk
> Bring the stars laden with a dream.
> With that dream you shall awake
> Between the laughters and the song."
>
> Yone Noguchi.

The Miraculous in Japanese Art

Among other legends is the story of Hidari Jingorō, the famous sculptor, whose masterpiece came to life when finished, which reminds us not a little of the story of Pygmalion. There are other legendary stories connected with the coming to life of Japanese works of art. On a certain occasion a number of peasants were much annoyed by the destruction of their gardens caused by some wild animal. Eventually they discovered that the intruder was a great black horse, and on giving chase it suddenly disappeared into a temple. When they entered the building they found Kanasoka's painting of a black steed steaming with its recent exertion ! The great artist at once painted in a rope tethering the animal to a post, and from that day to this the peasants' gardens have remained unmolested.

When the great artist Sesshiu was a little boy the story goes that he was, by way of punishment, securely bound in a Buddhist temple. Using his copious tears for ink and his toe for a brush, the little fellow sketched some rats upon the floor. Immediately they came to life and gnawed through the rope that bound their youthful creator.

Hokusai

There is something more than mere legend in these stories, if we may believe the words of the famous artist Hokusai, whose " Hundred Views of Fuji " are regarded as the finest examples of Japanese landscape-painting. He wrote in his Preface to this work : " At ninety I shall penetrate the mystery of things ; at a hundred I shall certainly have reached a marvellous stage ; and when I am a hundred and ten everything I do, be it a dot or a line, will be alive." Needless to say, Hokusai did not reach the age of a hundred and ten. In his last hours he wrote the following lines, which were afterwards inscribed upon his tomb :

" My soul, turned Will-o'-the-wisp,
Can come and go at ease over the summer fields."

With that strong poetic feeling so characteristic of the Japanese, Eternity meant for Hokusai an infinite time in which to carry on his beloved work—to perfect, to make alive all the wonderful strokes of his brush. As in ancient Egypt, so in Old Japan, the future life could only mean real happiness with periodic visits to this world again, and there is a subtle and almost pathetic paradox in this conception, suggesting, as it were, the continual loading of Eternity with fresh earthly memories. In both countries we find the spirit hankering after old human haunts. In Egypt the soul returned through the medium of its preserved body, and in Japan the Festival of the Dead, described elsewhere, afforded a joyous exit from the world of Emma-Ō, a three days' visit in the middle of July to Japan, a land more beautiful, more dear, it would seem, than any Japanese conception of a future world. But Hokusai appears to suggest that his visits would not be made merely in the summer season—rather a frequent coming and going at all times of the year.

A Japanese poet has written :

> " It is an awesome thing
>   To meet a-wandering,
>   In the dark night,
>   The dark and rainy night,
> A phantom greenish-grey,
>   Ghost of some wight,
>   Poor mortal wight !
>   Wandering
>   Lonesomely
>   Through
>   The black
>   Night."
>   Translated by Clara A. Walsh.

Ghosts and Goblins

It is scarcely less awesome to come across ghosts, goblins, and other supernatural beings in a Japanese picture. We find ghosts with long necks supporting horribly leering faces. Their necks are so long that it would seem that the ghastly heads could look above and into everything with a fiendish and dreadful relish. The ghoul, though represented in Japanese art as a three-year-old child, has reddish-brown hair, very long ears, and is often depicted as eating the kidneys of dead people. The horrible in this phase of Japanese art is emphasised to an almost unbearable degree, and a living Japanese artist's conception of a procession of ghosts[1] is so uncanny, so weird, that we certainly should not like to meet them in broad daylight, much less "through the dark night ! "

[1] See *Ancient Tales and Folk-lore of Japan*, by R. Gordon Smith.

THE DREAM OF ROSEI

A Garden of Skulls

The Japanese artist's conception of a garden, with
its pine-trees, and stone lanterns, and azalea-bordered
lakes, is usually extremely beautiful. Hiroshige, like
so many Japanese artists, has painted a garden touched
with snow ; but in one of his pictures he portrays the
snow as turning into a number of skulls, and has
borrowed this fantastic conception from the *Heike
Monogatari*.

It must not be thought that the Japanese artist,
when portraying some supernatural being, or in depicting some scene from a legendary story, exclusively
catches the grim and horrible. The grim and horrible
are certainly portrayed with considerable spirit and
dramatic force, but many of the Japanese works of art
depict the Gods and Goddesses of Old Japan with much
grace and charm.

The Dream of Rosei [1]

Japanese ornament frequently illustrates some ancient
legend. We may see on a certain *tsuba* (sword-guard)
a pine-tree with people sitting in the branches. One
man carries a banner, while two others are playing on
musical instruments. There is an exquisite legend connected with this quaint design, and, though it is of
Chinese origin, it deserves to find a place in this volume
because it is one of those fantastic Chinese legends that
has been woven into Japanese literature and art—has
become, in short, one of the favourite themes of
Japanese artists, and of those who witness the *No*, or
lyrical drama, of Nippon.

Rosei, in ancient times, reached the little inn of

---

[1] Adapted from the *No* drama, translated by B. H. Chamberlain.

Kantan, so weary with his travel that he fell asleep as soon as his head touched the pillow. It was no ordinary pillow, but might well be described as the Magic Pillow of Dreams, for directly Rosei was asleep an envoy approached him, and said : " I am sent by the Emperor of Ibara to inform you that his Majesty wishes to relinquish the throne and to install you in his place. Be pleased to enter the palanquin that awaits you, and the bearers will quickly carry you to the capital."

Rosei, much amazed by what he had heard and seen, entered the palanquin, "strewn with gems of radiant hue," and was borne to a wonderful country, best described in the following verse :

" For ne'er in those old vasty halls Imperial,
    Bath'd in the moonbeams bright,
  Or where the dragon soars on clouds ethereal,
    Was ought like this to entrance the sight :
  With golden sand and silvern pebbles white
  Was strewn the floor ;
  And at the corners four,
  Through gates inlaid
  With diamonds and jade,
Pass'd throngs whose vestments were of radiant light,—
So fair a scene,
That mortal eye might ween
It scann'd the very heav'ns' unknown delight.
Here countless gifts the folk came bearing,
Precious as myriad coins of finest gold ;
And there, the lesser with the greater sharing,
Advanc'd the vassals bold,
  Their banners to display
  That paint the sky with colours gay,
While rings the air as had a thunder roll'd."
                Trans. by B. H. Chamberlain.

Rosei found himself in a magical country where Nature either forgot her natural laws or was led into fresh wonders by the people of that land. In the east there was a silver hill over which the gold sun shone, and in the west there was a gold hill over which the moon shone.

> "No spring and autumn mark the time,
>   And o'er that deathless gate
>   The sun and moon their wonted speed forget."
>
> Trans. by B. H. CHAMBERLAIN.

The whole idea of this charming story seems to suggest that this country was not only a land of eternal youth, but a land, too, where Nature marshalled her seasons together, where there were always colour and blossom, and where no flower faded.

When Rosei had lived and reigned for fifty years in this glorious country a minister came to him one day and bade him drink of the Elixir of Life, in order that he might, like his subjects, live for ever.

The monarch drank the Elixir, "'Mid dazzling pomp and joys more ravishing than e'er before were shower'd on mortal sight." Rosei believed that he had cheated Death of his due, and lived the life of poetic, if sensuous, ecstasy. He gave sumptuous feasts to his courtiers, feasts which saw the sun and moon without intermission, where lovely maidens danced, and where there were endless music and song.

It so happened, however, that these joyous feasts, these pageants of colour, were not endless after all, for eventually Rosei awoke to find himself resting upon "Kantan's pillow." The moralist steps in at this juncture with the following :

> "But he that ponders well
>   Will find all life the self-same story tell,—
>   That, when death comes, a century of bliss
>   Fades like a dream."
>
> Trans. by B. H. CHAMBERLAIN.

Rosei, after this fantastic experience, came to the conclusion that "life is a dream," that ambition is a dream too, and, having accepted this Buddhistic teaching, he returned to his own home.

A Kakemono Ghost[1]

Sawara was a pupil in the house of the artist Tenko, who was a kind and able master, while Sawara, even at the commencement of his art studies, showed considerable promise. Kimi, Tenko's niece, devoted her time to her uncle and in directing the affairs of the household generally. Kimi was beautiful, and it was not long before she fell desperately in love with Sawara. This young pupil regarded her as very charming, one to die for if need be, and in his heart he secretly loved her. His love, however, unlike Kimi's, was not demonstrative, for he had his work to attend to, and so, to be sure, had Kimi; but work with Sawara came before his love, and with Kimi it was only love that mattered.

One day, when Tenko was paying a visit, Kimi came to Sawara, and, unable to restrain her feelings any longer, told him of her love, and asked him if he would like to marry her. Having made her request, she set tea before her lover, and awaited his answer.

Sawara returned her affection, and said that he would be delighted to marry her, adding, however, that marriage was not possible until after two or three years, when he had established a position for himself and had become a famous artist.

Sawara, in order to add to his knowledge of art, decided to study under a celebrated painter named Myokei, and, everything having been arranged, he bade farewell to his old master and Kimi, promising that he would return as soon as he had made a name for himself and become a great artist.

[1] *Ancient Tales and Folk-lore of Japan*, by R. Gordon Smith.

A KAKEMONO GHOST

Two years went by and Tenko and Kimi heard no news of Sawara. Many admirers of Kimi came to her uncle with offers of marriage, and Tenko was debating as to what he should do in the matter, when he received a letter from Myokei, saying that Sawara was doing good work, and that he desired that his excellent pupil should marry his daughter.

Tenko imagined, perhaps not without some reason, that Sawara had forgotten all about Kimi, and that the best thing he could do was to give her in marriage to Yorozuya, a wealthy merchant, and also to fulfil Miyokei's wish that Sawara should marry the great painter's daughter. With these intentions Tenko resolved to employ strategy, so he called Kimi to him, and said :

" Kimi, I have had a letter from Myokei, and I am afraid the sad news which it contains will distress you. Myokei wishes Sawara to marry his daughter, and I have told him that I fully approve of the union. I feel sure that Sawara has neglected you, and I therefore wish that you should marry Yorozuya, who will make, I am sure, a very good husband."

When Kimi heard these words she wept bitterly, and without a word went to her room.

In the morning Tenko entered Kimi's apartment, but his niece had gone, and the protracted search that followed failed to discover her whereabouts.

When Myokei had received Tenko's letter he told the promising young artist that he wished him to marry his daughter, and thus establish a family of painters ; but Sawara was amazed to hear this extraordinary news, and explained that he could not accept the honour of becoming his son-in-law because he was already engaged to Tenko's niece.

Sawara, all too late, sent letters to Kimi, and, receiving

no reply, he set out for his old home, shortly after the death of Myokei.

When he reached the little house where he had received his first lessons in the art of painting he learnt with anger that Kimi had left her old uncle, and in due time he married Kiku ("Chrysanthemum"), the daughter of a wealthy farmer.

Shortly after Sawara's marriage the Lord of Aki bade him paint the seven scenes of the Islands of Kabakari-jima, which were to be mounted on gold screens. He at once set out for these islands, and made a number of rough sketches. While thus employed he met along the shore a woman with a red cloth round her loins, her hair loose and falling about her shoulders. She carried shell-fish in her basket, and as soon as she saw Sawara she recognised him.

"You are Sawara and I am Kimi," said she, "to whom you are engaged. It was a false report about your marriage with Myokei's daughter, and my heart is full of joy, for now nothing prevents our union."

"Alas! poor, much-wronged Kimi, that cannot be!" replied Sawara. "I thought that you deserted Tenko, and that you had forgotten me, and believing these things to be true I have married Kiku, a farmer's daughter."

Kimi, without a word, sprang forward like a hunted animal, ran along the shore, and entered her little hut, Sawara running after her and calling her name over and over again. Before his very eyes he saw Kimi take a knife and thrust it into her throat, and in another moment she lay dead upon the ground. Sawara wept as he gazed upon her still form, noticed the wistful beauty of Death upon her cheek, and saw a new glory in her wind-blown hair. So fair and wonderful was her presence now that when he had controlled his

A Kakemono Ghost.

(See page 125)

Sengen, the Goddess of Mount Fuji.

(See page 132)

weeping he made a sketch of the woman who had loved him so well, but so pitifully. Above the mark of the tide he buried her, and when he reached his own home he took out the rough sketch, painted a picture of Kimi, and hung the *kakemono* on the wall.

Kimi Finds Peace

That very night he awoke to find that the figure on the *kakemono* had come to life, that Kimi with the wound in her throat, the dishevelled hair, stood beside him. Night after night she came, a silent, pitiful figure, until at last Sawara, unable to bear these visitations any longer, presented the *kakemono* to the Korinji Temple and sent his wife back to her parents. The priests of the Korinji Temple prayed every day for the soul of Kimi, and by and by Kimi found peace and troubled Sawara no more.

CHAPTER VIII : THE STAR LOVERS AND THE ROBE OF FEATHERS

The Star Lovers

ONE of the most romantic of the old Japanese festivals is the Festival of Tanabata, the Weaving Lady. It takes place on the seventh day of the seventh month, and on this occasion it was customary to place freshly cut bamboos either on the roofs of houses or to fix them in the ground close beside them. Coloured strips of paper were attached to these bamboos, and upon every strip of paper was a poem in praise of Tanabata and her husband Hikoboshi, such as : "As Tanabata slumbers with her long sleeves rolled up, until the reddening of the dawn, do not, O storks of the river-shallows, awaken her by your cries." This festival will more readily be understood when we have described the legend in connection with it.

The God of the Firmament had a lovely daughter, Tanabata by name, and she spent her time in weaving garments for her august father. One day, while she sat at her loom, she chanced to see a handsome lad leading an ox, and she immediately fell in love with him. Tanabata's father, reading her secret thoughts, speedily consented to their marriage. Unfortunately, however, they loved "not wisely, but too well," with the result that Tanabata neglected her weaving, and Hikoboshi's ox was allowed to wander at large over the High Plain of Heaven. The God of the Firmament became extremely angry, and commanded that these too ardent lovers should henceforth be separated by the Celestial River. On the seventh night of the seventh month, provided the weather was favourable, a great company of birds formed a bridge across the river, and by this means the lovers were able to meet. Their all too brief visit was not even a certainty, for if there were rain the Celestial River would become too wide for even a great bridge of magpies to span, and the lovers would be compelled to wait another weary year before there was even a chance of meeting each other again.

No wonder that on the Festival of the Weaving Maiden little children should sing, "*Tenki ni nari*" ("Oh, weather, be clear!"). Love laughs at locksmiths in our own country, but the Celestial River in flood is another matter. When the weather is fine and the Star Lovers meet each other after a weary year's waiting it is said that the stars, possibly Lyra and Aquila, shine with five different colours—blue, green, red, yellow, and white—and that is why the poems are written on paper of these colours.

The Robe of Feathers [1]

"Oh, magic strains that fill our ravish'd ears!
The fairy sings, and from the cloudy spheres,
Chiming in unison, the angels' lutes,
Tabrets, and cymbals, and sweet silv'ry flutes,
Ring through the heav'n that glows with purple hues,
As when Someiro's western slope endues
The tints of sunset, while the azure wave
From isle to isle the pine-clad shores doth lave.
From Yukishima's slope—a beauteous storm—
Whirl down the flow'rs: and still that magic form,
Those snowy pinions, flutt'ring in the light,
Ravish our souls with wonder and delight."

Ha-Goromo. (Trans. by B. H. CHAMBERLAIN.)

It was spring-time, and along Mio's pine-clad shore there came a sound of birds. The blue sea danced and

---

[1] The subject of this story resembles a certain Norse legend. See William Morris's *The Land East of the Sun and West of the Moon.*

sparkled in the sunshine, and Hairukoo, a fisherman, sat down to enjoy the scene. As he did so he chanced to see, hanging on a pine-tree, a beautiful robe of pure white feathers.

As Hairukoo was about to take down the robe he saw coming toward him from the sea an extremely lovely maiden, who requested that the fisherman would restore the robe to her.

Hairukoo gazed upon the lady with considerable admiration. Said he: "I found this robe, and I mean to keep it, for it is a marvel to be placed among the treasures of Japan. No, I cannot possibly give it to you."

"Oh," cried the maiden pitifully, "I cannot go soaring into the sky without my robe of feathers, for if you persist in keeping it I can never more return to my celestial home. Oh, good fisherman, I beg of you to restore my robe!"

The fisherman, who must have been a hard-hearted fellow, refused to relent. "The more you plead," said he, "the more determined I am to keep what I have found."

Thus the maiden made answer:

"Speak not, dear fisherman! speak not that word!
Ah! know'st thou not that, like the hapless bird
Whose wings are broke, I seek, but seek in vain,
Reft of my wings, to soar to heav'n's blue plain?"
                              Trans. by B. H. CHAMBERLAIN.

After further argument on the subject the fisherman's heart softened a little. "I will restore your robe of feathers," said he, "if you will at once dance before me."

Then the maiden replied: "I will dance it here— the dance that makes the Palace of the Moon turn round, so that even poor transitory man may learn its mysteries. But I cannot dance without my feathers."

128

"No," said the fisherman suspiciously. "If I give you this robe you will fly away without dancing before me."

This remark made the maiden extremely angry. "The pledge of mortals may be broken," said she, "but there is no falsehood among the Heavenly Beings."

These words put the fisherman to shame, and, without more ado, he gave the maiden her robe of feathers.

The Moon-Lady's Song

When the maiden had put on her pure white garment she struck a musical instrument and began to dance, and while she danced and played she sang of many strange and beautiful things concerning her far-away home in the Moon. She sang of the mighty Palace of the Moon, where thirty monarchs ruled, fifteen in robes of white when that shining orb was full, and fifteen robed in black when the Moon was waning. As she sang and played and danced she blessed Japan, "that earth may still her proper increase yield!"

The fisherman did not long enjoy this kindly exhibition of the Moon-Lady's skill, for very soon her dainty feet ceased to tap upon the sand. She rose into the air, the white feathers of her robe gleaming against the pine-trees or against the blue sky itself. Up, up she went, still playing and singing, past the summits of the mountains, higher and higher, until her song was hushed, until she reached the glorious Palace of the Moon.

CHAPTER IX : LEGENDS OF MOUNT FUJI

The Mountain of the Lotus and the Fan

MOUNT FUJI, or Fuji-yama ("The Never-dying Mountain"), seems to be typically Japanese. Its great snow-capped cone resembles a huge inverted fan, the fine streaks down its sides giving the appearance of fan-ribs. A native has thus fittingly described it : "Fuji dominates life by its silent beauty : sorrow is hushed, longing quieted, peace seems to flow down from that changeless home of peace, the peak of the white lotus." The reference here to a white lotus is as appropriate as that of the wide-stretched fan, for it refers to the sacred flower of the Lord Buddha, and its eight points symbolise to the devout Buddhist the Eight Intelligences of Perception, Purpose, Speech, Conduct, Living, Effort, Mindfulness, and Contemplation. The general effect of Fuji, then, suggests on the one hand religion, and on the other a fan vast enough and fair enough to coquet with stars and swift-moving clouds. Poets and artists alike have paid their tributes of praise to this peerless mountain, and we give the following exquisite poem on this apparently inexhaustible theme :

> " Fuji Yama,
>   Touched by thy divine breath,
>   We return to the shape of God.
>   Thy silence is Song,
>   Thy song is the song of Heaven :
>   Our land of fever and care
>   Turns to a home of mellow-eyed ease—
>   The home away from the land
>   Where mortals are born only to die.
>   We Japanese daughters and sons,
>   Chanting of thy fair majesty,

MOUNTAIN OF THE LOTUS AND THE FAN

The pride of God,
Seal our shadows in thy bosom,
The balmiest place of eternity,
O white-faced wonder,
O matchless sight,
O sublimity, O Beauty!
The thousand rivers carry thy sacred image
On their brows;
All the mountains raise their heads unto thee
Like the flowing tide,
As if to hear thy final command.
Behold! the seas surrounding Japan
Lose their hungry-toothed song and wolfish desire,
Kissed by lullaby-humming repose,
At sight of thy shadow,
As one in a dream of poem.
We being round thee forget to die:
Death is sweet,
Life is sweeter than Death.
We are mortals and also gods,
Innocent companions of thine,
O eternal Fuji!"

Yone Noguchi.

Mount Fuji has been a place of pilgrimage for hundreds of years, and Lafcadio Hearn has described its peak as "the Supreme Altar of the Sun." Many pilgrims still cling to the old Shintō custom of ascending this sacred mountain, wearing white clothes and very broad straw hats, and frequently ringing a bell and chanting : "May our six senses be pure, and the weather on the honourable mountain be fair."

Fuji was at one time an extremely active volcano. Her final outbreak took place in 1707–8, and covered Tōkyō, sixty miles distant, with six inches of ash. The very name Fuji is probably derived from Huchi, or Fuchi, the Aino Goddess of Fire ; "for," writes Professor Chamberlain, "down to times almost historical the country round Fuji formed part of Aino-land, and all Eastern Japan is strewn with names of Aino origin."

131

The Deities of Fuji

Sengen, the Goddess of Fuji, is also known as Ko-no-hana-saku-ya-hime[1] ("Radiant-blooming-as-the-flowers-of-the-trees"), and on the summit is her temple. In ancient days it is said that this Goddess hovered in a luminous cloud above the crater, tended by invisible servants, who were prepared to throw down any pilgrims who were not pure of heart. Another deity of this mountain is O-ana-mochi ("Possessor of the Great Hole," or "Crater"). In addition we have the Luminous Maiden, who lured a certain emperor to his doom. At the place of his vanishing a small shrine was erected, where he is still worshipped. It is said that on one occasion a shower of priceless jewels fell down from this mountain, and that the sand which during the day is disturbed by the feet of countless pilgrims falls to the base and nightly reascends to its former position.

Fuji, the Abode of the Elixir of Life

It is not surprising to find that legend has grown round this venerable and venerated mountain. Like so many mountains in Japan, and, indeed, in other Eastern countries, it was associated with the Elixir of Life. The Japanese poet's words, "We being round thee forget to die," though written in recent years, seem to reflect the old idea. We have already seen, in the legend of "The Bamboo-cutter and the Moon-Maiden," that Tsuki was commanded by the Lady Kaguya to ascend Fuji and there burn the Elixir of Life, together with a certain scroll.

The fame of Fuji, so an old legend informs us, reached the ears of an Emperor of China. When he was told that this mountain had come into being in a

---

[1] She married Ninigi, and is referred to in Chapter I.

single night[1] he conjectured that Mount Fuji must needs yield the Elixir of Life itself. He accordingly collected about him a number of handsome youths and maidens and set sail for the Land of the Rising Sun. The junks rushed before the roaring wind like a shower of gold petals ; but eventually the storm abated, and the Emperor and his people saw the white splendour of Fuji rise up before them. When the junks had run in upon the shore the Emperor formed his company in procession, and, walking very slowly, led the way up the mountain. Hour after hour the procession climbed, the gold-robed Emperor ever walking in advance, until the sound of the sea was lost, and the thousand feet trod softly on the snow where there was peace and life eternal. Nearing the journey's end, the old Emperor ran forward joyously, for he wanted to be the first to drink of the Elixir of Life. And he was the first to taste of that Life that never grows old ; but when the company found him they saw their Emperor lying on his back with a smile upon his face. He had indeed found Life Eternal, but it was through the way of Death.

Sentaro's Visit to the Land of Perpetual Youth

The desire to wrest from Mount Fuji the secret of perpetual life never seems to have met with success. A Chinese, Jofuku by name, reached the sacred mountain with this object in view. He failed, and never lived to return to his own country ; but he is looked upon as a saint, and those bound on the same quest pray earnestly at his shrine.

Sentaro on one occasion prayed at this shrine, and was presented with a small paper crane, which expanded to a vast size directly it had reached his hands. On

[1] See the last section of this chapter.

the back of this great crane flew Sentaro to the Land of Perpetual Youth, where, to his amazement, the people ate poisons and longed in vain to die! Sentaro soon grew weary of this land, returned to his own country, and resolved to be content with the ordinary span of years allotted to mankind—as well he may have been, considering that he had already spent three hundred years in the country where there was no death and no birth.

The Goddess of Fuji

Yosoji's mother, in common with many in the village where she lived, was stricken down with smallpox. Yosoji consulted the magician Kamo Yamakiko in the matter, for his mother grew so ill that every hour he expected her to be taken from him in death. Kamo Yamakiko told Yosoji to go to a small stream that flowed from the south-west side of Mount Fuji. "Near the source of this stream," said the magician, "is a shrine to the God of Long Breath. Go fetch this water, and give it to your mother, for this alone will cure her."

Yosoji, full of hope, eagerly set forth upon his journey, and when he had arrived at a spot where three paths crossed each other he was in difficulty as to the right one to take. Just as he was debating the matter a lovely girl, clad in white, stepped out from the forest, and bade him follow her to the place where the precious stream flowed near the shrine of the God of Long Breath.

When they reached the stream Yosoji was told to drink himself, as well as to fill the gourd with the sparkling water for his mother. When he had done these things the beautiful girl accompanied him to the place where he had originally seen her, and said: "Meet me again at this place in three days' time, for you will require a further supply of this water."

THE GODDESS OF FUJI

After five visits to this sacred shrine Yosoji rejoiced to find that his mother was quite well again, and not only his mother, but many of the villagers who had also been privileged to drink the water. Yosoji's bravery was loudly extolled, and presents were sent to the magician for his timely advice; but Yosoji, who was an honest lad, knew in his heart that all praise was really due to the beautiful girl who had been his guide. He desired to thank her more fully than he had hitherto done, and for this purpose he once more set out for the stream.

When Yosoji reached the shrine of the God of Long Breath he found that the stream had dried up. With much surprise and not a little sorrow he knelt down and prayed that she who had been so good to his mother would appear before him in order that he might thank her as she so richly deserved. When Yosoji arose he saw the maiden standing before him.

Yosoji expressed his gratitude in warm and elegant language, and begged to be told the name of her who had been his guide and restored his mother to health and strength again. But the maiden, smiling sweetly upon him, would not tell her name. Still smiling, she swung a branch of camellia in the air, so that it seemed that the fair blossom beckoned to some invisible spirit far away. In answer to the floral summons a cloud came down from Mount Fuji; it enveloped the lovely maiden, and carried her to the sacred mountain from which she had come. Yosoji knew now that his guide was none other than the Goddess of Fuji. He knelt with rapture upon his face as he watched the departing figure. As he gazed upon her he knew in his heart that with his thanks love had mingled too. While he yet knelt the Goddess of Fuji threw down the branch of camellia, a remembrance, perhaps a token, of her love for him.

The Rip van Winkle of Old Japan

We have already referred to the coming of Fuji in a single night, and the following legend gives an account of this remarkable event. We have added to this legend another, which is probably of Chinese origin, because the two fit in well together and furnish interesting material in regard to this mountain.

Many years ago there lived on the then barren plain of Suruga a woodman by the name of Visu. He was a giant in stature, and lived in a hut with his wife and children. One night, just as Visu was about to fall asleep, he heard a most extraordinary sound coming from under the earth, a sound louder and more terrible than thunder. Visu, thinking that he and his family were about to be destroyed by an earthquake, hastily snatched up the younger children and rushed to the door of the hut, where he saw a most wonderful sight. Instead of the once desolate plain he perceived a great mountain from whose head sprang tongues of flame and dense clouds of smoke ! So glorious was the sight of this mountain that had run under the earth for two hundred miles and then suddenly sprung forth on the plain of Suruga that Visu, his wife and family, sat down on the ground as if under a spell. When the sun rose the next morning Visu saw that the mountain had put on robes of opal. It seemed so impressive to him that he called it Fuji-yama ("The Never-dying Mountain"), and so it is called to this day. Such perfect beauty suggested to the woodman the eternal, an idea which no doubt gave rise to the Elixir of Life so frequently associated with this mountain.

Day after day Visu sat and gazed upon Fuji, and was just conjecturing how nice it would be for so imposing a mountain to be able to see her loveliness, when a great lake suddenly stretched before him, shaped like a lute, and so called Biwa.[1]

The Adventures of Visu

One day Visu received a visit from an old priest, who said to him : " Honourable woodman, I am afraid you never pray." Visu replied : " If you had a wife and a large family to keep you would never have time to pray." This remark made the priest angry, and the old man gave the woodcutter a vivid description of the horror of being reborn as a toad, or a mouse, or an insect for millions of years. Such lurid details were not to Visu's liking, and he accordingly promised the priest that in future he would pray. "Work and pray," said the priest as he took his departure.

Unfortunately Visu did nothing but pray. He prayed all day long and refused to do any work, so that his rice crops withered and his wife and family starved. Visu's wife, who had hitherto never said a harsh or bitter word to her husband, now became extremely angry, and, pointing to the poor thin bodies of her children, she exclaimed : " Rise, Visu, take up your axe and do something more helpful to us all than the mere mumbling of prayers ! "

Visu was so utterly amazed at what his wife had said that it was some time before he could think of a fitting reply. When he did so his words came hot and strong to the ears of his poor, much-wronged wife.

[1] There is some confusion here, for in actual fact Lake Biwa is a hundred and forty miles distant from Fuji—too great a distance, one would imagine, for even a miraculous mountain to look into. Legend asserts that Fuji came from the earth in a single night, while Lake Biwa sank simultaneously. Professor Chamberlain writes : " May we not have here an echo of some early eruption, which resulted in the formation, not indeed of Lake Biwa . . . but of one of the numerous small lakes at the foot of the mountain ? "

137

" Woman," said he, " the Gods come first. You are
an impertinent creature to speak to me so, and I will
have nothing more to do with you ! " Visu snatched
up his axe and, without looking round to say farewell,
he left the hut, strode out of the wood, and climbed
up Fuji-yama, where a mist hid him from sight.

When Visu had seated himself upon the mountain
he heard a soft rustling sound, and immediately after-
ward saw a fox dart into a thicket. Now Visu deemed
it extremely lucky to see a fox, and, forgetting his
prayers, he sprang up, and ran hither and thither in
the hope of again finding this sharp-nosed little
creature. He was about to give up the chase when,
coming to an open space in a wood, he saw two
ladies sitting down by a brook playing *go*.[1] The
woodman was so completely fascinated that he could
do nothing but sit down and watch them. There was
no sound except the soft click of pieces on the board
and the song of the running brook. The ladies took
no notice of Visu, for they seemed to be playing a
strange game that had no end, a game that entirely
absorbed their attention. Visu could not keep his
eyes off these fair women. He watched their long
black hair and the little quick hands that shot out
now and again from their big silk sleeves in order
to move the pieces. After he had been sitting there
for three hundred years, though to him it was but a
summer's afternoon, he saw that one of the players
had made a false move. " *Wrong*, most lovely lady ! "
he exclaimed excitedly. In a moment these women
turned into foxes[2] and ran away.

When Visu attempted to pursue them he found to

---

[1] " *Go* may with justice be considered more difficult than chess, its
wider field affording more numerous ramifications."—PROFESSOR B. H.
CHAMBERLAIN.   [2] Fox legends have been fully described in Chapter V.

Visu on Mount Fuji-yama.
(See page 138)

Kiyo and the Priest.

(See page 145)

his horror that his limbs were terribly stiff, that his hair was very long, and that his beard touched the ground. He discovered, moreover, that the handle of his axe, though made of the hardest wood, had crumbled away into a little heap of dust.

Visu's Return

After many painful efforts Visu was able to stand on his feet and proceed very slowly toward his little home. When he reached the spot he was surprised to see no hut, and, perceiving a very old woman, he said : " Good lady, I am amazed to find that my little home has disappeared. I went away this afternoon, and now in the evening it has vanished ! "

The old woman, who believed that a madman was addressing her, inquired his name. When she was told, she exclaimed : " Bah ! you must indeed be mad ! Visu lived three hundred years ago ! He went away one day, and he never came back again."

" *Three hundred years !* " murmured Visu. " It cannot be possible. Where are my dear wife and children ? "

" Buried ! " hissed the old woman, " and, if what you say is true, your children's children too. The Gods have prolonged your miserable life in punishment for having neglected your wife and little children."

Big tears ran down Visu's withered cheeks as he said in a husky voice : " I have lost my manhood. I have prayed when my dear ones starved and needed the labour of my once strong hands. Old woman, remember my last words: *if you pray, work too !* "

We do not know how long the poor but repentant Visu lived after he returned from his strange adventures. His white spirit is still said to haunt Fujiyama when the moon shines brightly.

139

CHAPTER X : BELLS

The Bell of Enkakuji

JAPANESE bells are among the finest in the world, for in their size, construction, and decoration the bell-maker of Nippon has reached a high level of efficiency. The largest bell in Japan belongs to the Jodo temple of Chion, at Kyōto. It weighs seventy-four tons, and requires seventy-five men to ring it in order to get the full effect from this great mass of metal. The bell of Enkakuji is the largest bell in Kamakura. It dates from the beginning of the thirteenth century, and is six inches thick, four feet seven inches in diameter, and about eight feet high. This bell, unlike our own, is the same diameter from top to bottom, a feature common to all big Japanese bells. It is rung by means of a beam suspended from the roof, and from the beam hangs a rope. When the beam is set swinging with sufficient velocity it strikes a lotus-moulding on the side of the bell, and a great note quivers forth, "deep as thunder, rich as the bass of a mighty organ."

The Return of Ono-no-Kimi

When Ono-no-Kimi died he went before the Judgment Seat of Emma-Ō, the Judge of Souls, and was told by that dread deity that he had quitted earthly life too soon, and that he must at once return. Ono-no-Kimi pleaded that he could not retrace his steps, as he did not know the way. Then Emma-Ō said : "By listening to the bell of Enkakuji you will be able to find your way into the world again." And Ono-no-Kimi went forth from the Judgment Seat, and, with the sound of the bell for guidance, once more found himself in his old home.

A WOMAN AND THE BELL OF MIIDERA

The Giant Priest

On one occasion it is said that a priest of giant stature was seen in the country, and no one knew his name or whence he had come. With unceasing zest he travelled up and down the land, from village to village, from town to town, exhorting the people to pray before the bell of Enkakuji. It was eventually discovered that this giant priest was none other than a personification of the holy bell itself. This extraordinary news had its effect, for numerous people now flocked to the bell of Enkakuji, prayed, and returned with many a wish fulfilled. On another occasion this sacred bell is said to have sounded a deep note of its own accord. Those who were incredulous and laughed at the miracle met with calamity, and those who believed in the miraculous power of the sacred bell were rewarded with much prosperity.

A Woman and the Bell of Miidera

In the ancient monastery of Miidera there was a great bronze bell. It rang out every morning and evening, a clear, rich note, and its surface shone like sparkling dew. The priests would not allow any woman to strike it, because they thought that such an action would pollute and dull the metal, as well as bring calamity upon them.

When a certain pretty woman who lived in Kyōto heard this she grew extremely inquisitive, and at last, unable to restrain her curiosity, she said : " I will go and see this wonderful bell of Miidera. I will make it sound forth a soft note, and in its shining surface, bigger and brighter than a thousand mirrors, I will paint and powder my face and dress my hair."

At length this vain and irreverent woman reached

the belfry in which the great bell was suspended at a time when all were absorbed in their sacred duties. She looked into the gleaming bell and saw her pretty eyes, flushed cheeks, and laughing dimples. Presently she stretched forth her little fingers, lightly touched the shining metal, and prayed that she might have as great and splendid a mirror for her own. When the bell felt this woman's fingers, the bronze that she touched shrank, leaving a little hollow, and losing at the same time all its exquisite polish.

Benkei and the Bell

Benkei,[1] the faithful retainer of Yoshitsune, may be fittingly described as the strong man of Old Japan. His strength was prodigious, as will be seen in the following legend.

When Benkei was a monk he very much desired to steal the bell of Miidera, and bring it to his own monastery. He accordingly visited Miidera, and, at an opportune moment, unhooked the great bell. Benkei's first thought was to roll it down the hill, and thus save himself the trouble of carrying such a huge piece of metal ; but, thinking that the monks would hear the noise, he was forced to set about carrying it down the steep incline. He accordingly pulled out the cross-beam from the belfry, suspended the bell at one end, and—humorous touch—his paper lantern at the other,[2] and in this manner he carried his mighty burden for nearly seven miles.

When Benkei reached his temple he at once demanded food. He managed to get through a concoction which filled an iron soup-pot five feet in diameter,

[1] See Chapter II.
[2] Hence the Japanese saying : " Lantern and bell, which is the heavier ? "

and when he had finished he gave permission for a few priests to strike the stolen bell of Miidera. The bell was struck, but in its dying murmur it seemed to cry : " I want to go back to Miidera ! I want to go back to Miidera ! "

When the priests heard this they were amazed. The abbot, however, thought that if the bell were sprinkled with holy water it would become reconciled to its new abode ; but in spite of holy water the bell still sobbed forth its plaintive and provoking cry. No one was more displeased by the sound than Benkei himself. It seemed that the bell mocked him and that arduous journey of his. At last, exasperated beyond endurance, he rushed to the rope, strained it till the beam was far from the great piece of metal, then let it go, hoping that the force of the swift-rushing beam would crack such a peevish and ill-bred bell. The whirling wood reached the bell with a terrific crash ; but it did not break. Through the air rang again : "I want to go back to Miidera ! " and whether the bell was struck harshly or softly it always spoke the same words.

At last Benkei, now in a towering rage, shouldered the bell and beam, and, coming to the top of a mountain, he set down his burden, and, with a mighty kick, sent it rolling into the valley beneath. Some time later the Miidera priests found their precious bell, and joyfully hung it in its accustomed place, and from that time it failed to speak, and only rang like other temple bells.

Karma

The power of Karma is one of the great Buddhist doctrines, and many are the stories, both true and legendary, told in connection with this theme. Of the former Lafcadio Hearn in " Kokoro " narrates the pitiful tale of a priest who had the misfortune to attract the love of many women. Rather than yield to their solicitations he committed suicide by kneeling in the middle of a railway track and allowing an express train to put an end to his temptations.

The story of "The Bamboo-cutter and the Moon-Maiden" gives us another representation of the working out of Karma. The Lady Kaguya was banished from her home in the moon owing to indulgence in some sensual passion. In her exile it will be remembered that her weakness was vanquished, and that she steadfastly resisted this particular sin during her earthly sojourn.

Karma by no means represents exclusively the power of evil thought, though it is most commonly applied to the human passions. In its fuller meaning it signifies cause and effect—all thoughts, all actions that are not spiritual, for by the working of Karma, according to Buddhist teaching, is the world and all it contains fashioned. The desire to be is Karma. The desire not to be is the breaking of the great wheel of birth and rebirth, and the attainment of Nirvana.

There are Japanese lovers who, owing to circumstance, are unable to marry; but they do not blame circumstance. They regard their misfortune as the result of an error in a previous existence, such as breaking their promise to wed, or because they were cruel to each other. Such lovers believe that if they bind themselves together with an under-girdle and spring into a river or lake they will become united in their next birth. This suicide of Japanese lovers is called *jōshi*, which means "love-death" or "passion-death." Buddhism is strongly opposed to self-destruction, and no less to a love of this kind, for in *jōshi* there is no desire to destroy, but rather to foster, the power of Karma. Such lovers may be united, but in the teaching of the Lord Buddha

144

a union of this kind is a delusion, while Nirvana alone is worth striving for. We read in the *Ratana Sutra :* "Their old Karma is exhausted, no new Karma is being produced : their hearts are free from the longing after future life ; the cause of their existence being destroyed, and no new yearnings springing up within them, they, the wise, are extinguished like this lamp."

A Bell and the Power of Karma

> "There are various paths leading to the attainment of complete happiness. When we find ourselves upon the wrong one it is our duty to quit it."
>
> BAKIN.

Near the banks of the Hidaka there once stood a far-famed tea-house nestling amid lovely scenery beside a hill called the Dragon's Claw. The fairest girl in this tea-house was Kiyo, for she was like "the fragrance of white lilies, when the wind, sweeping down the mountain heights, comes perfume-laden to the traveller."

Across the river stood a Buddhist temple where the abbot and a number of priests lived a simple and devout life. In the belfry of this temple reposed a great bell, six inches thick and weighing several tons. It was one of the monastery rules that none of the priests should eat fish or meat or drink *saké,* and they were especially forbidden to stop at tea-houses, lest they should lose their spirituality and fall into the sinful ways of the flesh.

One of the priests, however, on returning from a certain shrine, happened to see the pretty Kiyo, flitting hither and thither in the tea-garden, like a large, bright-winged butterfly. He stood and watched her for a moment, sorely tempted to enter the garden and speak to this beautiful creature, but, remembering his priestly calling, he crossed the river and entered his temple. That night, however, he could not sleep. The fever of a violent love had come upon him. He fingered his rosary and repeated passages from the Buddhist Scriptures, but these things brought him no peace of mind. Through all his pious thoughts there ever shone the winsome face of Kiyo, and it seemed to him that she was calling from that fair garden across the river.

His burning love grew so intense that it was not long before he stifled his religious feelings, broke one of the temple rules, and entered the forbidden tea-house. Here he entirely forgot his religion, or found a new one in contemplating the beautiful Kiyo, who brought him refreshment. Night after night he crept across the river and fell under the spell of this woman. She returned his love with equal passion, so that for the moment it appeared to this erring priest that he had found in a woman's charms something far sweeter than the possibility of attaining Nirvana.

After the priest had seen Kiyo on many nights conscience began to stir within him and to do battle with his unholy love. The power of Karma and the teaching of the Lord Buddha struggled within his breast. It was a fierce conflict, but in the end passion was vanquished, though, as we shall learn, not its awful consequences. The priest, having stamped out his carnal love, deemed it wise to deal with Kiyo as circumspectly as possible, lest his sudden change should make her angry.

When Kiyo saw the priest after his victory over the flesh she observed the far-away look in his eyes and the ascetic calm that now rested upon his face. She redoubled her feminine wiles, determined either to make the priest love her again, or, failing that, to put him to a cruel death by sorcery.

All Kiyo's blandishments failed to awaken love

within the priest's heart, and, thinking only of vengeance, she set out, arrayed in a white robe, and went to a certain mountain where there was a Fudo[1] shrine. Fudo sat, surrounded by fire, a sword in one hand and a small coil of rope in the other. Here Kiyo prayed with fearful vehemence that this hideous-looking God would show her how to kill the priest who had once loved her.

From Fudo she went to the shrine of Kompira,[2] who has the knowledge of magic and is able to teach sorcery. Here she begged that she might have the power to turn herself at will into a dragon-serpent. After many visits a long-nosed sprite (probably a *tengu*), who waited upon Kompira, taught Kiyo all the mysteries of magic and sorcery. He taught this once sweet girl how to change herself into the awful creature she desired to be for the purpose of a cruel vengeance.

Still the priest visited Kiyo ; but no longer was he the lover. By many exhortations he tried to stay the passion of this maiden he once loved ; but these priestly discourses only made Kiyo more determined to win the victory in the end. She wept, she pleaded, she wound her fair arms about him ; but none of her allurements had the slightest effect, except to drive away the priest for the last time.

Just as the priest was about to take his departure he was horrified to see Kiyo's eyes suddenly turn into

[1] Fudo is not, as is generally supposed, the God of Fire, but is identified, according to Sir Ernest Satow, with Dainichi, the God of Wisdom. It is not quite clear why Kiyo visited Fudo, whose sacred sword symbolises wisdom, while his fire represents power, and the coil of rope that which binds the passions.

[2] Kompira was originally an Indian God, which the mediæval Shintōists identified with Susa-no-o, brother of the Sun Goddess, who, as we have already seen, would be only too pleased to lend himself to mischief.

147

those of a serpent. With a shriek of fear he ran out of the tea-garden, swam across the river, and hid himself inside the great temple bell.

Kiyo raised her magic wand, murmured a certain incantation, and in a moment the sweet face and form of this lovely maiden became transformed into that of a dragon-serpent, hissing and spirting fire. With eyes as large and luminous as moons she crawled over the garden, swam across the river, and entered the belfry. Her weight broke down the supporting columns, and the bell, with the priest inside, fell with a deafening crash to the ground.

Kiyo embraced the bell with a terrible lust for vengeance. Her coils held the metal as in a vice; tighter and tighter she hugged the bell, till the metal became red-hot. All in vain was the prayer of the captive priest; all in vain, too, were the earnest entreaties of his fellow brethren, who implored that Buddha would destroy the demon. Hotter and hotter grew the bell, and it rang with the piteous shrieks of the priest within. Presently his voice was stilled, and the bell melted and ran down into a pool of molten metal. The great power of Karma had destroyed it, and with it the priest and the dragon-serpent that was once the beautiful Kiyo.

CHAPTER XI : YUKI-ONNA, THE LADY OF THE SNOW

" Midwinter gloom the earth enshrouds,
            Yet from the skies
            The blossoms fall
            A flutt'ring shower,
            White petals all !
            Can spring be come,
    So soon beyond the clouds ? "
    Kujohara No Fukayabu (Trans. by CLARA A. WALSH).

Yuki-Onna

SNOW-TIME in Japan has a beauty peculiarly its own, and it is a favourite theme of Japanese poets and artists. Both, for the most part, treat it artistically, as well they may do, seeing that in Nippon the white flakes fall upon the ornate roofs of Buddhist temples, upon the fairy-like bridges, resembling those we have seen on willow-pattern plates, and upon the exquisitely shaped stone lanterns that adorn so many Japanese gardens. The ideal snow-scene is to be found in Japan, and because it is so particularly beautiful it is surprising to find that Yuki-Onna,[1] the Lady of the Snow, is very far from being a benevolent and attractive spirit. All the artistry and poetry of snow vanish in her malignant presence, for she represents Death, with attributes not unlike that of a vampire. But Japan is full of sharp and surprising contrasts, and the delicate and beautiful jostle with the ugly and horrible. There is no promise of spring in the long white form of Yuki-Onna, for her mouth is the mouth of Death, and her ice-cold lips draw forth the life-blood of her unfortunate victims.

[1] See my *Land of the Yellow Spring*, p. 39.

The Snow-Bride

Mosaku and his apprentice Minokichi journeyed to a forest, some little distance from their village. It was a bitterly cold night when they neared their destination, and saw in front of them a cold sweep of water. They desired to cross this river, but the ferryman had gone away, leaving his boat on the other side of the water, and as the weather was too inclement to admit of swimming across the river they were glad to take shelter in the ferryman's little hut.

Mosaku fell asleep almost immediately he entered this humble but welcome shelter. Minokichi, however, lay awake for a long time listening to the cry of the wind and the hiss of the snow as it was blown against the door.

Minokichi at last fell asleep, to be soon awakened by a shower of snow falling across his face. He found that the door had been blown open, and that standing in the room was a fair woman in dazzlingly white garments. For a moment she stood thus; then she bent over Mosaku, her breath coming forth like white smoke. After bending thus over the old man for a minute or two she turned to Minokichi and hovered over him. He tried to cry out, for the breath of this woman was like a freezing blast of wind. She told him that she had intended to treat him as she had done the old man at his side, but forbore on account of his youth and beauty. Threatening Minokichi with instant death if he dared to mention to any one what he had seen, she suddenly vanished.

Then Minokichi called out to his beloved master : "Mosaku, Mosaku, wake ! Something very terrible has happened ! " But there was no reply. He touched the hand of his master in the dark, and found it was like a piece of ice. Mosaku was dead !

Yuki-Onna, the Lady of the Snow.
(See page 150*)*

Shingé and Yoshisawa by the Violet Well.

(See page 167)

During the next winter, while Minokichi was returning home, he chanced to meet a pretty girl by the name of Yuki. She informed him that she was going to Yedo, where she desired to find a situation as a servant. Minokichi was charmed with this maiden, and he went so far as to ask if she were betrothed, and hearing that she was not, he took her to his own home, and in due time married her.

Yuki presented her husband with ten fine and handsome children, fairer of skin than the average. When Minokichi's mother died her last words were in praise of Yuki, and her eulogy was echoed by many of the country folk in the district.

One night, while Yuki was sewing, the light of a paper lamp shining upon her face, Minokichi recalled the extraordinary experience he had had in the ferryman's hut. "Yuki," said he, "you remind me so much of a beautiful white woman I saw when I was eighteen years old. She killed my master with her ice-cold breath. I am sure she was some strange spirit, and yet to-night she seems to resemble you!"

Yuki flung down her sewing. There was a horrible smile on her face as she bent close to her husband and shrieked: "It was I, Yuki-Onna, who came to you then, and silently killed your master! Oh, faithless wretch, you have broken your promise to keep the matter secret, and if it were not for our sleeping children I would kill you now! Remember, if they have aught to complain of at your hands I shall hear, I shall know, and on a night when the snow falls I *will* kill you!"

Then Yuki-Onna, the Lady of the Snow, changed into a white mist, and, shrieking and shuddering, passed through the smoke-hole, never to return again.

Kyuzaemon's Ghostly Visitor

According to Mr. R. Gordon Smith, in his "Ancient Tales and Folk-lore of Japan," "all those who die by the snow and cold become spirits of snow." That is to say, all those who perish in this way become identified with Yuki-Onna, the Lady of the Snow. The following legend is adapted from Mr. Smith's book referred to above.

Kyuzaemon, a poor farmer, had closed the shutters of his humble dwelling and retired to rest. Shortly before midnight he was awakened by loud tapping. Going to the door, he exclaimed : "Who are you? What do you want?"

The strange visitor made no attempt to answer these questions, but persistently begged for food and shelter. The cautious Kyuzaemon refused to allow the visitor to enter, and, having seen that his dwelling was secure, he was about to retire to bed again, when he saw standing beside him a woman in white flowing garments, her hair falling over her shoulders.

"Where did you leave your *geta*?" demanded the frightened farmer.

The white woman informed him that she was the visitor who had tapped upon his door. "I need no *geta*," she said, "for I have no feet! I fly over the snow-capped trees, and should have proceeded to the next village, but the wind was blowing strongly against me, and I desired to rest awhile."

The farmer expressed his fear of spirits, whereupon the woman inquired if her host had a *butsudan* (a family altar). Finding that he had, she bade him open the *butsudan* and light a lamp. When this was done the woman prayed before the ancestral tablets, not forgetting to add a prayer for the still much-agitated Kyuzaemon.

KYUZAEMON'S GHOSTLY VISITOR

Having paid her respects at the *butsudan*, she informed the farmer that her name was Oyasu, and that she had lived with her parents and her husband, Isaburo. When she died her husband left her parents, and it was her intention to try to persuade him to go back again and support the old people.

Kyuzaemon began to understand as he murmured to himself: "Oyasu perished in the snow, and this is her spirit I see before me." However, in spite of this recollection he still felt much afraid. He sought the family altar with trembling footsteps, repeating over and over again: "Namu Amida Butsu!" ("Hail, Omnipotent Buddha!")

At last the farmer went to bed and fell asleep. Once he woke up to hear the white creature murmur farewell; but before he could make answer she had disappeared.

The following day Kyuzaemon went to the next village, and called upon Isaburo, whom he now found living with his father-in-law again. Isaburo informed him that he had received numerous visits from the spirit of his wife in the guise of Yuki-Onna. After carefully considering the matter Kyuzaemon found that this Lady of the Snow had appeared before Isaburo almost immediately after she had paid him such a mysterious visit. On that occasion Isaburo had promised to fulfil her wish, and neither he nor Kyuzaemon were again troubled with her who travels in the sky when the snow is falling fast.

CHAPTER XII : FLOWERS AND GARDENS

> " All the joy of my existence is concentrated around the
> pillow which giveth me nightly rest, all the hope of my
> days I find in the beauties of Nature that ever please my
> eyes."
>
> " *Hō-jō-ki* " (Trans. by F. V. DICKINS).

Japanese and English Gardens

THERE is nothing particularly æsthetic about the average English garden. When the bedding-out time comes a slow old gardener puts in his plants. Later on we see a crude blaze of colour—scarlet geraniums, yellow calceolarias, blue lobelias, the green grass and the ochre-coloured paths. And this is the colour effect of the average English garden, a colour effect that makes the eyes ache and shames the very flowers so unwisely set in this fashion. The truth of the matter is that we do not understand the art of flower arrangement. We buy flowers just to make the garden look bright, under the impression that brightness is an abstract quality with which we should like to spend our summer days. An Englishman once attempted to make a landscape garden after the Japanese manner. He was extremely proud of the result, and on one occasion he took a Japanese gentleman round to see it. The Japanese gentleman exclaimed, with extreme courtesy : " It is very beautiful ; we have nothing at all like it in Japan ! " The Englishman failed in his attempt to imitate because he considered gardening a hobby, while in Japan the garden is something indelibly associated with Japanese life itself. In Japan it is an ancient cult to which poets and artists have given years of thought, a cult

154

in which emotion, memory, and religion play their part.

The Love of Flowers, its Growth and Symbolism

One of the most striking, and certainly one of the most pleasing, characteristics of the Japanese is their intense love of flowers and trees. Merry parties set out to see the azaleas bloom, or the splendour of the pink-white cherry-blossom, or the scarlet glory of the maple-trees. This " flower-viewing " is an integral part of their existence. The very *kimono* of the laughing children look like little gardens of flowers themselves. Take away their landscape, and you take away at once their sense of poetry, and, we may almost add, the floral side of their religion too, for the Japanese worship flowers and trees in a way utterly impossible to the more prosaic Westerner.

During a recent spring the magnolia-trees in Kew Gardens afforded a wonderfully beautiful spectacle. But there were few to see these leafless trees with their profusion of lotus-like blossom. The most appreciative spectator was a child, who sat under the sweet-scented branches, gathered the fallen petals in her little brown hands, and made up a quaint story as she did so. But in Japan, where magnolia-trees bloom too, a hundred little poems would be threaded to the branches, and little cakes made in imitation of the petals. Perhaps, too, a branch of magnolia would be set in a vase, the object of silent admiration of the members of some tea ceremony. And afterwards the spray of blossom would be gently placed on a river or buried with joy and reverence for the beauty it had exhibited in its brief hour of life.

The love of flowers is only a small part of the Japanese love of Nature. There was an evolutionary growth in this worship as in every other, and we are inclined to think that the Japanese go very far back in this matter, and learnt first of all to love rocks and stones. To us rocks and stones are of interest only to the geologist and metallurgist, merely from a scientific point of view, and it seems almost incredible that rocks and stones have a poetical meaning. But it is otherwise to the Japanese. The Japanese garden is essentially a landscape garden. The owner of a garden falls in love with a certain view. It haunts him, and awakens in him some primitive feelings of delight that cannot be analysed. He brings that view perpetually before him in his garden, in miniature, perhaps, but a miniature of wonderful exactness. His garden thus becomes a place of happy memory, and not a plot laid out with gaudy flowers and terraces that can have no meaning, no poetry to his mind. Without a doubt Japanese gardens, with their gorgeous flowers, merry sunshine, and the sweet tinkle of dainty fairy-bells suspended from the branches of the trees, are the most delightful in the world.

Japanese Gardens

One thing that strikes us about Japanese gardens that we do not find in England is the wonderful economy displayed in their schemes. Suburbia often makes the excuse that their pocket-handkerchief of a garden is much too small to be made beautiful. Too small to be made beautiful? Why, the Japanese can make a wonderful little garden in a space no bigger than a soup-plate! Necessity is the mother of invention, and if we only loved Nature more we should soon find the means to make our smallest gardens attractive. The great Japanese designer of gardens, Kobori-Enshiu, said that an ideal garden should be like "the sweet solitude of a landscape clouded by moonlight, with a half-gloom between the trees."

JAPANESE GARDENS

Miss Florence Du Cane has much to say concerning Japanese rocks and stones. What poetry is suggested in the names of some of these garden stones—for example, "The Stone of Easy Rest." Then, among the lake stones we have one called "Wild Wave Stone," that at once suggests Matsushima, with its waves breaking against innumerable rocks.

The stone or wooden lamps are very important ornaments in a Japanese garden. The idea was borrowed from Korea, and they are still sometimes known as "Korean towers." They are seldom lit, except in temple gardens, but they need no jewel of light to make them beautiful. They are rich in amber and green moss, and in the winter they catch the snow and make ghost lanterns of exquisite beauty. Another feature of a Japanese garden is the *Torii*, a simple arch of wood shaped like a huge Chinese character. Shintō in origin, no one has as yet discovered what they were originally intended to represent, though there have been many diverse opinions on the subject. These gates to nowhere are extremely fascinating, and to look at them with the sea about their feet is to dream of a far-away fairy tale of childhood.

The lakes, cascades, tiny bridges, the stepping-stones over the winding ways of silver sand, form a place of retreat indeed. And then the colour of the Japanese garden! Every month has some fresh colour scene as the plum and cherry and peach-trees come into bloom. Trailing over the ground among the pine-needles or looking into the clear blue lake, one may see the azaleas. If there were ever a flower that personified colour then it is surely the azalea. It is the rainbow of flowers, and there seems scarcely a shade of colour not to be found in its blossoms. To look at the azaleas is to look into the very paint-box of Nature herself. Then at another season of the year we get the iris in purple and lavender, yellow and white, or the beautiful rose-coloured lotus that opens with a little explosion on the placid waters, as if to herald its coming to perfection. The last colour glory of the year is the splendour of the maple-trees. We have a fine crimson effect in our English blackberry leaves, but they lie hidden in the wet autumn hedges. In Japan the maples do not hide. They seem everywhere alive in a splendid flame. In the autumn it appears as if the maple-trees had conjured with the sunset, for at that time Japan is not the Land of the Rising Sun, but the land of the sun going down in a great pageant of red leaves. And is that the end of Nature's work for the year? No, indeed. Last of all comes the snow, and the beauty of its effect lies not so much in the soft flakes themselves, but in the way they are caught and held upon the beautiful little houses and temples and lanterns. See a Japanese garden then, and you see the white seal of Nature's approval upon it all. The snow scene is perhaps Nature's supreme touch in Japan, after all; and it is a scene dear to the hearts of the Japanese. In midsummer a Japanese emperor once had the miniature mountains in his gardens covered with white silk to suggest snow, and, no doubt, to give an imaginary coolness to the scene. A slight acquaintance with Japanese art will reveal the fact that snow affords a favourite theme for the artist's brush.

Nature in Miniature

The Japanese, for the most part, are little in stature, and have a love of things in miniature. Lafcadio Hearn tells a charming story of a Japanese nun who used to play with children and give them rice-cakes no bigger than peas and tea in very minute cups. Her love of

158

very small things came as the result of a great sorrow, but we see in this Japanese love of little objects something pathetic in the nation as a whole. Their love of dwarf trees, hundreds of years old, seems to say : " Be honourably pleased never to grow big. We are a little people, and so we love little things." The ancient pine, often less than a foot in height, does not render its age oppressive, and is not a thing to fear just because it is so very small. Westerners have been inclined to describe the dwarf Japanese tree as unnatural. It is no more unnatural than the Japanese smile, and reveals that the nation, like the Greeks of old, is still closely in touch with Nature.

The Pine-tree

The pine-tree is the emblem of good fortune and longevity. That is why we see this tree at almost every garden gate; and it must be admitted that a pine-tree is a more graceful talisman than a rusty old horse-shoe. In a certain Japanese play we find the following : " The emblem of unchangeableness—exalted is their fame to the end of time—the fame of the two pine-trees that have grown old together." This refers to the famous pines of Takasago. Mr. Conder tells us that at wedding feasts " a branch of the *male* pine is placed in one vessel and a branch of the *female* pine in the other. The general form of each design would be similar, but the branch of the *female* pine facing the opposite vase should stretch a little beneath the corresponding branch of the *male* pine." In other words, it shows that Woman's Suffrage exists not in Japan, and that the Japanese wife is subject to her lord and master, which is a very pretty way of suggesting what is in England a very dangerous subject. The design referred to above typifies " eternal union." The pine-tree really symbolises the comradeship of love, the Darby and Joan stage of old married people in Japan.

A Great Nature-lover

Kamo No Chōmei was a Buddhist recluse of the twelfth century, and he wrote a little book called *Hō-jō-ki* ("Notes from a Ten-feet-square Hut "). In this volume he describes how he left the ways of the world and took up his abode in a hut on the mountain-side. Chōmei used to sing and play and read his beloved books in the very heart of the country. He writes : " When the sixtieth year of my life, now vanishing as a dewdrop, approached, anew I made me an abode, a sort of last leap, as it were, just as a traveller might run himself up a shelter for a single night, or a decrepit silkworm weave its last cocoon." We see him, a happy old man, slowly trudging along the hills, gathering blossom as he went, ever watching with delighted eyes the ways and secrets of Nature. With all his musings, so full of poetry, his religious character plays a part. He writes with dry humour : " I do not need to trouble myself about the strict observance of the commandments, for, living as I do in complete solitude, how should I be tempted to break them ? " A very different expérience to that of some of the Indian anchorites, who find in solitude a veritable thunder-cloud of temptation ! But Chōmei was a happy soul, and we mention him here to show that the mainstay of his life were not the things of the world, but the workings of Nature on the hills and in the valleys, in the flowers and in the trees, in the running water and in the rising moon. To quote his own words : " You have fled from the world to live the life of a recluse amid the wild woods and hills, thus to bring peace to your soul and walk in the way of the Buddha."

JAPANESE FLAG AND THE CHRYSANTHEMUM

The Festival of the Dead

We find the Festival of the Dead the greatest argument of all in support of Japan's love of Nature. It was a woman's thought, this Festival of the Dead, and there is something about it so tender, so plaintive, that it could only have come from a woman. In July the spirits of the dead return from their dark abode. Little meals are prepared for this great company of ghosts, and the lanterns hang in the cemeteries and on the pine-trees of good fortune at the garden gates. The Japanese used to commit *hara-kiri*,[1] but let us not forget that their souls come back again to wander in a country that seems to be one great garden. And why do they come back? They come back with their soft footsteps over the hills and far away from over the sea to look at the flowers once more, to wander in the gardens where they spent so many happy hours. They come, that invisible host, when the sun shines brightly, when it seems that blossoms floating in the breeze suddenly turn into butterflies, when life is at its full, when Death and the dark place where Emma-O reigns cannot be endured. What a time to come back again! What a silent compliment to Nature that that great company of souls should wander back to her arms in the summer-time!

The Japanese Flag and the Chrysanthemum

Most of us are familiar with the Japanese flag depicting a red sun on a white ground, and we should naturally suppose that such an emblem was originally connected with the Sun Goddess. In this supposition, however, we should be entirely wrong. Astrological designs in

---

[1] *Hara-kiri*, or *seppuku*, is the term applied to suicide among the *samurai* class. For detailed account see *Tales of Old Japan*, by A. B. Mitford (Lord Redesdale).

ancient days figured upon the Chinese banners, and Professor B. H. Chamberlain describes them thus : " The Sun with the Three-legged Crow that inhabits it, the Moon with its Hare[1] and Cassia-tree, the Red Bird representing the seven constellations of the southern quarter of the zodiac, the Dark Warrior (a Tortoise) embracing the seven northern constellations, the Azure Dragon embracing the seven eastern, the White Tiger embracing the seven western, and a seventh banner representing the Northern Bushel (Great Bear)." The Chinese banners depicting the sun and moon were particularly noteworthy, because the sun represented the Emperor's elder brother and the moon his sister. In the seventh century the Japanese adopted these banners ; but as time went on they dropped many of the quaint astrological designs so dear to the heart of the Chinese. When in 1859 a national flag became necessary the sun banner pure and simple was adopted ; but a plain orb without rays was not sufficient, and a more elaborate design was executed—the sixteen-petalled chrysanthemum. We can only conjecture the connection between the sun and the chrysanthemum. Both were venerated in ancient China, and we may assume that the Japanese artist, in wishing to depict the sun's rays, found excellent material in copying the flower of a wild chrysanthemum.

The chrysanthemum is Japan's national flower, and we owe to Nippon its culture in our own country. Mythological scenes, particularly that of the Treasure Ship with the Gods of Luck on board is a favourite

---

[1] To this day Japanese peasants still believe in the Hare in the Moon. This animal employs its time in pounding rice in a mortar and making it into cakes. The origin of this conception is probably to be found in a pun, for " rice-cake " and " full moon " are both described by the word *mochi*.

device, fashioned entirely with innumerable chrysanthemums. Boats, castles, bridges, and various other objects are designed from the same flower with wonderful dexterity. Japan has always been happy in her use of names, and to no greater advantage than in the naming of her chrysanthemums. There is poetry in such names as " Sleepy Head," "Golden Dew," " White Dragon," and "Starlit Night."

The chrysanthemum is certainly a fitting symbolism for the Imperial standard. Once, like our English rose, it figured as a badge in the War of the Chrysanthemums, a protracted civil war that divided the nation into two hostile factions. Now the chrysanthemum stands for a united Empire.

Lady White and Lady Yellow

Long ago there grew in a meadow a white and a yellow chrysanthemum side by side. One day an old gardener chanced to come across them, and took a great fancy to Lady Yellow. He told her that if she would come along with him he would make her far more attractive, that he would give her delicate food and fine clothes to wear.

Lady Yellow was so charmed with what the old man said that she forgot all about her white sister and consented to be lifted up, carried in the arms of the old gardener, and to be placed in his garden.

When Lady Yellow and her master had departed Lady White wept bitterly. Her own simple beauty had been despised ; but, what was far worse, she was forced to remain in the meadow alone, without the converse of her sister, to whom she had been devoted.

Day by day Lady Yellow grew more fair in her master's garden. No one would have recognised the common flower of the field now ; but though her petals were long and curled and her leaves so clean and well cared for, she sometimes thought of Lady White alone in the field, and wondered how she managed to make the long and lonely hours pass by.

One day a village chief came to the old man's garden in quest of a perfect chrysanthemum that he might take to his lord for a crest design.[1] He informed the old man that he did not want a fine chrysanthemum with many long petals. What he wanted was a simple white chrysanthemum with sixteen petals. The old man took the village chief to see Lady Yellow ; but this flower did not please him, and, thanking the gardener, he took his departure.

On his way home he happened to enter a field, where he saw Lady White weeping. She told him the sad story of her loneliness, and when she had finished her tale of woe the village chief informed her that he had seen Lady Yellow and did not consider her half as beautiful as her own white self. At these cheering words Lady White dried her eyes, and she nearly jumped off her little feet when this kind man told her that he wanted her for his lord's crest !

In another moment the happy Lady White was being carried in a palanquin. When she reached the *Daimyō's* palace all warmly praised her remarkable perfection of form. Great artists came from far and near, sat about her, and sketched the flower with wonderful skill. She soon needed no mirror, for ere long she saw her pretty

---

[1] The sixteen-petalled chrysanthemum is one of the crests of the Imperial family, while the other represents the flowers and leaves of the paulownia. Crests in Japan are not confined to the wealthy classes. The crest is still worn upon the upper part of the native garment, to be seen on each breast and sleeve, and upon the back of the neck. Favourite designs are derived from the bamboo, birds, fans, Chinese characters, &c.

white face on all the *Daimyō's* most precious belongings. She saw it on his armour and lacquer boxes, on his quilts and cushions and robes. When she looked upward she could see her face in great carved panels. She was painted floating down a stream, and in all manner of quaint and beautiful ways. Every one acknowledged that the white chrysanthemum, with her sixteen petals, made the most wonderful crest in all Japan.

While Lady White's happy face lived for ever designed upon the *Daimyō's* possessions, Lady Yellow met with a sad fate. She had bloomed for herself alone and drunk in the visitors' praise as eagerly as she did the dew upon her finely curled petals. One day, however, she felt a stiffness in her limbs and a cessation of the exuberance of life. Her once proud head fell forward, and when the old man found her he lifted her up and threw her upon a rubbish heap.

"Chrysanthemum-Old-Man" [1]

Kikuo ("Chrysanthemum-Old-Man") was the faithful retainer of Tsugaru. One day his lord's force was overthrown, and the castle and fine estates were taken away by the enemy; but fortunately Tsugaru and Kikuo were able to escape to the mountains.

Kikuo, knowing his master's love of flowers, especially that of the chrysanthemum, resolved to cultivate this flower to the best of his ability, and in so doing to lessen a little of his master's remorse and humiliation in exile.

His efforts pleased Tsugaru, but unfortunately that lord soon fell sick and died, and the faithful Kikuo wept over his master's grave. Then once more he

---

[1] This story and those that follow in this chapter have been adapted from *Ancient Tales and Folk-lore of Japan*, by R. Gordon Smith.

returned to his work, and planted chrysanthemums about his master's tomb till he had made a border thirty yards broad, so that red, white, pink, yellow, and bronze blossoms scented the air, to the wonder of all who chanced to come that way.

When Kikuo was about eighty-two he caught cold and was confined to his humble dwelling, where he suffered considerable pain.

One autumn night, when he knew those beloved flowers dedicated to his master were at their best, he saw in the verandah a number of young children. As he gazed upon them he realised that they were not the children of this world.

Two of these little ones drew near to Kikuo, and said: "We are the spirits of your chrysanthemums, and have come to tell you how sorry we are to find you ill. You have guarded and loved us with such care. There was a man in China, Hozo by name, who lived eight hundred years by drinking the dew from chrysanthemum blossoms. Gladly would we lengthen out your days, but, alas! the Gods ordain otherwise. Within thirty days you will die."

The old man expressed the wish that he might die in peace, and the regret that he must needs leave behind him all his chrysanthemums.

"Listen," said one of the ghostly children: "we have all loved you, Kikuo, for what you have done for us. When you die we shall die too." As soon as these words were spoken a puff of wind blew against the dwelling, and the spirits departed.

Kikuo grew worse instead of better, and on the thirtieth day he passed away. When visitors came to see the chrysanthemums he had planted, all had vanished. The villagers buried the old man near his master, and, thinking to please Kikuo, they planted chrysanthemums near his grave ; but all died immediately they were put into the ground. Only grasses grow over the tombs now. The child-souls of the chrysanthemums chatter and sing and play with the spirit of Kikuo.

The Violet Well

Shingé and her waiting-maids were picnicking in the Valley of Shimizutani, that lies between the mountains of Yoshino and Tsubosaka. Shingé, full of the joy of spring, ran towards the Violet Well, where she discovered great clumps of purple, sweet-scented violets. She was about to pick the fragrant blossoms when a great snake darted forth, and she immediately fainted.

When the maidens found her they saw that her lips were purple, as purple as the violets that surrounded her, and when they saw the snake, still lurking in the vicinity, they feared that their mistress would die. Matsu, however, had sufficient presence of mind to throw her basket of flowers at the snake, which at once crawled away.

Just at that moment a handsome youth appeared, and, explaining to the maidens that he was a doctor, he gave Matsu some medicine, in order that she might give it to her mistress.

While Matsu forced the powder into Shingé's mouth the doctor took up a stick, disappeared for a few moments, and then returned with the dead snake in his hands.

By this time Shingé had regained consciousness, and asked the name of the physician to whom she was indebted for saving her life. But he politely bowed, evaded her question, and then took his departure. Only Matsu knew that the name of her mistress's rescuer was Yoshisawa.

When Shingé had been taken to her home she grew worse instead of better. All the cleverest doctors came to her bedside, but could do nothing to restore her to health.

Matsu knew that her mistress was gradually fading away for love of the handsome man who had saved her life, and she therefore talked the matter over with her master, Zembei. Matsu told him the story, and said that although Yoshisawa was of a low birth, belonging to the Eta, the lowest caste in Japan, who live by killing and skinning animals, yet nevertheless he was extremely courteous and had the manner and bearing of a *samurai*. "Nothing," said Matsu, "will restore your daughter to health unless she marries this handsome physician."

Both Zembei and his wife were dismayed at these words, for Zembei was a great *daimyō*, and could not for one moment tolerate the idea of his daughter marrying one of the Eta class. However, he agreed to make inquiries concerning Yoshisawa, and Matsu returned to her mistress with something like good news. When Matsu had told Shingé what her father was doing on her behalf she rallied considerably, and was able to take food.

When Shingé was nearly well again Zembei called her to him and said that he had made careful inquiries concerning Yoshisawa, and could on no account agree to her marrying him.

Shingé wept bitterly, and brooded long over her sorrow with a weary heart. The next morning she was not to be found in the house or in the garden. Search was made in every direction ; even Yoshisawa himself sought her everywhere ; but those who sought her found her not. She had mysteriously disappeared, burdened with a sorrow that now made her father realise the effect of his harsh decree.

After three days she was found lying at the bottom of the Violet Well, and shortly after Yoshisawa, overcome with grief, sought a similar end to his troubles. It is said that on stormy nights the ghost of Shingé is to be seen floating over the well, while near by comes the sound of the weeping of Yoshisawa.

The Ghost of the Lotus Lily

" O Resurrection, Resurrection of World and Life!
Lo, Sun ascend! The lotus buds flash with hearts parted,
With one chant ' Namu, Amida!'"

Yone Noguchi.

The lotus is the sacred flower of Buddhism. Because it grows out of mud, rears its stalk through water, and from such dark and slimy beginnings yields a lovely flower, it has been compared with a virtuous man dwelling in this wicked world. Sir Monier Williams writes : "Its constant use as an emblem seems to result from the wheel-like form of the flower, the petals taking the place of spokes, and thus typifying the doctrine of perpetual cycles of existence." Buddha is frequently portrayed as either standing or sitting upon a golden lotus, and the flower reminds us of the Buddhist *sutra*, known as the "Lotus of the Good Law."

Thus Lafcadio Hearn describes the lotus of Paradise : " They are gardening, these charming beings !—they are caressing the lotus buds, sprinkling their petals with something celestial, helping them to blossom. And what lotus-buds ! with colours not of this world. Some have burst open ; and in their luminous hearts, in a radiance like that of dawn, tiny naked infants are seated, each with a tiny halo. These are Souls, new Buddhas, *hotoke* born into bliss. Some are very, very small ; others larger ; all seem to be growing visibly, for their lovely nurses are feeding them with something ambrosial. I see one which has left its lotus-cradle, being conducted by a celestial Jizō toward the higher splendours far away."

So much, then, for the celestial lotus and for its intimate connection with Buddhism. In the following legend we find this flower possessed with the magical power of keeping away evil spirits.

A certain disease broke out in Kyōto from which many thousands of people died. It spread to Idzumi, where the Lord of Koriyama lived, and Koriyama, his wife and child, were stricken down with the malady.

One day Tada Samon, a high official in Koriyama's castle, received a visit from a *yamabushi*, or mountain recluse. This man was full of concern for the illness of the Lord Koriyama, and, addressing Samon, he said: " All this trouble has come about through the entrance of evil spirits in the castle. They have come because the moats about the abode are dry and contain no lotus. If these moats were at once planted with this sacred flower the evil spirits would depart, and your lord, his wife and child, grow well again."

Samon was much impressed by these wise words, and permission was given for this recluse to plant lotus about the castle. When he had accomplished his task he mysteriously disappeared.

Within a week the Lord Koriyama, his wife and son, were able to get up and resume their respective duties, for by this time the walls had been repaired, the moats filled with pure water, which reflected the nodding heads of countless lotus.

Many years later, and after the Lord Koriyama had died, a young *samurai* chanced to pass by the castle moats. He was gazing admiringly at these flowers when he suddenly saw two extremely handsome boys playing on the edge of the water. He was about to lead them to a safer place when they sprang into the air and, falling, disappeared beneath the water.

The astonished *samurai*, believing that he had seen a

couple of *kappas*,[1] or river goblins, made a hasty retreat
to the castle, and there reported his strange adventure.
When he had told his story the moats were dragged
and cleaned, but nothing could be found of the supposed
kappas.

A little later on another *samurai*, Murata Ippai, saw
near the same lotus a number of beautiful little boys.
He drew his sword and cut them down, breathing in as
he did so the heavy perfume of this sacred flower with
every stroke of his weapon. When Ippai looked about
him to see how many of these strange beings he had
killed, there arose before him a cloud of many colours,
a cloud that fell upon his face with a fine spray.

As it was too dark to ascertain fully the extent and
nature of his onslaught, Ippai remained all night by the
spot. When he awoke in the morning he found to his
disgust that he had only struck off the heads of a
number of lotus. Knowing that this beneficent flower
had saved the life of the Lord Koriyama, and now protected that of his son, Ippai was filled with shame and
remorse. Saying a prayer by the water's edge, he committed *hara-kiri*.

The Spirit of the Peony

It had been arranged that the Princess Aya should
marry the second son of Lord Ako. The arrangements,
according to Japanese custom, had been made entirely
without the consent or approval of the actual parties
concerned.

One night Princess Aya walked through the great
garden of her home, accompanied by her waiting-maids.
The moon shone brightly upon her favourite peony bed
near a pond, and covered the sweet-scented blooms in a

---

[1] Referred to elsewhere in the chapter dealing with Supernatural
Beings.

silver sheen. Here she lingered, and was stooping to breathe the fragrance of these flowers when her foot slipped, and she would have fallen had not a handsome young man, clad in a robe of embroidered peonies, rescued her just in time. He vanished as quickly and mysteriously as he had come, before, indeed, she had time to thank him.

It so happened that shortly after this event the Princess Aya became very ill, and in consequence the day for her marriage had to be postponed. All the medical aid available was useless to restore the feverish maiden to health again.

The Princess Aya's father asked his favourite daughter's maid, Sadayo, if she could throw any light upon this lamentable affair.

Sadayo, although hitherto bound to secrecy, felt that the time had come when it was wise, indeed essential, to communicate all she knew in the matter. She told her master that the Princess Aya was deeply in love with the young *samurai* wearing the robes embroidered with peonies, adding that if he could not be found she feared that her young mistress would die.

That night, while a celebrated player was performing upon the *biwa* in the hope of entertaining the sick Princess, there once more appeared behind the peonies the same young man in the same silk robe.

The next night, too, while Yae and Yakumo were playing on the flute and *koto*, the young man appeared again.

The Princess Aya's father now resolved to get at the root of the matter, and for this purpose he bade Maki Hiogo dress in black and lie concealed in the peony bed on the following night.

When the next night came Maki Hiogo lay hidden among the peonies, while Yae and Yakumo made sweet music. Not long after the music had sounded **the** mysterious young *samurai* again appeared. Maki Hiogo rose from his hiding-place with his arms tightly bound round this strange visitor. A cloud seemed to emanate from his captive. It made him dizzy, and he fell to the ground still tightly holding the handsome *samurai*.

Just as a number of guards came hurrying to the spot Maki Hiogo regained consciousness. He looked down expecting to see his captive. But all that he held in his arms was a large peony!

By this time Princess Aya and her father joined the astonished group, and the Lord Naizen-no-jo at once grasped the situation. " I see now," said he, " that the spirit of the peony flower had a moment ago, and on former occasions, taken the form of a young and handsome *samurai*. My daughter, you must take this flower and treat it with all kindness."

The Princess Aya needed to be told no more. She returned to the house, placed the peony in a vase, and stood it by her bedside. Day by day she got better, while the flower flourished exceedingly.

When the Princess Aya was quite well the Lord of Ako arrived at the castle, bringing with him his second son, whom she was to marry. In due time the wedding took place, but at that hour the beautiful peony suddenly died.

CHAPTER XIII : TREES

" One day Kinto Fujiwara, Great Adviser of State, dis-
puted with the Minister of Uji which was the fairest of
spring and autumn flowers. Said the Minister : ' The
Cherry is surely best among the flowers of spring, the
Chrysanthemum among those of autumn.' Then Kinto
said, ' How can the cherry-blossom be the best ? You
have forgotten the Plum.' Their dispute came at length
to be confined to the superiority of the Cherry and Plum,
and of other flowers little notice was taken. At length
Kinto, not wishing to offend the Minister, did not argue
so vehemently as before, but said, ' Well, have it so ; the
Cherry may be the prettier of the two ; but when once
you have seen the red plum-blossom in the snow at the
dawn of a spring morning, you will no longer forget its
beauty.' This truly was a gentle saying."

" *The Garden of Japan*," *by* Sir F. T. Piggott.

Cherry and Plum

THE supreme floral glory of Japan takes place in
April with the coming of the cherry-blossom, and,
as we have seen in the above quotation, it is the
cherry and plum that are regarded with the most favour.
The poet Motoöri wrote: " If one should ask you concerning the heart of a true Japanese, point to the wild
cherry flower glowing in the sun," and Lafcadio Hearn,
without the least exaggeration, but with true poetic insight, has compared Japan's cherry-blossom with a delicate sunset that has, as it were, strayed from the sky
and lingered about the leafless branches.

The really great wonders of Nature, to those who are
sufficiently susceptible to the beautiful, are apt to leave
behind an indefinable yearning, a regret that so much
loveliness must needs pass away, and this gentle touch of
sorrow mingled with the ecstasy is easily discovered in
much of the Japanese poetry. It is a point worthy of
emphasis because it reveals a temperament charged with

THE CAMELLIA

a supreme love of the beautiful, this craving for a petal that shall never wither, a colour that shall never fade. Thus sang Korunushi:

" No man so callous but he heaves a sigh
When o'er his head the withered cherry flowers
Come fluttering down. Who knows? the Spring's soft showers
May be but tears shed by the sorrowing sky."

Trans. by B. H. CHAMBERLAIN.

One of the greatest tributes Japan has paid to the cherry is as follows : " The cherry-trees in the far-away mountain villages should keep back their blooms until the flowers in the town have faded, for then the people will go out to see them too." A Japanese woman's beauty is frequently associated with the cherry-blossom, while her virtue is compared with the flower of the plum.

The Camellia

The Precious-Camellia of Yaegaki, with its double trunk and immense head, is of great age, and is regarded as so sacred that it is surrounded by a fence, and stone lamps are placed about it. The tree's unique shape, with the double trunk growing together in the middle, has given rise to the belief that this extraordinary tree symbolises a happy wedded life, and, moreover, that good spirits inhabit it, ever ready to answer the ardent prayers of lovers.

The camellia-tree is not always beneficent. A legend is recorded of a tree of this species walking about at night in a *samurai's* garden at Matsue. Its strange and restless wanderings became so frequent that at last the tree was cut down, and it is said that when it was struck it shot forth a stream of blood.

The Cryptomeria

Another tree held in high veneration is the imposing cryptomeria, and there is one avenue of these trees stretching from Utsunomiya to Nikkō, a distance of twenty miles. One of these trees is seven feet in diameter, and is said to have been planted " by a deputation representing eight hundred Buddhist nuns of the province of Wakasa." Later on in this chapter we give a legend connected with this particular tree.

A Pine-tree and the God of Roads

In the grounds of the great *hakaba* (cemetery) of the Kwannondera is a pine-tree standing upon four great roots that have the appearance of gigantic legs. About this tree is a fence, shrine, and a number of *torii*. Before the shrine repose miniature horses made from straw. These are offerings to Kōshin, the God of Roads, entreaties that the real horses which they symbolise may be preserved from death or sickness. The pine-tree, however, is not usually associated with Kōshin. It may be fittingly described as the most domestic of Japanese trees, for it takes a conspicuous place in the New Year festival [1] —a tree to plant at the garden gate, because it is said to bring good luck and, especially, happy marriages.

A Tree Spirit

As we shall see in the legends that follow, more than one variety of Japanese trees is endowed with supernatural power. There is a tree spirit known as Ki-no-o-baké that is capable of walking about and assuming various guises. The spirit of the tree speaks but little, and if disturbed disappears into the trunk or among the leaves. The spirit of the God Kōjin [2] resides

[1] See Chapter XVII.   [2] See Chapter XVI.

in the *enoki* tree, the God to whom very old dolls are
dedicated.

The Miraculous Chestnut

The Princess Hinako-Nai-Shinnō begged that chestnuts should be brought to her ; but she took but one,
bit it, and threw it away. It took root, and upon all
the chestnuts that it eventually bore there were the
marks of the Princess's small teeth. In honouring her
death the chestnut had expressed its devotion in this
strange way.

The Silent Pine

The Emperor Go-Toba, who strongly objected to the
croaking of frogs, was on one occasion disturbed by
a wind-blown pine-tree. When his Majesty loudly
commanded it to be still, the pine-tree never for a
moment moved again. So greatly impressed was this
obedient tree that the fiercest wind failed to stir its
branches, or even its myriad pine-needles.

Willow Wife [1]

"I have heard of the magical incense that summons the souls of the
absent ;
Would I had some to burn, in the nights when I wait alone."
From the Japanese.

In a certain Japanese village there grew a great willow-
tree. For many generations the people loved it. In
the summer it was a resting-place, a place where the
villagers might meet after the work and heat of the day
were over, and there talk till the moonlight streamed
through the branches. In winter it was like a great
half-opened umbrella covered with sparkling snow.

[1] This story and the one that follows have been adapted from
Ancient Tales and Folk-lore of Japan, by R. Gordon Smith.

MYTHS AND LEGENDS OF JAPAN

Heitaro, a young farmer, lived quite near this tree, and he, more than any of his companions, had entered into a deep communion with the imposing willow. It was almost the first object he saw upon waking, and upon his return from work in the fields he looked out eagerly for its familiar form. Sometimes he would burn a joss-stick beneath its branches and kneel down and pray.

One day an old man of the village came to Heitaro and explained to him that the villagers were anxious to build a bridge over the river, and that they particularly wanted the great willow-tree for timber.

"For timber?" said Heitaro, hiding his face in his hands. "My dear willow-tree for a bridge, one to bear the incessant patter of feet? Never, never, old man!"

When Heitaro had somewhat recovered himself, he offered to give the old man some of his own trees, if he and the villagers would accept them for timber and spare the ancient willow.

The old man readily accepted this offer, and the willow-tree continued to stand in the village as it had stood for so many years.

One night while Heitaro sat under the great willow he suddenly saw a beautiful woman standing close beside him, looking at him shyly, as if wanting to speak.

"Honourable lady," said he, "I will go home. I see you wait for some one. Heitaro is not without kindness towards those who love."

"He will not come now," said the woman, smiling.

"Can he have grown cold? Oh, how terrible when a mock love comes and leaves ashes and a grave behind!"

"He has not grown cold, dear lord."

"And yet he does not come! What strange mystery isthis?"

"He has come! His heart has been always here, here under this willow-tree." And with a radiant smile the woman disappeared.

Night after night they met under the old willow-tree. The woman's shyness had entirely disappeared, and it seemed that she could not hear too much from Heitaro's lips in praise of the willow under which they sat.

One night he said to her: "Little one, will you be my wife—you who seem to come from the very tree itself?"

"Yes," said the woman. "Call me Higo ("Willow") and ask no questions, for love of me. I have no father or mother, and some day you will understand."

Heitaro and Higo were married, and in due time they were blessed with a child, whom they called Chiyodō. Simple was their dwelling, but those it contained were the happiest people in all Japan.

While this happy couple went about their respective duties great news came to the village. The villagers were full of it, and it was not long before it reached Heitaro's ears. The ex-Emperor Toba wished to build a temple to Kwannon [1] in Kyōto, and those in authority sent far and wide for timber. The villagers said that they must contribute towards building the sacred edifice by presenting their great willow-tree. All Heitaro's argument and persuasion and promise of other trees were ineffectual, for neither he nor any one else could give as large and handsome a tree as the great willow.

Heitaro went home and told his wife. "Oh, wife," said he, "they are about to cut down our dear willow-tree! Before I married you I could not have borne it. Having you, little one, perhaps I shall get over it some day."

That night Heitaro was aroused by hearing a piercing

[1] See Chapter XV.

cry. " Heitaro," said his wife, " it grows dark ! The room is full of whispers. Are you there, Heitaro ? Hark ! They are cutting down the willow-tree. Look how its shadow trembles in the moonlight. I am the soul of the willow-tree ! The villagers are killing me. Oh, how they cut and tear me to pieces ! Dear Heitaro, the pain, the pain ! Put your hands here, and here. Surely the blows cannot fall now ? "

" My Willow Wife ! My Willow Wife ! " sobbed Heitaro.

" Husband," said Higo, very faintly, pressing her wet, agonised face close to his, " I am going now. Such a love as ours cannot be cut down, however fierce the blows. I shall wait for you and Chiyodo—— My hair is falling through the sky ! My body is breaking ! "

There was a loud crash outside. The great willow-tree lay green and dishevelled upon the ground. Heitaro looked round for her he loved more than anything else in the world. Willow Wife had gone !

The Tree of the One-eyed Priest

In ancient days there stood on the summit of Oki-yama a temple dedicated to Fudo, a god surrounded by fire, with sword in one hand and rope in the other. For twenty years Yenoki had performed his office, and one of his duties was to guard Fudo, who sat in a shrine, only accessible to the high-priest himself. During the whole of this period Yenoki had rendered faithful service and resisted the temptation to take a peep at this extremely ugly god. One morning, finding that the door of the shrine was not quite closed, his curiosity overcame him and he peeped within. No sooner had he done so than he became stone-blind in one eye and suffered the humiliation of being turned into a *tengu*.[1]

[1] A long-nosed creature referred to elsewhere.

THE TREE OF THE ONE-EYED PRIEST

He lived for a year after these deplorable happenings, and then died. His spirit passed into a great cryptomeria-tree standing on the east side of the mountain, and from that day Yenoki's spirit was invoked by sailors who were harassed by storms on the Chinese Sea. If a light blazed from the tree in answer to their prayers, it was a sure sign that the storm would abate.

At the foot of Oki-yama there was a village, where, sad to relate, the young people were very lax in their morals. During the Festival of the Dead they performed a dance known as the Bon Odori. These dances were very wild affairs indeed, and were accompanied by flirtations of a violent and wicked nature. The dances became more unrestrained as years went by, and the village got a bad name for immoral practices among the young people.

After a particularly wild celebration of the Bon a young maiden named Kimi set out to find her lover, Kurosuke. Instead of finding him she saw an extremely good-looking youth, who smiled upon her and continually beckoned. Kimi forgot all about Kurosuke; indeed, from that moment she hated him and eagerly followed the enticing youth. Nine fair but wicked maidens disappeared from the village in a similar way, and always it was the same youth who lured them astray in this mysterious manner.

The elders of the village consulted together, and came to the conclusion that the spirit of Yenoki was angry with the excesses connected with the Bon festival, and had assumed the form of a handsome youth for the purpose of administering severe admonition. The Lord of Kishiwada accordingly summoned Sonobé to his presence, and bade him journey to the great cryptomeria-tree on Oki-yama.

When Sonobé reached his destination he thus

addressed the ancient tree: "Oh, home of Yenoki's spirit, I upbraid you for carrying away our daughters. If this continues I shall cut down the tree, so that you will be compelled to seek lodging elsewhere."

Sonobé had no sooner spoken than rain began to fall, and he heard the rumblings of a mighty earthquake. Then from out of the tree Yenoki's spirit suddenly appeared. He explained that many of the young people of Sonobé's village had offended against the Gods by their misconduct, and that he had, as conjectured, assumed the form of a handsome youth in order to take away the principal offenders. "You will find them," added the spirit of Yenoki, "bound to trees on the second summit of this mountain. Go, release them, and allow them to return to the village. They have not only repented of their follies, but will now persuade others to live nobler and purer lives." And with these words Yenoki disappeared into his tree.

Sonobé set off to the second summit and released the maidens. They returned to their homes, good and dutiful daughters, and from that day to this the Gods have been well satisfied with the general behaviour of the village that nestles at the foot of Oki-yama.

The Burning of Three Dwarf Trees

In the reign of the Emperor Go-Fukakusa there lived a celebrated Regent, Saimyoji Tokiyori. When thirty years of age this Regent retired to a monastery for several years, and not infrequently his peace of mind was sadly disturbed by stories of peasants who suffered at the hands of tyrannical officials. Now Tokiyori loved above everything the welfare of his people, and after giving the matter careful consideration he determined to disguise himself, travel from place to place, and discover in an intimate way the heart of the poorer people, and later on to do all in his power to suppress malpractice on the part of various officials.

Tokiyori accordingly set out upon his excellent mission, and finally came to Sano, in the province of Kodzuke. Now it was the time of winter, and a heavy snowstorm caused the distinguished wanderer to lose his way. After wearily tramping about for several hours in the hope of finding shelter, he was about to make the best of the matter by sleeping under a tree when, to his joy, he noticed a small thatched cottage nestling under a hill at no great distance. To this cottage he went, and explained to the woman who greeted him that he had lost his way and would be much indebted to her if she would afford him shelter for the night. The good woman explained that as her husband was away from home, it would be disloyal as his wife to give shelter to a stranger. Tokiyori not only took this reply in good part, but he greatly rejoiced, in spite of a night in the snow, to find such a virtuous woman. But he had not gone far from the cottage when he heard a man calling to him. Tokiyori stood still, and presently he saw some one beckoning him. The man explained that he was the husband of the woman the ex-Regent had just left, and cordially invited one whom he took to be a wandering priest to return with him and accept such humble hospitality as was available.

When Tokiyori was sitting in the little cottage simple fare was spread before him, and as he had eaten nothing since the morning he did full justice to the meal. But the fact that millet and not rice was provided clearly conveyed to the observant Tokiyori that here was poverty indeed, but with it all a generosity that went straight to his heart. Nor was this all, for, the meal finished, they gathered round the fire that was fast dying out for want of fuel. The good man of the house turned to the fuel-box. Alas ! it was empty. Without a moment's hesitation he went out into the garden, heavily covered with snow, and brought back with him three pots of dwarf trees, pine, plum, and cherry. Now in Japan dwarf trees are held in high esteem ; much time and care is bestowed upon them, and their age and unique beauty have made them dear to the people of Nippon. In spite of Tokiyori's remonstrance his host broke up these little trees, and thus made a cheerful blaze.

It was this incident, scarcely to be fully appreciated by a Westerner, that caused Tokiyori to question his host, whose very possession of these valuable trees strongly suggested that this generous man was not a farmer by birth, but had taken to this calling by force of circumstance. The ex-Regent's conjecture proved to be correct, and his host, with some reluctance, finally explained that he was a *samurai* by the name of Sano Genzaemon Tsuneyo. He had been forced to take up farming owing to the dishonesty of one of his relatives.

Tokiyori readily recalled the name of this *samurai* before him, and suggested that he should make an appeal for redress. Sano explained that as the good and just Regent had died (so he thought), and as his successor was very young, he considered it was worse than useless to present a petition. But, nevertheless, he went on to explain to his interested listener that should there come a call to arms he would be the first to make an appearance at Kamakura. It was this thought of some day being of use to his country that had sweetened the days of his poverty.

The conversation, so rapidly suggested in this story, was in reality a lengthy one, and by the time it was concluded already a new day had begun. And when the storm-doors had been opened it was to reveal sunlight streaming over a world of snow. Before taking his departure Tokiyori warmly thanked his host and hostess for their hospitality. When this kindly visitor had gone Sano suddenly remembered that he had forgotten to inquire the name of his guest.

Now it happened that in the following spring a call to arms was instituted by the Government at Kamakura. No sooner had Sano heard the joyful news than he set out to obey the summons. His armour was shabby in the extreme, his halberd covered with rust, and his horse was in a very poor condition. He presented a sorry figure among the resplendent knights he found in Kamakura. Many of these knights made uncomplimentary remarks concerning him, but Sano bore this insolence without a word. While he stood, a forlorn figure, among the sparkling ranks of *samurai* about him, a herald approached riding on a magnificent horse, and carrying a banner bearing the house-crest of the Regent. With a loud, clear voice he bade the knight wearing the shabbiest armour to appear before his master. Sano obeyed the summons with a heavy heart. He thought that the Regent was about to rebuke him for appearing in such a gaily decked company clad in such miserable accoutrements.

This humble knight was surprised by the cordial welcome he received, and still more surprised when a servant pushed aside the screens of an adjoining room and revealed the Regent Saimyoji Tokiyori, who was none other than the priest who had taken shelter in his little home. Nor had Tokiyori forgotten the burning of the dwarf pine, plum, and cherry-trees. Out of that sacrifice, readily given without a thought of gain, came the thirty villages of which Sano had been robbed. This was only Sano's due, and in addition the grateful Tokiyori had the happy idea of presenting this faithful knight with the village of Matsu-idu, Umeda, and

Sakurai, *matsu*, *ume*, and *sakura* being the Japanese names for pine, plum, and cherry.

The Pine-tree Lovers

" The dawn is near,
And the hoar-frost falls
On the fir-tree twigs ;
But its leaves' dark green
Suffer no change.
Morning and evening
Beneath its shade
The leaves are swept away,
Yet they never fail.
True it is
That these fir-trees
Shed not all their leaves ;
Their verdure remains fresh
For ages long,
As the Masaka trailing vine ;
Even amongst evergreen trees—
The emblem of unchangeableness—
Exalted is their fame
As a symbol to the end of time—
The fame of the fir-trees that have grown
old together."
" *Takasago.*"   (Trans. by W. G. Aston.)

The *Takasago* is generally considered one of the finest of the *Nō*, or classical dramas.   The *Nō* was performed by statuesque players who chanted in an ancient dialect. It belonged to that period of Japanese formality fittingly described as " Heav'n to hear tell about, but Hell to see."   The theme of the *Takasago* seems to be a relic of a phallic cult common enough in the history of primitive nations.   The pine-tree of Takasago symbolises longevity, and in the following chorus from this drama we may gather the potency of this evergreen tree :

" And now, world without end,
The extended arms of the dancing maidens

THE PINE-TREE LOVERS

In sacerdotal robes
Will expel noxious influences;
Their hands folded to rest in their bosoms
Will embrace all good fortune;
The hymn of a thousand autumns
Will draw down blessings on the people,
And the song of ten thousand years
Prolong our sovereign's life.
And all the while
The voice of the breeze,
As it blows through the firs
That grow old together,
Will yield us delight."

The efficacy of the pine-tree is still believed in to this day. It is conspicuous in the festival of the San-ga-nichi, when pine branches decorate the gateways during the New Year festivities. Both this use of the pine-tree and that of this particular *Nō* drama owe their origin to the great pine-tree of Takasago, about which we narrate the following legend.

In ancient days there lived at Takasago a fisherman, his wife, and little daughter Matsue. There was nothing that Matsue loved to do more than to sit under the great pine-tree. She was particularly fond of the pine-needles that never seemed tired of falling to the ground. With these she fashioned a beautiful dress and sash, saying: "I will not wear these pine-clothes until my wedding-day."

One day, while Matsue was sitting under the pine-tree, she sang the following song:

"No man so callous but he heaves a sigh
When o'er his head the withered cherry flowers
Come fluttering down. Who knows? the Spring's soft showers
May be but tears shed by the sorrowing sky."

While she thus sang Teoyo stood on the steep shore of Sumiyoshi watching the flight of a heron. Up, up

187

it went into the blue sky, and Teoyo saw it fly over the village where the fisherfolk and their daughter lived.

Now Teoyo was a youth who dearly loved adventure, and he thought it would be very delightful to swim across the sea and discover the land over which the heron had flown. So one morning he dived into the sea and swam so hard and so long that the poor fellow found the waves spinning and dancing, and saw the great sky bend down and try to touch him. Then he lay unconscious on the water ; but the waves were kind to him after all, for they pressed him on and on till he was washed up at the very place where Matsue sat under the pine-tree.

Matsue carefully dragged Teoyo underneath the sheltering branches, and then set him down upon a couch of pine-needles, where he soon regained consciousness, and warmly thanked Matsue for her kindness.

Teoyo did not go back to his own country, for after a few happy months had gone by he married Matsue, and on her wedding morn she wore her dress and sash of pine-needles.

When Matsue's parents died her loss only seemed to make her love Teoyo the more. The older they grew the more they loved each other. Every night, when the moon shone, they went hand in hand to the pine-tree, and with their little rakes they made a couch for the morrow.

One night the great silver face of the moon peered through the branches of the pine-tree and looked in vain for the old lovers sitting together on a couch of pine-needles. Their little rakes lay side by side, and still the moon waited for the slow and stumbling steps of the Pine-Tree Lovers. But that night they did not come. They had gone home to an everlasting resting-place on the River of Souls. They had loved so well

Matsue rescues Teoyo.

(See page 188*)*

Shinzaburō recognised Tsuyu and her maid Yoné.

(See page 229*)*

and so splendidly, in old age as well as in youth, that the Gods allowed their souls to come back again and wander round the pine-tree that had listened to their love for so many years. When the moon is full they whisper and laugh and sing and draw the pine-needles together, while the sea sings softly upon the shore.

CHAPTER XIV : MIRRORS

"As the sword is the soul of a *samurai*, so is the mirror the soul of a woman."

"When the mirror is dim the soul is unclean."

Japanese Proverbs.

The Significance of Japanese Mirrors

OLD Japanese metal mirrors are circular, the surface convex, and the back adorned with elaborate designs in relief of flowers, birds, and other scenes from Nature. Professor B. H. Chamberlain writes : " An extraordinary peculiarity characterises some of these Japanese mirrors : sunlight reflected from their *face* displays a luminous image of the design on their *back !* So strange a phenomenon has naturally attracted the attention of men of science. After much speculation, it has been clearly proved by Professors Ayrton and Perry to arise from the fact that the curvature of the face of the mirror over the plain part of the back is greater than over the design." It is the phenomenon rather than the possible explanation of it that interests us, and no doubt this strange occurrence accounts in some measure for the magical significance of Nipponese mirrors.

The great legendary idea underlying Japanese mirrors is just this, that the mirror, through constant reflection of its owner's face, draws to itself the very soul of its possessor, and, as we shall see later on, something of the same idea is to be traced in regard to old but much-loved Japanese dolls.

Hidari Jingorō

The famous sculptor Hidari Jingorō on one occasion happened to fall in love with a very attractive woman whom he met in the street on his return to his studio. He

was so fascinated by her rare beauty that as soon as he had
reached his destination he commenced to carve a statue
of her. Between the chiselled robes he placed a mirror,
the mirror which the lovely woman had dropped, and
which her eager lover had at once picked up. Because
this mirror had reflected a thousand thousand times
that fair face, it had taken to its shining surface the very
body and soul of its owner, and because of these strange
things the statue came to life, to the extreme happiness
of sculptor and maid.

The Divine Mirror

Long before the Japanese mirror was a familiar object
in the house it had a very deep religious significance in
connection with Shintōism. The Divine Mirror into
which the Sun Goddess gazed reposes at Isé. Other
mirrors are to be found in Shintō shrines ; indeed,
these mirrors are the essential part of a shrine remarkable
for its simplicity. The mirror "typifies the human
heart, which, when perfectly placid and clear, reflects
the very image of the deity." In the *Kojiki* we are told
that Izanagi presented his children with a polished silver
disc, and bade them kneel before it every morning and
evening and examine their reflections. He told them
to think of heavenly things, to stifle passion and all evil
thought, so that the disc should reveal a pure and
lovely soul.

The Soul of a Mirror

The shrine of Ogawachi-Myōjin fell into decay, and
the Shintō priest in charge, Matsumura, journeyed to
Kyōto in the hope of successfully appealing to the
Shōgun for a grant for the restoration of the temple.

Matsumura and his family resided in a house in
Kyōto, said to be extremely unlucky, and many tenants

had thrown themselves into the well on the north-east side of the dwelling. But Matsumura took no notice of these tales, and was not the least afraid of evil spirits.

During the summer of that year there was a great drought in Kyōto. Though the river-beds dried up and many wells failed for want of rain, the well in Matsumura's garden was full to overflowing. The distress elsewhere, owing to want of water, forced many poor people to beg for it, and for all their drawing the water in this particular well did not diminish.

One day, however, a dead body was found lying in the well, that of a servant who had come to fetch water. In his case suicide was out of the question, and it seemed impossible that he should have accidentally fallen in. When Matsumura heard of the fatality he went to inspect the well. To his surprise the water stirred with a strange rocking movement. When the motion lessened he saw reflected in the clear water the form of a fair young woman. She was touching her lips with *beni*. At length she smiled upon him. It was a strange smile that made Matsumura feel dizzy, a smile that blotted out everything else save the beautiful woman's face. He felt an almost irresistible desire to fling himself into the water in order that he might reach and hold this enchanting woman. He struggled against this strange feeling, however, and was able after a while to enter the house, where he gave orders that a fence should be built round the well, and that from thenceforth no one, on any pretext whatever, should draw water there.

Shortly afterwards the drought came to an end. For three days and nights there was a continuous downpour of rain, and the city shook with an earthquake. On the third night of the storm there was a loud knocking at Matsumura's door. The priest himself inquired who his visitor might be. He half opened the door, and saw once more the woman he had seen in the well. He refused her admission, and asked why she had been guilty of taking the lives of so many harmless and innocent people.

Thus the woman made answer : " Alas ! good priest, I have never desired to lure human beings to their death. It is the Poison Dragon, who lived in that well, who forced me against my will to entice people to death. But now the Gods have compelled the Poison Dragon to live elsewhere, so that to-night I was able to leave my place of captivity. Now there is but little water in the well, and if you will search there you will find my body. Take care of it for me, and I shall not fail to reward your goodness." With these words she vanished as suddenly as she had appeared.

Next day well-cleaners searched the well, and discovered some ancient hair ornaments and an old metal mirror.

Matsumura, being a wise man, took the mirror and cleaned it, believing that it might reveal a solution to the mystery.

Upon the back of the mirror he discovered several characters. Many of the ideographs were too blurred to be legible, but he managed to make out "third month, the third day." In ancient time the third month used to be called *Yayoi*, or Month of Increase, and remembering that the woman had called herself Yayoi, Matsumura realised that he had probably received a visit from the Soul of the Mirror.

Matsumura took every care of the mirror. He ordered it to be resilvered and polished, and when this had been done he laid it in a box specially made for it, and mirror and box were placed in a particular room in the house.

193

One day, when Matsumura was sitting in the apartment where the mirror reposed, he once more saw Yayoi standing before him, looking more beautiful than ever, and the refulgence of her beauty was like summer moonlight. After she had saluted Matsumura she explained that she was indeed the Soul of the Mirror, and narrated how she had fallen into the possession of Lady Kamo, of the Imperial Court, and how she had become an heirloom of the Fujiwara House, until during the period of Hōgen, when the Taira and Minamoto clans were engaged in conflict, she was thrown into a well, and there forgotten. Having narrated these things, and all the horrors she had gone through under the tyranny of the Poison Dragon, Yayoi begged that Matsumura would present the mirror to the Shōgun, the Lord Yoshimasa, who was a descendant of her former possessors, promising the priest considerable good fortune if he did so. Before Yayoi departed she advised Matsumura to leave his home immediately, as it was about to be washed away by a great storm.

On the following day Matsumura left the house, and, as Yayoi had prophesied, almost immediately afterwards his late dwelling was swept away.

At length Matsumura was able to present the mirror to the Shōgun Yoshimasa, together with a written account of its strange history. The Shōgun was so pleased with the gift that he not only gave Matsumura many personal presents, but he also presented the priest with a considerable sum of money for the rebuilding of his temple.

A Mirror and a Bell

When the priests of Mugenyama required a large bell for their temple they asked the women in the vicinity to contribute their old bronze mirrors for the purpose of providing the necessary metal.

Hundreds of mirrors were given for this purpose, and all were offered gladly, except the mirror presented by a certain farmer's wife. As soon as she had given her mirror to the priests she began to regret having parted with it. She remembered how old it was, how it had reflected her mother's laughter and tears, and even her great-grandmother's. Whenever this farmer's wife went to the temple she saw her coveted mirror lying in a great heap behind a railing. She recognised it by the design on the back known as the *Shō-Chiku-Bai*, or the three emblems of the Pine, Bamboo, and Plum-flower. She yearned to stretch forth her arm between the railings and to snatch back her beloved mirror. Her soul was in the shining surface, and it mingled with the souls of those who had gazed into it before she was born.

When the Mugenyama bell was in course of construction the bell-founders discovered that one mirror would not melt. The workers said that it refused to melt because the owner had afterwards regretted the gift, which had made the metal hard, as hard as the woman's selfish heart.

Soon every one knew the identity of the giver of the mirror that would not melt, and, angry and ashamed, the farmer's wife drowned herself, first having written the following : "When I am dead you will be able to melt my mirror, and so cast the bell. My soul will come to him who breaks that bell by ringing it, and I will give him great wealth."

When the woman died her old mirror melted immediately, and the bell was cast and was suspended in its customary place. Many people having heard of the message written by the deceased farmer's wife, a great multitude came to the temple, and one by one rang the bell with the utmost violence in the hope of breaking it and winning great wealth. Day after day the ringing continued, till at last the noise became so unbearable that the priests rolled the bell into a swamp, where it lay hidden from sight.

The Mirror of Matsuyama

In ancient days there lived in a remote part of Japan a man and his wife, and they were blessed with a little girl, who was the pet and idol of her parents. On one occasion the man was called away on business in distant Kyōto. Before he went he told his daughter that if she were good and dutiful to her mother he would bring her back a present she would prize very highly. Then the good man took his departure, mother and daughter watching him go.

At last he returned to his home, and after his wife and child had taken off his large hat and sandals he sat down upon the white mats and opened a bamboo basket, watching the eager gaze of his little child. He took out a wonderful doll and a lacquer box of cakes and put them into her outstretched hands. Once more he dived into his basket, and presented his wife with a metal mirror. Its convex surface shone brightly, while upon its back there was a design of pine-trees and storks.

The good man's wife had never seen a mirror before, and on gazing into it she was under the impression that another woman looked out upon her as she gazed with growing wonder. Her husband explained the mystery and bade her take great care of the mirror.

Not long after this happy home-coming and distribution of presents the woman became very ill. Just before she died she called to her little daughter, and said: " Dear child, when I am dead take every care of your father. You will miss me when I have left you. But take this mirror, and when you feel most lonely look into it and you will always see me." Having said these words she passed away.

In due time the man married again, and his wife was not at all kind to her stepdaughter. But the little one, remembering her mother's last words, would retire to a corner and eagerly look into the mirror, where it seemed to her that she saw her dear mother's face, not drawn in pain as she had seen it on her death-bed, but young and beautiful.

One day this child's stepmother chanced to see her crouching in a corner over an object she could not quite see, murmuring to herself. This ignorant woman, who detested the child and believed that her stepdaughter detested her in return, fancied that this little one was performing some strange magical art—perhaps making an image and sticking pins into it. Full of these notions, the stepmother went to her husband and told him that his wicked child was doing her best to kill her by witchcraft.

When the master of the house had listened to this extraordinary recital he went straight to his daughter's room. He took her by surprise, and immediately the girl saw him she slipped the mirror into her sleeve. For the first time her doting father grew angry, and he feared that there was, after all, truth in what his wife had told him, and he repeated her tale forthwith.

When his daughter had heard this unjust accusation she was amazed at her father's words, and she told him that she loved him far too well ever to attempt or wish to kill his wife, who she knew was dear to him.

" What have you hidden in your sleeve ? " said her father, only half convinced and still much puzzled.

" The mirror you gave my mother, and which she on
197

her death-bed gave to me. Every time I look into its shining surface I see the face of my dear mother, young and beautiful. When my heart aches—and oh ! it has ached so much lately—I take out the mirror, and mother's face, with sweet, kind smile, brings me peace, and helps me to bear hard words and cross looks."

Then the man understood and loved his child the more for her filial piety. Even the girl's stepmother, when she knew what had really taken place, was ashamed and asked forgiveness. And this child, who believed she had seen her mother's face in the mirror, forgave, and trouble for ever departed from the home.

CHAPTER XV: KWANNON AND BENTEN. DAIKOKU, EBISU, AND HOTEI

> " Adoration to the great merciful Kwannon, who looketh
> down above the sound of prayer."
>
> *An Inscription.*

Kwannon

KWANNON, the Goddess of Mercy, resembles in many ways the no less merciful and gentle Jizō, for both renounced the joy of Nirvana that they might bring peace and happiness to others. Kwannon, however, is a much more complex divinity than Jizō, and though she is most frequently portrayed as a very beautiful and saintly Japanese woman, she nevertheless assumes a multitude of forms. We are familiar with certain Indian gods and goddesses with innumerable hands, and Kwannon is sometimes depicted as Senjiu-Kwannon, or Kwannon-of-the-Thousand-Hands.[1] Each hand holds an object of some kind, as if to suggest that here indeed was a goddess ready in her love to give and to answer prayer to the uttermost.

Then there is Jiu-ichi-men-Kwannon, the Kwannon-of-the-Eleven-Faces. The face of Kwannon is here represented as " smiling with eternal youth and infinite tenderness," and in her glowing presence the ideal of the divine feminine is presented with infinite beauty of conception. In the tiara of Jiu-ichi-men-Kwannon are exquisite faces, a radiation, as it were, of miniature Kwannons. Sometimes the tiara of Kwannon takes another form, as in Batō-Kwannon, or Kwannon-with-the-Horse's-Head. The title is a little misleading, for such a graceful creature is very far from possessing a

---

[1] The title is not accurate, for in reality this form of Kwannon possesses only forty hands. No doubt the name is intended to nsggest munificence on the part of this Goddess.

horse's head in any of her manifestations. Images of
this particular Kwannon depict a horse cut out in the
tiara. Batō-Kwannon is the Goddess to whom peasants
pray for the safety and preservation of their horses and
cattle, and Batō-Kwannon is not only said to protect
dumb animals, particularly those who labour for mankind, but she extends her power to protecting their
spirits and bringing them ease and a happier life than
they experienced while on earth. In sharp contrast with
the Kwannons we have already described is Hito-koto-
Kwannon, the Kwannon who will only answer one
prayer. The Gods of Love and Wisdom are frequently
represented in conjunction with this Goddess, and the
"Twenty-eight Followers" are personifications of certain
constellations. But in all the variations of Kwannon she
preserves the same virgin beauty, and this Goddess of
Mercy has not inappropriately been called the Japanese
Madonna.

Kwannon in Chinese Myth

In China Kwannon is known as Kwanjin, and is the
spiritual son of Amitâbha, but this divinity always
appears as a goddess, as her images in both China and
Japan testify. The Chinese claim that Kwanjin is of
native origin, and was originally the daughter of the
King of the Chow dynasty. She was sentenced to death
by her father because she refused to marry, but the
executioner's sword broke without inflicting a wound.
We are told that later on her spirit went to Hell. There
was something so radiantly beautiful about the spirit of
Kwanjin that her very presence turned Hell into Paradise.
The King of the Infernal Regions, in order to maintain
the gloomy aspect of his realm, sent Kwanjin back to
earth again, and he caused her to be miraculously
transported on a lotus flower to the Island of Pootoo.

THE THIRTY-THREE PLACES

An Incarnation of Kwannon

Chūjō Hime, a Buddhist nun, is generally regarded as the greatest early Japanese artist of embroidery, and, according to legend, she was an incarnation of Kwannon. Chūjō Hime met with much cruel treatment from her stepmother, until she finally retired to the temple of Tœema-dera, and there worked upon the wonderful lotus thread embroidery depicting the Buddhist Paradise. The design is so exquisite that we can easily understand the Japanese belief that the Gods helped this great artist in her work.

Kwannon the Mother

There is another remarkable embroidery, by Kano Hogai, depicting Kwannon as the Divine Mother, pouring forth from a crystal phial the water of creation. As this holy water falls in a series of bubbles, each bubble may be seen to contain a little babe with reverently folded hands. It is altogether a wonderful piece of work, and, turning from its pictorial beauty to study a description of its technicalities, we find that it took three years to execute, and that 12,100 different shades of silk, and twelve of gold thread, were used.

The "Thirty-three Places" Sacred to Kwannon

There are thirty-three shrines sacred to Kwannon. All are carefully numbered, and are to be found in the provinces near Kyōto. The following legend may possibly account for the reverence bestowed upon the *Saikoku Sanjū-san Sho* (the "Thirty-three Places").

When the great Buddhist abbot of the eighth century, Tokudō Shōnin, died, he was conducted into the presence of Emma-O, the Lord of the Dead. The castle in which Emma-O lived was resplendent with silver and gold, rosy pearls, and all manner of sparkling jewels. A light emanated from Emma-Ō too, and that dread God had a smile upon his face. He received the distinguished abbot with extreme courtesy, and thus addressed him :

" Tokudō Shōnin, there are thirty-three places where Kwannon reveals her special favour, for behold she has, in her boundless love, divided herself into many bodies, so that he who cries for aid shall not cry in vain. Alas ! men continue to go their evil ways, for they know not of these sacred shrines. They live their sordid lives and pass into Hell, a vast and countless number. Oh, how blind they are, how wayward, and how full of folly ! If they were to make but a single pilgrimage to these thirty-three shrines sacred to our Lady of Mercy, a pure and wonderful light would shine from their feet, feet made spiritually strong to crush down all evil, to scatter the hundred and thirty-six hells into fragments. If, in spite of this pilgrimage, one should chance to fall into Hell, I will take his place and receive into myself all his suffering, for if this happened my tale of peace would be false, and I should indeed deserve to suffer. Here is a list of the thirty-and-three sacred shrines of Kwannon. Take it into the troubled world of men and women, and make known the ever-lasting mercy of Kwannon."

Tokudō, having carefully listened to all Emma-Ō had told him, replied : " You have honoured me with such a mission, but mortals are full of doubts and fears, and they would ask for some sign that what I tell them is indeed true."

Emma-Ō at once presented the abbot with his jewelled seal, and, bidding him farewell, sent him on his way accompanied by two attendants.

While these strange happenings were taking place in the Underworld the disciples of Tokudō perceived that though their master's body had lain for three days and nights the flesh had not grown cold. The devoted followers did not bury the body, believing that their master was not dead. And such was indeed the case, for eventually Tokudō awakened from his trance, and in his right hand he held the jewelled seal of Emma-Ō.

Tokudō lost no time in narrating his strange adventures, and when he had concluded his story he and his disciples set off on a pilgrimage to the thirty-three holy places[1] over which the Goddess of Mercy presides.

List of the "Thirty-three Places"

The following is a complete list of the "Thirty-three Places" sacred to Kwannon :

1. Fudaraku-ji, at Nachi, in Kishū.
2. Kimii-dera, near Wakayama, in Kishū.
3. Kokawa-dera, in Kishū.
4. Sefuku-ji, in Izumi.
5. Fujii-dera, in Kawachi.
6. Tsubosaka-dera, in Yamato.
7. Oka-dera, in Yamato.
8. Hase-dera, in Yamato.
9. Nan-endō, at Nara, in Yamato.
10. Mimuroto-dera, at Uji, in Yamashiro.
11. Kami Daigo-dera, at Uji, in Yamashiro.
12. Iwama-dera, in Ōmi.
13. Ishiyama-dera, near Ōtsu, in Ōmi.
14. Miidera, near Ōtsu, in Ōmi.
15. Ima-Gumano, at Kyōto, in Yamashiro.
16. Kiyomizu-dera, at Kyōto.
17. Rokuhara-dera, at Kyōto.

---

[1] "In imitation of the original Thirty-three Holy Places, thirty-three other places have been established in Eastern Japan, and also in the district of Chichibu."—*Murray's Handbook for Japan*, by Basil Hall Chamberlain and W. B. Mason.

18. Rokkaku-dō, at Kyōto.
19. Kōdō, at Kyōto.
20. Yoshimine-dera, at Kyōto.
21. Anōji, in Tamba.
22. Sōjiji, in Settsu.
23. Katsuo-dera, in Settsu.
24. Nakayama-dera, near Kōbe, in Settsu.
25. Shin Kiyomizu-dera, in Harima.
26. Hokkeji, in Harima.
27. Shosha-san, in Harima.
28. Nareai-ji, in Tango.
29. Matsunoo-dera, in Wakasa.
30. Chikubu-shima, island in Lake Biwa, in Ōmi.
31. Chōmeiji, in Ōmi.
32. Kwannonji, in Ōmi.
33. Tanigumi-dera, near Tarui, in Mino.[1]

The "Hall of the Second Moon"

The Buddhist temple of Ni-gwarsu-dō (" Hall of the Second Moon ") contains a small copper image of Kwannon. It has the miraculous power of being warm like living flesh, and since the image was enshrined special services in honour of Kwannon take place in February, and on the 18th of each month the sacred image is exposed for worship.

Kwannon and the Deer

An old hermit named Saion Zenji took up his abode on Mount Nariai in order that he might be able to gaze upon the beauty of Ama-no-Hashidate, a narrow fir-clad promontory dividing Lake Iwataki and Miyazu Bay. Ama-no-Hashidate is still regarded as one of the *Sankei*, or "Three Great Sights," of Japan, and still Mount

---

[1] Compiled from *Murray's Handbook for Japan*.

KWANNON AND THE DEER

Nariai is considered the best spot from which to view this charming scene.

On Mount Nariai this gentle and holy recluse erected a little shrine to Kwannon not far from a solitary pine-tree. He spent his happy days in looking upon Ama-no-Hashidate and in chanting the Buddhist Scriptures, and his charming disposition and holy ways were much appreciated by the people who came to pray at the little shrine he had so lovingly erected for his own joy and for the joy of others.

The hermit's abode, delightful enough in mild and sunny weather, was dreary in the winter-time, for when it snowed the good old man was cut off from human intercourse. On one occasion the snow fell so heavily that it was piled up in some places to a height of twenty feet. Day after day the severe weather continued, and at last the poor old hermit found that he had no food of any kind. Chancing to look out one morning, he saw that a deer was lying dead in the snow. As he gazed upon the poor creature, which had been frozen to death, he remembered that it was unlawful in the sight of Kwannon to eat the flesh of animals ; but on thinking over the matter more carefully it seemed to him that he could do more good to his fellow creatures by partaking of this deer than by observing the strict letter of the law and allowing himself to starve in sight of plenty.

When Saion Zenji had come to this wise decision he went out and cut off a piece of venison, cooked it, and ate half, with many prayers of thanksgiving for his deliverance. The rest of the venison he left in his cooking-pot.

Eventually the snow melted, and several folk hastily wended their way from the neighbouring village, and ascended Mount Nariai, expecting to see that their good and much-loved hermit had forever passed away from this world. As they approached the shrine, however, they were rejoiced to hear the old man chanting, in a clear and ringing voice, the sacred Buddhist Scriptures.

The folk from the village gathered about the hermit while he narrated the story of his deliverance. When, out of curiosity, they chanced to peep into his cooking-pot, they saw, to their utter amazement, that it contained no venison, but a piece of wood covered with gold foil. Still wondering what it all meant, they looked upon the image of Kwannon in the little shrine, and found that a piece had been cut from her loins, and when they inserted the piece of wood the wound was healed. Then it was that the old hermit and the folk gathered about him realised that the deer had been none other than Kwannon, who, in her boundless love and tender mercy, had made a sacrifice of her own divine flesh.

Benten

> " The wild flowers fade, the maple-leaves,
> Touched by frost-fingers, float to earth ;
> But on the bosom of the sea
> The flowers to which her waves give birth
> Fade not, like blossoms on the land,
> Nor feel the chill of Autumn's hand."
> *Yasuhide.* (Trans. by CLARA A. WALSH.)

Benten, the Goddess of the Sea, is also one of the Seven Divinities of Luck ; and she is romantically referred to as the Goddess of Love, Beauty, and Eloquence. She is represented in Japanese art as riding on a dragon or serpent, which may account for the fact that in certain localities snakes are regarded as being sacred. Images of Benten depict her as having eight arms. Six hands are extended above her head and hold a bow, arrow, wheel, sword, key, and sacred jewel, while her two remaining hands are reverently crossed in prayer. She resembles Kwannon in many ways, and images of the two goddesses are frequently seen together, but the shrines of Benten are usually to be found on islands.

Benten and the Dragon

We have already referred to Benten riding on a dragon, and the following legend may possibly be connected with this particular representation.

In a certain cave there lived a formidable dragon, which devoured the children of the village of Koshigoe. In the sixth century Benten was determined to put a stop to this monster's unseemly behaviour, and having caused a great earthquake she hovered in the clouds over the cave where the dread dragon had taken up his abode. Benten then descended from the clouds, entered the cavern, married the dragon, and was thus able, through her good influence, to put an end to the slaughter of little children. With the coming of Benten there arose from the sea the famous Island of Enoshima,[1] which has remained to this day sacred to the Goddess of the Sea.

Benten-of-the-Birth-Water

Hanagaki Baishū, a young poet and scholar, attended a great festival to celebrate the rebuilding of the Amadera temple. He wandered about the beautiful grounds, and eventually reached the place of a spring from which he had often quenched his thirst. He found that what had originally been a spring was now a pond, and, moreover, that at one corner of the pond there was a tablet bearing the words *Tanjō-Sui* ("Birth-Water"), and also a small but attractive temple dedicated to Benten. While Baishū was noting the

[1] See *Glimpses of Unfamiliar Japan*, by Lafcadio Hearn, vol. i. pp. 62–104.

changes in the temple grounds the wind blew to his feet a charmingly written love-poem. He picked it up, and discovered that it had been inscribed by a female hand, that the characters were exquisitely formed, and that the ink was fresh.

Baishū went home and read and re-read the poem. It was not long before he fell in love with the writer, and finally he resolved to make her his wife. At length he went to the temple of Benten-of-the-Birth-Water, and cried : "Oh, Goddess, come to my aid, and help me to find the woman who wrote these wind-blown verses ! " Having thus prayed, he promised to perform a seven days' religious service, and to devote the seventh night in ceaseless worship before the sacred shrine of Benten, in the grounds of the Amadera.

On the seventh night of the vigil Baishū heard a voice calling for admittance at the main gateway of the temple grounds. The gate was opened, and an old man, clad in ceremonial robes and with a black cap upon his head, advanced and silently knelt before the temple of Benten. Then the outer door of the temple mysteriously opened, and a bamboo curtain was partially raised, revealing a handsome boy, who thus addressed the old man : "We have taken pity on a young man who desires a certain love-union, and have called you to inquire into the matter, and to see if you can bring the young people together."

The old man bowed, and then drew from his sleeve a cord which he wound round Baishū's body, igniting one end in a temple-lantern, and waving his hand the while, as if beckoning some spirit to appear out of the dark night. In a moment a young girl entered the temple grounds, and, with her fan half concealing her pretty face, she knelt beside Baishū.

Then the beautiful boy thus addressed Baishū : "We

have heard your prayer, and we have known that recently you have suffered much. The woman you love is now beside you." And having uttered these words the divine youth departed, and the old man left the temple grounds.

When Baishu had given thanks to Benten-of-the-Birth-Water he proceeded homeward. On reaching the street outside the temple grounds he saw a young girl, and at once recognised her as the woman he loved. Baishu spoke to her, and when she replied the gentleness and sweetness of her voice filled the youth with joy. Together they walked through the silent streets until at last they came to the house where Baishu lived. There was a moment's pause, and then the maiden said : "Benten has made me your wife," and the lovers entered the house together.

The marriage was an extremely fortunate one, and the happy Baishu discovered that his wife, apart from her excellent domestic qualities, was accomplished in the art of arranging flowers and in the art of embroidery, and that her delicate writing was not less pleasing than her charming pictures. Baishu knew nothing about her family, but as she had been presented to him by the Goddess Benten he considered that it was unnecessary to question her in the matter. There was only one thing that puzzled the loving Baishu, and that was that the neighbours seemed to be totally unaware of his wife's presence.

One day, while Baishu was walking in a remote quarter of Kyōto, he saw a servant beckoning to him from the gateway of a private house. The man came forward, bowed respectfully, and said : "Will you deign to enter this house ? My master is anxious to have the honour of speaking to you." Baishu, who knew nothing of the servant or his master, was not a little surprised by this strange greeting, but he allowed himself to be conducted to the guest-room, and thus his host addressed him :

"I most humbly apologise for the very informal manner of my invitation, but I believe that I have acted in compliance with a message I received from the Goddess Benten. I have a daughter, and, as I am anxious to find a good husband for her, I sent her written poems to all the temples of Benten in Kyōto. In a dream the Goddess came to me, and told me that she had secured an excellent husband for my daughter, and that he would visit me during the coming winter. I was not inclined to attach very much importance to this dream; but last night Benten again revealed herself to me in a vision, and said that to-morrow the husband she had chosen for my daughter would call upon me, and that I could then arrange the marriage. The Goddess described the appearance of the young man so minutely that I am assured that you are my daughter's future husband."

These strange words filled Baishū with sorrow, and when his courteous host proposed to present him to the lady he was unable to summon up sufficient courage to tell his would-be father-in-law that he already had a wife. Baishū followed his host into another apartment, and to his amazement and joy he discovered that the daughter of the house was none other than his own wife! And yet there was a subtle difference, for the woman who now smiled upon him was the body of his wife, and she who had appeared before the temple of Benten-of-the-Birth-Water was her soul. We are told that Benten performed this miracle for the sake of her worshippers, and thus it came to pass that Baishū had a strange dual marriage with the woman he loved.

DAIKOKU'S RAT

Daikoku

Daikoku, the God of Wealth, Ebisu, his son, the God of Labour, and Hotei, the God of Laughter and Contentment, belong to that cycle of deities known as the Gods of Luck. Daikoku is represented with a Magic Mallet, which bears the sign of the Jewel, embodying the male and female spirit, and signifies a creative deity. A stroke of his Mallet confers wealth, and his second attribute is the Rat. Daikoku is, as we should suppose, an extremely popular deity, and he is frequently portrayed as a prosperous Chinese gentleman, richly apparelled, and is usually shown standing on bales of rice, with a bag of precious things on his shoulder. This genial and beneficent God is also depicted as seated on bales of rice, or showing his treasures to some eager and expectant child, or holding the Red Sun against his breast with one hand and grasping the Magic Mallet with the other.

Daikoku's Rat

Daikoku's attribute, a Rat, has an emblematic and moral meaning in connection with the wealth hidden in the God's bag. The Rat is frequently portrayed either in the bale of rice with its head peeping out, or in it, or playing with the Mallet, and sometimes a large number of rats are shown.

According to a certain old legend, the Buddhist Gods grew jealous of Daikoku. They consulted together, and finally decided that they would get rid of the too popular Daikoku, to whom the Japanese offered prayers and incense. Emma-Ō, the Lord of the Dead, promised to send his most cunning and clever *oni*, Shiro, who, he said, would have no difficulty in conquering the God of Wealth. Shiro, guided by a sparrow, went to

Daikoku's castle, but though he hunted high and low he could not find its owner. Finally Shiro discovered a large storehouse, in which he saw the God of Wealth seated. Daikoku called his Rat and bade him find out who it was who dared to disturb him. When the Rat saw Shiro he ran into the garden and brought back a branch of holly, with which he drove the *oni* away, and Daikoku remains to this day one of the most popular of the Japanese Gods. This incident is said to be the origin of the New Year's Eve charm, consisting of a holly leaf and a skewer, or a sprig of holly fixed in the lintel of the door of a house to prevent the return of the *oni*.

The Six Daikoku

1. Makura Daikoku, ordinary form with Mallet on lotus leaf.

2. Ojikara Daikoku, with sword and *vajra*.

3. Bika Daikoku, a priest, with Mallet in right hand, *vajra*-hilted sword in left.

4. Yasha Daikoku, with Wheel of the Law in his right hand.

5. Shinda Daikoku, a boy seated with a crystal in his left hand.

6. Mahakara Daikoku, seated female, with small bale of rice on her head.

Ebisu

Ebisu and his father Daikoku are usually pictured together : the God of Wealth seated upon bales of rice, pressing the Red Sun against his breast with one hand, and with the other holding the wealth-giving Mallet, while Ebisu is depicted with a fishing-rod and a great *tai* fish under his arm.

HOTEI

Hotei

Hotei, the God of Laughter and Contentment, is one of the most whimsical of the Japanese Gods. He is represented as extremely fat, carrying on his back a linen bag (*ho-tei*), from which he derives his name. In this bag he stows the Precious Things, but when in a particularly playful mood he uses it as a receptacle for merry and inquisitive children. Sometimes Hotei is represented in a broken-down and extremely shabby carriage drawn by boys, and is then known as the Waggon Priest. Again he is portrayed as carrying in one hand a Chinese fan and in the other his bag, or balancing at either end of a pole the bag of Precious Things and a boy.

CHAPTER XVI : DOLLS AND BUTTERFLIES

> "I asked a charming Japanese girl : 'How can a doll
> live ?' 'Why,' she answered, '*if you love it enough*, it will
> live ! ' "
>
> LAFCADIO HEARN.

The English and Japanese Doll

OUR English dolls, with their flaxen hair, blue eyes, and simpering faces, are certainly not a credit to the toy-maker's art if they are to be regarded as bearing even a remote likeness to living children. Put in a horizonal position, something will click in their little heads and their blue eyes will close, or more correctly roll backward ; a pinch will make them emit a tolerable imitation of the words "Papa !" "Mamma !" and yet in spite of these mechanical devices they have nothing more to their credit than a child's short-lived love. They are speedily broken, or liable at any moment to be decapitated by a little brother who has learnt too well the story of Lady Jane Grey !

In Japan, however, the doll is not merely a plaything by which little children may become make-believe mothers, but in earlier days it was regarded as a means to make a wife a mother. Lafcadio Hearn writes : "And if you see such a doll, though held quite close to you, being made by a Japanese mother to reach out its hands, to move its little bare feet, and to turn its head, you would be almost afraid to venture a heavy wager that it was only a doll." It is this startling likeness that is perhaps accountable for the quaint and beautiful love connected with Japanese dolls.

LIVE DOLLS

Live Dolls

At one time certain dolls were actually said to become alive, to take to their small bodies a human soul, and the belief is merely an echo of the old idea that much love will quicken to life the image of a living thing. In Old Japan the doll was handed down from one generation to another, and sometimes remained in an excellent condition for over a hundred years. A hundred years spent in little children's arms, served with food, put to bed regularly every night, and the object of constant endearments, will no doubt work wonders in the poetic imagination of a happy and child-like people.

The tiny doll known as O-Hina-San does not come within the region of our present study ; it was simply a toy and nothing more. It is the life-size dolls we must deal with, those dolls so cunningly representing little children two or three years old. The girl doll of this class is known as O-Toku-San and the boy doll as Tokutarō-San. It was believed that if these dolls were ill-treated or neglected in any way they would weep, become angry, and bring misfortune upon their possessors. They had in addition many other supernatural powers.

In a certain old family there was a Tokutarō-San which received a reverence almost equal to that shown to Kishibōjin, the Goddess to whom Japanese wives pray for offspring. This Tokutarō-San was borrowed by childless couples. They gave it new clothes and tended it with loving care, assured that such a doll which had a soul would make them happy by answering their prayers for a child. Tokutarō-San, according to legend, was very much alive, for when the house caught fire it speedily ran into the garden for safety !

215

A Doll's Last Resting-place

What happens to a Japanese doll when after a very long and happy life it eventually gets broken ? Though finally regarded as dead, its remains are treated with the utmost respect. It is not thrown away with rubbish, or burned, or even reverently laid upon running water, as is often the case with dead Japanese flowers. It is not buried, but dedicated to Kōjin, frequently represented as a deity with many arms. Kōjin is supposed to reside in the *enoki* tree, and in front of this tree there is a small shrine and *torii*. Here, then, the remains of a very old Japanese doll are reverently laid. Its little face may be scratched, its silk dress torn and faded and its arms and legs broken, but it once had a soul, once had the mysterious *desire* to give maternity to those who longed for it.

On March 3 the Girls' Festival takes place. It is known as *Jōmi no Sekku*, or *Hina Matsuri*, the Feast of Dolls.

Butterflies

> " Where the soft drifts lie
> Of fallen blossoms, dying,
> Did one flutter now,
> From earth to its brown bough ?
> Ah, no ! 'twas a butterfly,
> Like fragile blossom flying ! "
>
> *Arakida Mortitake.*
> (Trans. by CLARA A. WALSH.)

It is in China rather than in Japan that the butterfly is connected with legend and folk-lore. The Chinese scholar Rōsan is said to have received visits from two spirit maidens who regaled him with ghostly stories about these bright-winged insects.

It is more than probable that the legends concerning

butterflies in Japan have been borrowed from China. Japanese poets and artists were fond of choosing for their professional appellation such names as "Butterfly-Dream," "Solitary Butterfly," "Butterfly-Help," and so on. Though probably of Chinese origin, such ideas naturally appealed to the æsthetic taste of the Japanese people, and no doubt they played in early days the romantic game of butterflies. The Emperor Gensō used to make butterflies choose his loves for him. At a wine-party in his garden fair ladies would set caged butterflies free. These bright-coloured insects would fly and settle upon the fairest damsels, and those maidens immediately received royal favours.

Butterflies of Good and Evil Omen

In Japan the butterfly was at one time considered to be the soul of a living man or woman. If it entered a guest-room and pitched behind the bamboo screen it was a sure sign that the person whom it represented would shortly appear in the house. The presence of a butterfly in the house was regarded as a good omen, though of course everything depended on the individual typified by the butterfly.

The butterfly was not always the harbinger of good. When Taira-no-Masakado was secretly preparing for a revolt Kyōto was the scene of a swarm of butterflies, and the people who saw them were much frightened. Lafcadio Hearn suggests that these butterflies may have been the spirits of those fated to fall in battle, the spirits of the living who were stirred by a premonition of the near approach of death. Butterflies may also be the souls of the dead, and they often appear in this form in order to announce their final leave-taking from the body.

"The Flying Hairpin of Kochō"

The Japanese drama contains reference to the ghostly significance of butterflies. In the play known as *The Flying Hairpin of Kochō*, the heroine, Kochō, kills herself on account of false accusations and cruel treatment. Her lover seeks to discover who has been the cause of her untimely death. Eventually Kochō's hairpin turns into a butterfly and hovers over the hiding-place of the villain who has caused all the trouble.

The White Butterfly

There is a quaint and touching Japanese legend connected with the butterfly. An old man named Takahama lived in a little house behind the cemetery of the temple of Sōzanji. He was extremely amiable and generally liked by his neighbours, though most of them considered him to be a little mad. His madness, it would appear, entirely rested upon the fact that he had never married or evinced desire for intimate companionship with women.

One summer day he became very ill, so ill, in fact, that he sent for his sister-in-law and her son. They both came and did all they could to bring comfort during his last hours. While they watched Takahama fell asleep; but he had no sooner done so than a large white butterfly flew into the room, and rested on the old man's pillow. The young man tried to drive it away with a fan; but it came back three times, as if loth to leave the sufferer.

At last Takahama's nephew chased it out into the garden, through the gate, and into the cemetery beyond, where it lingered over a woman's tomb, and then mysteriously disappeared. On examining the tomb the young man found the name "Akiko" written upon it, together with a description narrating how Akiko died when she was eighteen. Though the tomb was covered with moss and must have been erected fifty years previously, the boy saw that it was surrounded with flowers, and that the little water-tank had been recently filled.

When the young man returned to the house he found that Takahama had passed away, and he returned to his mother and told her what he had seen in the cemetery.

"Akiko?" murmured his mother. "When your uncle was young he was betrothed to Akiko. She died of consumption shortly before her wedding-day. When Akiko left this world your uncle resolved never to marry and to live ever near her grave. For all these years he has remained faithful to his vow, and kept in his heart all the sweet memories of his one and only love. Every day Takahama went to the cemetery, whether the air was fragrant with summer breeze or thick with falling snow. Every day he went to her grave and prayed for her happiness, swept the tomb and set flowers there. When Takahama was dying, and he could no longer perform his loving task, Akiko came for him. That white butterfly was her sweet and loving soul."

Just before Takahama passed away into the Land of the Yellow Spring he may have murmured words like those of Yone Noguchi:

> "Where the flowers sleep,
> Thank God! I shall sleep to-night.
> Oh, come, butterfly!" [1]

[1] Legends concerning other insects will be found in Chapter XXIII.

CHAPTER XVII : FESTIVALS

The New Year

THE *San-ga-nichi*, or "three days" of the New Year, is one of the most important of the Japanese festivals, for the Japanese make far more of the New Year than we do in this country. They regard the first three days of the year as a fitting occasion when it is most important to insure good luck and happiness for the days that follow, and in order to bring this about many quaint and ancient observances take place. Before the houses are decorated a thorough winter cleaning is carried out. "In ancient times," writes Mrs. C. M. Salwey, "from the Court of the Emperor to the hut of the peasant, this attention was observed to such an extent that the Shōgun's Court provided overseers, who visited with ornamented dusting poles, to overhaul the labour of the servants, passing their official brooms over ledges and crevices, and in so doing flourishing in a certain manner their mystic wands to demonstrate the Chinese ideograph which signified water." Not only is the house thoroughly cleaned and everything put in order, but evil spirits are got rid of by throwing out peas and beans from the open *shoji*, or paper slides.

On the festival of the New Year the houses and gate-posts are adorned with straw ropes, and these are often made to represent such lucky Chinese numbers as three, five, and seven. The food chiefly eaten on this occasion comprises lobsters (their bent and ancient appearance suggesting long life), oranges, and certain varieties of edible seaweeds. In addition there are mirror cakes, associated with the Sun Goddess, and these cakes, composed of rice, are eaten with the oranges and lobster, and served on pure white trays. One other important

220

decoration must not be overlooked, and that is the branches of the pine-tree. These branches symbolise long life, and for some unknown reason they are burnt when the festival is over.

One of the most picturesque customs associated with this festival, and one particularly appealing to children, is the Treasure Ship with the Seven Gods of Good Luck on board, to which we have referred elsewhere.[1]

The Boys' Festival

The *Tango no Sekku*, or Boys' Festival, takes place on May 5, and is intended to inspire the youth of Japan with warlike qualities. It is the day when flags are to be seen in every direction, when the roofs of the houses are decorated with the leaves of iris, so that Nature's flag and the flag made by human hands are both conspicuous on this joyous festival, which is popularly known as the Feast of Flags. Boys are presented with small figures representing certain great heroes of the past, while ancient swords, bows, arrows, spears, &c., are handed down from one generation of children to another.

Perhaps the dominant feature of this festival is the paper flag shaped like a carp. It is hollow, and when inflated with wind has the appearance of vigorously flying through the air. The carp symbolises something more than the crude spirit of warfare, for it typifies tenacity of purpose and indomitable courage. As the carp swims against the stream, so is the Japanese youth expected to fight against all the fierce currents of adversity. This idea is probably derived from the fascinating Chinese legend of the Dragon Carp which, after a long struggle, succeeded in swimming past the Dragon Gate rapids, lived a thousand years, and finally rose into the sky.

[1] Chapter VII. : "Legend in Japanese Art."

The Festival of the Dead

The Festival of the Dead, or *Bommatsuri*, deserves mention here because it contains much that is legendary. The Japanese peasant's conception of a future life is not a very delightful one. At death the body is washed and shaven and then arrayed in a pure white garment—indeed, in the garment of a pilgrim. Round the neck is hung a wallet containing three or six *rin*, according to the custom of the place in which the death occurs, and these *rin* are buried with the deceased. The idea of burying coin with the dead is to be found in the belief that all who die, children alone excepted, must journey to the Sanzu-no-Kawa, or "The River of the Three Roads." On the bank of this dismal river Sodzu-Baba, the Old Woman of the Three Roads, awaits the coming of souls, together with her husband, Ten Datsu-Ba. If three *rin* are not paid to the Old Woman she takes away the white garments of the dead and, regardless of entreaties, hangs them on trees. Then there is the no less formidable Emma-Ō, the Lord of the Dead; and when we add to these dread figures some of the terrors of the Buddhist hells it is not surprising that the gentle and poetical Japanese should have founded a festival that will afford a pleasant, if all too brief, respite from the horrors of Hades.

The festival takes place from July 13 to 15. At such a time most of the houses are mere skeletons, being open to the summer breeze on all sides. People saunter about in the lightest of garments. Butterflies and dragon-flies disport in countless numbers, flying over a cool stretch of lotus or settling on the purple petal of an iris. Fuji rears her great head into the clear blue sky, bearing like a white scarf a patch of fast-fading snow.

THE FESTIVAL OF THE DEAD

When the morning of the 13th arrives new mats of rice straw are spread upon all Buddhist altars and on the little household shrines. Every Japanese home on that day is provided with a quaint, minute meal in readiness for the great company of ghosts.

At sunset the streets are bright with the flames of torches, and the entrances of houses gay with brightly coloured lanterns. Those to whom this festival applies in a particular sense and not in a general one—that is to say, those who have recently lost some dear one—go out on this night to the cemeteries, and there pray, make offerings, burn incense, and pour out water. Lanterns are lit and bamboo vases filled with flowers.

On the evening of the 15th the ghosts of the Circle of Penance or Gakidō are fed, and in addition those ghosts who have no friends among the living to care for them. There is a legend bearing upon this particular phase of the Festival of the Dead. Dai-Mokenren, a great disciple of Buddha, was once permitted to see the soul of his mother in the Gakidō. He grieved so much on account of intense suffering that he gave her a bowl containing choice food. Every time she tried to eat the food would suddenly turn into fire, and finally to ashes. Then Mokenren asked Buddha to tell him what he could do to ease his mother's suffering. He was told to feed the ghosts of the great priests of all countries " on the fifteenth day of the seventh month." When this had been done Mokenren returned, to find his mother dancing for joy. In this happy dance after much tribulation we trace the origin of the *Bon-odori*, which takes place on the third night of the festival.

When the evening of the third day arrives preparations are made for the departure of the ghosts. Thousands of little boats are packed with food and loving messages of farewell. Into these boats step the departing ghosts. Loving hands set these frail craft upon river, lake, or sea. A small lantern glows at the prow, while pale blue clouds of incense float up from the stern. Hearn writes: "Down all the creeks and rivers and canals the phantom fleets go glimmering to the sea; and all the sea sparkles to the horizon with the lights of the dead, and the sea wind is fragrant with incense."

There is a pathetic charm about this festival. It is by no means unique, for it corresponds to the Indian *Sraddha*; but in Japan it is touched with a more delicate and haunting beauty. No one has been able to solve conclusively the origin of the *Torii*, that wonderful gateway that leads nowhere. What a charming entrance or exit for a company of wandering souls! What a place for ghosts to play and dream awhile is a Japanese garden, with its lake and moon-shaped bridge, its stone lantern, its paths of silver sand! And what a street for ghosts to wander in is the Street Everlasting that is so near to the Street of Aged Men! Thus Yone Noguchi sums up the magic of a Japanese night, one of those three nights when souls come in touch with old earthly memories:

"The scented purple breezes of the Japanese night!
The old moon like a fairy ship of gold
Softly through the dream sea begins to rock on:
(I hear the unheard song of Beauty in the moon ship,
I hear even the whisper of her golden dress.)
The hundred lanterns burning in love and prayer,
Float on the streets like haunting memories.
The silvery music of wooden clogs of the Japanese girls!
Are they not little ghosts out of the bosom of ancient age?
Are they returning to fulfil their thousand fancies forgotten?
O the fancy world of the Japanese night
Born out of the old love and unfulfilled desires!
The crying love-song of the Japanese night,
The *samisen* music of hungry passion and tears!
O the long wail of heart through the darkness and love!"

THE TORII

The Laughing Festival of Wasa

Numerous other Japanese festivities take place during the year, and two, the Festival of Dolls and the Festival of Tanabata, the Weaving Maiden, have been referred to elsewhere. Perhaps in some way the Laughing Festival of Wasa is the most quaint of all the Japanese festivities. During the month of October a number of old men form a procession carrying two boxes full of oranges and persimmons spitted on sticks. These old men are followed by children with similar fruit on bamboo rods. Just as the leader reaches the shrine he turns round and makes a most ludicrous grimace, which is immediately followed by a merry peal of laughter, and this irresistible merriment has its origin in the following legend.

In the month of October the Gods used to assemble in a great temple at Izumo, and they met for the purpose of arranging the love-affairs of the people. When the Gods were sitting in the temple one of them said: "Where is Miwa Daimyō-jin?" All the Gods looked everywhere for him, but he was not to be found. Now Miwa Daimyō-jin was extremely deaf, and, owing to this defect, he had mistaken the great day when the Gods met together. When he reached Izumo the meeting had been dissolved, and all the Gods laughed very much when they heard about it, a laughter that is imitated year by year in the Laughing festival to which we have referred.

The Torii

We have referred in this chapter and elsewhere to the *torii*, and though authorities agree to differ in regard to its use and origin, the theme is a fascinating one and well worthy of study. According to a popular

225

account the word *torii* means "fowl-dwelling" or "bird-rest." On the top beam of this imposing gateway the fowls heralded the approach of dawn, and in their cry bade the priests attend to their early morning prayers. In one legend we are informed that the sun descends to earth in the form of the Ho-Ho Bird, messenger of love, peace, and goodwill, and rests upon one of the *torii*.

Professor B. H. Chamberlain regards the "bird-rest" etymology and the theories derived from it as erroneous, and believes that the *torii* came originally from Asia. He writes, in *Things Japanese* : "The Koreans erect somewhat similar gateways at the approach of their royal palaces ; the Chinese *p'ai lou*, serving to record the virtues of male or female worthies, seem related in shape as well as in use ; and the occurrence of the word *turan* in Northern India and of the word *tori* in Central India, to denote gateways of strikingly cognate appearance, gives matter for reflection." Dr. W. G. Aston also believes that the *torii* came from abroad, "but holds that it was fitted with a pre-existing name, which would have originally designated 'a lintel' before it came to have its present sacred associations." [1]

In regard to the construction of these gateways, Mrs. C. M. Salwey writes : "The oldest *torii* of Japan . . . were constructed of plain unvarnished wood. In fact, they were built of straight, upright trunks of trees in their natural state, though sometimes bereft of the outer bark. Later on the wood was painted a deep, rich vermilion, possibly to heighten the effect when the background was densely wooded." Though the *torii* was originally associated with Shintōism, it was later on adopted by the Buddhists, who considerably altered its simple but beautiful construction by turning up the

[1] *Things Japanese*, by Professor B. H. Chamberlain.

corners of the horizontal beams, supplying inscriptions and ornaments of various kinds.

"The Footstool of the King"

Whatever the origin and significance of the Shintō *torii* may be, no one will deny its exquisite beauty, and many will agree in believing it to be the most perfect gateway in the world. Perhaps the most wonderful *torii* is the one that stands before the Itsukushima shrine on the Island of Myajima, and it is called "The Footstool of the King," "The Gateway of Light," or "The Water Gate of the Sacred Island."

Mrs. Salwey writes: "Is not this Gateway the symbol of the Right Direction, according to the dogmas of the Shintō Cult, the Goal towards which the face should be turned—'The Way of the Gods.' Are they not monitors writing their mystic message as an ideographic sign over the Lord of the Gods before the rising and setting sun, enhancing by their presence the dense luxuriance of cryptomerian avenue, reflecting within dark, still rivers or the silver ripples of the In-land Sea?" We must be content with this pleasing interpretation of the symbolism of the *torii*, for it takes us through the gate of conflicting theories, and gives us something more satisfying than the ramifications of etymology.

CHAPTER XVIII : THE PEONY-LANTERN [1]

"Morning Dew"

TSUYU ("Morning Dew") was the only daughter of Iijima. When her father married again she found she could not live happily with her stepmother, and a separate house was built for her, where she lived with her servant-maid Yoné.

One day Tsuyu received a visit from the family physician, Yamamoto Shijō, accompanied by a handsome young *samurai* named Hagiwara Shinzaburō. These young people fell in love with each other, and at parting Tsuyu whispered to Shinzaburō : "*Remember! if you do not come to see me again I shall certainly die!*"

Shinzaburō had every intention of seeing the fair Tsuyu as frequently as possible. Etiquette, however, would not allow him to visit her alone, so that he was compelled to rely on the old doctor's promise to take him to the villa where his loved one lived. The old doctor, however, having seen more than the young people had supposed, purposely refrained from keeping his promise.

Tsuyu, believing that the handsome young *samurai* had proved unfaithful, slowly pined away and died. Her faithful servant Yoné also died soon afterwards, being unable to live without her mistress, and they were buried side by side in the cemetery of Shin-Banzui-In.

Shortly after this sad event had taken place the old

[1] This story, though inspired by a Chinese tale, is Japanese in local colour, and serves to illustrate, in an extremely weird way, the power of Karma, or human desire, referred to in Chapter X. We have closely followed Lafcadio Hearn's rendering, to be found in *In Ghostly Japan*.

doctor called upon Shinzaburō and gave him full particulars of the death of Tsuyu and her maid.

Shinzaburō felt the blow keenly. Night and day the girl was in his thoughts. He inscribed her name upon a mortuary tablet, placed offerings before it, and repeated many prayers.

The Dead Return

When the first day of the Festival of the Dead[1] arrived he set food on the Shelf of Souls and hung out lanterns to guide the spirits during their brief earthly sojourn. As the night was warm and the moon at her full, he sat in his verandah and waited. He felt that all these preparations would not be in vain, and in his heart he believed that the soul of Tsuyu would come to him.

Suddenly the stillness was broken by the sound of *kara-kon*, *kara-kon*, the soft patter of women's *geta*. There was something strange and haunting about the sound. Shinzaburō rose and peeped over the hedge. He saw two women. One was carrying a long-shaped lantern with silk peonies stuck in at the upper end; the other wore a lovely robe covered with designs of autumnal blossom. In another moment he recognised the sweet figure of Tsuyu and her maid Yoné.

When Yoné had explained that the wicked old doctor had told them that Shinzaburō was dead, and the young *samurai* had likewise informed his visitors that he, too, had learnt from the same source that his loved one and her maid had departed this life, the two women entered the house, and remained there that night, returning home a little before sunrise. Night after night they came in this mysterious manner, and always Yoné carried the shining peony-lantern, always she and her mistress departed at the same hour.

[1] See Chapter XVII.

A Spy

One night Tomozō, one of Shinzaburō's servants, who lived next door to his master, chanced to hear the sound of a woman's voice in his lord's apartment. He peeped through a crack in one of the sliding doors, and perceived by the night-lantern within the room that his master was talking with a strange woman under the mosquito-net. Their conversation was so extraordinary that Tomozō was determined to see the woman's face. When he succeeded in doing so his hair stood on end and he trembled violently, for he saw the face of a dead woman, a woman long dead. There was no flesh on her fingers, for what had once been fingers were now a bunch of jangling bones. Only the upper part of her body had substance; below her waist there was but a dim, moving shadow. While Tomozō gazed with horror upon such a revolting scene a second woman's figure sprang up from within the room. She made for the chink and for Tomozō's eye behind it. With a shriek of terror the spying Tomozō fled to the house of Hakuōdō Yusai.

Yusai's Advice

Now Yusai was a man well versed in all manner of mysteries; but nevertheless Tomozō's story made considerable impression upon him, and he listened to every detail with the utmost amazement. When the servant had finished his account of the affair Yusai informed him that his master was a doomed man if the woman proved to be a ghost, that love between the living and the dead ended in the destruction of the living.

However, apart from critically examining this strange event, Yusai took practical steps to rescue this young

230

samurai from so horrible a fate. The next morning he discussed the matter with Shinzaburō, and told him pretty clearly that he had been loving a ghost, and that the sooner he got rid of that ghost the better it would be for him. He ended his discourse by advising the youth to go to the district of Shitaya, in Yanaka-no-Sasaki, the place where these women had said they lived.

The Mystery is Revealed

Shinzaburō carried out Yusai's advice, but nowhere in the quarter of Yanaka-no-Sasaki could he find the dwelling-place of Tsuyu. On his return home he happened to pass through the temple Shin-Banzui-In. There he saw two tombs placed side by side, one of no distinction, and the other large and handsome, adorned with a peony-lantern swinging gently in the breeze. Shinzaburō remembered that this lantern and the one carried by Yoné were identical, and an acolyte informed him that the tombs were those of Tsuyu and Yoné. Then it was that he realised the strange meaning of Yoné's words: "*We went away, and found a very small house in Yanaka-no-Sasaki. There we are now just barely able to live by doing a little private work.*" Their house, then, was a grave. The ghost of Yoné carried the peony-lantern, and the ghost of Tsuyu wound her fleshless arms about the neck of the young *samurai.*

Holy Charms

Shinzaburō, now fully aware of the horror of the situation, hastily retraced his steps and sought counsel from the wise, far-seeing Yusai. This learned man confessed his inability to help him further in the matter, but advised him to go to the high-priest Ryōseki, of

Shin-Banzui-In, and gave him a letter explaining what had taken place.

Ryōseki listened unmoved to Shinzaburō's story, for he had heard so many bearing on the same theme, the evil power of Karma. He gave the young man a small gold image of Buddha, which he instructed him to wear next his skin, telling him that it would protect the living from the dead. He also gave him a holy *sutra*, called "Treasure-Raining Sutra," which he was commended to recite in his house every night ; and lastly he gave him a bundle of sacred texts. Each holy strip he was to paste over an opening in his house.

By nightfall everything was in order in Shinzaburō's house. All the apertures were covered with sacred texts, and the air resounded with the recitation of the "Treasure-Raining Sutra," while the little gold Buddha swayed upon the *samurai's* breast. But somehow or other peace did not come to Shinzaburō that night. Sleep refused to close his weary eyes, and just as a temple bell ceased booming he heard the old *karan-koron, karan-koron*—the patter of ghostly *geta* ! Then the sound ceased. Fear and joy battled within Shinzaburō's heart. He stopped reciting the holy *sutra* and looked forth into the night. Once more he saw Tsuyu and her maid with the peony-lantern. Never before had Tsuyu looked so beautiful or so alluring ; but a nameless terror held him back. He heard with bitter anguish the women speaking together. He heard Yoné tell her mistress that his love had changed because his doors had been made fast against them, followed by the plaintive weeping of Tsuyu. At last the women wandered round to the back of the house. But back and front alike prevented their entry, so potent were the sacred words of the Lord Buddha.

The Betrayal

As all the efforts of Yoné to enter Shinzaburō's house were of no avail, she went night after night to Tomozō and begged him to remove the sacred texts from his master's dwelling. Over and over again, out of intense fear, Tomozō promised to do so, but with the coming of daylight he grew brave and decided not to betray one to whom he owed so much. One night, however, Yoné refused to be trifled with. She threatened Tomozō with awful hatred if he did not take away one of the sacred texts, and in addition she pulled such a terrible face that Tomozō nearly died of fright.

Tomozō's wife Miné happened to awake and hear the voice of a strange woman speaking to her husband. When the ghost-woman had vanished Miné gave her lord cunning counsel to the effect that he should consent to carry out Yoné's request provided that she would reward him with a hundred *ryō*.

Two nights later, when this wicked servant had received his reward, he gave Yoné the little gold image of Buddha, took down from his master's house one of the sacred texts, and buried in a field the *sutra* which his master used to recite. This enabled Yoné and her mistress to enter the house of Shinzaburō once more, and with their entry began again this horrible love of the dead, presided over by the mysterious power of Karma.

When Tomozō came the next morning to call his master as usual, he obtained no response to his knocking. At last he entered the apartment, and there, under the mosquito-net, lay his master dead, and beside him were the white bones of a woman. The bones of "Morning Dew" were twined round the neck of one who had loved her too well, of one who had loved her with a fierce passion that at the last had been his undoing.

CHAPTER XIX : KŌBŌ DAISHI, NICHIREN, AND SHŌDŌ SHONIN

"When he died it was as though a bright light had
gone out in the midst of a black night."
"Namudaishi." (Trans. by ARTHUR LLOYD.)

The "Namudaishi"

K ŌBŌ DAISHI[1] ("Glory to the Great Teacher"),
who was born A.D. 774, was the most holy and
most famous of the Japanese Buddhist saints.
He founded the Shingon-shū, a Buddhist sect remarkable for its magical formulæ and for its abstruse and
esoteric teachings, and he is also said to have invented
the *Hiragana* syllabary, a form of running script. In
the *Namudaishi,* which is a Japanese poem on the life
of this great saint, we are informed that Kōbō Daishi
brought back with him from China a millstone and
some seeds of the tea-plant, and thus revived the drinking of this beverage, which had fallen into disuse. We
are also told in the same poem that it was Kōbō Daishi
who "demonstrated to the world the use of coal." He
was renowned as a great preacher, but was not less
famous as a calligraphist, painter, sculptor, and traveller.

"A Divine Prodigy"

Kōbō Daishi, however, is essentially famous for the
extraordinary miracles which he performed, and numerous are the legends associated with him. His conception was miraculous, for when he was born in the
Baron's Hall, on the shore of Byōbu, a bright light shone,
and he came into the world with his hands folded as if
in prayer. When but five years of age he would sit

[1] The saint's name when living was Kūkai. Kōbō Daishi was a
posthumous title, and it is by this title that he is generally known.

among the lotuses and converse with Buddhas, and he kept secret all the wisdom he thus obtained. His heart was troubled by the sorrow and pain of humanity. While on Mount Shashin he sought to sacrifice his own life by way of propitiation, but he was prevented from doing so by a number of angels who would not allow this ardent soul to suffer death until he had fulfilled his destiny. His very games were of a religious nature. On one occasion he built a clay pagoda, and he was immediately surrounded by the Four Heavenly Kings (originally Hindu deities). The Imperial Messenger, who happened to pass by when this miracle took place, was utterly amazed, and described the young Kōbo Daishi as "a divine prodigy." While at Muroto, in Tosa, performing his devotions, we are told in the *Namu-daishi* that a bright star fell from Heaven and entered his mouth, while at midnight an evil dragon came forth against him, "but he spat upon it, and with his saliva he killed it."

In his nineteenth year he wore the black silk robes of a Buddhist priest, and with a zeal that never failed him sought for enlightenment. "Many are the ways," he said; "but Buddhism is the best of all." During his mystical studies he came across a book containing the Shingon doctrine, a doctrine that closely resembles the old Egyptian speculations. The book was so abstruse that even Kōbo Daishi failed to master it; but, nothing daunted, he received permission from the Emperor to visit China, where he ultimately unravelled its profound mysteries, and attained to that degree of saintship associated with the miraculous.

Gohitsu-Oshō

When Kōbo Daishi was in China the Emperor, hearing of his fame, sent for him and bade him rewrite the name of a certain room in the royal palace, a name that had become obliterated by the effacing finger of Time. Kōbō Daishi, with a brush in each hand, another in his mouth, and two others between the toes, wrote the characters required upon the wall, and for this extraordinary performance the Emperor named him Gohitsu-Oshō ("The Priest who writes with Five Brushes").

Writing on Sky and Water

While still in China Kōbō Daishi met a boy standing by the side of a river. "If you be Kōbō Daishi," said he, "be honourably pleased to write upon the sky, for I have heard that no wonder is beyond your power."

Kōbō Daishi raised his brush; it moved quickly in the air, and writing appeared in the blue sky, characters that were perfectly formed and wonderfully beautiful.

When the boy had also written upon the sky with no less skill, he said to Kōbō Daishi: "We have both written upon the sky. Now I beg that you will write upon this flowing river."

Kōbō Daishi readily complied. Once again his brush moved, and this time a poem appeared on the water, a poem written in praise of that particular river. The letters lingered for a moment, and then were carried away by the swift current.

There seems to have been a contest in magical power between these two workers of marvels, for no sooner had the letters passed out of sight than the boy also wrote upon the running water the character of the Dragon, and it remained stationary.

Kōbō Daishi, who was a great scholar, at once perceived that the boy had omitted the *ten*, a dot which rightly belonged to this character. When Kōbō Daishi pointed out the error, the boy told him that he had forgotten to insert the *ten*, and begged that the famous saint would put it in for him. No sooner had Kōbō Daishi done so than the Dragon character became a Dragon. Its tail lashed the waters, thunder-clouds sped across the sky, and lightning flashed. In another moment the Dragon arose from the water and ascended to heaven.

Though Kōbō Daishi's powers of magic excelled those of the boy, he inquired who this youth might be, and the boy replied: " I am Monju Bosatsu, the Lord of Wisdom." Having spoken these words, he became illumined by a radiant light ; the beauty of the Gods shone upon his countenance, and, like the Dragon, he ascended into heaven.

How Kōbō Daishi Painted the Ten

On one occasion Kōbō Daishi omitted the *ten* on a tablet placed above one of the gates of the Emperor's palace.[1] The Emperor commanded that ladders should be brought; but Kōbō Daishi, without making use of them, stood upon the ground, and threw up his brush, which, after making the *ten*, fell into his hand.

Kino Momoye and Onomo Toku

Kino Momoye once ridiculed some of Kōbō Daishi's characters, and said that one of them resembled a conceited wrestler. On the night he made this foolish jest Momoye dreamed that a wrestler struck him blow upon blow—moreover, that his antagonist leapt upon his body, causing him considerable pain. Momoye awoke, and cried aloud in his agony, and as he cried he saw the wrestler suddenly change into the character he had so unwisely jeered at. It rose into the air, and went back to the tablet from whence it had come.

[1] Hence the Japanese proverb : " Even Kōbō Daishi sometimes wrote wrong."

Momoye was not the only man who imprudently scoffed at the great Kōbō Daishi's work. Legend records that one named Onomo Toku said that the saint's character *Shu* was far more like the character " rice." That night Onomo Toku had good reason to regret his folly, for in a dream the character *Shu* took bodily form and became a rice-cleaner, who moved up and down the offender's body after the manner of hammers that were used in beating this grain. When Onomo Toku awoke it was to find that his body was covered with bruises and that his flesh was bleeding in many places.

Kōbō Daishi's Return

When Kōbō Daishi was about to leave China and return to his own country he went down to the seashore and threw his *vajra* [1] across the ocean waves, and it was afterwards found hanging on the branch of a pine-tree at Takano, in Japan.

We are not told anything about Kōbō Daishi's voyage to his own land; but directly he arrived in Japan he gave thanks for the divine protection he had received during his travels. On the Naked Mountain he offered incantations of so powerful a nature that the once barren mountain became covered with flowers and trees.

Kōbō Daishi, as time advanced, became still more holy. During a religious discussion the Divine Light streamed from him, and he continued to perform many great marvels. He made brackish water pure, raised the dead to life, and continued to commune with certain gods. On one occasion Inari,[2] the God of Rice,

---

[1] An instrument of incantation somewhat resembling a thunderbolt.

[2] At a later period Inari was known as the Fox God. See Chapter V.

appeared on Mount Fushimé and took from the great saint the sacrifice he offered. "Together, you and I," said Kōbō Daishi, "we will protect this people."

The Death of Kōbō Daishi

In A.D. 834 this remarkable saint died, and we are told that a very great gathering, both lay and priestly, wept at the graveyard of Okunoin, in Kōya, where he was buried. His death, however, by no means meant a sudden cessation of miracles on his part, for when the Emperor Saga died "his coffin was mysteriously borne through the air to Kōya, and Kōbō himself, coming forth from his grave, performed the funeral obsequies." Nor did the wonders cease with this incident, for the Emperor Uda received from Kōbō Daishi the sacred Baptism. When the Imperial Messenger to the temple where Kōbō Daishi was worshipped was unable to see the face of this great saint, Kōbō "guided the worshipper's hand to touch his knee. Never, as long as he lived, did the Messenger forget that feeling!"

A Miraculous Image

At Kawasaki there is a temple dedicated to Kōbō Daishi. "Local legend attributes the sanctity of this place to an image of Kōbō Daishi carved by that saint himself while in China, and consigned by him to the waves. It floated to this coast, where it was caught in a fisherman's net, and, being conveyed ashore, performed numerous miracles. The trees in the temple grounds, trained in the shape of junks under sail, attest the devotion paid to this holy image by the seafaring folk."[1]

[1] *Murray's Handbook for Japan*, by B. H. Chamberlain and W. B. Mason.

Nichiren

Nichiren was the founder of the Buddhist sect which
bears his name. His name means Sun Lotus, and was
given to him because his mother dreamt that the sun
rested on a lotus when she conceived him. Nichiren
was an iconoclast of very marked character. He received,
by revelation, a complete knowledge of Buddhist mysteries, though in reading the story of his life one would
have supposed that he acquired his remarkable religious
wisdom through arduous study. During his lifetime
Japan was visited by a terrible earthquake, followed by
a destructive hurricane, pestilence, and famine. So great
were these calamities that men prayed to die rather than
live amidst such universal misery. Nichiren saw in these
great disasters the hand of Fate. He saw that religion
and politics had become corrupt, and that Nature had
rebelled against the numerous evils that existed at that
time. Nichiren realised that Buddhism was no longer
the simple teaching of the Lord Buddha. In the various
Buddhist sects he had studied so diligently he found
that the priests had neglected Shaka Muni (the Buddha),
and worshipped Amida, a manifestation of the Lord
Buddha, instead. Nor did their heresy end there, for
he found that priests and people also worshipped Kwannon and other divinities. Nichiren desired to sweep
these deities aside and to restore Buddhism to its old
purity and singleness of purpose. He cried in one of
his sermons : " Awake, men, awake ! Awake and look
around you. No man is born with two fathers or two
mothers. Look at the heavens above you : there are
no two suns in the sky. Look at the earth at your
feet : no two kings can rule a country." In other
words, he implied that no one can serve two masters,
and the only master he found to be worthy of service

and worship was Buddha himself. With this belief he sought to replace the ordinary *mantra*, *Namu Amida Butsu*, by *Namu Myōhō Renge Kyō* ("Oh, the Scripture of the Lotus of the Wonderful Law !").

Nichiren wrote *Risshō Ankōku Ron* ("Book to Tranquillise the Country"), which contained the prediction of a Mongol invasion and many bitter attacks against the other Buddhist sects. At length Hōjō Tokiyori was compelled to exile him to Ito for thirty years. He escaped, however, and renewed his heated attacks upon the rival sects. Nichiren's enemies sought assistance from the Regent Tokimune, who decided to have the monk beheaded, and the vindictive Nichiren was finally sent to the beach of Koshigoye to be executed. While awaiting the fatal stroke Nichiren prayed to Buddha, and the sword broke as it touched his neck. Nor was this the only miracle, for immediately after the breaking of the sword a flash of lightning struck the palace at Kamakura, and a heavenly light surrounded the saintly Nichiren. The official entrusted with the deed of execution was considerably impressed by these supernatural events, and he sent a messenger to the Regent for a reprieve. Tokimune, however, had sent a horseman bearing a pardon, and the two men met at a river now called Yukiai ("Place of Meeting.")

Nichiren's miraculous escape was followed by an even more vigorous attack on those whom he considered were not of the true religion. He was again exiled, and finally took up his abode on Mount Minobu. It is said that a beautiful woman came to this mountain whilst Nichiren was praying. When the great saint saw her, he said : "Resume your natural state." After the woman had drunk water she changed into a snake nearly twenty feet long, with iron teeth and golden scales.

Shōdō Shonin

Shōdō Shonin was the founder of the first Buddhist temple at Nikko, and the following legend is supposed to have led to the construction of the sacred bridge of Nikko. One day, while Shōdō Shonin was on a journey, he saw four strange-looking clouds rise from the earth to the sky. He pressed forward in order to see them more clearly, but could not go far, for he found that his road was barred by a wild torrent. While he was praying for some means to continue his journey a gigantic figure appeared before him, clad in blue and black robes, with a necklace of skulls. The mysterious being cried to him from the opposite bank, saying: "I will help you as I once helped Hiuen." Having uttered these words, the Deity threw two blue and green snakes across the river, and on this bridge of snakes the priest was able to cross the torrent. When Shōdō Shonin had reached the other bank the God and his blue and green snakes disappeared.

CHAPTER XX : FANS

The Significance of the Japanese Fan

HER weapons are a smile and a little fan. This quotation from Mr. Yone Noguchi only illustrates one phase of the Japanese fan, the phase with which we are familiar in our own country. The Japanese fan is not merely a dainty feminine trifle to be used in conjunction with a smile or with eyes peeping behind some exquisite floral design. Nippon's fan has a fascinating history quite outside the gentle art of coquetry, and those who are interested in this subject would do well to consult Mrs. C. M. Salwey's *Fans of Japan*. Here the reader will find that the fan of the Land of the Rising Sun has performed many important offices. It has been used by ancient warriors on the battlefield as a means of giving emphasis to their commands. On one occasion it was the mark of Nasu no Yoichi's bow, and although the sun-marked fan was whirling in the wind, tied to a staff in the gunwale of one of the Taira ships, Yoichi brought it down:

> " Alas ! the fan !
> Now driftwood on the sea.
> The lord Nasu,
> Skilful with the bow,
> Yoichi's fame is spread."

A certain Japanese fan, of gigantic size, is used in the festival of the Sun Goddess in Ise, and there is a pretty story told of the widow of Atsumori becoming a nun and curing a priest by fanning him with the first folding fan, which is said to have been her own invention.

One of the most important parts of the Japanese fan, as of any other, is the rivet, and concerning the rivet there is the following legend. Kashima on one occasion stuck his sword through the earth, with the idea of steadying the world and thus preventing earthquakes, phenomena still prevalent in Japan. Eventually the sword turned into stones, and it was called *Kaname ishi*, or the Rivet Rock, and this was the origin of the name *kaname* as applied to Japanese fans.

Mrs. C. M. Salwey tells us in an article entitled *On Symbolism and Symbolic Ceremonies of the Japanese*[1] that the folding fan symbolises life itself. She writes : " The rivet end typifies the starting-point, the radiating limbs the road of life. . . . The outside frame-sticks specify the parents, the inside limbs the children, to show that children must be under control all their life long." On the frame there is often a cat's eye, suggesting the rapid passing of time, or, again, |there is a series of circles, one linked into the other—an incomplete design, showing that " life and wisdom can never be exhausted."

There is a legend concerning the Japanese fan that is extremely pleasing, and neither war nor philosophy figures in it. Though the story of the Japanese fan is wide and varied, it appeals to us most in its more tender aspect. The Japanese fan that has a love-poem upon it and a love-story behind it is the fan that will always be the most precious to those who still keep a place for romance in their hearts. The following legend is from *The Diary of a Convolvulus*.

The Love of Asagao

> " The morning glory
> Her leaves and bells has bound
> My bucket-handle round.
> I would not break the bands
> Of those soft hands.

[1] *Asiatic Quarterly Review*, October 1894.

THE LOVE OF ASAGAO

The bucket and the well to her I left:
Lend me some water, for I come bereft."

From the Japanese. (Trans. by SIR EDWIN ARNOLD.)

Komagawa Miyagi, a retainer of one of the *daimyōs*, came to a suburb of Kyōto. As it happened to be a warm summer evening he hired a boat, and, forgetting all his worries, he watched many bright-robed little ladies catching fireflies. In the air and on the grass these bright insects shone, so that the laughing ladies had many opportunities of catching these living jewels and placing them for a moment in their hair, upon poised finger, or against a silk flower on a *kimono*.

While Komagawa watched this pretty scene he saw that one of the ladies was in difficulty with her boat. Komagawa at once came to her assistance, and there and then fell desperately in love with her. They lingered together in a cool recess on the river, and no longer troubled about fireflies, for both were eager to express their love.

In order to pledge their vows these two lovers, according to an ancient custom, exchanged fans. On Miyuki's fan there was a painting of a convolvulus. Komagawa wrote a poem about this lovely flower upon his own fan before presenting it to the woman he loved. So it was that their fans and their vows were exchanged, and the convovulus, in picture and in verse, became the pledge of their troth.

Eventually the lovers separated, to meet again a few days later at Akasha, where it chanced that their ships touched each other. When they had exchanged many a fair and loving word they returned to their respective homes.

When Miyuki reached her home, radiant with thoughts of her true love, she discovered that her parents had already arranged a marriage for her with some one the poor little woman had never seen.

Miyuki heard this piece of news with an aching heart. She knew that children must obey their parents, and when she was lying down on her *futon* she did her utmost to comply with her parents' wish. But the struggle proved useless, for the form of her lover kept on coming back to her, and the river and the gleaming fireflies. So she arose, crept out of the house, and walked towards a certain town, hoping to find Komagawa, only to discover on her arrival that he had departed, no one knew whither.

This bitter disappointment much affected Miyuki, and she wept for many days. Her salt tears flowed so persistently that she soon became quite blind, as helpless a creature as " a bird without feathers or a fish without fins."

Miyuki, after she had given way to grief for some time, discovered that if she did not wish to starve she must do something to earn a living. She made up her mind to make use of her excellent voice and to sing in streets or in tea-houses. Her voice, combined with her beautiful and pathetic face, won instant recognition. People wept over her plaintive singing without knowing why. She loved to sing the little poem about the convolvulus Komagawa had written on his fan, so the people who heard her called her Asagao ("Convolvulus").

The blind maiden was led from place to place by her friend Asaka ("Slight Fragrance"), till some one killed her, and Asagao was left alone to tap out her dark journeys without a loving hand to guide her. There was only one thought that consoled Asagao, and that was that she might, in her wanderings, eventually meet her lover.

When a few years had passed by it chanced that Komagawa, accompanied by Iwashiro Takita, was sent on business by his *Daimyō*. While on their journey they happened to enter a certain tea-house. Iwashiro Takita was sullen and morose, and sat in gloomy silence, not deigning to notice his surroundings. Komagawa, on the other hand, looked about him, and saw on a screen the very poem he had written about the convolvulus, the poem he had so lovingly inscribed for Asagao. While pondering the matter in his mind the master of the tea-house entered the apartment. Komagawa questioned him concerning this little love-poem, and the master of the tea-house told the following story:

"It is a very sad story," said he. "The poem was sung by a poor blind lady. She ran away from her home because she could not marry the man her parents had chosen for her. She was unable to consent to the union because she already had a lover, and this lover she sought up and down the country, ever singing this little poem about the convolvulus, in the hope that some day she might have the good fortune to meet him. Honourable sir, at this very moment she is in my tea-garden!"

Komagawa could scarcely conceal his joy when he requested that the master of the tea-house would bring in the blind woman.

In another moment Asagao stood before him. He saw in her delicate face an added beauty, the beauty of a hope, of a love kept bright and clear through the long, sorrowful years of waiting.

Asagao touched the *samisen*.[1] Very gently she sang:

"Down fell the shower of silver rain and wet the poor Convolvulus,
The sweet dew on the leaves and flowers being taken away by the jealous sun."

[1] "The *samisen*, or 'three strings,' now the favourite instrument of the singing-girls and of the lower classes generally, seems to have been introduced from Manila as recently as the year 1700."—*Things Japanese*, by B. H. Chamberlain.

Komagawa listened intently, longing to speak, longing
to reveal his love, yet keeping silent because his ill-bred
companion still remained in the room. He watched her
dark eyes fixed upon him, but they were without expression, for they could not see. Still the *samisen* tinkled,
and still the voice sounded sweet and low and un-
speakably pathetic in the apartment. With an aching
heart and without a word of love he dismissed her with
the usual fee. She walked out of the room as if conscious
of a new, acute sorrow. There was something in her
patron's voice that was extremely tender, something that
moved her deeply, and it made her heart ache and yearn
without knowing why.

The next day Komagawa gave the master of the tea-
house a fan, saying: "Give this fan and money to
Asagao. She will understand." With these words
Komagawa and his companion proceeded on their
journey.

When Asagao had received the fan she felt it eagerly
with her small white fingers. "Who has given me this
fan and money?" she inquired. "Oh, tell me what
the fan is like. Has it a drawing of a convolvulus?"

The master of the tea-house looked at her gently.
"He to whom you sang last night gave you this fan,"
said he. "There is a drawing of a convolvulus upon it."

Asagao gave a cry of joy. "Last night," she said
softly, "I was with my lover again! And now, and
now . . ."

At this very moment a servant from Asagao's old
home arrived, asserting that he had been sent by her
parents to bring her back again. But Asagao, true to
her old love, determined to fight down all opposition.

Now it happened that the master of this tea-house
had once been employed by Asagao's father. He had
committed a great wrong in that capacity, a wrong

worthy of death ; but Asagao's father had taken pity upon him.   He had dismissed him with money, which had enabled the wrongdoer to set up in business for himself.   During this crisis the master of the tea-house thought over the kindness that had been shown him, and resolved to commit *seppuku* in order that his old master's child might receive her sight again by means of this brave man's liver.[1]

So the master of the tea-house killed himself, and Asagao received her sight.   That very night, though there was a fierce tempest raging, she set out in search of her lover, accompanied by a faithful little band of servants.   All night the maiden journeyed over rough and rugged roads.   She scarcely noticed the heavy rain or her bleeding feet.   She was urged on by a joyous love, by the fond hope of finding her lover again.

As she climbed a mountain, now bathed in sunlight, she fancied she heard a voice calling her name.   She looked about her and discovered Komagawa.   Peace came to her then.   All the weariness of long search and almost endless waiting were over for ever, and in a little while the lovers were married.   The convolvulus, or morning glory, is a flower that only blooms for a few hours ; but Asagao's love had the beauty of the convolvulus combined with the strength and long life of the pine.   In their happy union they had remained true to the pledge of love upon their fans, and out of blindness and much suffering Asagao could hold up her fair head to the dew and sunshine of her lover's sheltering arms.

---

[1] The liver, both of man and animal, was supposed to have remarkable medicinal properties.   It frequently occurs in Japanese legends, but the idea was probably borrowed from the strangest pharmacopœia in the world, that of the Chinese.

CHAPTER XXI : THUNDER

"The earth is full of saltpetre and sulphur, which rise in the form of mist, and, uniting in the sky, become a vapour that possesses the properties of gunpowder. When this nears the intense heat of the sun it explodes, like a natural gas ; and the terrible sound is heard by all the world. The shock, striking animals and birds wandering in the clouds, hurls them to the ground. Therefore thunder, and lightning, and the creatures that tumble from the clouds during a storm, are not one and the same thing."

"*Shin-rai-ki*" (*Record of Thunder*).

Raiden

THERE are many quaint legends in regard to thunder, and in Bakin's *Kumono Tayema Ama Yo No Tsuki*[1] ("The Moon, shining through a Cloud-rift, on a Rainy Night") the famous Japanese novelist, who is an ardent believer in many of the superstitions of his country, has much to say in regard to Raiden, the God of Thunder, and the supernatural beings associated with him. Raiden is usually depicted as having red skin, the face of a demon, with two claws on each foot, and carrying on his back a great wheel or arc of drums. He is often found in company with Fugin, or with his son, Raitaro. When the Mongols attempted to invade Japan they were prevented from doing so by a great storm, and, according to legend, only three men escaped to tell the tale. Raiden's assistance in favour of Japan is often portrayed in Japanese art. He is depicted sitting on the clouds emitting lightning, and sending forth a shower of arrows upon the invaders. In China the Thunder God is regarded as a being ever on the look-out for wicked people. When he finds

---

[1] See translation, entitled *A Captive of Love*, by Edward Greey.

them, the Goddess of Lightning flashes a mirror upon those whom the God wishes to strike.

The Thunder Animal

Raijū, or Thunder Animal, appears to be more closely associated with lightning than with thunder. He is seen in forms resembling a weasel, badger, or monkey. In the *Shin-rai-ki* ("Thunder Record") we read the following : " On the twenty-second day of the sixth month of the second year of Meiwa [July 1766] a Thunder Animal fell at Ōyama [Great Mountain], in the province of Sagami. It was captured by a farmer, who brought it to Yedo, and exhibited it for money on the Riyo-goku Bridge. The creature was a little larger than a cat, and resembled a weasel : it had black hair, and five claws on each paw. During fine weather it was very tame and gentle ; but, before and during a storm, exceedingly savage and unmanageable." In China the Thunder Animal is described as having " the head of a monkey, with crimson lips, eyes like mirrors, and two sharp claws on each paw." During a storm the Thunder Animal of Japan springs from tree to tree, and if any of the trees are found to have been struck by lightning it is believed to be the savage work of the Thunder Animal's claws. This being, in common with the Thunder God himself, is said to have a weakness for human navels, so that for this reason many superstitious people endeavour, if possible, to lie flat on their stomachs during a thunderstorm. Bark torn by the Thunder Animal is carefully preserved, and is supposed to be an excellent remedy for toothache.

The Thunder Bird and Thunder Woman

Raicho, Thunder Bird, resembles a rook, but it has spurs of flesh, which, when struck together, produce a horrible sound. This is the bird to which the Emperor of Goto-bain referred in the following poem:

> " In the shadow of the pine-tree of Shiro-yama
> Thunder-birds rest, and spend the night."

These birds feed upon the tree-frog named *rai* (thunder), and are always seen flying about in the sky during a thunderstorm.

Little is known concerning Kaminari (Thunder Woman), except that on one occasion she is said to have appeared in the guise of a Chinese Empress.

A Strange Belief

Bakin remarks that those who are afraid of thunder have the *In*, or female principle, predominating, while those who are not afraid have the *Yo*, or the male principle, in the ascendency. The same writer gives the following custom in regard to those who have suffered as the result of a thunderstorm, and we must note that emphasis is laid upon *thunder* as the destructive power— noise rather than light : " When any one is struck by thunder make him lie upon his back, and place a live carp in his bosom. If the carp jumps and moves the patient will recover. This is infallible. When thunder scorches the flesh burn *Ko* (incense) under the sufferer's nose. This will cause him to cough, and break the spell of the Thunder God."

The Child of the Thunder God

Most of the legends relating to Raiden and his kindred spirits are of a malevolent nature ; but in the following story we learn that the Thunder God's child brought considerable prosperity.

Near Mount Hakuzan there once lived a very poor farmer named Bimbo. His plot of land was extremely small, and though he worked upon it from dawn till sunset he had great difficulty in growing sufficient rice for himself and his wife.

One day, after a protracted drought, Bimbo dismally surveyed his dried-up rice sprouts. As he thus stood fearing starvation in the near future, rain suddenly descended, accompanied by loud claps of thunder. Just as Bimbo was about to take shelter from the storm he was nearly blinded by a vivid flash of lightning, and he prayed fervently to Buddha for protection. When he had done so he looked about him, and to his amazement saw a little baby boy laughing and crooning as he lay in the grass.

Bimbo took the infant in his arms, and gently carried him to his humble dwelling, where his wife greeted him with surprise and pleasure. The child was called Raitaro, the Child of Thunder, and lived with his foster-parents a happy and dutiful boy. He never played with other children, for he loved to roam in the fields, to watch the stream and the swift flight of clouds overhead.

With the coming of Raitaro there came prosperity to Bimbo, for Raitaro could beckon to clouds and bid them throw down their rain-drops only on his foster-father's field.

When Raitaro had grown into a handsome youth of eighteen he once again thanked Bimbo and his wife for all they had done for him, and told them that he must now bid farewell to his benefactors.

Almost before the youth had finished speaking, he suddenly turned into a small white dragon, lingered a moment, and then flew away.

The old couple ran to the door. As the white dragon ascended into the sky it grew bigger and bigger, till it was hidden behind a great cloud.

When Bimbo and his wife died a white dragon was carved upon their tomb in memory of Raitaro, the Child of Thunder.

Shokuro and the Thunder God

Shokuro, in order to stand well with Toru, the magistrate of his district, promised him that he would catch the Thunder God. "If," said Shokuro, "I were to tie a human navel to the end of a kite, and fly it during a stormy day, I should be sure to catch Raiden, for the Thunder God would not be able to resist such a repast. The most difficult part of the whole business is to secure the meal."

With this scheme in view Shokuro set out upon a journey in quest of food for the Thunder God. On reaching a wood he chanced to see a beautiful woman named Chiyo. The ambitious Shokuro, without the least compunction, killed the maid, and, having secured his object, flung her corpse into a deep ditch. He then proceeded on his way with a light heart.

Raiden, while sitting on a cloud, happened to notice the woman's body lying in a ditch. He descended quickly, and, being fascinated by the beauty of Chiyo, he took from his mouth a navel, restored her to life, and together they flew away into the sky.

Some days later Shokuro was out hunting for the Thunder God, his kite, with its gruesome relic, soaring high over the trees as it flew hither and thither in a strong wind. Chiyo saw the kite, and descended nearer and nearer to the earth. At last she held it in her hands and saw what was attached. Filled with indignation, she looked down in order to see who was flying the kite, and was much astonished to recognise her murderer. At this juncture Raiden descended in a rage, only to receive severe chastisement at the hands of Shokuro, who then made his peace with Chiyo, and afterwards became a famous man in the village. Truly an astonishing story!

CHAPTER XXII : ANIMAL LEGENDS

Magical Animals

MANY of the following stories are the tales a
Japanese mother narrates to her child, for
animal stories make a universal appeal to the
child-mind. They are generally regarded as fairy stories,
but they contain so much legendary material that it is
necessary to include them in a book of this kind, for
they tend to illustrate our subject in a lighter vein, where
the miraculous is mingled with the humorous. We
have devoted a separate chapter to fox legends on
account of the importance of the subject, but it must be
borne in mind that the supernatural characteristics of
this animal apply also to the badger and cat, for in
Japanese legend all three animals have been associated
with an incalculable amount of mischief.

The Hare

The hare is supposed to attain, like the fox, tortoise,
crane, and tiger, a fabulous age, extending to no less
than a thousand years. In Taoist legends the hare is
said to live in the moon, and is occupied in pounding,
with pestle and mortar, the drugs that compose the
Elixir of Life, while in other legends, as we have seen
elsewhere, this animal is represented as pounding rice.
Shaka Muni (the Lord Buddha), according to legend, is
said to have sacrificed himself as a hare in order that he
might appease the hunger of Indra, who drew the animal
upon the moon by way of showing his admiration. The
fur of the hare becomes white when it has lived for five
hundred years, and we give below the famous legend
from the *Kojiki* known as " The White Hare of
Inaba."

The White Hare of Inaba

In ancient days there were eighty-one brothers, who were Princes in Japan. With the exception of one brother they were quarrelsome fellows, and spent their time in showing all manner of petty jealousy, one toward the other. Each wanted to reign over the whole kingdom, and, in addition, each had the misfortune to wish to marry the Princess of Yakami, in Inaba. Although these eighty Princes were at variance in most things, they were at one in persistently hating the brother who was gentle and peaceful in all his ways.

At length, after many angry words, the eighty brothers decided to go to Inaba in order to visit the Princess of Yakami, each brother fully resolved that he and he alone should be the successful suitor. The kind and gentle brother accompanied them, not, indeed, as a wooer of the fair Princess, but as a servant who carried a large and heavy bag upon his back.

At last the eighty Princes, who had left their much-wronged brother far behind, arrived at Cape Keta. They were about to continue their journey when they saw a white hare lying on the ground looking very miserable and entirely divested of fur.

The eighty Princes, who were much amused by the sorry plight of the hare, said : "If you want your fur to grow again, bathe in the sea, and, when you have done so, run to the summit of a high mountain and allow the wind to blow upon you." With these words the eighty heartless Princes proceeded on their way.

The hare at once went down to the sea, delighted at the prospect of regaining his handsome white fur. Having bathed, he ran up to the top of a mountain and lay down upon it ; but he quickly perceived that the cold wind blowing on a skin recently immersed in salt water was beginning to crack and split. In addition to the humiliation of having no fur he now suffered considerable physical pain, and he realised that the eighty Princes had shamefully deceived him.

While the hare was lying in pain upon the mountain the kind and gentle brother approached, slowly and laboriously, owing to the heavy bag he carried. When he saw the weeping hare he inquired how it was that the poor animal had met with such a misfortune.

"Please stop a moment," said the hare, "and I will tell you how it all happened. I wanted to cross from the Island of Oki to Cape Keta, so I said to the crocodiles: 'I should very much like to know how many crocodiles there are in the sea, and how many hares on land. Allow me first of all to count you.' And having said these words the crocodiles formed themselves into a long line, stretching from the Island of Oki to Cape Keta. I ran across their horny bodies, counting each as I passed. When I reached the last crocodile, I said : 'O foolish crocodiles, it doesn't matter to me how many there are of you in the sea, or how many hares on land ! I only wanted you for a bridge in order that I might reach my destination.' Alas ! my miserable boast cost me dear, for the last crocodile raised his head and snapped off all my fur !"

"Well," said the gentle brother, "I must say you were in the wrong and deserved to suffer for your folly. Is that the end of your story ?"

"No," continued the hare. "I had no sooner suffered this indignity than the eighty Princes came by, and lyingly told me that I might be cured by salt water and wind. Alas ! not knowing that they deceived me, I carried out their instructions, with the result that my body is cracked and extremely sore."

"Bathe in fresh water, my poor friend," said the

good brother, "and when you have done so scatter the pollen of sedges upon the ground and roll yourself in it. This will indeed heal your sores and cause your fur to grow again."

The hare walked slowly to the river, bathed himself, and then rolled about in sedge pollen. He had no sooner done so than his skin healed and he was covered once more with a thick coat of fur.

The grateful hare ran back to his benefactor. "Those eighty wicked and cruel brothers of yours," said he, "shall never win the Princess of Inaba. It is you who shall marry her and reign over the country."

The hare's prophecy came true, for the eighty Princes failed in their mission, while the brother who was good and kind to the white hare married the fair Princess and became King of the country.

The Crackling Mountain

An old man and his wife kept a white hare. One day a badger came and ate the food provided for the pet. The mischievous animal was about to scamper away when the old man, seeing what had taken place, tied the badger to a tree, and then went to a neighbouring mountain to cut wood.

When the old man had gone on his journey the badger began to weep and to beg that the old woman would untie the rope. She had no sooner done so than the badger proclaimed vengeance and ran away.

When the good white hare heard what had taken place he set out to warn his master; but during his absence the badger returned, killed the old woman, assumed her form, and converted her corpse into broth.

"I have made such excellent broth," said the badger, when the old man returned from the mountain. "You must be hungry and tired : pray sit down and make a good meal !"

The old man, not suspecting treachery of any kind, consumed the broth and pronounced it excellent.

"Excellent ?" sneered the badger. "You have eaten your wife! Her bones lie over there in that corner," and with these words he disappeared.

While the old man was overcome with sorrow, and while he wept and bewailed his fate, the hare returned, grasped the situation, and scampered off to the mountain fully resolved to avenge the death of his poor old mistress.

When the hare reached the mountain he saw the badger carrying a bundle of sticks on his back. Softly the hare crept up, and, unobserved, set light to the sticks, which began to crackle immediately.

"This is a strange noise," said the badger. "What is it ?"

"The Crackling Mountain," replied the hare.

The fire began to burn the badger, so he sprang into a river and extinguished the flames ; but on getting out again he found that his back was severely burnt, and the pain he suffered was increased by a cayenne poultice which the delighted hare provided for that purpose.

When the badger was well again he chanced to see the hare standing by a boat he had made.

"Where are you going in that vessel ?" inquired the badger.

"To the moon," replied the hare. "Perhaps you would like to come with me ?"

"Not in your boat !" said the badger. "I know too well your tricks on the Crackling Mountain. But I will build a boat of clay for myself, and we will journey to the moon."

Down the river went the wooden boat of the hare

and the clay boat of the badger. Presently the badger's vessel began to come to pieces. The hare laughed derisively, and killed his enemy with his oar. Later on, when the loyal animal returned to the old man, he justly received much praise and loving care from his grateful master.

The Badger

The badger in legend has much in common with the fox. It can adopt human form and assume the shape of the moon ; but in many legends it is described as a humorous creature, an animal intensely fond of a practical joke. The badger is frequently depicted in legend and art as playing a tattoo on its protuberant and drum-like stomach, and it is for this reason that Japanese jesters are sometimes called badgers.

Kadzutoyo and the Badger

On one occasion Kadzutoyo and his retainer went fishing. They had had excellent sport, and were about to return home, when a violent shower came on, and they were forced to take shelter under a willow-tree. After waiting for some time the rain showed no sign of abating, and as it was already growing dark they decided to continue their journey in spite of the inclement weather. They had not proceeded far when they perceived a young girl weeping bitterly. Kadzutoyo regarded her with suspicion, but his retainer was charmed by the maiden's great beauty, and inquired who she was and why she lingered on such a stormy night.

"Alas ! good sir," said the maiden, still weeping, "my tale is a sad one. I have long endured the taunts and cruelties of my wicked stepmother, who hates me. To-night she spat upon me and beat me. I could bear

KADZUTOYO AND THE BADGER

the bitter humiliation no longer, and I was on the way
to my aunt, who lives in yonder village, there to receive
peace and shelter, when I was stricken down with a
strange malady, and compelled to remain here until the
pain subsided."

These words much affected the kind-hearted retainer,
and he fell desperately in love with this fair maiden ;
but Kadzutoyo, after carefully considering the matter,
drew his sword and cut off her head.

"Oh! my lord," said the retainer, "what awful deed
is this? How can you kill a harmless girl? Believe
me, you will have to pay for your folly."

"You do not understand," replied Kadzutoyo, "but
all I ask is that you keep silence in the matter."

When they reached home Kadzutoyo soon fell asleep ;
but his retainer, after brooding over the murder of the
fair maiden, went to his lord's parents and told them
the whole pitiful story.

Kadzutoyo's father was stricken with anger when he
heard the dreadful tale. He at once went to his son's
room, roused him, and said: "Oh, miserable murderer!
How could you slay an innocent girl without the least
provocation? You have shamed the honourable name
of *samurai*, a name that stands for true chivalry and
for the defence of the weak and helpless. You have
brought dishonour upon our house, and it is my duty
to take your life." Having said these words, he drew
his sword.

"Sir," replied Kadzutoyo, without flinching at the
shining weapon, "you, like my retainer, do not understand. It has been given me to solve certain mysteries,
and with that knowledge I assure you that I have not
been guilty of so foul a crime as you suppose, but have
been loyal to the fair calling of a *samurai*. The girl I
cut down with my sword was no mortal. Be pleased

to go to-morrow with your retainers to the spot where this scene occurred. If you find the corpse of a girl you will have no need to take my life, for I will disembowel myself."

Early next day, when the sun had scarce risen in the sky, Kadzutoyo's father, together with his retainers, set out upon the journey. When they reached the place where the tragedy had taken place the father saw lying by the roadside, not the corpse of a fair maiden as he had feared, but the body of a great headless badger.

When the father reached home again he questioned his son: "How is it," said he, "that what appeared to be a girl to your retainer seemed to you to be a badger?"

"Sir," replied Kadzutoyo, "the creature I saw last night appeared to me as a girl; but her beauty was strange, and not like the beauty of earthly women. Moreover, although it was raining hard, I observed that the garments of this being did not get wet, and having noticed this weird occurrence, I knew at once that the woman was none other than some wicked goblin. The creature took the form of a lovely maiden with the idea of bewitching us with her many charms, in the hope that she might get our fish."

The old Prince was filled with admiration for his son's cleverness. Having discovered so much foresight and prudence, he resolved to abdicate, and proclaim Kadzutoyo Prince of Tosa in his stead.

The Miraculous Tea-kettle

One day a priest of the Morinji temple put his old tea-kettle on the fire in order that he might make himself a cup of tea. No sooner had the kettle touched the fire than it suddenly changed into the head, tail, and legs of a badger. The novices of the temple were called in to see the extraordinary sight. While they gazed in utter astonishment, the badger, with the body of a kettle, rushed nimbly about the room, and finally flew into the air: Round and round the room went the merry badger, and the priests, after many efforts, succeeded in capturing the animal and thrusting it into a box.

Shortly after this event had taken place a tinker called at the temple, and the priest thought it would be an excellent idea if he could induce the good man to buy his extraordinary tea-kettle. He therefore took the [kettle out of its box, for it had now resumed its ordinary form, and commenced to bargain, with the result that the unsuspecting tinker purchased the kettle, and took it away with him, assured that he had done a good day's work in buying such a useful article at so reasonable a price.

That night the tinker was awakened by hearing a curious sound close to his pillow. He looked out from behind his quilts and saw that the kettle he had purchased was not a kettle at all, but a very lively and clever badger:

When the tinker told his friends about his remarkable companion, they said : " You are a fortunate fellow, and we advise you to take this badger on show, for it is clever enough to dance and walk on the tight-rope. With song and music you certainly have in this very strange creature a series of novel entertainments which will attract considerable notice, and bring you far more money than you would earn by all the tinkering in the world."

The tinker accordingly acted upon this excellent advice, and the fame of his performing badger spread far and wide. Princes and princesses came to see the show, and from royal patronage and the delight of the common people he amassed a great fortune. When the tinker had made his money he restored the kettle to the Morinji temple, where it was worshipped as a precious treasure.

The Cat

> " Feed a dog for three days and he will remember your kindness for three years ; feed a cat for three years and she will forget your kindness in three days."
>
> *A Japanese Proverb.*

The Japanese cat, with or without a tail, is very far from being popular, for this animal and the venomous serpent were the only two creatures that did not weep when the Lord Buddha died. Nipponese cats seem to be under a curse, and for the most part they are left to their own resourccs, resources frequently associated with supernatural powers. Like foxes and badgers, they are able to bewitch human beings. Professor B. H. Chamberlain writes in *Things Japanese :* " Among Europeans an irreverent person may somtimes be heard to describe an ugly, cross old woman as a cat. In Japan, the land of topsy-turvydom, that nickname is colloquially applied to the youngest and most attractive —the singing-girls." The comparison seems strange to us, but the allusion no doubt refers to the power of witchery common alike to the singing-girl and the cat.

The Japanese cat, however, is regarded with favour among sailors, and the *mike-neko,* or cat of three colours, is most highly prized. Sailors the world over are said to be superstitious, and those of Japan do their utmost to secure a ship's cat, in the belief that this animal will keep off the spirits of the deep. Many sailors believe that those who are drowned at sea never find spiritual repose ; they believe that they everlastingly lurk in the waves and shout and wail as junks pass by.

To such men the breakers beating on the seashore are the white, grasping hands of innumerable spirits, and they believe that the sea is crowded with *O-baké*, honourable ghosts. The Japanese cat is said to have control over the dead.

The Vampire Cat

The Prince of Hizen, a distinguished member of the Nabéshima family, lingered in the garden with O Toyo, the favourite among his ladies. When the sun set they retired to the palace, but failed to notice that they were being followed by a large cat.

O Toyo went to her room and fell asleep. At midnight she awoke and gazed about her, as if suddenly aware of some dreadful presence in the apartment. At length she saw, crouching close beside her, a gigantic cat, and before she could cry out for assistance the animal sprang upon her and strangled her. The animal then made a hole under the verandah, buried the corpse, and assumed the form of the beautiful O Toyo.

The Prince, who knew nothing of what had happened, continued to love the false O Toyo, unaware that in reality he was caressing a foul beast. He noticed, little by little, that his strength failed, and it was not long before he became dangerously ill. Physicians were summoned, but they could do nothing to restore the royal patient. It was observed that he suffered most during the night, and was troubled by horrible dreams. This being so his councillors arranged that a hundred retainers should sit with their lord and keep watch while he slept.

The watch went into the sick-room, but just before ten o'clock it was overcome by a mysterious drowsiness. When all the men were asleep the false O Toyo crept into the apartment and disturbed the Prince until sunrise. Night after night the retainers came to guard their master, but always they fell asleep at the same hour, and even three loyal councillors had a similar experience.

During this time the Prince grew worse, and at length a priest named Ruiten was appointed to pray on his behalf. One night, while he was engaged in his supplications, he heard a strange noise proceeding from the garden. On looking out of the window he saw a young soldier washing himself. When he had finished his ablutions he stood before an image of Buddha, and prayed most ardently for the recovery of the Prince.

Ruiten, delighted to find such zeal and loyalty, invited the young man to enter his house, and when he had done so inquired his name.

" I am Ito Soda," said the young man, " and serve in the infantry of Nabéshima. I have heard of my lord's sickness and long to have the honour of nursing him ; but being of low rank it is not meet that I should come into his presence. I have, nevertheless, prayed to the Buddha that my lord's life may be spared. I believe that the Prince of Hizen is bewitched, and if I might remain with him I would do my utmost to find and crush the evil power that is the cause of his illness."

Ruiten was so favourably impressed with these words that he went the next day to consult with one of the councillors, and after much discussion it was arranged that Ito Soda should keep watch with the hundred retainers.

When Ito Soda entered the royal apartment he saw that his master slept in the middle of the room, and he also observed the hundred retainers sitting in the chamber quietly chatting together in the hope that they would be able to keep off approaching drowsiness. By ten o'clock all the retainers, in spite of their efforts, had fallen asleep. Ito Soda tried to keep his eyes open, but a heaviness was gradually overcoming him, and he realised that if he wished to keep awake he must resort to extreme measures. When he had carefully spread oil-paper over the mats he stuck his dirk into his thigh. The sharp pain he experienced warded off sleep for a time, but eventually he felt his eyes closing once more. Resolved to outwit the spell which had proved too much for the retainers, he twisted the knife in his thigh, and thus increased the pain and kept his loyal watch, while blood continually dripped upon the oil-paper.

While Ito Soda watched he saw the sliding doors drawn open and a beautiful woman creep softly into the apartment. With a smile she noticed the sleeping re-tainers, and was about to approach the Prince when she observed Ito Soda. After she had spoken curtly to him she approached the Prince and inquired how he fared, but the Prince was too ill to make a reply. Ito Soda watched every movement, and believed she tried to bewitch the Prince, but she was always frustrated in her evil purpose by the dauntless eyes of Ito Soda, and at last she was compelled to retire.

In the morning the retainers awoke, and were filled with shame when they learnt how Ito Soda had kept his vigil. The councillors loudly praised the young soldier for his loyalty and enterprise, and he was commanded to keep watch again that night. He did so, and once more the false O Toyo entered the sick-room, and, as on the previous night, she was compelled to retreat without being able to cast her spell over the Prince.

It was discovered that immediately the faithful Soda had kept guard the Prince was able to obtain peaceful slumber, and, moreover, that he began to get better, for the false O Toyo, having been frustrated on two occasions, now kept away altogether, and the guard was not troubled with mysterious drowsiness. Soda, impressed by these strange circumstances, went to one of the councillors and informed him that the so-called O Toyo was a goblin of some kind.

That night Soda planned to go to the creature's room and try to kill her, arranging that in case she should escape there should be eight retainers outside waiting to capture her and despatch her immediately.

At the appointed hour Soda went to the creature's apartment, pretending that he bore a message from the Prince.

"What is your message?" inquired the woman.

"Kindly read this letter," replied Soda, and with these words he drew his dirk and tried to kill her.

The false O Toyo seized a halberd and endeavoured to strike her adversary. Blow followed blow, but at last perceiving that flight would serve her better than battle she threw away her weapon, and in a moment the lovely maiden turned into a cat and sprang on to the roof. The eight men waiting outside in case of emergency shot at the animal, but the creature succeeded in eluding them.

The cat made all speed for the mountains, and caused trouble among the people who lived in the vicinity, but was finally killed during a hunt ordered by the Prince Hizen. The Prince became well again, and Ito Soda received the honour and reward he so richly deserved.

The Dog

Generally speaking the dog in Japan is looked upon as a friendly animal, and in most legends he acquits himself well; but in the Oki Islands many of the inhabitants believe that all dogs have supernatural power, attributed to the fox elsewhere. Professor B. H. Chamberlain writes: "The human beings in league with them are termed *inu-gami-mochi*—that is, 'dog-god owners.' When the spirit of such a magic dog goes forth on an errand of mischief its body remains behind, growing gradually weaker, and sometimes dying and falling to decay. When this happens the spirit on its return takes up its abode in the body of a wizard, who thereupon becomes more powerful than ever."

Shippeitarō and the Phantom Cats

A certain knight took shelter in a lonely and dilapidated mountain temple. Towards midnight he was awakened by hearing a strange noise. Gazing about him, he saw a number of cats dancing and yelling and shrieking, and over and over again he heard these words: "*Tell it not to Shippeitarō !*"

At midnight the cats suddenly disappeared, stillness reigned in the ruined temple, and our warrior was able to resume his slumber.

The next morning the young knight left the haunted building, and came to one or two small dwellings near a village. As he passed one of these houses he heard great wailing and lamentation, and inquired the cause of the trouble.

"Alas !" said those who thronged about the knight, "well may you ask why we are so sorely troubled. This very night the mountain spirit will take away our fairest maiden in a great cage to the ruined temple where you have spent the night, and in the morning she will be devoured by the wicked spirit of the mountain. Every year we lose a girl in this way, and there is none to help us."

The knight, greatly moved by these pitiful words, and anxious to be of service, said: "Who or what is Shippeitarō ? The evil spirits in the ruined temple used the name several times."

" Shippeitarō," said one of the people, " is a brave and very fine dog, and belongs to the head man of our Prince."

The knight hastened off, was successful in securing Shippeitarō for one night, and took the dog back with him to the house of the weeping parents. Already the cage was prepared for the damsel, and into this cage he put Shippeitarō, and, with several young men to assist him, they reached the haunted temple. But the young men would not remain on the mountain, for they were full of fear, and, having performed their task, they took their departure, so that the knight and the dog were left alone.

At midnight the phantom cats again appeared, this time surrounding a tomcat of immense size and of great fierceness. When the monster cat saw the cage he sprang round it with screams of delight, accompanied by his companions.

The warrior, choosing a suitable opportunity, opened the cage, and Shippeitarō sprang out and held the great cat in his teeth. In another moment his master drew forth his sword and slew the wicked creature. The other cats were too amazed at what they had seen to make good their escape, and the valiant Shippeitarō soon made short work of them. Thus the village was no longer troubled with ravages of the mountain spirit, and the knight, in true courtly fashion, gave all the praise to the brave Shippeitarō.

The Old Man Who Made the Trees to Blossom

One day, while an old man and his wife were in the garden, their dog suddenly became very excited as he lowered his head and sniffed the ground in one particular place. The old people, believing that their pet had detected something good to eat, brought a spade and commenced to dig, and to their amazement they dug up a great number of gold and silver pieces and a variety of

precious treasures as well. With this newly acquired
wealth the old couple lost no time in distributing alms
among the poor.

When the people next door heard about their neighbours' good fortune they borrowed the dog, and spread
before him all manner of delicacies in the hope that the
animal would do them a good turn too. But the dog,
who had been on previous occasions ill-treated by his
hosts, refused to eat, and at length the angry couple
dragged him into the garden. Immediately the dog
began to sniff, and exactly where he sniffed the greedy
couple began to dig; but they dug up no treasure, and
all they could find was very objectionable refuse. The
old couple, angry and disappointed, killed the dog and
buried him under a pine-tree.

The good old man eventually learnt what had befallen
his faithful dog, and, full of sorrow, he went to the place
where his pet was buried, and arranged food and flowers
on the grave, weeping as he did so.

That night the spirit of the dog came to his master,
and said : "Cut down the tree where I am buried, and
from the wood fashion a mortar, and think of me whenever you use it."

The old man carried out these instructions, and he
found that when he ground the grains of rice in the pine
mortar every grain turned into a precious treasure.

The wicked old couple, having borrowed the dog,
had no compunction in borrowing the mortar too, but
with these wicked people the rice immediately turned
into filth, so that in their anger they broke and burnt
the precious vessel.

Once again the spirit of the dog appeared before his
master, and informed him what had taken place, adding:
"If you will sprinkle the ashes of the mortar over
withered trees they will immediately become full of

blossom," and having uttered these words the spirit departed.

The kind-hearted old man secured the ashes, and, placing them in a basket, journeyed from village to village and from town to town, and over withered trees he threw the ashes, and, as the dog had promised, they suddenly came into flower. A prince heard of these wonders, and commanded the old man to appear before him, requesting that he would give an exhibition of his miraculous power. The old man did so, and joyfully departed with the many royal gifts bestowed upon him.

The old man's neighbours, hearing of these miracles, collected together the remaining ashes of the wonderful mortar, and the wicked fellow went about the country claiming to be able to revive withered or dead trees. Like the original worker of wonders, the greedy old man appeared in the palace, and was commanded to restore a withered tree. The old man climbed up into a tree and scattered the ashes, but the tree still remained withered, and the ashes almost blinded and suffocated the Prince. Upon this the old impostor was almost beaten to death, and he went away in a very miserable state indeed.

The kind old man and his wife, after rebuking their neighbours for their wickedness, allowed them to share in their wealth, and the once mean, cruel, and crafty couple led good and virtuous lives.

The Jelly-fish and the Monkey [1]

Rin-Jin, the King of the Sea, took to wife a young and beautiful Dragon Princess. They had not been

---

[1] The Three Mystic Apes figure in Japanese legend. Mizaru is represented with his hands over his eyes, Kikazaru with his hands covering his ears, and Iwazaru with his hands laid upon his mouth. These mystic apes symbolise (1) He who sees no evil, (2) He who hears no evil, (3) He who speaks no evil.

married long when the fair Queen fell ill, and all the advice and attention of the great physicians availed nothing.

"Oh," sobbed the Queen, "there is only one thing that will cure me of my illness!"

"What is that?" inquired Rin-Jin.

"If I eat the liver of a live monkey I shall immediately recover. Pray get me a monkey's liver, for I know that nothing else will save my life."

So Rin-Jin called a jelly-fish to his side, and said: "I want you to swim to the land and return with a live monkey on your back, for I wish to use his liver that our Queen may be restored to health again. You are the only creature who can perform this task, for you alone have legs and are able to walk about on shore. In order to induce the monkey to come you must tell him of the wonders of the deep and of the rare beauties of my great palace, with its floor of pearl and its walls of coral."

The jelly-fish, delighted to think that the health and happiness of his mistress depended upon the success of his enterprise, lost no time in swimming to an island. He had no sooner stepped on shore than he observed a fine-looking monkey playing about in the branches of a pine-tree.

"Hello!" said the jelly-fish, "I don't think much of this island. What a dull and miserable life you must lead here! I come from the Kingdom of the Sea, where Rin-Jin reigns in a palace of great size and beauty. It may be that you would like to see a new country where there is plenty of fruit and where the weather is always fine. If so, get on my back, and I shall have much pleasure in taking you to the Kingdom of the Sea."

"I shall be delighted to accept your invitation," said

the monkey, as he got down from the tree and comfortably seated himself on the thick shell of the jelly-fish.

"By the way," said the jelly-fish, when he had accomplished about half of the return journey, "I suppose you have brought your liver with you, haven't you?"

"What a personal question!" replied the monkey. "Why do you ask?"

"Our Sea Queen is dangerously ill," said the foolish jelly-fish, "and only the liver of a live monkey will save her life. When we reach the palace a doctor will make use of your liver and my mistress will be restored to health again."

"Dear me!" exclaimed the monkey, "I wish you had mentioned this matter to me before we left the island."

"If I had done so," replied the jelly-fish, "you would most certainly have refused my invitation."

"Believe me, you are quite mistaken, my dear jelly-fish. I have several livers hanging up on a pine-tree, and I would gladly have spared one in order to save the life of your Queen. If you will bring me back to the island again I will get it. It was most unfortunate that I should have forgotten to bring a liver with me."

So the credulous jelly-fish turned round and swam back to the island. Directly the jelly-fish reached the shore the monkey sprang from his back and danced about on the branches of a tree.

"*Liver*," said the monkey, chuckling, "did you say *liver*? You silly old jelly-fish, you'll certainly never get mine!"

The jelly-fish at length reached the palace, and told Rin-Jin his dismal tale. The Sea King fell into a great passion. "Beat him to a jelly!" he cried to those about him. "Beat this stupid fellow till he hasn't a bone left in his body!"

The Jelly-Fish and the Monkey.

(See page 273)

The Firefly Battle.
(See page 285)

THE HORSE OF BRONZE

So the jelly-fish lost his shell from that unfortunate hour, and all the jelly-fishes that were born in the sea after his death were also without shells, and have remained nothing but jelly to this day.

The Horse of Bronze

Upon the festival of the *Minige*, or "The Body-escaping," the Deity of Kitzuki, Oho-kuninushi, is said to ride through the streets on the Bronze Horse. The rite connected with the festival is of so mysterious a kind that the officiating priest can only impart the secret after his death to his son through the medium of the deceased man's spirit. The great carved dragon of Kitzuki was supposed at one time to crawl over the roofs of many houses, but when his wooden throat was cut he remained simply a work of art and no longer troubled the inhabitants. Bronze deer of Matsue, a stag and a doe, also had miraculous power and were able to run about the streets at night. These visitations were so frequent and so disturbing that eventually their heads were cut and their escapades came to an end. The gigantic tortoise of the Gesshōji temple, a stone colossus very nearly sixteen feet in height, was on many occasions seen endeavouring to swim across a pond covered with lotus. This creature, like those we have just mentioned, was mutilated, and his midnight wanderings permanently checked.

CHAPTER XXIII : BIRD AND INSECT LEGENDS

Birds

WE have already noticed certain birds mentioned in Japanese legend, the pheasant in the story of Momotaro, the *Ho-Ho* Bird, the Bridge or Magpies in the account of Tanabata, the mysterious light said to shine from the blue heron, the Thunder Bird, &c. The *sekirei*, or wagtails, are sacred to Izanagi and Izanami, for it was through these birds that these divinities first learnt the art of love, and not even the God of Scarecrows can frighten them. When the great hero Yamato-take died he was supposed to have been transformed into a white bird, and we read in the *Hō-jō-ki*[1] that Chōmei fancied he heard in the note of a copper pheasant the cry of his mother. Mythical creatures such as the *Tengu* possess certain bird-like qualities, but they cannot be classed under the heading of birds, and for this reason they are dealt with elsewhere.

The Cock

The God of Mionoseki detests cocks and hens and everything pertaining to these birds, and the inhabitants respect his very marked dislike. On one occasion a certain steamer, shortly after making for the open sea, encountered a severe storm, and it was thought that the God of Mionoseki, who is the God of Mariners, must have been seriously offended. At length the captain discovered that one of his passengers was smoking a pipe adorned with the figure of a crowing cock. The pipe was immediately thrown into the sea, and the storm abated.

[1] Translated by F. Victor Dickins.

HOW YORITOMO WAS SAVED BY TWO DOVES

We are able to gather the reason for the hatred of the cock from the following legend. In the *Kojiki* we are informed that the son of the Deity of Kitsuki spent many an hour at Mionoseki in catching birds and fish. At that time the cock was his trusted friend, and it was the duty of this bird to crow lustily when it was time for the God to return from his sport. On one occasion, however, the cock forgot to crow, and in consequence, in the God's hurry to go back in his boat he lost his oars, and was compelled to propel the vessel with his hands, which were severely bitten by fishes.

How Yoritomo was Saved by Two Doves

Yoritomo, having been defeated in a battle against Oba Kage-chika, was forced to retreat with six of his followers. They ran with all speed through a forest, and, finding a large hollow tree, crept inside for shelter.

In the meantime Oba Kage-chika said to his cousin, Oba Kagetoki: "Go and search for Yoritomo, for I have good reason to believe that he lies hidden in this forest. I will so arrange my men that the flight of our enemy will be impossible."

Oba Kagetoki departed, none too pleased with the mission, for he had once been on friendly terms with Yoritomo. When he reached the hollow tree and saw through a hole in the trunk that his old friend lay concealed within, he took pity on him, and returned to his cousin, saying: "I believe that Yoritomo, our enemy, is not in this wood."

When Oba Kage-chika heard these words he cried fiercely: "You lie! How could Yoritomo make his escape so soon and with my men standing on guard about the forest? Lead the way, and I and some of my men will follow you. No cunning this time, cousin, or you shall severely suffer for it."

In due time the party reached the hollow tree, and Kage-chika was about to enter it, when his cousin cried : "Stay ! What folly is this ? Cannot you see that there is a spider's web spun across the opening ? How could any one enter this tree without breaking it ? Let us spend our time more profitably elsewhere."

Kage-chika, however, was still suspicious concerning his cousin, and he thrust his bow into the hollow trunk. It almost touched the crouching Yoritomo, when two white doves suddenly flew out of the cavity.

"Alas ! " exclaimed Kage-chika, " you are right, our enemy cannot lie concealed here, for doves and a cob-web would not admit of such a thing."

By the timely aid of two doves and a spider's web the great hero Yoritomo made good his escape, and when, in later years, he became Shōgun he caused shrines to be erected to Hachiman, the God of War, in recognition of his deliverance, for the doves of Japan are recognised as the messengers of war, and not of peace, as is the case in our own country.

The Hototogisu

> "A solitary voice !
> Did the Moon cry ?
> 'Twas but the *hototogisu*."
> *From the Japanese.*

There is a mysterious bird called the *hototogisu* which plaintively cries its own name, dividing it into syllables thus: " *ho-to-to-gi-su*." According to legend it is no earthly bird, but wanders from the Realm of the Dead at the end of May, and warns all peasants who see it that it is time to sow the rice. Some interpret the bird's note as meaning, " Has the *kakemono* been suspended ? " others that it gently repeats : " Surely it is better to return home." The latter intrepretation is characteristically Japanese, for if it is believed that souls return in the summer-time, it is reasonable to suppose that at least one of the birds should fly back to the old woods and streams and hills of Nippon.

The Tongue-cut Sparrow

A cross old woman was at her wash-tub when her neighbour's pet sparrow ate up all the starch, mistaking it for ordinary food. The old woman was so angry at what had happened that she cut out the sparrow's tongue, and the unfortunate bird flew away to a mountain.

When the old couple to whom the sparrow belonged heard what had taken place they left their home and journeyed a great distance until they had the good fortune to find their pet again.

The sparrow was no less delighted to meet his master and mistress, and begged them to enter his house. When they had done so they were feasted with an abundance of fish and *saké*, were waited upon by the sparrow's wife, children, and grandchildren, and, not content with these deeds of hospitality, the feathered host danced a jig called the Sparrow's Dance.

When it was time for the old couple to return home the sparrow brought forth two wicker baskets, saying : " One is heavy, and the other is light. Which would you rather have ? "

" Oh, the light one," replied the old couple, " for we are aged and the journey is a long one."

When the old people reached their home they opened the basket, and to their delight and amazement discovered gold and silver, jewels and silk. As fast as they took the precious things out an inexhaustible supply came to their place, so that the wonderful basket of treasure could not be emptied, and the happy old couple grew rich and prosperous.

It was not long before the old woman who had cut out the sparrow's tongue heard about the good fortune of her neighbours, and she hastened to inquire where this wonderful sparrow was to be seen.

Having gained the information, she had no difficulty in finding the sparrow. When the bird saw her he asked which of two baskets she would prefer to take away with her, the heavy or light one? The cruel and greedy old woman chose the heavy one, believing that this basket would contain more treasure than the light one; but when, after much labour, she reached home and opened it, devils sprang upon her and tore her to pieces.

A Noble Sacrifice

There was once a man who was extremely fond of shooting birds. He had two daughters, good Buddhists, and each in turn pointed out the folly of their father's cruel sport, and begged him not to destroy life wantonly. However, the man was obstinate and would not listen to his daughters' entreaties. One day a neighbour asked him to shoot two storks, and he promised to do so. When the women heard what their father was about to do, they said: "Let us dress in pure white garments and go down upon the shore to-night, for it is a place much frequented by storks. If our father should kill either of us in mistake for the birds, it will teach him a lesson, and he will surely repent his evil ways, which are contrary to the gentle teaching of the Lord Buddha."

That night the man went to the shore, and the cloudy sky made it difficult for him to discover any storks. At last, however, he saw two white objects in the distance. He fired; the bodies fell immediately, and he ran to where they lay, only to discover that he had shot both his noble, self-sacrificing daughters.

Stricken with sorrow, the man erected a funeral pyre and burnt the bodies of his poor children. Having done these things, he shaved his head, went into the woods, and became a hermit.

A Pair of Phœnix

A clever woman named Saijosen was engaged in embroidery. One day an old man called upon her, and said : "Work for me on a piece of cloth a pair of phœnix." Saijosen readily complied, and when the birds were worked the old man closed his eyes and pointed at the phœnix with his finger. Immediately the birds became alive, and the girl and the old man mounted upon their backs and disappeared into the sky.

Insects

Much has been written about the Japanese *semi*, or tree-crickets, and it seems strange to us that these little creatures should be bought and placed in minute cages, where they sing with extraordinary sweetness. Lafcadio Hearn in *Kottō* gives us a pathetic story concerning one of these insects. He tells us that his servant forgot to feed it, and that gradually it ceased to sing, being forced at last to eat its own minute limbs.

The *minminzemi's* singing resembles the chanting of a Buddhist priest, while the green *semi*, or *higurashi*, makes a sound like the trilling of a tiny bell. The carrying of a dried beetle is said to increase one's wardrobe. It must be remembered in the legends that follow that according to Buddhist teaching all life is sacred, and, moreover, that on account of some sin the Buddhists believe that the soul of a man or woman can enter even the minute form of an insect.

Dragon-flies

> " The gold sun shimmering in noontide skies
> Shines down, where the red-burnished dragon-flies
> Flit to and fro in the translucent haze
> Over the village of eventless days ! "
>
> Trans. by CLARA A. WALSH.

The dragon-fly is frequently mentioned in Japanese poetry, but nowhere more pathetically than in the following lines written by Chiyo after the death of her little son :

> " How far, I wonder, did he stray,
> Chasing the burnished dragon-fly to-day ? "

Chiyo, in this exquisite fragment, suggests a very great deal, for in her mother-love there is no dismal concepion of Death. She regards the future life of her little one as the happiest hour of playtime. Once more in these lines there is the Japanese idea of the soul coming back again.

The most charming Japanese dragon-fly is called *Tenshi-tombō*, " the Emperor's dragon-fly." There is a larger variety particularly sought after by children, and of this species there are many more females than males. Boys tie a female to a tree, and sing : " Thou, the male, King of Korea, dost thou not feel shame to flee away from the Queen of the East ? " This quaint song is an allusion to the legendary conquest of Korea, to which we shall refer later on, and it succeeds in attracting the male dragon-fly. It is also believed that if a certain ideograph is traced in the air it has the power to paralyse the dragon-fly one wishes to catch.

Tama's Return

Kazariya Kyūbei, a merchant, had a maid-servant called Tama. Tama worked well and cheerfully, but

282

she was negligent in regard to her dress. One day, when she had been five years in Kyūbei's house, her master said to her : "Tama, how is it that, unlike most girls, you seem to have no desire to look your best ? When you go out you wear your working dress. Surely you should put on a pretty robe on such occasions."

"Good master," said Tama, "you do well to rebuke me, for you do not know why, during all these years, I have worn old clothes and have made no attempt to wear pretty ones. When my father and mother died I was but a child, and as I had no brothers or sisters it rested upon me to have Buddhist services performed on behalf of my parents. In order that this might come to pass I have saved the money you have given me, and spent as little upon myself as possible. Now my parents' mortuary tablets are placed in the Jōrakuji temple, and, having given my money to the priests, the sacred rites have now been performed. I have fulfilled my wish, and, begging for your forgiveness, I will in future dress more becomingly."

Before Tama died she asked her mistress to keep the remaining money she had saved. Shortly after her death a large fly entered Kyūbei's house. Now at that time of the year, the Period of the Greatest Cold, it was unusual for flies to appear, and the master of the house was considerably puzzled. He carefully put the insect outside the house ; but it flew back immediately, and every time it was ejected it came back again. "This fly," said Kyūbei's wife, "may be Tama." Kyūbei cut a small piece out of the insect's wings, and this time carried it some distance from his abode. But the next day it returned once more, and this time the master painted the fly's wings and body with rouge, and took it even further away from his dwelling. Two days later the fly returned, and the nick in its wings and the rouge with which it was covered left no doubt in the minds of Kyūbei and his wife that this persistent insect was indeed Tama.

"I believe," said Kyūbei's wife, "that Tama has returned to us because she wants us to do something for her. I have the money she asked me to keep. Let us give it to the priests in order that they may pray for her soul." When these words had been spoken the fly fell dead upon the floor.

Kyūbei and his wife placed the fly in a box, and with the girl's money they went to the priests. A *sutra* was recited over the body of the insect, and it was duly buried in the temple grounds.

Sanemori and Shiwan

Sanemori, who was a great warrior, was on one occasion, while riding on a horse, engaged in fighting an enemy. During the conflict his horse slipped and rolled into a rice-field. As the result of this mishap his antagonist was able to slay him, and from that hour Sanemori became a rice-devouring insect, known by the peasantry of Izumo as Sanemori-San. During certain summer nights the peasants light fires in their rice-fields in order to attract the insect, play upon flutes and beat gongs, crying : " O Sanemori, augustly deign to come hither ! " A religious rite is then performed, and a straw representation of a rider upon a horse is either burnt or thrown into water. It is believed that this ceremony will successfully free the fields from the rice-devouring insect.

The *shiwan*, a small yellow insect that feeds upon cucumbers, is said to have once been a physician. This physician, guilty of some intrigue, was forced to leave his home, but in attempting to make his escape his foot caught in the sinuous coils of a cucumber vine, and he was killed by his pursuers. His angry ghost became a *shiwan*, and from that day to this the insect feeds upon cucumbers.

Fireflies

> " For this willow-tree the season of budding would seem to have returned in the dark—look at the fireflies."

In ancient days firefly-hunting was one of the amusements of great nobles, but to-day it is the pastime of children only. These hunting parties, however, have lost none of their picturesqueness, and the flashing insect has been the theme of many an exquisite poem, such as : " Ah, the cunning fireflies ! being chased, they hide themselves in the moonlight ! "

Grown-up people, however, go out to see the fireflies with the same ardour with which they indulge in flower-viewing. To the minds of these great Nature-lovers the fireflies resemble dazzling petals of some strange fire-flower or a host of wondering stars that has left the sky to wander upon the earth. During the summer thousands of people visit Uji in order to see the *Hotaru-Kassen,* or Firefly Battle. From the river-bank dart myriads of these flashing insects, and in a moment they form a great silver-shining cloud. The cloud breaks and the flowing river, once dark as black velvet, becomes a winding stretch of gleaming jewels. No wonder the Japanese poet cries : "Do I see only fireflies drifting with the current ? Or is the Night itself drifting, with its swarming of stars ?"

There is a legend connected with this fascinating spectacle. It is believed that the Minamoto-Firefly and the Taira-Firefly are the ghosts of the old warriors or the Minamoto and Taira clans. On the night of the twentieth day of the fourth month they fight a great battle on the Uji River. On that night all caged fire-flies are set free in order that they may fight again the old clan battles of the twelfth century. The ghostly significance of fireflies is further strengthened by the fact that these insects are fond of swarming round willow-trees—the most eerie trees in Japan. Fireflies in ancient days were supposed to possess medicinal pro-perties. Firefly ointment was said to render all poisons harmless, and, moreover, it had the power to drive away evil spirits and to preserve a house from the attacks of robbers.

A Strange Dream

A young man of Matsue was returning home from a wedding-party when he saw, just in front of his house, a firefly. He paused a moment, surprised to see such an insect on a cold winter's night with snow on the ground. While he stood and meditated the firefly flew toward him, and the young man struck at it with his stick, but the insect flew away and entered the garden adjoining his own.

The next day he called at his neighbour's house, and was about to relate the experience of the previous night when the eldest daughter of the family entered the room, and exclaimed : " I had no idea you were here, and yet a moment ago you were in my mind. Last night I dreamt that I became a firefly. It was all very real and very beautiful, and while I was darting hither and thither I saw you, and flew toward you, intending to tell you that I had learnt to fly, but you thrust me aside with your stick, and the incident still frightens me."

The young man, having heard these words from the lips of his betrothed, held his peace.

THE VENGEANCE OF KANSHIRO

The Vengeance of Kanshiro[1]

In the village of Funakami there lived a devout old farmer called Kanshiro. Every year the old man made various pilgrimages to certain shrines, where he prayed and asked the blessings of the deities. At last, however, he became so infirm that he realised that his earthly days were numbered, and that he would probably only have strength to pay one more visit to the great shrines at Ise. When the people of the village heard this noble resolution they generously gave him a sum of money in order that the respected old farmer might present it to the sacred shrines.

Kanshiro set off upon his pilgrimage carrying the money in a bag, which he hung round his neck. The weather was extremely hot, and the heat and fatigue of the journey made the old man so ill that he was forced to remain for a few days in the village of Myojo. He went to a small inn and asked Jimpachi, the innkeeper, to take care of his money, explaining that it was an offering to the Gods at Ise. Jimpachi took the money, and assured the old man that he would take great care of it, and, moreover, that he himself would attend upon him.

On the sixth day the old man, though still far from well, paid his bill, took the bag from the innkeeper, and proceeded on his journey. As Kanshiro observed many pilgrims in the vicinity he did not look into the bag, but carefully concealed it in the sack containing spare raiment and food.

When Kanshiro at length rested under a pine-tree he took out the bag and looked inside. Alas! the money had been stolen, and stones of the same weight inserted

1 Adapted from *Ancient Tales and Folk-lore of Japan*, by R. Gordon Smith.

287

in its place. The old man hastily returned to the inn-keeper and begged him to restore the money. Jimpachi grew extremely angry, and gave him a severe beating.

The poor old man crawled away from the village, and three days later, with indomitable courage, he succeeded in reaching the sacred shrines at Ise. He sold his property in order to refund the money his good neighbours had given him, and with what remained he continued his pilgrimage, till at last he was forced to beg for food.

Three years later Kanshiro went to the village of Myoto, and found that the innkeeper who had treated him so badly was now comparatively well off, and lived in a large house. The old man went to him, and said: "You have stolen sacred money from me, and I have sold my little property in order that I might refund it to those who had given it to me. Ever since that time I have been a beggar, but be assured vengeance shall fall upon you!"

Jimpachi cursed the old man and told him that he had not stolen his money. During the heated dispute a watchman seized Kanshiro, dragged him away from the house, and told him that he would be arrested if he dared to return. At the end of the village the old man died, and a kindly priest took his body to a temple, respectfully burnt it, and offered up many holy prayers for his good and loyal soul.

Immediately after Kanshiro's death Jimpachi grew afraid of what he had done, and became so ill that he was forced to take to his bed. When he had lost all power of movement a great company of fireflies flew out of the farmer's tomb and surrounded Jimpachi's mosquito-curtain, and tried to break it down. Many of the villagers came to Jimpachi's assistance and killed a number of fireflies, but the stream of shining insects that flew from Kanshiro's tomb never lessened. Hundreds were killed, but thousands came to take their place. The room was ablaze with firefly light, and the mosquito-curtain sank beneath their ever-increasing weight. At this remarkable sight some of the villagers murmured : "Jimpachi stole the old man's money after all. This is the vengeance of Kanshiro."

Even while they spoke the curtain broke and the fire-flies rushed into the eyes, ears, mouth, and nose of the terrified Jimpachi. For twenty days he screamed aloud for mercy ; but no mercy came. Thicker and thicker grew the stream of flashing, angry insects, till at last they killed the wicked Jimpachi, when from that hour they completely disappeared.

CHAPTER XXIV : CONCERNING TEA [1]

> " The first cup moistens my lips and throat, the second cup breaks my loneliness, the third cup searches my inmost being. . . . The fourth cup raises a slight perspiration—all the wrong of life passes away through my pores. At the fifth cup I am purified; the sixth cup calls me to the realms of immortals. The seventh cup—ah, but I could take no more ! I only feel the breath of cool wind that rises in my sleeves. Where is Horaisan ? [2] Let me ride on this sweet breeze and waft away thither."

Lotung.

Tea-drinking in England and Japan

IN England we regard tea simply as a beverage, a refreshing and mild stimulant over which ladies are wont to gossip with their neighbours. There is nothing romantic about our tea-pots and kettles and spoons ; they come from the kitchen and are returned to the kitchen with prescribed regularity. We have a few stock comments on the subject of tea, and can quote the exact price our grandmothers paid for this beverage. We have our opinions as to whether it is best taken with or without sugar, and have sometimes found it efficacious in driving away a headache.

When tea reached our own country in 1650 it was referred to as "that excellent and by all physicians approved China drink, called by the Chineans Tcha, and by other nations Tay, alias Tee." In 1711 the *Spectator* remarked : " I would therefore in a particular manner recommend these my speculations to all well-regulated families that set apart an hour every morning for tea, bread and butter ; and would earnestly advise them for

---

[1] We have derived most of the material for this chapter from *The Book of Tea*, by Okakura-Kakuzo, and we warmly commend this very charming volume to those who are interested in the subject.

[2] The Chinese Paradise.

their good to order this paper to be punctually served up and to be looked upon as a part of the tea-equipage.' Dr. Johnson described himself as "a hardened and shameless tea-drinker, who for twenty years diluted his meals with only the infusion of the fascinating plant ; who with tea amused the evening, with tea solaced the midnight, and with tea welcomed the morning." But there is no romance, no old tradition associated with our tea-drinking in this country. Perhaps it is as well that the ladies sitting in our fashionable drawing-rooms are unacquainted with the grim and pathetic legend that narrates how a Buddhist priest fell asleep during his meditations. When he awoke he cut off his offending eyelids and flung them on the ground, where they were immediately transformed into the first tea-plant.

In Japan tea-drinking has become a ritual. It is not so much a social function as a time for peaceful medi-tation. The elaborate tea ceremonies, *cha-no-yu*, have their tea-masters, etiquette, and numerous observances. A cup of Japanese tea is combined with spiritual and artistic enlightenment. But before discussing these very interesting ceremonies we must learn something about the significance of tea in China, for it was the drinking of this beverage in the Celestial Kingdom, associated with the rarest porcelain and æsthetic and religious thought, that inspired the tea cult in the Land of the Gods.

Tea in China

The tea-plant, a native of Southern China, was origi-nally regarded as a medicine. It was referred to in the classics by such names as *Tou*, *Tseh*, *Chung*, *Kha*, and *Ming*, and was much esteemed on account of its medi-cinal properties. It was regarded as an excellent lotion for strengthening the eyes, and, moreover, had the power to banish fatigue, strengthen the will, and delight the soul. It was sometimes made in the form of a paste, and was believed to be efficacious in reducing rheumatic pain. The Taoists went so far as to claim that tea was one of the ingredients of the Elixir of Life, while the Buddhist priests drank it whenever it was necessary for them to meditate during the long hours of the night.

Luwuh and the "Chaking"

In the fourth and fifth centuries we find that tea became a highly favoured beverage among the people of the Yangtse-Kiang valley. At this time, too, poets waxed eloquent in its praise, and described it as the "froth of the liquid jade." But tea at that time was a very horrible concoction indeed, for it was boiled with rice, salt, ginger, orange-peel, and not infrequently with onions! However, Luwuh, who lived in the eighth century, discountenanced the strange mixture we have just referred to. He was the first Chinese tea-master, and not only did he idealize tea, but he saw, with keen poetic insight, that the ceremony of drinking it made for harmony and order in daily life.

In his *Chaking* ("The Holy Scripture of Tea") he describes the nature of the tea-plant, and how its leaves should be gathered and selected. He was of the opinion that the best leaves should have "creases like the leathern boot of Tartar horsemen, curl like the dewlap of a mighty bullock, unfold like a mist rising out of a ravine, gleam like a lake touched by a zephyr, and be wet and soft like fine earth newly swept by rain." Luwuh describes the various utensils connected with the tea ceremony, and asserts that the green beverage should be drunk from blue porcelain cups. He discourses on the subject of the choice of water and the manner of boiling it. In poetical language he describes the three stages of boiling. He compares the little bubbles of the first boil with the eyes of fishes, the bubbles of the second boil with a fountain crowned with clustering crystal beads, and the final boil is described as resembling the surge of miniature billows. The concluding chapters of the *Chaking* deal with the vulgar and unorthodox methods of drinking tea, and the ardent master gives a list of celebrated tea-drinkers, and enumerates the famous Chinese tea plantations. Luwuh's fascinating book was regarded as a master-piece. He was sought after by the Emperor Taisung, attracted many disciples, and was regarded as the greatest authority on tea and tea-drinking. His fame did not die with him, for since his death Chinese tea-merchants have worshipped him as a tutelary god.

The Japanese Tea Ceremony

It is believed that the great Buddhist saint, Dengyŏ Daishi, introduced tea into Japan from China in A.D. 805. In any case tea-drinking in Nippon was associated with Buddhism, and most particularly with the Zen sect, which had incorporated so many of the Taoist doctrines. The priests of this order drank tea from a single bowl before the image of Bodhi Dharma (Daruma). They did so in the spirit of reverence, and regarded the tea-drinking as a holy sacrament. It was this Zen observance, strictly of a religious nature, which finally developed into the Japanese tea ceremony.

"The tea ceremonies," writes Professor B. H. Chamberlain, "have undergone three transformations during the six or seven hundred years of their existence. They have passed through a medico-religious stage, a luxurious stage, and, lastly, an æsthetic stage." In the religious stage the Buddhist priest Eisai wrote a

293

pamphlet entitled *The Salutary Influence of Tea-drinking*, in which he asserted that this beverage had the power to drive away evil spirits. He introduced a religious ceremonial in regard to the worship of ancestors, accompanied by the beating of drums and the burning of incense. Eisai wrote his tract with the intention of converting Minamoto-no-Sanetomo from his vicious love of the wine-cup, and endeavoured to show the superiority of the tea-plant over the juice of the grape.

We find that the tea ceremonies for the time being lost their religious significance. "The Daimyōs," writes Professor Chamberlain, "who daily took part in them reclined on couches spread with tiger-skins and leopard-skins. The walls of the spacious apartments in which the guests assembled were hung, not only with Buddhist pictures, but with damask and brocade, with gold and silver vessels, and swords in splendid sheaths. Precious perfumes were burnt, rare fishes and strange birds were served up with sweetmeats and wine, and the point of the entertainment consisted in guessing where the material for each cup of tea had been produced ; for as many brands as possible were brought in, to serve as a puzzle or *jeu de société*. . . . Every right guess procured for him who made it the gift of one of the treasures that were hung round the room. But he was not allowed to carry it away himself. The rules of the tea ceremonies, as then practised, ordained that all the things rich and rare that were exhibited must be given by their winners to the singing- and dancing-girls, troupes of whom were present to help the company in their carousal."

This variety of tea ceremony, which appears to have been more of an orgy than anything else, reflected the luxurious and dissolute age in which it was practised.

THE JAPANESE TEA CEREMONY

The tea ceremony, in its more enduring and characteristic form, was destined to abandon all vulgar display, to embrace a certain amount of religion and philosophy, and above all to afford a means of studying art and the beauty of Nature. The tea-room became, not a place of carousal, but a place where the wayfarer might find peace in solemn meditation. Even the garden path leading to the tea-room had its symbolic meaning, for it signified the first stage of self-illumination. The following was Kobori-Enshiu's idea of the path leading to the tea-room :

> " A cluster of summer trees,
> A bit of the sea,
> A pale evening moon."

Such a scene was intended to convey to the wayfarer a sense of spiritual light. The trees, sea, and moon awakened old dreams, and their presence made the guest eager to pass into the greater joys of the tea-room. No *samurai* was allowed to take his sword into the fragrant sanctuary of peace, and in many tea-rooms there was a low door through which the guests entered with bowed head, as a sign of humility. In silence the guests made obeisance before a *kakemono,* or some simple and beautiful flower on the *tokonoma* (alcove), and then seated themselves upon the mats. When they had done so the host entered and the water was heard to boil in the kettle with a musical sound, because of some pieces of iron which it contained. Even the boiling of the kettle was associated with poetical ideas, for the song of water and metal was intended to suggest " the echoes of a cataract muffled by clouds, of a distant sea breaking among the rocks, a rainstorm sweeping through a bamboo forest, or of the soughing of pines on some far-away hill." There was a sense of harmony in the tea-room. The light was like the mellow light of evening, and the garments of the

295

company were as quiet and unobtrusive as the grey wings of a moth. In this peaceful apartment the guests drank their tea and meditated, and went forth into the world again better and stronger for having contemplated in silence the beautiful and the noble in religion, art, and nature. " Seeking always to be in harmony with the great rhythm of the universe, they were ever prepared to enter the unknown."

The Passing of Rikiu

Rikiu was one of the greatest of tea-masters, and for long he remained the friend of Taiko-Hideyoshi ; but the age in which he lived was full of treachery. There were many who were jealous of Rikiu, many who sought his death. When a coldness sprang up between Hideyoshi and Rikiu, the enemies of the great tea-master made use of this breach of friendship by spreading the report that Rikiu intended to add poison to a cup of tea and present it to his distinguished patron. Hideyoshi soon heard of the rumour, and without troubling to examine the matter he condemned Rikiu to die by his own hand.

On the last day of the famous tea-master's life he invited many of his disciples to join with him in his final tea ceremony. As they walked up the garden path it seemed that ghosts whispered in the rustling leaves. When the disciples entered the tea-room they saw a *kakemono* hanging in the *tokonoma*, and when they raised their sorrowful eyes they saw that the writing described the passing of all earthly things. There was poetry in the singing of the tea-kettle, but it was a sad song like the plaintive cry of an insect. Rikiu came into the tea-room calm and dignified, and, according to custom, he allowed the chief guest to admire the various articles associated with the tea ceremony. When all the guests had gazed upon them, noting their beauty with a heavy heart, Rikiu presented each disciple with a souvenir. He took his own cup in his hand, and said : " Never again shall this cup, polluted by the lips of misfortune, be used by man." Having spoken these words, he broke the cup as a sign that the tea ceremony was over, and the guests bade a sad farewell and departed. Only one remained to witness, not the drinking of another cup of tea, but the passing of Rikiu. The great master took off his outer garment, and revealed the pure white robe of Death. Still calm and dignified, he looked upon his dagger, and then recited the following verse with unfaltering voice :

> " Welcome to thee,
> O sword of eternity !
> Through Buddha
> And through Daruma alike
> Thou hast cleft thy way."

He who loved to quote the old poem, " To those who long only for flowers fain would I show the full-blown spring which abides in the toiling buds of snow-covered hills," has crowned the Japanese tea ceremony with an immortal flower.

The Legend of the Tea-plant[1]

Daruma was an Indian sage, whose image, as we have already seen, was associated with the ritualistic drinking of tea by the Zen sect in Japan. He is said to have been the son of a Hindu king, and received instruction from Panyatara. When he had completed his studies he retired to Lo Yang, where he remained seated in meditation for nine years. During this period the sage was tempted after the manner of St. Anthony. He wrestled with these temptations by continually reciting sacred scriptures ; but the frequent repetition of the

[1] A full account of this beautiful legend will be found in Lafcadio Hearn's *Some Chinese Ghosts*.

word "jewel" lost its spiritual significance, and became associated with the precious stone worn in the ear of a certain lovely woman. Even the word "lotus," so sacred to all true Buddhists, ceased to be the symbol of the Lord Buddha and suggested to Daruma the opening of a girl's fair mouth. His temptations increased, and he was transported to an Indian city, where he found himself among a vast crowd of worshippers. He saw strange deities with horrible symbols upon their foreheads, and Rajahs and Princes riding upon elephants, surrounded by a great company of dancing-girls. The great crowd of people surged forward, and Daruma with them, till they came to a temple with innumerable pinnacles, a temple covered with a multitude of foul forms, and it seemed to Daruma that he met and kissed the woman who had changed the meaning of jewel and lotus. Then suddenly the vision departed, and Daruma awoke to find himself sitting under the Chinese sky. The sage, who had fallen asleep during his meditation, was truly penitent for the neglect of his devotions, and, taking a knife from his girdle, he cut off his eyelids and cast them upon the ground, saying : "O Thou Perfectly Awakened!" The eyelids were transformed into the tea-plant, from which was made a beverage that would repel slumber and allow good Buddhist priests to keep their vigils.

Daruma

Daruma is generally represented without legs, for according to one version of the legend we have just given he lost his limbs as the result of the nine-year meditation. *Netsuke*[1]-carvers depict him in a full, bag-

---

[1] "Originally a kind of toggle for the medicine-box or tobacco-pouch, carved out of wood or ivory."—*Things Japanese*, by B. H. Chamberlain.

like garment, with a scowling face and lidless eyes.
He is sometimes presented in Japanese art as being
surrounded with cobwebs, and there is a very subtle
variation of the saint portrayed as a female Daruma,
which is nothing less than a playful jest against Japanese
women, who could not be expected to remain silent
for nine years! An owl is frequently associated with
Daruma, and in his journey to Japan he is pictured as
standing on waves, supported by a millet stalk. Three
years after Daruma's death he was seen walking across
the western mountains of China, and it was observed
that he carried one shoe in his right hand. When
Daruma's tomb was opened by the order of the
Emperor it was found only to contain a shoe, which
the saint had forgotten to take away with him.[1]

[1] Reference to Yuki-Daruma, or Snow-Daruma, and toy-Daruma,
called *Okiagari-koboshi* ("The Getting-up Little Priest"), will be
found in Lafcadio Hearn's *A Japanese Miscellany.*

CHAPTER XXV : LEGENDS OF THE WEIRD[1]

"Hōichi-the-Earless"

IN the stories concerning Yoshitsune and his loyal retainer Benkei we have already referred to the battle of Dan-no-ura, the last conflict between the Taira and Minamoto clans.[2] In this great sea-fight the Taira perished, including their infant Emperor, Antoku Tenno. Thus is the memorable scene described in the *Heike Monogatari*, translated by Dr. W. G. Aston :

" 'This world is the region of sorrow, a remote spot small as a grain of millet. But beneath the waves there is a fair city called the Pure Land of Perfect Happiness. Thither it is that I am taking you.' With such words she soothed him. The child then tied his top-knot to the Imperial robe of the colour of a mountain-dove, and tearfully joined together his lovely little hands. First he turned to the East, and bade adieu to the shrine of the great God of Ise and the shrine of Hachiman. Next he turned to the West, and called upon the name of Buddha. When he had done so, Niidono made bold to take him in her arms, and, soothing him with the words, 'There is a city away below the waves,' sank down to the bottom one thousand fathoms deep."

It is said that for seven hundred years after this great battle the sea and coast in the vicinity have been haunted by the ghosts of the Taira clan. Mysterious fires shone on the waves, and the air was filled with the noise of warfare. In order to pacify the unfortunate spirits the temple of Amidaji was built at Akamagaséki, and a cemetery was made close by, in which were various

---

[1] The legends in this chapter are adapted from stories in Lafcadio Hearn's *Kwaidan* and *Glimpses of Unfamiliar Japan*.

[2] See Chapter II.

monuments inscribed with the names of the drowned Emperor and his principal followers. This temple and cemetery pacified the ghostly visitants to a certain extent, but from time to time many strange things happened, as we shall gather from the following legend.

There once lived at the Amidaji temple a blind priest named Hoïchi. He was famous for his recitation and for his marvellous skill in playing upon the *biwa* (a four-stringed lute), and he was particularly fond of reciting stories in connection with the protracted war between the Taira and Minamoto clans.

One night Hoïchi was left alone in the temple, and as it was a very warm evening he sat out on the verandah, playing now and again upon his *biwa*. While thus occupied he heard some one approaching, some one stepping across the little back garden of the temple. Then a deep voice cried out from below the verandah : "Hoïchi !" Yet again the voice sounded : "Hoïchi !"

Hoïchi, now very much alarmed, replied that he was blind, and would be glad to know who his visitor might be.

"My lord," began the stranger, "is now staying at Akamagaséki with many noble followers, and he has come for the purpose of viewing the scene of the battle of Dan-no-ura. He has heard how excellently you recite the story of the conflict, and has commanded me to escort you to him in order that you may show him your skill. Bring your *biwa* and follow me. My lord and his august assembly now await your honourable presence."

Hoïchi, deeming that the stranger was some noble *samurai*, obeyed immediately. He donned his sandals and took his *biwa*. The stranger guided him with an iron hand, and they marched along very quickly. Hoïchi heard the clank of armour at his side ; but all fear left him, and he looked forward to the honour of showing his skill before a distinguished company.

Arriving at a gate, the stranger shouted : "*Kaimon !*" Immediately the gate was unbarred and opened, and the two men passed in. Then came the sound of many hurrying feet, and a rustling noise as of screens being opened. Hoïchi was assisted in mounting a number of steps, and, arriving at the top, he was commanded to leave his sandals. A woman then led him forward by the hand till he found himself in a vast apartment, where he judged that a great company of people were assembled. He heard the subdued murmur of voices and the soft movement of silken garments. When Hoïchi had seated himself on a cushion the woman who had led him bade him recite the story of the great battle of Dan-no-ura.

Hoïchi began to chant to the accompaniment of his *biwa.* His skill was so great that the strings of his instrument seemed to imitate the sound of oars, the movement of ships, the shouting of men, the noise of surging waves, and the whirring of arrows. A low murmur of applause greeted Hoïchi's wonderful performance. Thus encouraged, he continued to sing and play with even greater skill. When he came to chant of the perishing of the women and children, the plunge of Niidono into the sea with the infant Emperor in her arms, the company began to weep and wail.

When the performance was over the woman who had led Hoïchi told him that her lord was well pleased with his skill, and that he desired him to play before him for the six following nights. "The retainer," added she, "who brought you to-night will visit your temple at the same hour to-morrow. You must keep these visits secret, and may now return to your abode."

Once more the woman led Hoïchi through the apart-

Hōïchi-the-Earless.

(See page 301*)*

The Maiden of Unai.

(See page 314)

ment, and having reached the steps the same retainer
led him back to the verandah at the back of the temple
where he lived.

The next night Hōïchi was again led forth to enter-
tain the assembly, and he met with the same success.
But this time his absence was detected, and upon his
return his fellow priest questioned him in regard to the
matter. Hōïchi evaded his friend's question, and told
him that he had merely been out to attend some private
business.

His questioner was by no means satisfied. He
regretted Hōïchi's reticence and feared that there was
something wrong, possibly that the blind priest had
been bewitched by evil spirits. He bade the men-
servants keep a strict watch upon Hōïchi, and to follow
him if he should again leave the temple during the
night.

Once more Hōïchi left his abode. The men-servants hastily lit their lanterns and followed him with all
speed; but though they walked quickly, looked everywhere, and made numerous inquiries, they failed to
discover Hōïchi, or learn anything concerning him. On
their return, however, they were alarmed to hear the
sound of a *biwa* in the cemetery of the temple, and on
entering this gloomy place they discovered the blind
priest. He sat at the tomb of Antoku Tenno, the infant
Emperor, where he twanged his *biwa* loudly, and as
loudly chanted the story of the battle of Dan-no-ura.
About him on every side mysterious fires glowed, like
a great gathering of lighted candles.

"Hōïchi! Hōïchi!" shouted the men. "Stop your
playing at once! You are bewitched, Hōïchi!" But
the blind priest continued to play and sing, rapt, it
seemed, in a strange and awful dream.

The men-servants now resorted to more extreme

measures. They shook him, and shouted in his ear: "Hōïchi, come back with us at once!"

The blind priest rebuked them, and said that such an interruption would not be tolerated by the noble assembly about him.

The men now dragged Hōïchi away by force. When he reached the temple his wet clothes were taken off and food and drink set before him.

By this time Hōïchi's fellow priest was extremely angry, and he not unjustly insisted upon a full explanation of his extraordinary behaviour. Hōïchi, after much hesitation, told his friend all that had happened to him. When he had narrated his strange adventures, the priest said:

"My poor fellow! You ought to have told me this before. You have not been visiting a great house of a noble lord, but you have been sitting in yonder cemetery before the tomb of Antoku Tenno. Your great skill has called forth the ghosts of the Taira clan. Hōïchi, you are in great danger, for by obeying these spirits you have assuredly put yourself in their power, and sooner or later they will kill you. Unfortunately I am called away to-night to perform a service, but before I go I will see that your body is covered with sacred texts."

Before night approached Hōïchi was stripped, and upon his body an acolyte inscribed, with writing-brushes, the text of the *sutra* known as *Hannya-Shin-Kyō*. These texts were written upon Hōïchi's breast, head, back, face, neck, legs, arms, and feet, even upon the soles thereof.

Then the priest said: "Hōïchi, you will be called again to-night. Remain silent, sit very still, and continually meditate. If you do these things no harm will befall you."

That night Hōïchi sat alone in the verandah, scarcely moving a muscle and breathing very softly.

Once more he heard the sound of footsteps. "Hōïchi!" cried a deep voice. But the blind priest made no answer. He sat very still, full of a great fear.

His name was called over and over again, but to no effect. "This won't do," growled the stranger. "I must see where the fellow is." The stranger sprang into the verandah and stood beside Hōïchi, who was now shaking all over with the horror of the situation.

"Ah!" said the stranger. "This is the *biwa*, but in place of the player I see—only two ears! Now I understand why he did not answer. He has no mouth, only his two ears! Those ears I will take to my lord!"

In another moment Hōïchi's ears were torn off, but in spite of the fearful pain the blind priest remained mute. Then the stranger departed, and when his footsteps had died away the only sound Hōïchi heard was the trickling of blood upon the verandah, and thus the priest found the unfortunate man upon his return.

"Poor Hōïchi!" cried the priest. "It is all my fault. I trusted my acolyte to write sacred texts on every part of your body. He failed to do so on your ears. I ought to have seen that he carried out my instructions properly. However, you will never be troubled with those spirits in future." From that day the blind priest was known as *Mimi-nashi-Hōïchi*, "Hōïchi-the-Earless."

The Corpse-eater

Musō Kokushi, a priest, lost his way while travelling through the province of Mino. Despairing of finding a human abode, he was about to sleep out in the open, when he chanced to discover a little hermitage, called *anjitsu*

An aged priest greeted him, and Musō requested that he
would give him shelter for the night. "No," replied the
old priest angrily, "I never give shelter to any one. In
yonder valley you will find a certain hamlet; seek a
night's repose there."

With these rather uncivil words, Musō took his
departure, and reaching the hamlet indicated he was
hospitably received at the headman's dwelling. On
entering the principal apartment, the priest saw a number
of people assembled together. He was shown into a
separate room, and was about to fall asleep, when he
heard the sound of lamentation, and shortly afterwards a
young man appeared before him, holding a lantern in
his hand.

"Good priest," said he, "I must tell you that my
father has recently died. We did not like to explain the
matter upon your arrival, because you were tired and
much needed rest. The number of people you saw in
the principal apartment had come to pay their respects to
the dead. Now we must all go away, for that is the
custom in our village when any one dies, because strange
and terrible things happen to corpses when they are left
alone; but perhaps, being a priest, you will not be afraid
to remain with my poor father's body."

Musō replied that he was in no way afraid, and told
the young man that he would perform a service, and
watch by the deceased during the company's absence.
Then the young man, together with the other mourners,
left the house, and Musō remained to perform his
solitary night vigil.

After Musō had undertaken the funeral ceremonies,
he sat meditating for several hours. When the night
had far advanced, he was aware of the presence of a
strange Shape, so terrible in aspect that the priest could
neither move nor speak. The Shape advanced, raised

the corpse, and quickly devoured it. Not content with this horrible meal, the mysterious form also ate the offerings, and then vanished.

The next morning the villagers returned, and they expressed no surprise on hearing that the corpse had disappeared. After Musō had narrated his strange adventure he inquired if the priest on the hill did not sometimes perform the funeral service. " I visited him last night at his *anjitsu*, and though he refused me shelter, he told me where I might rest."

The villagers were amazed at these words, and informed Musō that there was certainly no priest and no *anjitsu* on yonder hill. They were positive in their assertion, and assured Musō that he had been deluded in the matter by some evil spirit. Musō did not reply, and shortly afterwards he took his departure, determined if possible to unravel the mystery.

Musō had no difficulty in finding the *anjitsu* again. The old priest came out to him, bowed, and exclaimed that he was sorry for his former rudeness. " I am ashamed," added he, " not only because I gave you no shelter, but because you have seen my real shape. You have seen me devour a corpse and the funeral offerings. Alas ! good sir, I am a *jikininki* [man-eating goblin], and if you will bear with me I will explain my wretched condition.

" Many years ago I used to be a priest in this district, and I performed a great number of burial services ; but I was not a good priest, for I was not influenced by true religion in performing my tasks, and thought only of the good and fine clothes I could get out of my calling. For that reason I was reborn a *jikininki*, and have ever since devoured the corpses of all those who died in this district. I beg that you will have pity on my miserable plight, and repeat certain prayers on my behalf, that I

may speedily find peace and make an end of my great
wickedness."

Immediately after these words had been spoken, the
recluse and his hermitage suddenly vanished, and Musō
found himself kneeling beside a moss-covered tomb,
which was probably the tomb of the unfortunate
priest.

The Ghost Mother

A pale-faced woman crept down a street called
Nakabaramachi, entered a certain shop, and purchased
a small quantity of *midzu-ame*.[1] Every night, at a late
hour, she came, always haggard of countenance and
always silent. The shopkeeper, who took a kindly
interest in her, followed her one night, but seeing that
she entered a cemetery, he turned back, puzzled and
afraid.

Once again the mysterious woman came to the little
shop, and this time she did not buy *midzu-ame*, but
beckoned the shopkeeper to follow her. Down the
street went the pale-faced woman, followed by the seller
of amber syrup and some of his friends. When they
reached the cemetery the woman disappeared into a
tomb, and those without heard the weeping of a child.
When the tomb was opened they saw the corpse of the
woman they had followed, and by her side a living
child, laughing at the lantern-light and stretching forth
its little hands towards a cup of *midzu-ame*. The
woman had been prematurely buried and her babe born
in the tomb. Every night the silent mother went forth
from the cemetery in order that she might bring back
nourishment for her child.

[1] A syrup made from malt and given to children when milk is not
available.

THE FUTON OF TOTTORI

The Futon of Tottori

In Tottori there was a small and modest inn. It was
a new inn, and as the landlord was poor he had been
compelled to furnish it with goods purchased from a
second-hand shop in the vicinity. His first guest was
a merchant, who was treated with extreme courtesy and
given much warm *saké*. When the merchant had drunk
the refreshing rice wine he retired to rest and soon fell
asleep. He had not slumbered long when he heard the
sound of children's voices in his room, crying pitifully :
" Elder Brother probably is cold ? " " Nay, thou probably art cold ? " Over and over again the children
repeated these plaintive words. The merchant, thinking
that children had strayed into his room by mistake,
mildly rebuked them and prepared to go to sleep again.
After a moment's silence the children again cried :
" Elder Brother probably is cold ? " " Nay, thou probably art cold ? "

The guest arose, lit the *andon* (night-light), and proceeded to examine the room. But there was no one in
the apartment ; the cupboards were empty, and all the
shōji (paper-screens) were closed. The merchant lay
down again, puzzled and amazed. Once more he heard
the cry, close to his pillow : " Elder Brother probably
is cold ? " " Nay, thou probably art cold ? " The
cries were repeated, and the guest, cold with horror,
found that the voices proceeded from his *futon* (quilt).

He hurriedly descended the stairs and told the innkeeper what had happened. The landlord was angry.
" You have drunk too much warm *saké*," said he.
" Warm *saké* has brought you evil dreams." But the
guest paid his bill and sought lodging elsewhere.

On the following night another guest slept in the
haunted room, and he, too, heard the same mysterious

voices, rated the innkeeper, and hastily took his departure. The landlord then entered the apartment himself. He heard the pitiful cries of children coming from one *futon*, and now was forced to believe the strange story his two guests had told him.

The next day the landlord went to the second-hand shop where he had purchased the *futon*, and made inquiries. After going from one shop to another, he finally heard the following story of the mysterious *futon* :

There once lived in Tottori a poor man and his wife, with two children, boys of six and eight years respectively. The parents died, and the poor children were forced to sell their few belongings, until one day they were left with only a thin and much-worn *futon* to cover them at night. At last they had no money to pay the rent, and not even the wherewithal to purchase food of any kind.

When the period of the greatest cold came, the snow gathered so thickly about the humble dwelling that the children could do nothing but wrap the *futon* about them, and murmur to each other in their sweet, pathetic way : "Elder Brother probably is cold ?" "Nay, thou probably art cold ?" And sobbing forth these words they clung together, afraid of the darkness and of the bitter, shrieking wind.

While their poor little bodies nestled together, striving to keep each other warm, the hard-hearted landlord entered, and finding that there was no one to pay the rent, he turned the children out of the house, each clad only in one thin *kimono*. They tried to reach a temple of Kwannon, but the snow was too heavy, and they hid behind their old home. A *futon* of snow covered them and they fell asleep on the merciful bosom of the Gods, and were finally buried in the cemetery of the Temple of Kwannon-of-the-Thou-sand-Arms.

When the innkeeper heard this sad story he gave the *futon* to the priests of the Kwannon temple, prayers were recited for the children's souls, and from that hour the *futon* ceased to murmur its plaintive cries.

The Return

In the village of Mochida-no-ura there lived a peasant. He was extremely poor, but, notwithstanding, his wife bore him six children. Directly a child was born, the cruel father flung it into a river and pretended that it had died at birth, so that his six children were murdered in this horrible way.

At length, as years went by, the peasant found himself in a more prosperous position, and when a seventh child was born, a boy, he was much gratified and loved him dearly.

One night the father took the child in his arms, and wandered out into the garden, murmuring ecstatically: " What a beautiful summer night ! "

The babe, then only five months old, for a moment assumed the speech of a man, saying : " The moon looks just as it did when you last threw me in the river ! "

When the infant had uttered these words he became like other children ; but the peasant, now truly realising the enormity of his crime, from that day became a priest.

A Test of Love

There was once a certain fair maiden who, contrary to Japanese custom, was permitted to choose her own husband. Many suitors sought her hand, and they brought her gifts and fair poems, and said many loving words to her. She spoke kindly to each suitor, saying : " I will marry the man who is brave enough to bear a

certain test I shall impose upon him, and whatever that
test of love may be, I expect him, on the sacred honour
of a *samurai*, not to divulge it." The suitors readily
complied with these conditions, but one by one they left
her, with horror upon their faces, ceased their wooing,
but breathed never a word concerning the mysterious
and awful secret.

At length a poor *samurai*, whose sword was his only
wealth, came to the maiden, and informed her that he was
prepared to go through any test, however severe, in order
that he might make her his wife.

When they had supped together the maiden left
the apartment, and long after midnight returned clad
in a white garment. They went out of the house
together, through innumerable streets where dogs
howled, and beyond the city, till they came to a great
cemetery. Here the maiden led the way while the *samurai*
followed, his hand upon his sword.

When the wooer was able to penetrate the darkness he
saw that the maiden was digging the ground with a spade.
She dug with extreme haste, and eventually tore off
the lid of a coffin. In another moment she snatched up
the corpse of a child, tore off an arm, broke it, and commenced to eat one piece, flinging the other to her wooer,
crying : " If you love me, eat what I eat ! "

Without a moment's hesitation the *samurai* sat down by
the grave and began to eat one half of the arm. " Excellent ! " he cried, " I pray you give me more ! " At this
point of the legend the horror happily disappears, for
neither the *samurai* nor the maiden ate a corpse—the arm
was made of delicious confectionery !

The maiden, with a cry of joy, sprang to her feet, and
said : " At last I have found a brave man ! I will marry
you, for you are the husband I have ever longed for, and
until this night have never found."

CHAPTER XXVI : THREE MAIDENS

The Maiden of Unai

THE Maiden of Unai dwelt with her parents in the village of Ashinóya. She was extremely beautiful, and it so happened that she had two most ardent and persistent lovers—Mubara, who was a native of the same countryside, and Chinu, who came from Izumi. These two lovers might very well have been twins, for they resembled each other in age, face, figure, and stature. Unfortunately, however, they both loved her with an equal passion, so that it was impossible to distinguish between them. Their gifts were the same, and there appeared to be no difference in their manner of courting. We get a good idea of the formidable aspect of these two lovers in the following, taken from Mushi-maro's poem on the subject :

> " With jealous love these champions twain
> The beauteous girl did woo ;
> Each had his hand on the hilt of his sword,
> And a full-charged quiver, too,

> " Was slung o'er the back of each champion fierce,
> And a bow of snow-white wood
> Did rest in the sinewy hand of each ;
> And the twain defiant stood."
> Trans. by B. H. CHAMBERLAIN.

In the meantime, the Maiden of Unai grew sick at heart. She never accepted the gifts of either Mubara or Chinu, and yet it distressed her to see them standing at the gate month after month, never relaxing for a moment the ardent expression of their feeling toward her.

The Maiden of Unai's parents do not seem to have appreciated the complexity of the situation, for they said to her : " Sad it is for us to have to bear the burden of thine unseemly conduct in thus carelessly from month to month, and from year to year, causing others to sorrow. If thou wilt accept the one, after a little time the other's love will cease."

These well-meant words brought no consolation or assistance to the poor Maiden of Unai, so her parents sent for the lovers, explained the pitiful situation, and decided that he who should shoot a water-bird swimming in the river Ikuta, which flowed by the platform on which the house was built, should have their daughter in marriage.

The lovers were delighted at this decision, and anxious to put an end to this cruel suspense. They pulled their bow-strings at the same instant, and together their arrows struck the bird, one in the head and the other in the tail, so that neither could claim to be the better marksman. When the Maiden of Unai saw how entirely hopeless the whole affair was, she exclaimed :

> " Enough, enough ! yon swiftly flowing wave
> Shall free my soul from her long anxious strife :
> Men call fair Settsu's stream the stream of life,
> But in that stream shall be the maiden's grave ! "
>
> Trans. by B. H. CHAMBERLAIN.

With these melodramatic words she flung herself from the platform into the surging water beneath.

The maid's parents, who witnessed the scene, shouted and raved on the platform, while the devoted lovers sprang into the river. One held the maiden's foot, and the other her hand, and in a moment the three sank and perished. In due time the maiden was buried with her lovers on either side, and to this day the spot is known as the "Maiden's Grave." In the grave or Mubara there was a hollow bamboo-cane, together with a bow, a quiver, and a long sword ; but nothing had been placed in the grave of Chinu.

THE GRAVE OF THE MAIDEN OF UNAI

Some time afterwards a stranger happened to pass one night in the neighbourhood of the grave, and he was suddenly disturbed by hearing the sound of fighting. He sent his retainers to inquire into the matter, but they returned to him saying they could hear or see nothing of an unusual nature. While the stranger pondered over the love-story of the Maiden of Unai he fell asleep. He had no sooner done so than he saw before him, kneeling on the ground, a blood-stained man, who told him that he was much harassed by the persecutions of an enemy, and begged that the stranger would lend him his sword. This request was reluctantly granted. When the stranger awoke he was inclined to think the whole affair a dream ; but it was no passing fantasy of the night, for not only was his sword missing, but he heard near at hand the sound of a great combat. Then the clash of weapons suddenly ceased, and once more the blood-stained man stood before him, saying : "By thine honourable assistance have I slain the foe that had oppressed me during these many years." So we may infer that in the spirit world Chinu fought and slew his rival, and after many years of bitter jealousy was finally able to call the Maiden of Unai his own.

The Grave of the Maiden of Unai

" I stand by the grave where they buried
The Maiden of Unai,
Whom of old the rival champions
Did woo so jealously.

" The grave should hand down through the ages
Her story for evermore,
That men yet unborn might love her,
And think on the days of yore.

" And so beside the causeway
    They piled up the boulders high;
Nor e'er, till the clouds that o'ershadow us
    Shall vanish from the sky,

" May the pilgrim along the causeway
    Forget to turn aside,
And mourn o'er the grave of the Maiden;
    And the village folk, beside,

" Ne'er cease from their bitter weeping,
    But cluster around her tomb;
And the ages repeat her story,
    And bewail the Maiden's doom.

" Till at last e'en I stand gazing
    On the grave where she lies low,
And muse with unspeakable sadness
    On the old days long ago."
        Sakimaro. (Trans. by B. H. CHAMBERLAIN.)

The Maiden of Katsushika

" Where in the far-off eastern land
    The cock first crows at dawn,
The people still hand down a tale
    Of days long dead and gone.

" They tell of Katsushika's maid,
    Whose sash of country blue
Bound but a frock of home-spun hemp,
    And kirtle coarse to view;

" Whose feet no shoe had e'er confined,
    Nor comb passed through her hair;
Yet all the queens in damask robes
    Might nevermore compare

" With this dear child, who smiling stood,
    A flow'ret of the spring—
In beauty perfect and complete,
    Like to the full moon's ring.

THE MAIDEN WITH THE WOODEN BOWL

" And, as the summer moths that fly
　　Towards the flame so bright,
Or as the boats that seek the port
　　When fall the shades of night,

" So came the suitors ; but she said :
　　' Why take me for your wife ?
Full well I know my humble lot,
　　I know how short my life.'

" So where the dashing billows beat
　　On the loud-sounding shore,
Hath Katsushika's tender maid
　　Her home for evermore.

" Yes ! 'tis a tale of days long past ;
　　But, list'ning to the lay,
It seems as I had gazed upon
　　Her face but yesterday."

Trans. by B. H. CHAMBERLAIN.

To the translation of this Japanese ballad Professor
B. H. Chamberlain adds the following note : " To the
slight, but undoubtedly very ancient, tradition preserved
in the foregoing ballad, there is nothing to add from
any authentic source.　Popular fancy, however, has
been busy filling up the gaps, and introduces a cruel
stepmother, who, untouched by the piety of the maiden
in drawing water for her every day from the only well
whose water she cares to drink, is so angry with her for,
by her radiant beauty, attracting suitors to the house,
that the poor girl ends by drowning herself, upon which
the neighbours declare her to be a goddess, and erect a
temple in her honour.　Both the temple and the well
are still among the show-places in the environs of
Tōkyō."

The Maiden with the Wooden Bowl

In ancient days there lived an old couple with their
only child, a girl of remarkable　charm and beauty.

When the old man fell sick and died his widow became more and more concerned for her daughter's future welfare.

One day she called her child to her, and said : " Little one, your father lies in yonder cemetery, and I, being old and feeble, must needs follow him soon. The thought of leaving you alone in the world troubles me much, for you are beautiful, and beauty is a temptation and a snare to men. Not all the purity of a white flower can prevent it from being plucked and dragged down in the mire. My child, your face is all too fair. It must be hidden from the eager eyes of men, lest it cause you to fall from your good and simple life to one of shame."

Having said these words, she placed a lacquered bowl upon the maiden's head, so that it veiled her attractions. " Always wear it, little one," said the mother, " for it will protect you when I am gone."

Shortly after this loving deed had been performed the old woman died, and the maiden was forced to earn her living by working in the rice-fields. It was hard, weary work, but the girl kept a brave heart and toiled from dawn to sunset without a murmur. Over and over again her strange appearance created considerable comment, and she was known throughout the country as the " Maiden with the Bowl on her Head." Young men laughed at her and tried to peep under the vessel, and not a few endeavoured to pull off the wooden covering ; but it could not be removed, and laughing and jesting, the young men had to be content with a glimpse of the lower part of the fair maiden's face. The poor girl bore this rude treatment with a patient but heavy heart, believing that out of her mother's love and wisdom would come some day a joy that would more than compensate for all her sorrow.

THE MAIDEN WITH THE WOODEN BOWL

One day a rich farmer watched the maiden working in his rice-fields. He was struck by her diligence and the quick and excellent way she performed her tasks. He was pleased with that bent and busy little figure, and did not laugh at the wooden bowl on her head. After observing her for some time, he came to the maiden, and said : "You work well and do not chatter to your companions. I wish you to labour in my rice-fields until the end of the harvest."

When the rice harvest had been gathered and winter had come the wealthy farmer, still more favourably impressed with the maiden, and anxious to do her a service, bade her become an inmate of his house. "My wife is ill," he added, "and I should like you to nurse her for me."

The maiden gratefully accepted this welcome offer. She tended the sick woman with every care, for the same quiet diligence she displayed in the rice-fields was characteristic of her gentle labour in the sick-room. As the farmer and his wife had no daughter they took very kindly to this orphan and regarded her as a child of their own.

At length the farmer's eldest son returned to his old home. He was a wise young man who had studied much in gay Kyōto, and was weary of a merry life of feasting and frivolous pleasure. His father and mother expected that their son would soon grow tired of his father's house and its quiet surroundings, and every day they feared that he would come to them, bid farewell, and return once more to the city of the Mikado. But to the surprise of all the farmer's son expressed no desire to leave his old home.

One day the young man came to his father, and said : "Who is this maiden in our house, and why does she wear an ugly black bowl upon her head ?"

When the farmer had told the sad story of the maiden his son was deeply moved ; but, nevertheless, he could not refrain from laughing a little at the bowl. The young man's laughter, however, did not last long. Day by day the maiden became more fascinating to him. Now and again he peeped at the girl's half-hidden face, and became more and more impressed by her gentleness of manner and her nobility of nature. It was not long before his admiration turned into love, and he resolved that he would marry the Maiden with the Bowl on her Head. Most of his relations were opposed to the union. They said : "She is all very well in her way, but she is only a common servant. She wears that bowl in order to captivate the unwary, and we do not think it hides beauty, but rather ugliness. Seek a wife elsewhere, for we will not tolerate this ambitious and scheming maiden."

From that hour the maiden suffered much. Bitter and spiteful things were said to her, and even her mistress, once so good and kind, turned against her. But the farmer did not change his opinion. He still liked the girl, and was quite willing that she should become his son's wife, but, owing to the heated remarks of his wife and relations, he dared not reveal his wishes in the matter.

All the opposition, none too kindly expressed, only made the young man more desirous to achieve his purpose. At length his mother and relations, seeing that their wishes were useless, consented to the marriage, but with a very bad grace.

The young man, believing that all difficulties had been removed, joyfully went to the Maiden with the Bowl on her Head, and said : "All troublesome opposition is at an end, and now nothing prevents us from getting married."

THE MAIDEN WITH THE WOODEN BOWL

"No," replied the poor maiden, weeping bitterly, "I cannot marry you. I am only a servant in your father's house, and therefore it would be unseemly for me to become your bride."

The young man spoke gently to her. He expressed his ardent love over and over again, he argued, he begged ; but the maiden would not change her mind. Her attitude made the relations extremely angry. They said that the woman had made fools of them all, little knowing that she dearly loved the farmer's son, and believed, in her loyal heart, that marriage could only bring discord in the home that had sheltered her in her poverty.

That night the poor girl cried herself to sleep, and in a dream her mother came to her, and said : "My dear child, let your good heart be troubled no more. Marry the farmer's son and all will be well again." The maiden woke next morning full of joy, and when her lover came to her and asked once more if she would become his bride, she yielded with a gracious smile.

Great preparations were made for the wedding, and when the company assembled, it was deemed high time to remove the maiden's wooden bowl. She herself tried to take it off, but it remained firmly fixed to her head. When some of the relations, with not a few unkind remarks, came to her assistance, the bowl uttered strange cries and groans. At length the bridegroom approached the maiden, and said : "Do not let this treatment distress you. You are just as dear to me with or without the bowl," and having said these words, he commanded that the ceremony should proceed.

Then the wine-cups were brought into the crowded apartment and, according to custom, the bride and bridegroom were expected to drink together the "Three times three" in token of their union. Just as the maiden put the wine-cup to her lips the bowl on her head broke with a great noise, and from it fell gold and silver and all manner of precious stones, so that the maiden who had once been a beggar now had her marriage portion. The guests were amazed as they looked upon the heap of shining jewels and gold and silver, but they were still more surprised when they chanced to look up and see that the bride was the most beautiful woman in all Japan.

CHAPTER XXVII : LEGENDS OF THE SEA

> "Oh ! that the white waves far out
> On the sea of Ise
> Were but flowers,
> That I might gather them
> And bring them as a gift to my love."
> *Prince Aki.* (Trans. by W. G. Aston.)

The Tide of the Returning Ghosts

ON the last day of the Festival of the Dead the sea is covered with countless *shōryōbune* (soul-ships), for on that day, called *Hotoke-umi*, which means Buddha-Flood, or the Tide of the Returning Ghosts, the souls go back to their spirit world again. The sea shines with the light of the departed, and from over the waves comes the sound of ghosts whispering together. No human being would dream of putting out to sea amid such sacred company, for the sea that night belongs to the dead ; it is their long pathway to the realm where Emma-Ō reigns supreme.

It sometimes happens, however, that a vessel fails to come to port before the departure of the soul-ships, and on such occasions the dead arise from the deep, stretch forth their arms, and implore that buckets may be given them. Sailors comply with this request, but present the ghosts with one that has no bottom, for if they gave the dead sound buckets, the angry spirits would use them for the purpose of sinking the vessel.

Urashima

> " 'Tis Spring, and the mists come stealing
> O'er Suminóye's shore,
> And I stand by the seaside musing
> On the days that are no more.

MYTHS AND LEGENDS OF JAPAN

"I muse on the old-world story,
    As the boats glide to and fro,
Of the fisher-boy Urashima,
    Who a-fishing lov'd to go."
                Trans. by B. H. CHAMBERLAIN.

"The legend of Urashima," writes Professor B. H. Chamberlain in *Japanese Poetry*, "is one of the oldest in the language, and traces of it may even be found in the official annals." In the popular version, which we give below, " the Evergreen Land," recorded in the Japanese ballad, "The Fisher Boy Urashima," appears as the Dragon Palace. Professor Chamberlain writes : "The word Dragon Palace is in Japanese *ryūgū*, or, more properly, *ryūkyū*, which is likewise the Japanese pronunciation of the name of the islands we call Luchu, and the Chinese Liu-kiu ; and it has been suggested that the Dragon Palace may be but a fanciful name given by some shipwrecked voyager to those sunny southern isles, whose inhabitants still distinguish themselves, even above their Chinese and Japanese neighbours, by their fondness for the dragon as an artistic and architectural adornment. There is one ode in the *Man-yōshū* which would favour this idea, speaking as it does of the orange having first been brought to Japan from the 'Evergreen Land' lying to the south."

Urashima and the Tortoise

One day Urashima, who lived in a little fishing village called Midzunoe, in the province of Tango, went out to fish. It so happened that he caught a tortoise, and as tortoises are said to live many thousands of years, the thoughtful Urashima allowed the creature to return to the sea, rebaited his hook, and once more waited for the bite of a fish. Only the sea gently waved his line

324

to and fro. The sun beat down upon his head till at last Urashima fell asleep.

He had not been sleeping long when he heard some one calling his name : "Urashima, Urashima !"

It was such a sweet, haunting voice that the fisher-lad stood up in his boat and looked around in every direction, till he chanced to see the very tortoise he had been kind enough to restore to its watery home. The tortoise, which was able to speak quite fluently, profusely thanked Urashima for his kindness, and offered to take him to the *ryūkyū*, or Palace of the Dragon King.

The invitation was readily accepted, and getting on the tortoise's back, Urashima found himself gliding through the sea at a tremendous speed, and the curious part about it was he discovered that his clothes remained perfectly dry.

In the Sea King's Palace

Arriving at the Sea King's Palace, red bream, flounder, sole, and cuttlefish came out to give Urashima a hearty welcome. Having expressed their pleasure, these vassals of the Dragon King escorted the fisher-lad to an inner apartment, where the beautiful Princess Otohime and her maidens were seated. The Princess was arrayed in gorgeous garments of red and gold, all the colours of a wave with the sunlight upon it.

This Princess explained that she had taken the form of a tortoise by way of testing his kindness of heart. The test had happily proved successful, and as a reward for his virtue she offered to become his bride in a land where there was eternal youth and everlasting summer.

Urashima bashfully accepted the high honour bestowed upon him. He had no sooner spoken than a great company of fishes appeared, robed in long ceremonial garments, their fins supporting great coral trays loaded with rare delicacies. Then the happy couple drank the wedding cup of *saké*, and while they drank, some of the fishes played soft music, others sang, and not a few, with scales of silver and golden tails, stepped out a strange measure on the white sand.

After the festivities were over, Otohime showed her husband all the wonders of her father's palace. The greatest marvel of all was to see a country where all the seasons lingered together.[1] Looking to the east, Urashima saw plum- and cherry-trees in full bloom, with bright-winged butterflies skimming over the blossom, and away in the distance it seemed that the pink petals and butterflies had suddenly been converted into the song of a wondrous nightingale. In the south he saw trees in their summer glory, and heard the gentle note of the cricket. Looking to the west, the autumn maples made a fire in the branches, so that if Urashima had been other than a humble fisher-lad he might have recalled the following poem :

> " Fair goddess of the paling Autumn skies,
> Fain would I know how many looms she plies,
> Wherein through skilful tapestry she weaves
> Her fine brocade of fiery maple leaves—
> Since on each hill, with every gust that blows,
> In varied hues her vast embroidery glows ? "
>
> Trans. by CLARA A. WALSH.

It was, indeed, a "vast embroidery," for when Urashima looked toward the north he saw a great stretch of snow and a mighty pond covered with ice. All the seasons lingered together in that fair country where Nature had yielded to the full her infinite variety of beauty.

After Urashima had been in the Sea King's Palace for

---

[1] Compare "The Dream of Rosei" in Chapter VII.

Urashima and the Sea King's Daughter.

(See page 325*)*

Tokoyo and the Sea Serpent.

(See page 335*)*

three days, and seen many wonderful things, he suddenly remembered his old parents, and felt a strong desire to go and see them. When he went to his wife, and told her of his longing to return home, Otohime began to weep, and tried to persuade him to stop another day. But Urashima refused to be influenced in the matter. " I must go," said he, " but I will leave you only for a day. I will return again, dear wife of mine."

The Home-coming of Urashima

Then Otohime gave her husband a keepsake in remembrance of their love. It was called the *Tamate-Bako* (" Box of the Jewel Hand)." She explained that he was on no account to open the box, and Urashima, promising to fulfil her wish, said farewell, mounted a large tortoise, and soon found himself in his own country. He looked in vain for his father's home. Not a sign of it was to be seen. The cottage had vanished, only the little stream remained.

Still much perplexed, Urashima questioned a passerby, and he learnt from him that a fisher-lad, named Urashima, had gone to sea three hundred years ago and was drowned, and that his parents, brothers, and their grandchildren had been laid to rest for a long time. Then Urashima suddenly remembered that the country of the Sea King was a divine land, where a day, according to mortal reckoning, was a hundred years.

Urashima's reflections were gloomy in the extreme, for all whom he had loved on earth were dead. Then he heard the murmur of the sea, and recalled the lovely Otohime, as well as the country where the seasons joined hands and made a fourfold pageant of their beauty—the land where trees had emeralds for leaves and rubies for berries, where the fishes wore long robes and sang and danced and played. Louder the sea

sounded in Urashima's ears. Surely Otohime called
him ? But no path opened out before him, no obliging
tortoise appeared on the scene to carry him to where his
wife waited for him. "The box ! the box ! " said
Urashima softly, " if I open my wife's mysterious gift,
it may reveal the way."

Urashima untied the red silk thread and slowly,
fearfully opened the lid of the box. Suddenly there
rushed out a little white cloud ; it lingered a moment,
and then rolled away far over the sea. But a sacred
promise had been broken, and Urashima from a handsome youth became old and wrinkled. He staggered
forward, his white hair and beard blowing in the wind.
He looked out to sea, and then fell dead upon the
shore.

Professor Chamberlain writes : " Urashima's tomb,
together with his fishing-line, the casket given him by
the maiden, and two stones said to be precious, are
still shown at one of the temples in Kanagawa."

The Land of the Morning Calm

Chosen, the Land of the Morning Calm, was the old
name for Korea,[1] and however poetical the phrase may
be, it was, nevertheless, totally inapplicable to actual
fact. In its early history it was a country divided
against itself, and later on it was troubled with the
invading armies of China and Japan, to say nothing of
minor skirmishes with other countries. There is certainly a pathetic calm in Korea to-day, but it is the calm
of a long-vanquished and persecuted nation. It now rests
with Japan whether or not the Koreans rise from
serfdom and regain something of that old hardihood
that was at one time so prominent a feature of her
northern men.

[1] See *The Story of Korea*, by Joseph H. Longford.

THE LAND OF THE MORNING CALM

Long ago Korea came under the glamour of the Chinese civilisation, and it haunts her people to this day. Japan borrowed from Korea what Korea had borrowed from China. It was because Japan went on borrowing from the West when she had exhausted all that Korea and China could teach her that she eventually became, with the progressive stream of thought and action flowing vigorously through her, a world-power, while Korea remained a forlorn example of an almost stagnant country.

When Japan had succeeded in convincing Korea that she alone could be her faithful guide, Russia came, like a thief in the night, and established a military outpost at Wiju. The Russo-Japanese War resulted, and Korea became a Japanese colony, an experimental ground for social and political reform. Japan has waited long for Korea. May she find it at last, not a turbulent and rebellious country, but in very deed the Land of the Morning Calm. Korea in the past has contributed to the making of Japan's greatness in handing on the religion, art, and literature of China. Now it is Japan's turn to succour an impoverished country, and if the Morning Calm is united with the Rising Sun, there should be peace and prosperity in her new possession.

Professor J. H. Longford, in *The Story of Korea*, writes in regard to the invasion of the Empress Jingo : " Dr. Aston . . . contemptuously dismisses the whole as a myth founded on two very distinct historical facts—that there was, at the time of the alleged invasion, an Empress of Japan, a woman of real determination and ability, and that not one, but several Japanese invasions of Korea did occur, though at later periods, in which the Japanese did not invariably meet with the triumphant success that they claim for the Empress." We give

329

below the picturesque legend of Japan's first invasion of Korea.

The Tide Jewels

One night the Empress Jingo, as she lay asleep in her tent, had a strange dream. She dreamt that a spirit came to her and told her of a wonderful land, a land in the West, full of treasures of gold and silver, a dazzling land, fair to look upon as a beautiful woman. The spirit informed her that the name of this country was Chosen (Korea), and that it might belong to Japan if she would set out and conquer this wealthy land.

The next day the Empress Jingo informed her husband about her dream; but the Emperor, a stolid, matter-of-fact man, did not believe in dreams. However, as his wife persisted in thrusting upon him what he deemed to be a foolish scheme, he climbed a high mountain, and looking toward the setting sun saw no land in the West. When the Emperor had come down from the mountain, he informed his wife that he would on no account give his consent to invade and conquer a country which simply owed its existence to a disordered dream. But the Gods were angry with the Emperor, and shortly after he had uttered his prohibition he died in battle.

The Gift of the Dragon King

When the Empress Jingo became sole ruler she was determined to go to this country she had heard about in a dream; but as she was resolved to make her expedition no puny and tame affair, she called upon the Spirit of the Mountain to give her timber and iron for her ships. The Spirit of Fields gave her rice and other grain for her army, while the Spirit of Grass presented her with hemp for rope. The Wind God looked favourably upon her scheme, and promised to blow her ships towards Korea. All the spirits appeared in compliance with the Empress Jingo's wishes except Isora, the Spirit of the Seashore.

Isora was a lazy fellow, and when he finally appeared above the waves of the sea, he did so without gorgeous apparel, for he was covered with slime and shells, and seaweed adorned his unkempt person. When the Empress saw him she bade him go to his master, the Dragon King, and ask him to give her the Tide Jewels.

Isora obeyed, dived down into the water, and presently stood before the Dragon King and made his request.

The Dragon King took out the Tide Jewels from a casket, placed them on a great shell, and bade Isora promptly return to the Empress Jingo with this precious gift.

Isora sprang from his master's palace to the surface of the sea, and the Empress Jingo placed the Tide Jewels in her girdle.

The Voyage

Now that the Empress had obtained the Jewel of the Flood-Tide and the Jewel of the Ebb-Tide she had three thousand ships built and launched, and during the tenth month she started on her great expedition. Her fleet had not proceeded far when a mighty storm arose, so that the vessels crashed together and were likely to sink to the bottom of the sea. The Dragon King, however, commanded great sea-monsters to go to the rescue; some bore up the ships with their great bodies, others pushed their heads against the sterns of many vessels, thus propelling them through a heavy sea which had very nearly driven them back whence they came. Powerful dragon-fishes lent their aid to those pushing and snorting in the rear by holding the ships' cables in their mouths and towing the vessels forward at a surprising speed. Directly the storm ceased, the sea-monsters and dragon-fishes disappeared.

The Throwing of the Tide Jewels

At last the Empress Jingo and her army saw the distant mountains of Korea loom out on the horizon. On nearing the coast they perceived that the whole of the Korean army stood upon the shore with their ships ready to be launched at the word of command. As soon as the Korean sentinels perceived the Japanese fleet, they gave the signal for embarking, and immediately a great line of war-vessels shot out over the water.

The Empress stood watching these proceedings with unruffled calm. She knew that the victory or defeat of her army lay in her power. When the Korean vessels drew near to her fleet she threw into the sea the Jewel of the Ebb-Tide. Directly it touched the water it caused the tide to recede from under the very keels of the Korean ships, so that they were left stranded upon dry land. The Koreans, suspecting no magic and believing their stranded condition to have been the result of a tidal wave and, moreover, that the Japanese vessels would succumb to the back-wash, sprang from their vessels and rushed over the sand. Now the Japanese bowmen twanged their bow-strings, and a great cloud of arrows flew into the air, killing many hundreds of the enemy. When the Koreans were quite near the Japanese vessels, the Empress flung forth the Jewel of the Flood-Tide. Immediately a great wave rushed over and destroyed nearly the whole of the Korean army. It was now an easy matter for the Japanese to land and capture the country. The King of Korea surrendered, and the Empress returned to her own kingdom laden with silk and jewels, books and pictures, tiger-skins and precious robes.

When the Tide Jewels had been thrown by the Empress, they did not lie long on the bed of the ocean. Isora speedily rescued them and carried them back to the Dragon King.

Prince Ojin

Soon after the Empress Jingo's return she gave birth to a son named Ojin. When Ojin had grown into a fair and wise little boy, his mother told him about the wonderful Tide Jewels, and expressed a wish that he, too, should possess them in order that he might bring honour and glory to Japan.

One day the Prime Minister, who was said to be three hundred and sixty years old, and the counsellor of no less than five Mikados, took Ojin with him in a royal war-barge. The vessel skimmed over the sea with its gold silk sails. The Prime Minister in a loud voice called on the Dragon King to give young Ojin the Tide Jewels.

Immediately the waves about the vessel were churned into foam, and amid a great thunderous roar the Dragon King himself appeared with a living creature of dreadful countenance for a helmet. Then out of the water arose a mighty shell, in the recess of which glittered the Tide Jewels. After presenting these jewels, and making a pretty little speech, he returned to his great green kingdom.

The Slaughter of the Sea Serpent [1]

Oribe Shima had offended the great ruler Hojo Takatoki, and was in consequence banished to Kami-

[1] This legend, and those that follow in this chapter, are adapted from *Ancient Tales and Folk-lore of Japan*, by R. Gordon Smith.

shima, one of the Oki Islands, and forced to leave his beautiful daughter Tokoyo, whom he deeply loved.

At last Tokoyo was unable to bear the separation any longer, and she was determined to find her father. She therefore set out upon a long journey, and arriving at Akasaki, in the province of Hoki, from which coast town the Oki Islands are visible on a fine day, she besought many a fisherman to row her to her destination. But the fisher-folk laughed at Tokoyo, and bade her relinquish her foolish plan and return home. The maiden, however, would not listen to their advice, and at nightfall she got into the lightest vessel she could find, and by dint of a fair wind and persistent rowing the brave girl came to one of the rocky bays of the Oki Islands.

That night Tokoyo slept soundly, and in the morning partook of food. When she had finished her meal she questioned a fisherman as to where she might find her father. " I have never heard of Oribe Shima," replied the fisherman, " and if he has been banished, I beg that you will desist from further search, lest it lead to the death of you both."

That night the sorrowful Tokoyo slept beneath a shrine dedicated to Buddha. Her sleep was soon disturbed by the clapping of hands, and looking up she saw a weeping maiden clad in a white garment with a priest standing beside her. Just as the priest was about to push the maiden over the rocks into the roaring sea, Tokoyo sprang up and held the maiden's arm.

The priest explained that on that night, the thirteenth of June, the Serpent God, known as Yofuné-Nushi, demanded the sacrifice of a young girl, and that unless this annual sacrifice was made the God became angry and caused terrible storms.

THE SLAUGHTER OF THE SEA SERPENT

"Good sir," said Tokoyo, "I am glad that I have been able to save this poor girl's life. I gladly offer myself in her place, for I am sad of heart because I have been unable to find my father. Give him this letter, for my last words of love and farewell go to him."

Having thus spoken, Tokoyo took the maiden's white robe and clad herself in it, and having prayed to the image of Buddha, she placed a small dagger between her teeth and plunged into the tempestuous sea. Down she went through the moonlit water till she came to a mighty cave where she saw a statue of Hojo Takatoki, who had sent her poor father into exile. She was about to tie the image on her back when a great white serpent crept out from the cave with eyes gleaming angrily. Tokoyo, realising that this creature was none other than Yofuné-Nushi, drew her dagger and thrust it through the right eye of the God. This unexpected attack caused the serpent to retire into the cave, but the brave Tokoyo followed and struck another blow, this time at the creature's heart. For a moment Yofuné-Nushi blindly stumbled forward, then with a shriek of pain fell dead upon the floor of the cavern.

During this adventure the priest and the maiden stood on the rocks watching the spot where Tokoyo had disappeared, praying fervently for the peace of her sorrowful soul. As they watched and prayed they saw Tokoyo come to the surface of the water carrying an image and a mighty fish-like creature. The priest hastily came to the girl's assistance, dragged her upon the shore, placed the image on a high rock, and secured the body of the White Sea Serpent.

In due time the remarkable story was reported to Tameyoshi, lord of the island, who in turn reported the strange adventure to Hojo Takatoki. Now Takatoki had for some time been suffering from a disease which defied the skill of the most learned doctors ; but it was observed that he regained his health precisely at the hour when his image, which had been cursed and thrown into the sea by some exile, had been restored. When Hojo Takatoki heard that the brave girl was the daughter of the exiled Oribe Shima, he sent him back with all speed to his own home, where he and his daughter lived in peace and happiness.

The Spirit of the Sword

One night a junk anchored off Fudo's Cape, and when various preparations had been made, the Captain, Tarada by name, and his crew fell asleep on deck. At about midnight Tarada was awakened by hearing an extraordinary rumbling sound that seemed to proceed from the bottom of the sea. Chancing to look in the direction of the bow of the vessel, he saw a fair girl clad in white and illumined by a dazzling light.

When Tarada had awakened his crew he approached the maiden, who said : " My only wish is to be back in the world again." Having uttered these words, she disappeared among the waves.

The next day Tarada went on shore and asked many who lived in Amakura if they had ever heard of a wondrous maiden bathed, as it were, in a phosphorescent light. One of the villagers thus made answer : " We have never seen the maiden you describe, but for some time past we have been disturbed by rumbling noises that seem to come from Fudo's Cape, and ever since, these mysterious sounds have prevented fish from entering our bay. It may be that the girl you saw was the ghost of some poor maiden drowned at sea, and the noise we hear none other than the anger of the Sea God on account of a corpse or human bones polluting the water."

It was eventually decided that the dumb Sankichi should dive into the sea and bring up any corpse he might find there. So Sankichi went on board Tarada's junk, and having said farewell to his friends, he plunged into the water. He searched diligently, but could see no trace of corpse or human bones. At length, however, he perceived what looked like a sword wrapped in silk, and on untying the wrapping he found that it was indeed a sword, of great brightness and without a flaw of any kind. Sankichi came to the surface and was quickly taken aboard. The poor fellow was gently laid on the deck, but he fainted from exhaustion. His cold body was rubbed vigorously and fires were lit. In a very short time Sankichi became conscious and was able to show the sword and give particulars of his adventure.

An official, by the name of Naruse Tsushimanokami, was of the opinion that the sword was a sacred treasure, and on his recommendation it was placed in a shrine and dedicated to Fudo. Sankichi faithfully guarded the precious weapon, and Fudo's Cape became known as the Cape of the Woman's Sword. To the delight of the fisher-folk, the spirit of the weapon now being satisfied, the fish came back into the bay again.

The Love of O Cho San

"To-day is the tenth of June. May the rain fall in torrents!
For I long to see my dearest O Cho San."
Trans. by R. Gordon Smith.

In the isolated Hatsushima Island, celebrated for its *suisenn* (jonquils), there once lived a beautiful maiden called Cho, and all the young men on the island were eager to marry her. One day the handsome Shinsaku, who was bolder than the rest, went to Gisuke, the brother of Cho, and told him that he much desired to marry his fair sister. Gisuke offered no objections, and calling Cho to him, when the suitor had gone, he said : " Shinsaku wishes to become your husband. I like the fisherman, and think that in him you will make an excellent match. You are now eighteen, and it is quite time that you got married."

O Cho San fully approved of what her brother had said, and the marriage was arranged to take place in three days' time. Unfortunately, those days were days of discord on the island, for when the other fishermen lovers heard the news they began to hate the once popular Shinsaku, and, moreover, they neglected their work and were continually fighting each other. These lamentable scenes cast such a gloom upon the once happy Hatsushima Island that O Cho San and her lover decided that for the peace of the many they would not marry after all.

This noble sacrifice, however, did not bring about the desired effect, for the thirty lovers still fought each other and still neglected their fishing. O Cho San determined to perform a still greater sacrifice. She wrote loving letters of farewell to her brother and Shinsaku, and having left them by the sleeping Gisuke, she softly crept out of the house on a stormy night or the 10th of June. She dropped big stones into her pretty sleeves, and then flung herself into the sea.

The next day Gisuke and Shinsaku read their letters from O Cho San, and, overcome by grief, they searched the shore, where they found the straw sandals of Cho. The two men realised that the fair maid had indeed taken her precious life, and shortly after her body was taken from the sea and buried, and over her tomb Shinsaku placed many flowers and wept continually.

THE SPIRIT OF THE GREAT AWABI

One evening, Shinsaku, unable to bear his sorrow any longer, decided to take his life, believing that by doing so he would meet the spirit of O Cho San. As he lingered by the girl's grave, he seemed to see her white ghost, and, murmuring her name over and over again, he rushed toward her. At this moment Gisuke, awakened by the noise, came out of his house, and found Shinsaku clinging to his lover's gravestone.

When Shinsaku told his friend that he had seen the spirit of O Cho San, and intended to take his life in order to be with her for ever, Gisuke made answer thus : " Shinsaku, great is your love for my poor sister, but you can love her best by serving her in this world. When the great Gods call, you will meet her, but await with hope and courage till that hour comes, for only a brave, as well as a loving, heart is worthy of O Cho San. Let us together build a shrine and dedicate it to my sister, and keep your love strong and pure by never marrying any one else."

The thirty lovers who had shown such unmanly feeling now fully realised the sorrow they had caused, and in order to show their contrition they too helped to build the shrine of the unfortunate maiden, where to this day a ceremony takes place on the 10th of June, and it is said that the spirit of O Cho San comes in the rain.

The Spirit of the Great Awabi

The morning after a great earthquake had devastated the fishing village of Nanao, it was observed that about two miles from the shore a rock had sprung up as the result of the seismic disturbance and, moreover, that the sea had become muddy. One night a number of fishermen were passing by the rock, when they observed, near at hand, a most extraordinary light that

appeared to float up from the bottom of the sea with a
glory as bright as the sun. The fishermen shipped
their oars and gazed upon the wonderful spectacle with
considerable surprise, but when the light was suddenly
accompanied by a deep rumbling sound, the sailors
feared another earthquake and made all speed for
Nanao.

On the third day the wondrous rays from the deep
increased in brilliance, so that folk standing on the shore
of Nanao could see them distinctly, and the superstitious fishermen became more and more frightened.
Only Kansuke and his son Matakichi had sufficient
courage to go fishing. On their return journey they
reached the Rock Island, and were drawing in their line
when Kansuke lost his balance and fell into the sea.

Though old Kansuke was a good swimmer, he went
down like a stone and did not rise to the surface.
Matakichi, deeming this strange, dived into the water,
almost blinded by the mysterious rays we have already
described. When he at length reached the bottom he
discovered innumerable *awabi* (ear-shells), and in the
middle of the group one of vast size. From all these
shells there poured forth a brilliant light, and though
it was like day under the water, Matakichi could find
no trace of his father. Eventually he was forced to rise
to the surface, only to find that the rough sea had
broken his boat. However, scrambling upon a piece
of wreckage, with the aid of a favourable wind and
current he at last reached the shore of Nanao, and gave
the villagers an account of his remarkable adventure,
and of the loss of his old father.

Matakichi, grieving sorely over the death of his
parent, went to the old village priest and begged that
worthy that he would make him one of his disciples in
order that he might pray the more efficaciously for the

spirit of his father. The priest readily consented, and about three weeks later they took boat to the Rock Island, where both prayed ardently for the soul of Kansuke.

That night the old priest awoke with a start and saw an ancient man standing by his bedside. With a profound bow the stranger thus spoke : " I am the Spirit of the Great Awabi, and I am more than one thousand years old. I live in the sea near the Rock Island, and this morning I heard you praying for the soul of Kansuke. Alas ! good priest, your prayers have deeply moved me, but in shame and sorrow I confess that I ate Kansuke. I have bade my followers depart elsewhere, and in order to atone for my sin I shall take my own wretched life, so that the pearl that is within me may be given to Matakichi." And having uttered these words, the Spirit of the Great Awabi suddenly disappeared.

When Matakichi awoke next morning and opened the shutters he discovered the enormous *awabi* he had seen near the Rock Island. He took it to the old priest, who, after listening to his disciple's story, gave an account of his own experience. The great pearl and shell of the *awabi* were placed in the temple, and the body was reverently buried.

CHAPTER XXVIII : SUPERSTITIONS

Japanese Superstition

THE subject of Japanese superstition is of special importance, because it serves to indicate the channel by which many myths and legends, but more particularly folk-lore, have evolved. Superstition is, as it were, the raw material out of which innumerable strange beliefs are gradually fashioned into stories, and an inquiry into the subject will show us the peasant mind striving to counteract certain supernatural forces, or to turn them to advantage in every-day life. Many superstitions have already been recorded in these pages, and in the present chapter we shall deal with those that have not been treated elsewhere. It is scarcely necessary to point out that these superstitions, selected from a vast store of quaint beliefs, are necessarily of a primitive kind and must be regarded, excluding, perhaps, those associated with the classic art of divination, as peculiar to the more ignorant classes in Japan.

Human Sacrifice

In prehistoric times the bow was believed to possess supernatural power. It would miraculously appear on the roof of a man's house as a sign that the eldest unmarried daughter must be sacrificed. She was accordingly buried alive in order that her flesh might be consumed by the Deity of Wild Beasts. Later on, however, the bow was no longer the message of a cruel divinity, for it gradually lost its horrible significance, and has now become a symbol of security. To this day it may be seen fixed to the ridge-pole of a roof, and is regarded as a lucky charm.

We have another example of human sacrifice in the old repulsive custom of burying a man alive with the

342

idea of giving stability to a bridge or castle. In the early days, when forced labour existed, there was unfortunately scant regard for the sacredness of human life. Those who laboured without reward were under the control of a merciless superintendent, who emphasised his orders by means of a spear. He was ready to kill all those who were idle or in any way rebellious, and many corpses were flung into the masonry. When a river had to be dammed, or a fortification constructed with the utmost despatch, this deplorable deed was not unusual.

When a new bridge was built its utility and long life were assured, not always by human sacrifice or sorrow, but sometimes by happiness. The first persons allowed to walk over a new bridge were those of a particularly happy disposition. We are told that two genial old men, who each had a family of twelve children, first crossed the Matsue bridge, accompanied by their wives, children, grandchildren, and great-grandchildren. This joyous procession took place amid much rejoicing and a display of fireworks. The idea of happiness contributing to the success of a Japanese bridge is a pretty conception, but, unfortunately, the old bridge of Matsue, now replaced by one far less picturesque, is associated with a very unpleasant tradition.

When Horiō Yoshiharu became *Daimyō* of Izumo he arranged to build a bridge over the turbulent river at Matsue. Many laboured to carry out his wishes, but the work did not prosper. Countless great stones were flung into the rushing water with the idea of making a solid base on which to construct the pillars, but many of the stones were washed away, and as soon as the bridge took tangible form it was wrecked by the fierce torrent. It was believed that the spirits of the flood were angry, and in order to appease them it was deemed necessary to offer a human sacrifice. A man was accordingly buried alive below the central pillar where the water was most turbulent. When this had been done the work prospered, and the bridge remained intact for three hundred years. Gensuke was the unfortunate victim, and this was the name given to the central pillar. It is said that on moonless nights a mysterious red fire shines from this pillar—the ghostly emanations of poor Gensuke.

Classical Divination

One of the most popular forms of Japanese superstition is associated with divination, and Confucianism has no doubt contributed much to its popularity. The *Yih-King*, or " Book of Changes," is the main source of the art, and Confucius devoted so much time to the study of this mysterious work that it is said that the leathern thongs used to hold the leaves together were replaced three times during his lifetime. The *Yih-King* was commenced by Fu Hsi two thousand years before the birth of Christ, and Confucius added much fresh material. A more complicated method of reading the future than by means of eight trigrams and sixty-four diagrams cannot be imagined. So involved a system of divination naturally became the art of the learned few, but in course of time it underwent various modifications. It lost, to a certain extent, its most classic aspect, and many Japanese diviners sprang up in the country professing to read the future for a small fee, and without the qualification of having deeply pondered over the instruction to be found in the *Yih-King*. A comparatively simple form of divination is with fifty divining rods, shuffled in a particular way, and the final position of the rods is supposed to answer the various

OTHER FORMS OF DIVINATION

questions of the inquirer. Many diviners in Japan to-day are mere charlatans working upon the credulity of their patrons, without fully understanding the art they practise. But in ancient times divination was associated with a sacred ritual. It was necessary for the diviner, like the old swordsmith, to prepare and fit himself for his task. It was required of him that he should thoroughly cleanse his body, seat himself in a private apartment, and go through the elaborate process of holding the rods in the spirit of reverence. At a certain moment he was instructed to close his eyes, suspend breathing for a time, and concentrate his thoughts on his work of divination, for the old diviner, like the old Shintō priest, believed that he was calling the supernatural to his aid.

Other Forms of Divination

In other forms of divination, requiring no expert interpretation, we find that the future is supposed to be revealed in the cracks and lines of a slightly burnt shoulder-bone of a deer, a method which closely resembles the old English custom of "reading the speal-bone." It was not always easy to secure a deer's shoulder-bone, and as the markings were of more importance than the bone itself, in course of time burnt tortoise-shell took its place. As hair-combs were usually made of this material, a woman, by charring it, was able to read the lines and ascertain the constancy or otherwise of her lover, &c. Girls used to read the riddle of the future and see what it had in store for them by going out at night and stringing together the fragmentary remarks of passers-by. This method is known as *tsuji-ura*, but it is by no means peculiar to Japan, for it is still frequently practised by superstitious people in our own country. A love-sick maiden tried to discover whether or not her love would be requited by placing a rod in the ground, surrounding it with various offerings, and listening to the conversation of wayfarers who chanced to come that way.[1]   A later and more elaborate development of this form of divination required three maidens, and the method employed is as follows.   The young women went to where roads crossed each other, and thrice repeated an invocation to the God of Roads.   When they had supplicated this Deity, they flung rice on the ground, for rice has the power of driving away evil spirits.   The maidens then rubbed their fingers against the teeth of a boxwood comb, because *tsuge*, the Japanese name for this wood, also means " to tell."   After these preparations they each stood in a different position and pieced together the remarks of passers-by.   Occasionally some message from the future was received while the inquirer stood under a bridge and listened to the clatter of feet, and sometimes a priest whistling by inhalation was supposed to reveal an omen of some kind.

Unlucky Years and Days

It is believed that certain periods of life are extremely unlucky.   The twenty-fifth, forty-second, and sixty-first years of a man's life are considered unfortunate, while the unlucky years of a woman's life are the nineteenth, thirty-third, and thirty-seventh.   In order to prevent calamity during these periods, it is necessary to devote much time to religious exercises.   Men and women are advised not to take a journey during the

---

[1] This variety of divination is of particular interest, for the rod symbolises the God of Roads, the Deity created from Izanagi's staff, which, it will be remembered, he flung behind him when pursued in the Under-world by the Eight Ugly Females.

sixteenth, twenty-fifth, thirty-fourth, forty-third, fifty-second, and sixty-first year. When superstitious women wish to make a new garment, they utter an invocation, and later on sprinkle three pinches of salt on the shoulder gusset. No woman should use her needle on a "monkey" day, but rather on a "bird" day. If the work is undertaken on the former day, the garment is in danger of being burnt or rent; but if the apparel is made on the latter day, it will have the beauty and durability of the feathers of a bird.

Children

When a child's tooth falls out, it is thrown away under the eaves, with the wish that it may be replaced by the tooth of a demon. Sometimes the tooth of a little boy or girl is thrown on the floor with the request that it may be replaced by the tooth of a rat. Children may be immune from nightmare if the word "puppy" is written on their foreheads; and if to this precaution is added a sketch of the *Baku*, Eater of Dreams, the little one's slumber will be sure to be of a peaceful kind. The word "dog" inscribed on a child's forehead is a protection against the magic of foxes and badgers.

Some of the nostrums that are supposed to cure children's ailments are very curious. Blood extracted from a cock's comb cures indigestion, while an eruption on the head may be driven away by repeating these words: "In the long days of spring weeds may be removed, but those in the garden must be cut down at once." Even a Japanese baby cries occasionally, but if a red bag containing dog's hair is fastened on its back, it will immediately cease to cry, and the plaintive wailing will give place to smiles. Blindness is frequently the result of smallpox, but this calamity may be prevented by throwing seven peas into a well, reciting seven prayers, and then drawing off all the water from the well.

Charms

Many Japanese charms are pieces of paper bearing an inscription designed to avert evil. Another variety is inscribed with the name of a god. It takes the form of a long strip which the poor fasten on the outside of their houses, while those who have not to contend with poverty regard it as a part of their domestic altar. The imprint of a child's hand, "obtained," writes Professor Chamberlain, "by first wetting the hand with ink and then applying it to a sheet of paper, is believed to avert malign influences." Fragments of temples, rice-grains carved to represent the Gods of Luck, minute *sutras*, copies of Buddha's footprint, and many other quaint conceits are among the multitudinous charms of Japan.

The Beckoning Leaf

There is a certain Japanese tree, called *tegashiwa*, and its leaves in shape are not unlike a hand. In ancient days, when it was necessary for a *samurai* to leave his home, he received just before his departure a *tai* (perch), which was served on the leaf of a *tegashiwa* tree. This was his farewell repast, and when the *samurai* had eaten the fish the leaf was hung over the door, in the belief that it would guard him on his journey, and bring him safely back to his home again. It was not the shape, but the movement of the *tegashiwa* leaf that gave rise to this pleasing fancy, for the leaf, when blown by the wind, appeared to beckon after the graceful Japanese manner.

348

BIMBOGAMI

Bimbogami

Dry peas are usually found to be efficacious in driving away evil spirits, but Bimbogami, the God of Poverty, is not so easily overcome. There is something pathetic in the idea that poverty should be regarded as an obstinate and most unwelcome fellow, for at this point we touch reality. However, though Bimbogami takes no notice of dry peas, he may be vanquished by other means.

The charcoal fire in a Japanese kitchen is blown into a cheerful glow by means of a utensil called *hifukidake*, a bamboo tube—a more artistic and simple form of bellows, where the inflated cheeks take the place of our hand-moved leather bag. Before long the bamboo tube cracks with the intense heat. When this takes place a copper coin is put inside the tube, an incantation is uttered, and then the "fire-blow-tube" is thrown either into the street or into a stream. This throwing away of the useless bamboo of the kitchen is always supposed to signify the forced departure of Bimbogami. Most of us are familiar with what is known as the Death-spider that ticks like a watch in our walls. In Japan it is called *Bimbomushi*, "Poverty-Insect." Its ticking does not foretell the coming of Death, as is the belief in our own country, but it denotes the unwelcome presence of the God of Poverty in the Japanese home.

CHAPTER XXIX : SUPERNATURAL BEINGS

The Kappa

THE *Kappa* is a river goblin, a hairy creature with the body of a tortoise and scaly limbs. His head somewhat resembles that of an ape, in the top of which there is a cavity containing a mysterious fluid, said to be the source of the creature's power. The chief delight of the *Kappa* is to challenge human beings to single combat, and the unfortunate man who receives an invitation of this kind cannot refuse. Though the *Kappa* is fierce and quarrelsome, he is, nevertheless, extremely polite. The wayfarer who receives his peremptory summons gives the goblin a profound bow. The courteous *Kappa* acknowledges the obeisance, and in inclining his head the strength-giving liquid runs out from the hollow in his cranium, and becoming feeble, his warlike characteristics immediately disappear. To defeat the *Kappa*, however, is just as unfortunate as to receive a beating at his hands, for the momentary glory of the conquest is rapidly followed by a wasting away of the unfortunate wayfarer. The *Kappa* possesses the propensities of a vampire, for he strikes people in the water, as they bathe in lake or river, and sucks their blood. In a certain part of Japan the *Kappa* is said to claim two victims every year. When they emerge from the water their skin becomes blanched, and they gradually pine away as the result of a terrible disease.

In Izumo the village people refer to the *Kappa* as *Kawako* ("The Child of the River"). Near Matsue there is a little hamlet called Kawachi-mura, and on the bank of the river Kawachi there is a small temple known as Kawako-no-miya, that is, the temple of the *Kawako* or

THE TENGU

Kappa, said to contain a document signed by this river goblin. Concerning this document the following legend is recorded.

The Kappa's Promise

In ancient days a *Kappa* dwelt in the river Kawachi, and he made a practice of seizing and destroying a number of villagers, and in addition many of their domestic animals. On one occasion a horse went into the river, and the *Kappa*, in trying to capture it, in some way twisted his neck, but in spite of considerable pain he refused to let his victim go. The frightened horse sprang up the river bank and ran into a neighbouring field with the *Kappa* still holding on to the terrified animal. The owner of the horse, together with many villagers, securely bound the Child of the River. " Let us kill this horrible creature," said the peasants, " for he has assuredly committed many horrible crimes, and we should do well to be rid of such a dreadful monster." " No," replied the owner of the horse, " we will not kill him. We will make him swear never to destroy any of the inhabitants or the domestic animals of this village." A document was accordingly prepared, and the *Kappa* was asked to peruse it, and when he had done so to sign his name. " I cannot write," replied the penitent *Kappa*, " but I will dip my hand in ink and press it upon the document." When the creature had made his inky mark, he was released and allowed to return to the river, and from that day to this the *Kappa* has remained true to his promise.

The Tengu

We have already referred to the *Tengu* in the story of Yoshitsune and Benkei.[1] In this legend it will

[1] *See* Chapter II.

be remembered that Yoshitsune, one of the greatest warriors of Old Japan, learnt the art of swordsmanship from the King of the *Tengu*. Professor B. H. Chamberlain describes the *Tengu* as "a class of goblins or gnomes that haunt the mountains and woodlands, and play many pranks. They have an affinity to birds ; for they are winged and beaked, sometimes clawed. But often the beak becomes a large and enormously long human nose, and the whole creature is conceived as human, nothing bird-like remaining but the fan of feathers with which it fans itself. It is often dressed in leaves, and wears on its head a tiny cap." In brief, the *Tengu* are minor divinities, and are supreme in the art of fencing, and, indeed, in the use of weapons generally. The ideographs with which the name is written signify "heavenly dog," which is misleading, for the creature bears no resemblance to a dog, and is, as we have already described, partly human and partly bird-like in appearance. There are other confusing traditions in regard to the word *Tengu*, for it is said that the Emperor Jomei gave the name to a certain meteor "which whirled from east to west with a loud detonation." Then, again, a still more ancient belief informs us that the *Tengu* were emanations from Susa-no-o, the Impetuous Male, and again, that they were female demons with heads of beasts and great ears and noses of such enormous length that they could carry men on them and fly with their suspended burden for thousands of miles without fatigue, and in addition their teeth were so strong and so sharp that these female demons could bite through swords and spears. The *Tengu* is still believed to inhabit certain forests and the recesses of high mountains. Generally speaking, the *Tengu* is not a malevolent being, for he possesses a keen sense of humour, and is fond of a practical joke. Sometimes, however, the *Tengu*

The Kappa and his Victim.

(See page 351)

Kato Sayemon in his Palace of the Shōgun Ashikaga.

(See page 370*)*

mysteriously hides human beings, and when finally they return to their homes they do so in a demented condition. This strange occurrence is known as *Tengu-kakushi*, or hidden by a *Tengu*.

Tobikawa Imitates a Tengu

Tobikawa, an ex-wrestler who lived in Matsue, spent his time in hunting and killing foxes. He did not believe in the various superstitions concerning this animal, and it was generally believed that his great strength made him immune from the witchcraft of foxes. However, there were some people of Matsue who prophesied that Tobikawa would come to an untimely end as the result of his daring deeds and disbelief in supernatural powers. Tobikawa was extremely fond of practical jokes, and on one occasion he had the hardihood to imitate the general appearance of a *Tengu*, feathers, long nose, claws, and all. Having thus disguised himself, he climbed up into a tree belonging to a sacred grove. Presently the peasants observed him, and deeming the creature they saw to be a *Tengu*, they began to worship him and to place many offerings about the tree. Alas ! the dismal prophecy came true, for while the merry Tobikawa was trying to imitate the acrobatic antics of a *Tengu*, he slipped from a branch and was killed.

The Adventures of Kiuchi Heizayemon

We have already referred to the *Tengu-kakushi*, and the following legend gives a graphic account of this supernatural occurrence.

One evening, Kiuchi Heizayemon, a retainer, mysteriously disappeared. Kiuchi's friends, when they heard of what had taken place, searched for him in every direction. Eventually they discovered the missing man's clogs, scabbard, and sword ; but the sheath was bent like the curved handle of a tea-kettle. They had no sooner made this lamentable discovery than they also perceived Kiuchi's girdle, which had been cut into three pieces. At midnight, those who searched heard a strange cry, a voice calling for help. Suzuki Shichiro, one of the party, chanced to look up, and he saw a strange creature with wings standing upon the roof of a temple. When the rest of the band had joined their comrade, they all looked upon the weird figure, and one said: "I believe it is nothing but an umbrella flapping in the wind." "Let us make quite sure," replied Suzuki Shichiro, and with these words he lifted up his voice, and cried loudly: "Are you the lost Kiuchi?" "Yes," was the reply, "and I pray that you will take me down from this temple as speedily as possible."

When Kiuchi had been brought down from the temple roof, he fainted, and remained in a swoon for three days. At length, gaining consciousness, he gave the following account of his strange adventure:

"The evening when I disappeared I heard some one shouting my name over and over again, and going out I discovered a black-robed monk, bawling 'Heizayemon!' Beside the monk stood a man of great stature; his face was red, and his dishevelled hair fell upon the ground. 'Climb up on yonder roof,' he shouted fiercely. I refused to obey such an evil-faced villain, and drew my sword, but in a moment he bent the blade and broke my scabbard into fragments. Then my girdle was roughly torn off and cut into three pieces. When these things had been done, I was carried to a roof, and there severely chastised. But this was not the end of my trouble, for after I had been beaten, I was forced to seat myself on a round tray. In a moment I was whirled into the air, and the tray carried me with great speed to many regions. When it appeared to me that I had

travelled through space for ten days, I prayed to the
Lord Buddha, and found myself on what appeared to
be the summit of a mountain, but in reality it was the
roof of the temple whence you, my comrades, rescued
me."

A Modern Belief in the Tengu

Captain Brinkley, in *Japan and China*, informs us
that as late as 1860 the officials of the Yedo Government showed their belief in supernatural beings. Prior
to the visit of the *Shōgun* to Nikko, they caused the
following notice to be exhibited in the vicinity of the
mausolea :

"TO THE TENGU AND OTHER DEMONS

" Whereas our *Shōgun* intends to visit the Nikko Mausolea
next April, now therefore ye *Tengu* and other Demons
inhabiting these mountains must remove elsewhere until
the *Shōgun's* visit is concluded.
"(Signed)   MIZUNO, Lord of Dewa.
" Dated July 1860."

The local officials were not content with a notice of
this kind. After duly notifying the *Tengu* and other
demons of the coming of the *Shōgun*, the exact mountains were specified where these creatures might live
during the ruler's visit.

The Mountain Woman and the Mountain Man

The Mountain Woman's body is covered with long
white hair. She is looked upon as an ogre (*kijo*), and, as
such, figures in Japanese romance. She has cannibalistic
tendencies, and is able to fly about like a moth and
traverse pathless mountains with ease.

The Mountain Man is said to resemble a great dark-

haired monkey. He is extremely strong, and thinks
nothing of stealing food from the villages. He is, however, always ready to assist woodcutters, and will gladly
carry their timber for them in exchange for a ball of rice.
It is useless to capture or kill him, for an attack of any
kind upon the Mountain Man brings misfortune, and
sometimes death, upon the assailants.

Sennin

The *Sennin* are mountain recluses, and many are the
legends told in connection with them. Though they
have human form, they are, at the same time, immortal,
and adepts in the magical arts. The first great Japanese
sennin was Yōshō, who was born at Noto A.D. 870.
Just before his birth his mother dreamt that she had
swallowed the sun, a dream that foretold the miraculous
power of her child. Yōshō was studious and devout,
and spent most of his time in studying the "Lotus of
the Law." He lived very simply indeed, and at length
reduced his diet to a single grain of millet a day. He
departed from the earth A.D. 901, having attained
much supernatural power. He left his mantle hanging
on the branch of a tree, together with a scroll bearing
these words : "I bequeath my mantle to Emmei of
Dogen-ji." In due time Emmei became a *sennin*, and,
like his master, was able to perform many marvels.
Shortly after Yōshō's disappearance his father became
seriously ill, and he prayed most ardently that he might
see his well-loved son again. In reply to his prayers,
Yōshō's voice was heard overhead reciting the "Lotus
of the Law." When he had concluded his recitations,
he said to his stricken father: "If flowers are offered
and incense burned on the 18th of every month, my
spirit will descend and greet you, drawn by the perfume
of the flowers and the blue smoke of incense."

A GLOBE OF FIRE

Sennin in Art

Sennin are frequently depicted in Japanese art:
Chokoro releasing his magic horse from a gigantic
gourd; Gama with his wizard toad; Tekkai blowing
his soul into space; Roko balancing himself on a
flying tortoise; and Kumé, who fell from his chariot of
cloud because, contrary to his holy calling, he loved
the image of a fair girl reflected in a stream.

Miraculous Lights

There are many varieties of fire apparitions in Japan.
There is the ghost-fire, demon-light, fox-flame, flash-
pillar, badger-blaze, dragon-torch, and lamp of Buddha.
In addition supernatural fire is said to emanate from
certain birds, such as the blue heron, through the skin,
mouth, and eyes. There are also fire-wheels, or messengers from Hades, sea-fires, besides the flames that
spring from the cemetery.

A Globe of Fire

From the beginning of March to the end of June
there may be seen in the province of Settsu a globe of
fire resting on the top of a tree, and within this globe
there is a human face. In ancient days there once
lived in Nikaido district of Settsu province a priest
named Nikōbō, famous for his power to exorcise evil
spirits and evil influences of every kind. When the
local governor's wife fell sick, Nikōbō was requested to
attend and see what he could do to restore her to health
again. Nikōbō willingly complied, and spent many days
by the bedside of the suffering lady. He diligently
practised his art of exorcism, and in due time the
governor's wife recovered. But the gentle and kind-
hearted Nikōbō was not thanked for what he had done;

on the contrary, the governor became jealous of him, accused him of a foul crime, and caused him to be put to death. The soul of Nikōbō flashed forth in its anger and took the form of a miraculous globe of fire, which hovered over the murderer's house. The strange light, with the justly angry face peering from it, had its effect, for the governor was stricken with a fever that finally killed him. Every year, at the time already indicated, Nikōbō's ghost pays a visit to the scene of its suffering and revenge.

The Ghostly Wrestlers

In Omi province, at the base of the Katada hills, there is a lake. During the cloudy nights of early autumn a ball of fire emerges from the margin of the lake, expanding and contracting as it floats toward the hills. When it rises to the height of a man it reveals two shining faces, to develop slowly into the torsos of two naked wrestlers, locked together and struggling furiously. The ball of fire, with its fierce combatants, floats slowly away to a recess in the Katada hills. It is harmless so long as no one interferes with it, but it resents any effort to retard its progress. According to a legend concerning this phenomenon, we are informed that a certain wrestler, who had never suffered a defeat, waited at midnight for the coming of this ball of fire. When it reached him he attempted to drag it down by force, but the luminous globe proceeded on its way, and hurled the foolish wrestler to a considerable distance.

Baku

In Japan, among superstitious people, evil dreams are believed to be the result of evil spirits, and the supernatural creature called *Baku* is known as Eater of Dreams. The *Baku*, like so many mythological beings, is a curious mingling of various animals. It has the face of a lion, the body of a horse, the tail of a cow, the forelock of a rhinoceros, and the feet of a tiger. Several evil dreams are mentioned in an old Japanese book, such as two snakes twined together, a fox with the voice of a man, blood-stained garments, a talking rice-pot, and so on. When a Japanese peasant awakens from an evil nightmare, he cries : "Devour, O *Baku*! devour my evil dream." At one time pictures of the *Baku* were hung up in Japanese houses and its name written upon pillows. It was believed that if the *Baku* could be induced to eat a horrible dream, the creature had the power to change it into good fortune.

The Shojō's White Saké [1]

The *Shojō* is a sea monster with bright red hair, and is extremely fond of drinking large quantities of sacred white *saké*. The following legend will give some account of this creature and the nature of his favourite beverage.

We have already referred to the miraculous appearance of Mount Fuji.[2] On the day following this alleged miracle a poor man named Yurine, who lived near this mountain, became extremely ill, and feeling that his days were numbered, he desired to drink a cup of *saké* before he died. But there was no rice wine in the little hut, and his boy, Koyuri, desiring if possible to fulfil his father's dying wish, wandered along the shore with a gourd in his hand. He had not gone far when he heard some one calling his name. On looking about him he discovered two strange-looking creatures with long red hair and skin the colour of pink cherry-blossom,

---

[1] Adapted from *Ancient Tales and Foll.-lore of Japan*, by R. Gordon Smith.

[2] *See* Chapter IX.

wearing green seaweed girdles about their loins. Drawing nearer, he perceived that these beings were drinking
white *saké* from large flat cups, which they continually
replenished from a great stone jar.

"My father is dying," said the boy, and he much
desires to drink a cup of *saké* before he departs this life.
But alas! we are poor, and I know not how to grant
him his last request."

"I will fill your gourd with this white *saké*," replied
one of the creatures, and when he had done so Koyuri
ran with haste to his father.

The old man drank the white *saké* eagerly. "Bring
me more," he cried, "for this is no common wine. It
has given me strength, and already I feel new life flowing through my old veins."

So Koyuri returned to the seashore, and the red-haired
creatures gladly gave him more of their wine; indeed,
they supplied him with the beverage for five days, and
by the end of that time Yurine was restored to health
again.

Now Yurine's neighbour was a man called Mamikiko,
and when he heard that Yurine had recently obtained a
copious supply of *saké* he grew jealous, for above all
things he loved a cup of rice wine. One day he called
Koyuri and questioned him in regard to the matter,
saying: "Let me taste the *saké*." He roughly snatched
the gourd from the boy's hand and began to drink,
making a wry face as he did so. "This is not *saké!*"
he exclaimed fiercely; "it is filthy water," and having
said these words, he began to beat the boy, crying:
"Take me to those red people you have told me about.
I will get from them fine *saké*, and let the beating I have
given you warn you never again to play a trick upon
me."

Koyuri and Mamikiko went along the shore together,

and presently they came to where the red-haired creatures were drinking. When Koyuri saw them he
began to weep.

" Why are you crying ? " said one of the creatures.
" Surely your good father has not drunk all the *sake*
already ? "

" No," replied the boy, " but I have met with
misfortune. This man I bring with me, Mamikiko by
name, drank some of the *sake*, spat it out immediately,
and threw the rest away, saying that I had played a trick
upon him and given him foul water to drink. Be so
good as to let me have some more *sake* for my father."

The red-haired man filled the gourd, and chuckled
over Mamikiko's unpleasant experience.

" I should also like a cup of *sake*," said Mamikiko.
" Will you let me have some ? "

Permission having been granted, the greedy Mamikiko filled the largest cup he could find, smiling over
the delicious fragrance. But directly he tasted the *sake*
he felt sick, and angrily remonstrated with the red-
haired creature.

The red man thus made answer : " You are evidently
not aware that I am a *Shojō*, and that I live near the
Sea Dragon's Palace. When I heard of the sudden
appearance of Mount Fuji I came here to see it, assured
that such an event was a good omen and foretold of
the prosperity and perpetuity of Japan. While enjoying the beauty of this fair mountain I met Koyuri, and
had the good fortune to save his honest father's life by
giving him some of our sacred white *sake* that restores
youth to human beings, together with an increase in
years, while to *Shojō* it vanquishes death. Koyuri's father
is a good man, and the *sake* was thus able to exert its
full and beneficent power upon him ; but you are greedy
and selfish, and to all such this *sake* is poison."

"*Poison?*" groaned the now contrite Mamikiko.
"Good *Shōjō*, have mercy upon me and spare my life!"

The *Shōjō* gave him a powder, saying: "Swallow
this in *saké* and repent of your wickedness."

Mamikiko did so, and this time he found that the
white *saké* was delicious. He lost no time in making
friends with Yurine, and some years later these men
took up their abode on the southern side of Mount
Fuji, brewed the *Shōjō's* white *saké*, and lived for three
hundred years.

The Dragon

The Dragon is undoubtedly the most famous of
mythical beasts, but, though Chinese in origin, it has
become intimately associated with Japanese mythology.
The creature lives for the most part in the ocean, river,
or lake, but it has the power of flight and rules over
clouds and tempests. The Dragon of China and
Japan resemble each other, with the exception that the
Japanese variety has three claws, while that of the
Celestial Kingdom has five. The Chinese Emperor
Yao was said to be the son of a dragon, and many
rulers of that country were metaphorically referred to
as "dragon-faced." The Dragon has the head of a
camel, horns of a deer, eyes of a hare, scales of a carp,
paws of a tiger, and claws resembling those of an eagle.
In addition it has whiskers, a bright jewel under its
chin, and a measure on the top of its head which
enables it to ascend to Heaven at will. This is merely
a general description and does not apply to all dragons,
some of which have heads of so extraordinary a kind
that they cannot be compared with anything in the
animal kingdom. The breath of the Dragon changes
into clouds from which come either rain or fire. It is
able to expand or contract its body, and in addition it

has the power of transformation and invisibility. In both Chinese and Japanese mythology the watery principle is associated with the Dragon, as we have already seen in the story of Urashima, the Empress Jingo, and the adventures of Hoori, &c.

The Dragon (*Tatsu*) is one of the signs of the zodiac, and the four seas, which in the old Chinese conception limited the habitable earth, were ruled over by four Dragon Kings. The Celestial Dragon ruled over the Mansions of the Gods, the Spiritual Dragon presided over rain, the Earth Dragon marked the courses or rivers, and the Dragon of Hidden Treasure guarded precious metals and stones.

A white Dragon, which lived in a pond in Yamashiro, transformed itself every fifty years into a bird called *O-Goncho*, with a voice resembling the howling of a wolf. Whenever this bird appeared it brought with it a great famine. On one occasion, while Fuk Hi was standing by the Yellow River, the Yellow Dragon presented him with a scroll inscribed with mystic characters. This tradition is said to be the legendary origin of the Chinese system of writing.

CHAPTER XXX : THE TRANSFORMA-TION OF ISSUNBOSHI, AND KINTARO, THE GOLDEN BOY

A Prayer to the Empress Jingo

AN old married couple went to the shrine of the deified Empress Jingo,[1] and prayed that they might be blessed with a child, even if it were no bigger than one of their fingers. A voice was heard from behind the bamboo curtain of the shrine, and the old people were informed that their wish would be granted.

In due time the old woman gave birth to a child, and when she and her husband discovered that this miniature piece of humanity was no bigger than a little finger, they became extremely angry, and thought that the Empress Jingo had treated them very meanly indeed, though, as a matter of fact, she had fulfilled their prayer to the letter.

'One-Inch Priest"

The little fellow was called Issunboshi ("One-Inch Priest"), and every day his parents expected to see him suddenly grow up as other boys ; but at thirteen years of age he still remained the same size as when he was born. Gradually his parents became exasperated, for it wounded their vanity to hear the neighbours describe their son as Little Finger, or Grain-of-Corn. They were so much annoyed that at last they determined to send Issunboshi away.

The little fellow did not complain. He requested his mother to give him a needle, a small soup-bowl, and a chop-stick, and with these things he set off on his adventures.

[1] Deifying the mighty dead is one of the teachings of Shintōism.

AN ENCOUNTER WITH ONI

Issunboshi becomes a Page

His soup-bowl served as a boat, which he propelled along the river with his chop-stick. In this fashion he finally reached Kyōto. Issunboshi wandered about this city until he saw a large roofed gate. Without the least hesitation he walked in, and having reached the porch of a house, he cried out in a very minute voice : " I beg an honourable inquiry ! "

Prince Sanjo himself heard the little voice, and it was some time before he could discover where it came from. When he did so he was delighted with his discovery, and on the little fellow begging that he might live in the Prince's house, his request was readily granted. The boy became a great favourite, and was at once made the Princess Sanjo's page. In this capacity he accompanied his mistress everywhere, and though so very small, he fully appreciated the honour and dignity of his position.

An Encounter with Oni

One day the Princess Sanjo and her page went to the Temple of Kwannon, the Goddess of Mercy, " under whose feet are dragons of the elements and the lotuses of Purity." As they were leaving the temple two *oni* (evil spirits) sprang upon them. Issunboshi took out his needle-sword from its hollow straw, and loudly denouncing the *oni*, he flourished his small weapon in their evil-looking faces.

One of the creatures laughed. " Why," said he scornfully, " I could swallow you, as a cormorant swallows a trout, and what is more, my funny little bean-seed, I will do so ! "

The *oni* opened his mouth, and Issunboshi found himself slipping down a huge throat until he finally stood in the creature's great dark stomach. Issunboshi, nothing daunted, began boring away with his needle-sword. This made the evil spirit cry out and give a great cough, which sent the little fellow into the sunny world again.

The second *oni*, who had witnessed his companion's distress, was extremely angry, and tried to swallow the remarkable little page, but was not successful. This time Issunboshi climbed up the creature's nostril, and when he had reached the end of what seemed to him to be a very long and gloomy tunnel, he began piercing the *oni's* eyes. The creature, savage with pain, ran off as fast as he could, followed by his yelling companion.

Needless to say, the Princess was delighted with her page's bravery, and told him that she was sure her father would reward him when he was told about the terrible encounter.

The Magic Mallet

On their way home the Princess happened to pick up a small wooden mallet. "Oh!" said she, "this must have been dropped by the wicked *oni*, and it is none other than a lucky mallet. You have only to wish and then tap it upon the ground, and your wish, no matter what, is always granted. My brave Issunboshi, tell me what you would most desire, and I will tap the mallet on the ground."

After a pause the little fellow said : "Honourable Princess, I should like to be as big as other people."

The Princess tapped the mallet on the ground, calling aloud the wish of her page. In a moment Issunboshi was transformed from a bijou creature to a lad just like other youths of his age.

These wonderful happenings excited the curiosity of the Emperor, and Issunboshi was summoned to his presence. The Emperor was so delighted with the youth that he gave him many gifts and made him a high official. Finally, Issunboshi became a great lord and married Prince Sanjo's youngest daughter.

Kintaro, the Golden Boy

Sakata Kurando was an officer of the Emperor's bodyguard, and though he was a brave man, well versed in the art of war, he had a gentle disposition, and during his military career chanced to love a beautiful lady named Yaégiri. Kurando eventually fell into disgrace, and was forced to leave the Court and to become a travelling tobacco merchant. Yaégiri, who was much distressed by her lover's flight, succeeded in escaping from her home, and wandered up and down the country in the hope of meeting Kurando. At length she found him, but the unfortunate man, who, no doubt, felt deeply his disgrace and his humble mode of living, put an end to his humiliation by taking his miserable life.

Animal Companions

When Yaégiri had buried her lover she went to the Ashigara Mountain, where she gave birth to a child, called Kintaro, or the Golden Boy. Now Kintaro was remarkable for his extreme strength. When only a few years old his mother gave him an axe, with which he felled trees as quickly and easily as an experienced woodcutter. Ashigara Mountain was a lonely and desolate spot, and as there were no children with whom Kintaro could play, he made companions of the bear, deer, hare, and monkey, and in a very short time was able to speak their strange language.

One day, when Kintaro was sitting on the mountain, with his favourites about him, he sought to amuse
367

himself by getting his companions to join in a friendly wrestling match. A kindly old bear was delighted with the proposal, and at once set to work to dig up the earth and arrange it in the form of a small daïs. When this had been made a hare and a monkey wrestled together, while a deer stood by to give encouragement and to see that the sport was conducted fairly. Both animals proved themselves to be equally strong, and Kintaro tactfully rewarded them with tempting rice-cakes.

After spending a pleasant afternoon in this way, Kintaro proceeded to return home, followed by his devoted friends. At length they came to a river, and the animals were wondering how they should cross such a wide stretch of water, when Kintaro put his strong arms round a tree which was growing on the bank, and pulled it across the river so that it formed a bridge. Now it happened that the famous hero, Yorimitsu, and his retainers witnessed this extraordinary feat of strength, and said to Watanabé Isuna : " This child is truly remarkable. Go and find out where he lives and all about him."

A Famous Warrior

So Watanabé Isuna followed Kintaro and entered the house where he lived with his mother. " My master," said he, "Lord Yorimitsu, bids me find out who your wonderful son is." When Yaégiri had narrated the story of her life and informed her visitor that her little one was the son of Sakata Kurando, the retainer departed and told Yorimitsu all he had heard.

Yorimitsu was so pleased with what Watanabé Isuna told him that he went himself to Yaégiri, and said : " If you will give me your child I will make him my retainer." The woman gladly consented, and the

A FAMOUS WARRIOR

Golden Boy went away with the great hero, who named him Sakata Kintoki. He eventually became a famous warrior, and the stories of his wonderful deeds are recited to this day. Children regard him as their favourite hero, and little boys, who would fain emulate the strength and bravery of Sakata Kintoki, carry his portrait in their bosoms.

CHAPTER XXXI : MISCELLANEOUS LEGENDS

Kato Sayemon

KATO SAYEMON lived in the palace of the Shōgun Ashikaga, where he had his separate apartments, and as there was no war at that time, he remained contentedly with his wife and concubines. Kato Sayemon was a man who loved luxury and ease, and he regarded domestic peace as the greatest of all earthly blessings. He honestly believed that among all his smiling, courteous women there was nothing but harmony, and this thought made life particularly sweet to him.

One evening Kato Sayemon went into the palace garden and was enchanted by the ever-moving cloud of fireflies, and he was scarcely less pleased with the gentle song of certain insects. "What a charming scene," murmured Sayemon, "and what a charming world we live in ! Bows and smiles and abject humility from my women. Oh, it's all very wonderful and very delightful ! I would have life always so."

Thus voicing his thoughts in this self-satisfied manner, he chanced to pass his wife's room, and peeped in with a loving and benevolent eye. He observed that his wife was playing *go* with one of his concubines. "Such polite decorum," murmured Sayemon. "Surely their words are as sweet as honey and as soft and fair as finely spun silk. But stay ! What strange thing is this ? The hair of my wife and the hair of my concubine have turned into snakes that twist and rear their heads in anger. All the time these women smile and bow and move their pieces with well-ordered charm and grace. Gentle words come from their lips, but the snakes of their hair mock them, for

370

these twisting reptiles tell of bitter jealousy in their hearts."

Sayemon's beautiful dream of domestic happiness was for ever shattered. "I will go forth," said he, "and become a Buddhist priest. I will leave behind the hot malice and envy of my wife and concubines, and in the teaching of the Blessed One I shall indeed find true peace."

The next morning Sayemon left the palace secretly, and though search was made for him, he could not be found. About a week later Sayemon's wife reduced the establishment and lived quietly with her little son, Ishidomaro. Two years went by and still there came no news of her husband.

At length Sayemon's wife and child went in search of the missing man. For five years they wandered about the country, till at length they came to a little village in Kishu, where an old man informed the weary and travel-stained wanderers that Sayemon was now a priest, and that a year ago he lived in the temple of Kongobuji, on Mount Koya.

The next day the woman and her son found that at the temple of Kongobuji no women were permitted to enter, so Ishidomaro, after carefully listening to his mother's instructions, ascended the mountain alone. When the boy, after a long and arduous climb, reached the temple, he saw a monk, and said : "Does a priest called Kato Sayemon live here ? I am his little son, and my good mother awaits me in yonder valley. Five years we have sought for him, and the love that is in our hearts will surely find him."

The priest, who was none other than Sayemon himself, thus addressed his son : "I am sorry to think that your journey has been in vain, for no one of the name of Kato Sayemon lives in this temple."

Sayemon spoke with outward coldness, but within his heart there was a struggle between his religion and love for his son. Knowing, however, that he had left his wife and child well provided for, he yielded to the teaching of the Lord Buddha and crushed out his parental feelings.

Ishidomaro, however, was not satisfied, for he felt instinctively that the man before him was in reality his father, and once again he addressed the priest : " Good sir, on my left eye there is a mole, and my mother told me that on the left eye of my father there is a similar mark, by which I might at once recognise him. You have the very mark, and in my heart I know that you are my father." And having said these words the boy wept bitterly, longing for arms that never came to caress and soothe the unhappy little fellow.

Sayemon's feelings were again stirred ; but with a great effort to conceal his emotion, he said : " The mark of which you speak is very common. I am certainly not your father, and you had better dry your eyes and seek him elsewhere." With these words the priest left the boy in order to attend an evening service.

Sayemon continued to live in the temple. He had found peace in serving the Lord Buddha, and he cared not what became of his wife and child.

How an Old Man lost his Wen

There was once an old man who had a wen on his right cheek. This disfigurement caused him a good deal of annoyance, and he had spent a considerable sum of money in trying to get rid of it. He took various medicines and applied many lotions, but instead of the wen disappearing or even diminishing, it increased in size.

One night, while the old man was returning home laden with firewood, he was overtaken by a terrible thunderstorm, and was forced to seek shelter in a hollow tree. When the storm had abated, and just as he was about to proceed on his journey, he was surprised to hear a sound of merriment close at hand. On peeping out from his place of retreat, he was amazed to see a number of demons dancing and singing and drinking. Their dancing was so strange that the old man, forgetting caution, began to laugh, and eventually left the tree in order that he might see the performance better. As he stood watching, he saw that a demon was dancing by himself, and, moreover, that the chief of the company was none too pleased with his very clumsy antics. At length the leader of the demons said : "Enough ! Is there no one who can dance better than this fellow ? "

When the old man heard these words, it seemed that his youth returned to him again, and having at one time been an expert dancer, he offered to show his skill. So the old man danced before that strange gathering of demons, who congratulated him on his performance, offered him a cup of *saké*, and begged that he would give them the pleasure of several other dances.

The old man was extremely gratified by the way he had been received, and when the chief of the demons asked him to dance before them on the following night, he readily complied. "That is well," said the chief, "but you must leave some pledge behind you. I see that you have a wen on your right cheek, and that will make an excellent pledge. Allow me to take it off for you." Without inflicting any pain, the chief removed the wen, and having accomplished this extraordinary feat, he and his companions suddenly vanished.

The old man, as he walked towards his home, kept on feeling his right cheek with his hand, and could scarcely realise that after many years of disfigurement he had at last the good fortune to lose his troublesome and unsightly wen. At length he entered his humble abode, and his old wife was none the less pleased with what had taken place.

A wicked and cantankerous old man lived next door to this good old couple. For many years he had been afflicted with a wen on his left cheek, which had failed to yield to all manner of medical treatment. When he heard of his neighbour's good fortune, he called upon him and listened to the strange adventures with the demons. The good old man told his neighbour where he might find the hollow tree, and advised him to hide in it just before sunset.

The wicked old man found the hollow tree and entered it. He had not remained concealed more than a few minutes when he rejoiced to see the demons. Presently one of the company said : " The old man is a long time coming. I made sure he would keep his promise."

At these words the old man crept out of his hiding-place, flourished his fan, and began to dance ; but, unfortunately, he knew nothing about dancing, and his extraordinary antics caused the demons to express considerable dissatisfaction. " You dance extremely ill," said one of the company, " and the sooner you stop the better we shall be pleased ; but before you depart we will return the pledge you left with us last night." Having uttered these words, the demon flung the wen at the right cheek of the old man, where it remained firmly fixed, and could not be removed. So the wicked old man, who had tried to deceive the demons, went away with a wen on either side of his face.

A Japanese Gulliver [1]

Shikaiya Wasōbiōye was a man of Nagasaki, and possessed considerable learning, but disliked visitors.

[1] Adapted from Professor B. H. Chamberlain's translation in the *Transactions of the Asiatic Society of Japan*, vol. vii.

A JAPANESE GULLIVER

On the eighth day of the eighth month, in order to escape the admirers of the full moon, he set off in his boat, and had proceeded some distance, when the sky looked threatening, and he attempted to return, but the wind tore his sail and broke his mast. The poor man was tossed for three months on the waves, until at last he came to the Sea of Mud, where he nearly died of hunger, for there were no fishes to be caught.

At length he reached a mountainous island, where the air was sweet with the fragrance of many flowers, and in this island he found a spring, the waters of which revived him. At length Wasōbiōye met Jofuku, who led him through the streets of the main city, where all the inhabitants were spending their time in pursuit of pleasure. There was no death or disease on this island ; but the fact that here life was eternal was regarded by many as a burden, which they tried to shake off by studying the magic art of death and the power of poisonous food, such as globe-fish sprinkled with soot and the flesh of mermaids.

When twenty years had passed by Wasōbiōye grew weary of the island, and as he had failed in his attempts to take his life, he started upon a journey to the Three Thousand Worlds mentioned in Buddhist Scriptures. He then visited the Land of Endless Plenty, the Land of Shams, the Land of the Followers of the Antique, the Land of Paradoxes, and, finally, the Land of Giants.

After Wasōbiōye had spent five months riding on the back of a stork through total darkness, he at length reached a country where the sun shone again, where trees were hundreds of feet in girth, where weeds were as large as bamboos, and men sixty feet in height. In this strange land a giant picked up Wasōbiōye, took him to his house, and fed him from a single grain of monster rice, with chopsticks the size of a small tree.

For a few weeks Wasōbiōye attempted to catechise his host in regard to the doctrines of the old world whence he came, but the giant laughed at him and told him that such a small man could not be expected to understand the ways of big people, for their intelligences were in like proportion to their size.

The Jewel-tears of Samébito

One day, while Tōtarō was crossing the Long Bridge of Séta, he saw a strange-looking creature. It had the body of a man, with a skin blacker than that of a negro ; its eyes glowed like emeralds, and its beard was like the beard of a dragon. Tōtarō was not a little startled at seeing such an extraordinary being ; but there was so much pathos in its green eyes that Tōtarō ventured to ask questions, to which the strange fellow replied:

"I am Samébito ["A Shark-Person "], and quite recently I was in the service of the Eight Great Dragon Kings as a subordinate officer in the Dragon Palace. I was dismissed from this glorious dwelling for a very slight fault, and I was even banished from the sea. Ever since I have been extremely miserable, without a place of shelter, and unable to get food. Pity me, good sir ! Find me shelter, and give me something to eat ! "

Tōtarō's heart was touched by Samébito's humility, and he took him to a pond in his garden and there gave him a liberal supply of food. In this quiet and secluded spot this strange creature of the sea remained for nearly half a year.

Now in the summer of that year there was a great female pilgrimage to the temple called Miidera, situated in the neighbouring town of Ōtsu. Tōtarō attended the festival, and there saw an extremely charming girl. "Her face was fair and pure as snow ; and the loveliness of her lips assured the beholder that their very utterance

Tōtarō and Samébito.

(See page 376)

would sound 'as sweet as the voice of a nightingale singing upon a plum-tree.'"

Tōtarō at once fell in love with this maiden. He discovered that her name was Tamana, that she was unmarried, and would remain so unless a young man could present her with a betrothal gift of a casket containing no fewer than ten thousand jewels.

When Tōtarō learnt that this fair girl was only to be won by what seemed to him an impossible gift, he returned home with a heavy heart. The more he thought about the beautiful Tamana, the more he fell in love with her. But alas! no one less wealthy than a prince could make such a betrothal gift—ten thousand jewels!

Tōtarō worried himself into an illness, and when a physician came to see him, he shook his head, and said : "I can do nothing for you, for no medicine will cure the sickness of love." And with these words he left him.

Now Samébito gained tidings of the sickness of his master, and when the sad news reached him, he left the garden pond and entered Tōtarō's chamber.

Tōtarō did not speak about his own troubles. He was full of concern for the welfare of this creature of the sea. "Who will feed you, Samébito, when I am gone?" said he mournfully.

When Samébito saw that his good master was dying, he uttered a strange cry, and began to weep. He wept great tears of blood, but when they touched the floor they suddenly turned into glowing rubies.

When Tōtarō saw these jewel-tears he shouted for joy, and new life came back to him from that hour. "I shall live! I shall live!" he cried with great delight. "My good friend, you have more than repaid me for the food and shelter I have given you. Your wonderful tears have brought me untold happiness."

Then Samébito stopped weeping, and asked his master to be so good as to explain the nature of his speedy recovery.

So Tōtarō told the Shark-Man of his love-affair and of the marriage-gift demanded by the family of Tamana. "I thought," added Tōtarō, "that I should never be able to get ten thousand jewels, and it was that thought that brought me so near to death. Now your tears have turned into jewels, and with these the maid will become my wife."

Tōtarō proceeded to count the jewels with great eagerness. "Not enough! Not enough!" he exclaimed with considerable disappointment. "Oh, Samébito, be so good as to weep a little more!"

These words made Samébito angry. "Do you think," said he, "I can weep at will like women? My tears come from the heart, the outward sign of true and deep sorrow. I can weep no longer, for you are well again. Surely the time has come for laughter and merrymaking, and not for tears."

"Unless I get ten thousand jewels, I cannot marry the fair Tamana," said Tōtarō. "What am I to do? Oh, good friend, weep, weep!"

Samébito was a kindly creature. After a pause, he said: "I can shed no more tears to-day. Let us go to-morrow to the Long Bridge of Séta, and take with us a good supply of wine and fish. It may be that as I sit on the bridge and gaze toward the Dragon Palace, I shall weep again, thinking of my lost home, and longing to return once more."

On the morrow they went to the Séta Bridge, and after Samébito had taken a good deal of wine, he gazed in the direction of the Dragon Kingdom. As he did so his eyes filled with tears, red tears that turned into rubies as soon as they touched the bridge. Tōtarō, without very much concern for his friend's sorrow, picked up the jewels, and found at last that he had ten thousand lustrous rubies.

Just at that moment they heard a sound of sweet music, and from the water there rose a cloud-like palace, with all the colours of the setting sun shining upon it. Samébito gave a shout of joy and sprang upon the parapet of the bridge, saying : " Farewell, my master ! The Dragon Kings are calling ! " With these words he leaped from the bridge and returned to his old home again.

Tōtarō lost no time in presenting the casket containing ten thousand jewels to Tamana's parents, and in due season he married their lovely daughter.

A NOTE ON JAPANESE POETRY

THERE is a subtle charm about Japanese poetry peculiarly its own. I recall with pleasure the unforgettable hours I spent in reading Mr. Yone Noguchi's *The Pilgrimage*. I was compelled, through sheer delight, to read the two volumes at a sitting. It is true that Mr. Noguchi is very much under the influence of Walt Whitman, and it has left its impress upon his work; but that only tends to heighten the effect of the purely Japanese element. A brief, haunting phrase of Mr. Noguchi has far more charm than an imitation of his American master's torrential manner. Japan has no need to imitate as far as her poetry is concerned. In the old days one of the characteristics of that country's poetry was its almost entire freedom from outside influences, not even excepting that of China, from whom, in other directions, she borrowed so much. I have mentioned Mr. Yone Noguchi because his work forms an excellent starting-point for the study of Japanese poetry. This charming poet, writing in English, has given us for the first time an intimate knowledge of the very spirit of Japanese poetry. When a book is written on comparative poetry, that of Japan will take a very high place.

It is far easier to describe what Japanese poetry is not than what it actually is. To begin with, there are no Japanese epics, such as the *Iliad* and *Odyssey*, the *Kalevala*, and the *Mahabharata*, and their phrase *naga-uta* ("long poetry") is to us a misnomer, for they have no really long poems. Philosophy, religion, satire are not themes for the Japanese poet; he even goes so far as to consider war no fit subject for a song.

380

The Tanka and Hokku

Where, then, are the charm and wonder of Japan's Pegasus ? The real genius is to be found in the *tanka*, a poem of five lines or phrases and thirty-one syllables. In many ways the *tanka* shows far more limitation than an English sonnet, and our verbose poets would do well to practise a form that engenders suppression and delicately gives suggestion the supreme place. It is surprising what music and sentiment are expressed within these limits. The *tanka* is certainly brief in form, but it frequently suggests, with haunting insistency, that the fragment really has no end, when imagination seizes it and turns it into a thousand thousand lines. The *tanka* belongs as much to Japan as Mount Fuji itself. One cannot regard it without thinking that a Japanese poet must essentially have all the finer instincts of an artist. In him the two arts seem inseparable. He must convey in five lines, in the most felicitous language at his disposal, the idea he wishes to express. That he does so with extraordinary success is beyond dispute. These brief poems are wonderfully characteristic of the Japanese people, for they have such a love for little things. The same love that delights in carving a *netsuke*, the small button on a Japanese tobacco-pouch, or the fashioning of a miniature garden in a space no bigger than a soup-plate is part of the same subtle genius.

There is an even more Lilliputian form of verse. It is called the *hokku*, and contains only seventeen syllables, such as : " What I saw as a fallen blossom returning to the branch, lo ! it was a butterfly." Butterflies were no mere flying insects in Old Japan. The sight of such a brightly coloured creature heralded the approach of some dear friend. On one occasion great clouds of butterflies were thought to be the souls of an army.

The Hyaku-nin-isshiu

Those who are familiar with the *Hyaku-nin-isshiu* [1] ("Single Verses by a Hundred People"), written before the time of the Norman Conquest, will recognise that much of the old Japanese poetry depended on the dexterous punning and the use of "pivot" and "pillow" words. The art was practised, not with the idea of provoking laughter, which was the aim of Thomas Hood, but rather with the idea of winning quiet admiration for a clever and subtle verbal ornament. No translation can do full justice to this phase of Japanese poetry; but the following *tanka*, by Yasuhide Bunya, may perhaps give some idea of their word-play:

> " The mountain wind in autumn time
> Is well called ' hurricane ' ;
> It *hurries canes* and twigs along,
> And whirls them o'er the plain
> To scatter them again."

The cleverness of this verse lies in the fact that *yama kaze* (" mountain wind ") is written with two characters. When these characters are combined they form the word *arashi* (" hurricane "). Clever as these "pillow" and "pivot" words were, they were used but sparingly by the poets of the classical period, to be revived again in a later age when their extravagant use is to be condemned as a verbal display that quite overshadowed the spirit of the poetry itself.

Love Poems

There are Japanese love poems, but they are very different from those with which we are familiar. The

[1] *See* translation by William N. Porter.

tiresome habit of enumerating a woman's charms, either briefly or at length, is happily an impossibility in the *tanka*. There is nothing approaching the sensuousness of a Swinburne or a D. G. Rossetti in Japanese poetry, but the sentiments are gentle and pleasing nevertheless. No doubt there were love-lorn poets in Japan, as in every other country, poets who possibly felt quite passionately on the subject; but in their poetry the fire is ghostly rather than human, always polite and delicate. What could be more naïve and dainty than the following song from the " Flower Dance " of Bingo province ?

> " If you want to meet me, love,
>   Only we twain,
>   Come to the gate, love,
>   Sunshine or rain ;
>   And if people pry
>   Say that you came, love,
>   To watch who went by.

> " If you want to meet me, love,
>   Only you and I,
>   Come to the pine-tree, love,
>   Clouds or clear sky ;
>   Stand among the spikelets, love,
>   And if folks ask why,
>   Say that you came, love,
>   To catch a butterfly."

Or again, the following *tanka* by the eleventh-century official, Michimasa :

> " If we could meet in privacy,
>   Where no one else could see,
>   Softly I'd whisper in thy ear
>   This little word from me—
>   I'm dying, Love, for thee."

There is a good deal more ingenuity in this poem than would appear on the surface. It was addressed to the Princess Masako, and though *omoi-taenamu* may be correctly translated, " I'm dying, Love, for thee," it may also mean, " I shall forget about you." The poem was purposely written with a double meaning, in case it miscarried and fell into the hands of the palace guards.

Nature Poems

Charming as are many of the Japaneses love poems, they are not so pleasing or so distinguished as those describing some mood, some scene from Nature, for the Japanese poets are essentially Nature poets. Our National Anthem is very far from being poetry. Here is Japan's, literally rendered into English : " May our Lord's Empire live through a thousand ages, till tiny pebbles grow into giant boulders covered with emerald mosses." It is based on an ancient song mentioned in the *Kokinshiu*, and, like all ancient songs in praise of kingship, expresses a desire for an Emperor whose very descent from the Sun shall baffle Death, one who shall live and rule past mortal reckoning. There is a symbolic meaning attached to Japanese rocks and stones, closely associated with Buddhism. They represent something more than mere stolidity ; they represent prayers. It is the Nature poems of Japan that are supremely beautiful, those describing plum- and cherry-blossom, moonlight on a river, the flight of a heron, the murmuring song of a blue pine, or the white foam of a wave. The best of these poems are touched with pathos. Here is one by Isé :

> " Cold as the wind of early Spring,
> Chilling the buds that still lie sheathed
> In their brown armour with its sting,
> And the bare branches withering—
> So seems the human heart to me !
> Cold as the March wind's bitterness ;
> I am alone, none comes to see
> Or cheer me in these days of stress."

CHŌMEI

Chōmei

I often think of that twelfth-century Japanese recluse Chōmei. He lived in a little mountain hut far
away from City Royal, and there he read and played
upon the *biwa*, went for walks in the vicinity, picking
flowers and fruit and branches of maple-leaves, which
he set before the Lord Buddha as thankofferings.
Chōmei was a true lover of Nature, for he understood
all her many moods. In the spring he gazed upon " the
festoons of the wistaria, fine to see as purple clouds."
In the west wind he heard the song of birds, and when
autumn came he saw the gold colouring of the trees,
while the piling and vanishing of snow caused him to
think of "the ever waxing and waning volume of the
world's sinfulness." He wrote in his charming *Hō-jō-ki*,
the most tender and haunting autobiography in the
Japanese language : " All the joy of my existence is
concentrated around the pillow which giveth me
nightly rest ; all the hope of my days I find in the
beauties of Nature that ever please my eyes." He
loved Nature so well that he would fain have taken all
the colour and perfume of her flowers through death
into the life beyond. That is what he meant when
he wrote :

> " Alas ! the moonlight
> Behind the hill is hidden
> In gloom and darkness !
> Oh, would her radiance ever
> My longing eyes rejoiced ! "

Here is a touching *hokku*, written by Chiyo, after the
death of her little son :

> " How far, I wonder, did he stray,
> Chasing the burnished dragon-fly to-day ? "

The souls of Japanese children are often pictured as playing in a celestial garden with the same flowers and butterflies they used to play with while on earth. It is just this subtle element of the childlike disposition in Japanese people that has helped them to discover the secrets of flowers, and birds, and trees, has enabled them to catch their timorous, fleeting shadows, and to hold them, as if by magic, in a picture, on a vase, or in a delicate and wistful poem.

"The Ah-ness of Things"

There is a Japanese phrase, *mono no aware wo shiru* ("the Ah-ness of things"), which seems to describe most accurately the whole significance of Japanese poetry. There is a plaintive and intimate union between the poet and the scene from Nature he is writing about. Over and over again he suggests that Spring, with all her wealth of cherry- and plum-blossom, will continue to grace his country long after he has departed. Nearly all Japan's people, from the peasant to the Mikado himself, are poets. They write poetry because they live poetry every day of their lives—that is to say, before Japan dreamed of wearing a bowler hat and frock-coat, or became a wholesale buyer of everything Western. They live poetry, always that poetry steeped in an intimate communion with Nature. And when in July the Festival of the Dead takes place, there comes a great company of poet souls to see Nippon's blossom again, to wander down old familiar gardens, through red *torii*, or to lean upon a stone lantern, and drink in the glory of a summer day, which is sweeter to them than life beyond the grave.

GODS AND GODDESSES

AIZEN MYŌ-Ō.	The God of Love.
AJI-SHI-KI.	A Shintō God who was mistaken for his deceased friend *Ame-waka.*
AMA-NO-HO.	The first of the Divine Messengers sent to prepare the way for the coming of *Ninigi.*
AMA-TERASU.	The Sun Goddess.
AME-WAKA.	" Heaven-young-Prince," and one of the Divine Messengers.
AMIDA.	A Buddhist deity, originally an abstraction, the ideal of boundless light. The *Daibutsu* at Kamakura represents this God.
ANAN.	A cousin of Buddha, and, like Bishamon, gifted with great knowledge and a wonderful memory.
BENTEN.	One of the Seven Deities of Luck.
BIMBOGAMI.	The God of Poverty.
BINZURU.	A disciple of Buddha, and worshipped by the lower classes on account of his miraculous power to cure all human ailments.
BISHAMON.	The God of Wealth and also of War.
BOSATSU.	A term applied to Buddhist saints.
BUDDHA.	See *Shaka.*
DAIKOKU.	The God of Wealth.
DAINICHI NYORAI.	A personification of purity and wisdom. One of the Buddhist Trinity.
DAISHI.	" Great Teacher," a term applied to many Buddhist saints.
DARUMA.	A follower of Buddha.
DŌSOJIN.	The God of Roads.
EBISU.	A God of Luck and of Daily Food. He is the patron of honest labour, and is represented as a fisherman carrying in his hand a *tai*-fish.
EKIBIOGAMI.	The God of Pestilence.

Emma-ō.	The Lord of Hell and Judge of the Dead.
Fu Daishi	A deified Chinese priest.
Fudō.	The God of Wisdom.
Fugen.	The divine patron of those who practise a special kind of ecstatic meditation. He is usually depicted as sitting on the right hand of *Shaka*.
Fukurokuju.	A God of Luck, and typifies longevity and wisdom.
Gaki.	Evil Gods.
Go-chi Nyorai.	The Five Buddhas of Contemplation, viz.: *Yakushi, Tahō, Dainichi, Ashuku,* and *Shaka*.
Gongen.	A generic name for the Shintō incarnations of Buddhas. It is also applied to deified heroes.
Gwakkō Bosatsu.	A Buddhist moon-deity.
Hachiman.	The God of War. He is the deified Emperor Ōjin, patron of the Minamoto clan.
Hoderi.	" Fire Shine," and son of *Ninigi.*
Hoori.	" Fire Fade," and son of *Ninigi.*
Hoso-no-Kami.	The God of Smallpox.
Hotei.	A God of Luck who typifies contentment.
Hotoke.	The name of all Buddhas, and frequently applied to the dead generally.
Ida Ten.	A protector of Buddhism.
Iha-naga.	" Princess Long-as-the-Rocks," eldest daughter of the Spirit of Mountains.
Inari.	The Goddess of Rice, and also associated with the Fox God.
Isora.	The Spirit of the Seashore.
Izanagi and Izanami.	The Creator and Creatress of Japan, and from them the deities of the Shintō pantheon are descended.
Jizō	The God of Children.

GODS AND GODDESSES

Jurōjin.	A God of Luck.
Kami.	A general name for all Shintō deities.
Kashō.	One of the greatest disciples of Buddha.
Kaze-no-Kami.	The God of Wind and Bad Colds.
Kengyū.	The Herdsman lover of the Weaving Maiden.
Ken-ro-ji-jin.	The Earth God.
Kishi Bojin.	An Indian Goddess, worshipped by the Japanese as the protectress of children.
Kōbō Daishi.	A deified Buddhist sage.
Kodomo-no-Inari.	The children's Fox God.
Kōjin.	The God of the Kitchen. Worn-out dolls are offered to this deity.
Kokuzō Bosatsu.	A female Buddhist saint.
Kompira.	A Buddhist deity of obscure origin, identified with *Susa-no-o* and other Shintō Gods.
Kōshin.	The God of Roads. A deification of the day of the Monkey, represented by the Three Mystic Apes.
Kuni-toko-tachi.	"The Earthly Eternally Standing One." A self-created Shintō God.
Kwannon.	The Goddess of Mercy, represented in various forms :

1. *Shō-Kwannon* (Kwannon the Wise).
2. *Jū-ichi-men Kwannon* (Eleven-Faced).
3. *Sen-ju Kwannon* (Thousand-Handed).
4. *Ba-tō-Kwannon* (Horse-Headed).
5. *Nyo-i-rin Kwannon* (Omnipotent).

Marishiten.	In Japanese and Chinese Buddhism she is represented as the Queen of Heaven. She has eight arms, two of which hold the symbols of the sun and moon. In Brahminical theology she is the personification of Light, and also a name of Krishna.
Maya Bunin.	The mother of Buddha.

389

Miroku.	Buddha's successor, and known as the Buddhist Messiah.
Miwa-daimyō-jin.	The deity associated with the Laughing Festival of Wasa.
Monju Bosatu.	The Lord of Wisdom.
Musubi-no-Kami.	The God of Marriage.
Nikkō Bosatsu.	A Buddhist solar deity.
Ninigi.	The grandson of Amer-terasu, the Sun Goddess.
Ni-ō.	Two gigantic and fierce kings who guard the outer gates of temples.
Nominosukune.	Patron deity of wrestlers.
Nyorai.	An honorific title applied to all Buddhas.
O-ana-mochi.	"Possessor of the Great Hole" of Mount Fuji.
Oho-yama.	The Spirit of the Mountains.
Onamuji or Okuni-nushi.	Son of *Susa-no-o*. He ruled in Izumo, but retired in favour of *Ninigi*.
Oni.	A general name for evil spirits.
Otohime.	The daughter of the Dragon King.
Raiden.	The God of Thunder.
Raitaro.	The son of the Thunder God.
Rakan.	A name used to designate the perfected saint and also the immediate disciples of Buddha.
Roku-bu-ten.	A collective name for the Buddhist Gods *Bonten, Taishaku,* and the *Shi-Tennō*.
Rin-jin.	The Dragon, or Sea, King.
Saruta-hiko.	A terrestrial deity who greeted *Ninigi*.
Sengen.	The Goddess of Mount Fuji. She is also known as *Asama* or *Ko-no-Hana-Saku-ya-Hime*, "The Princess who makes the Flowers of the Trees to Blossom."
Shaka Muni.	The founder of Buddhism, also called Gautama, but most generally known as the Buddha.

GODS AND GODDESSES

SHARIHOTSU.	The wisest of Buddha's ten chief disciples.
SHICHI FUKUJIN.	The Seven Gods of Luck, viz.: *Ebisu, Daikoku, Benten, Fukurokuju, Bishamon, Jurōjin,* and *Hotei.*
SHITA-TERU-HIME.	"Lower-shine-Princess," and wife of *Ame-waka.*
SHI-TENNŌ.	The Four Heavenly Kings who protect the earth from demons, each defending one quarter of the horizon. Their names are *Jikoku,* East; *Kōmoku,* South; *Zōchō,* West; and *Tamon,* also called *Bishamon,* North. Their images are placed at the inner gate of the temple.
SHŌDEN.	The Indian Ganesa, God of Wisdom.
SOHODO-NO-KAMI.	The God of Scarecrows.
SUKUNA-BIKONA.	A deity sent from Heaven to assist *Onamuji* in pacifying his realm.
SUSA-NO-O.	"The Impetuous Male," brother of the Sun Goddess.
TAISHAKU.	The Brahminical God Indra.
TANABATA or SHOKUJO.	The Weaving Maiden.
TEN.	A title equivalent to the Sanskrit *Dêva.*
TENJIN.	The God of Calligraphy.
TENNIN.	Female Buddhist Angels.
TŌSHŌGU.	The deified name of the great Shōgun Ieyasu or Gongen Sama.
TOYOKUNI.	The deified name of Hideyoshi.
TOYO-TAMA.	The Dragon King's daughter.
TOYO-UKE-BIME.	The Shintō Goddess of Earth or Food.
TSUKI-YUMI.	The Moon God.
UZUME.	The Goddess of Dancing.
YAKUSHI NYORAI.	"The Healing Buddha."
YOFUNÉ-NUSHI.	The Serpent God.
YUKI-ONNA.	The Lady of the Snow.

GENEALOGY OF THE AGE OF THE GODS

The Heavenly parent, Ame yudzuru hi ame no sa-giri kuni yudzuru tsuki kuni no sa-giri Mikoto.

FIRST GENERATION.

Companion-born heavenly Gods.

Ame no mi-naka-nushi no Mik'oto.
Heaven middle master.

Umashi-ashi-kabi hikoji no Mikoto.
Sweet reed-shoot prince elder.

SECOND GENERATION.

Companion-born heavenly Gods.

Kuni no toko tachi no Mikoto.
Land eternal stand.

Toyo-kuni-nushi no Mikoto.
Rich land master.

A Branch.

Ame-ya-kudari no Mikoto.
Heaven eight descend.

THIRD GENERATION.

Heavenly Gods born as mates.

Tsuno-gui no Mikoto.
Horn stake.

Iku-gui no Mikoto, his younger sister or wife.
Live stake.

A Branch.

Ame mi kudari no Mikoto.
Heaven three descend.

FOURTH GENERATION.

Heavenly Gods born as mates.

Uhiji-ni no Mikoto.
Mud earth (honorific affix).

Suhiji-ni no Mikoto, his younger sister or wife.
Sand earth.

A BRANCH.

Ama-ahi no Mikoto.
Heaven meet.

FIFTH GENERATION.

Heavenly Gods born as mates.

Oho-toma-hiko no Mikoto.
Great mat prince.

Oho-toma-he no Mikoto, his younger sister or wife.
Great mat place.

A BRANCH.

Ame ya-wo-hi no Mikoto.
Heaven eight hundred days.

SIXTH GENERATION.

Heavenly Gods born as mates.

Awo-kashiki ne no Mikoto.
Green awful (honorific).

Aya-kashiki ne no Mikoto, his younger sister or wife.
Ah! awful.

A BRANCH.

Ame no ya-so-yorodzu-dama no Mikoto.
Eighty myriad spirits.

SEVENTH GENERATION.

Heavenly Gods born as mates.

Izanagi no Mikoto.
Izanami no Mikoto, his younger sister or wife.

GENEALOGY OF THE AGE OF THE GODS

A Branch.

Taka mi-musubi no Mikoto.
High august growth.

Children.

Ama no omohi-game no Mikoto.
Heaven thought-compriser.

Ama no futo-dama no Mikoto.
Big jewel.

Ama no woshi-hi no Mikoto.
Endure sun.

Ama no kamu-dachi no Mikoto.
God stand.

Next there was—

Kamu mi musubi no Mikoto.
Above growth.

Children.

Ame no mi ke mochi no Mikoto.
August food hold.

Ame no michi ne no Mikoto.
Road (honorific).

Ame no kami-dama no Mikoto.
God jewel.

Iku-dama no Mikoto.
Live jewel.

Next there was—

Tsu-haya-dama no Mikoto.
Port quick jewel.

Children.

Ichi-chi-dama no Mikoto.
Market thousand jewel.

Kogoto-dama no Mikoto.
Ama no ko-yane no Mikoto.
Child-roof.

Takechi-nokori no Mikoto.
Brave milk remnant.

Next there was—

Furu-dama no Mikoto.
Shake jewel.

CHILDREN.

Saki-dama no Mikoto.
First jewel.

Ama no woshi-dachi no Mikoto.
Endure stand.

Next there was—

Yorodzu-dana no Mikoto.
Myriad jewel.

CHILD.

Ama no koha-kaha no Mikoto
Hard river.

BIBLIOGRAPHY

ANDERSON, WILLIAM.
The Pictorial Arts of Japan.
Descriptive and Historical Catalogue of Japanese and Chinese
Paintings in the British Museum.
History of Japanese Art.

ASTON, W. G.
A History of Japanese Literature.
A Grammar of the Japanese Written Language.
A Grammar of the Japanese Spoken Language.
The Nihongi. Transactions of the Japan Society, 1896.

AUDSLEY, G. A.
Ornamental Arts of Japan.

AUDSLEY, G. A., and TOMKINSON, M.
The Art Carvings of Japan.

AYRTON, W. E., and PERRY, J.
On the Magic Mirrors of Japan. Proceedings of the Royal Society,
Vol. xxvii.

BACON, A. M.
In the Land of the Gods.
Japanese Girls and Women.

BALLARD, S.
Fairy-Tales from Far Japan.

BATCHELOR, Rev. J.
The Ainu of Japan.

BINYON, LAURENCE.
The Flight of the Dragon.

BISHOP, Mrs.
Unbeaten Tracks in Japan.

BRINKLEY, Captain F.
Japan and China.

CHAMBERLAIN, BASIL HALL.
Things Japanese.
Japanese Poetry.
The Language, Mythology, and Geographical Nomenclature of Japan,
Viewed in the Light of Aino Studies.
Handbook of Colloquial Japanese.
Practical Introduction to Study of Japanese Writing.
Murray's Handbook for Japan. (In collaboration with W. B.
Mason.)

397

BIBLIOGRAPHY

CHAMBERLAIN, BASIL HALL (*continued*).
>*A Translation of the " Kojiki," or " Records of Ancient Matters,"
with Introduction and Commentary.* Published as Supplement
to Vol. **x.** of the *Transactions of the Asiatic Society of Japan.*
The Japanese Fairy-Tales Series.

CONDER, J.
>*The Floral Art of Japan.*
>*Flowers of Japan.*
>*Landscape Gardening in Japan.*

DAVIDSON, J. W.
>*The Island of Formosa, Past and Present: History, People, Resources,
and Commercial Prospects.*

DAVIS, F. HADLAND.
>*The Land of the Yellow Spring, and other Japanese Stories.*

DE BENNEVILLE, JAMES S.
>*Saitō Musashi-Bō Benkei. Tales of the Wars of Gempei.*

DENNING, WALTER.
>*Life of Hideyoshi.*
>*Japan in Days of Yore.*

DICK, STEWART.
>*Arts and Crafts of Old Japan.*

DICKINS, F. VICTOR.
>*The Old Bamboo-hewer's Story.* (A translation of the *Taketori
Monogatari.*)
>*Primitive and Mediæval Japanese Texts.*
>*Hō-Jō-Ki* ("Notes from a Ten Feet Square Hut"). From
the Japanese of Kamo No Chōmei.
>*The Chiushingura; or, The Loyal League.* Translated with Notes
and an Appendix containing *The Ballad of Takasago.*

DU CANE, FLORENCE.
>*Flowers and Gardens of Japan.*

EDWARDS, OSMAN.
>*Japanese Plays and Playfellows.*

GILES, H. A.
>*A History of Chinese Literature.*
>*Strange Stories from a Chinese Studio.*

GONSE, LOUIS.
>*L'Art Japonais.*

GOWLAND, W.
>*Dolmens and Burial Mounds in Japan.*

BIBLIOGRAPHY

GRIFFIS, Rev. W. E.
The Japanese Nation in Evolution.
The Mikado's Empire.
Japan in History, Folklore, and Art.
Fairy-Tales of Old Japan.

GULIC, Rev. S. L.
Evolution of the Japanese.

HEARN, LAFCADIO.
Glimpses of Unfamiliar Japan.
Out of the East.
In Ghostly Japan.
Shadowings.
Gleanings in Buddha-Fields.
Kokoro : Hints and Echoes of Japanese Inner Life.
A Japanese Miscellany.
Exotics and Retrospectives.
Kottō.
Kwaidan.
The Romance of the Milky Way.
Japan : An Interpretation.
The Life and Letters of Lafcadio Hearn. By ELIZABETH BISLAND.
The Japanese Letters of Lafcadio Hearn. Edited by ELIZABETH
BISLAND.

HINCKS, M. A.
The Japanese Dance.

HUISH, M. B.
Japan and its Art..

INOUE, JUKICHI.
Sketches of Tōkyō Life.

JAMES, GRACE.
Green Willow, and other Japanese Fairy-Tales.

JOLY, HENRI L.
Legend in Japanese Art.

KAEMPFER, E.
History of Japan.

KNAPP, A. M.
Feudal and Modern Japan.

LAY, A. H.
*Japanese Funeral Rites. Transactions of the Asiatic Society of
Japan,* Vol. xix.

BIBLIOGRAPHY

LEECH, J. H.
    Butterflies from Japan.

LLOYD, REV. ARTHUR.
    The Creed of Half Japan.

LONGFORD, JOSEPH H.
    The Story of Old Japan.
    The Story of Korea.

LOWELL, PERCIVAL.
    The Soul of the Far East.
    Occult Japan.

McCLATCHIE, T. R. H.
    Japanese Heraldry.

MITFORD, A. B. (LORD REDESDALE).
    Tales of Old Japan.

MORRISON, ARTHUR.
    The Painters of Japan.

MUNRO, N. G.
    Coins of Japan.

NITOBE, INAZO.
    Bushido : The Soul of Japan.

NOGUCHI, YONE.
    From the Eastern Sea.
    The Pilgrimage.
    Lafcadio Hearn in Japan.

OKAKURA, K.
    The Book of Tea.
    Ideals of the East.

OKAKURA, Y.
    The Japanese Spirit.

OKUMA, Count.
    Fifty Years of New Japan. English edition. Edited by MARCUS
        B. HUISH.

OZAKI, Y. T.
    The Japanese Fairy Book.
    Warriors of Old Japan.
    Buddha's Crystal.

PASTEUR, VIOLET M.
    Gods and Heroes of Old Japan.

BIBLIOGRAPHY

PIGGOT, Sir F. T.
  The Garden of Japan.
  The Music and Musical Instruments of Japan.

PORTER, ROBERT P.
  The Full Recognition of Japan.

PORTER, WILLIAM N.
  A Year of Japanese Epigrams.
  A Hundred Verses from Old Japan. A translation of the *Hyaku-nin-isshiu,* or " Single Verses by a Hundred People."

REIN, J. J.
  Japan.
  The Industries of Japan.

RINDER, F.
  Old-world Japan.

SALWEY, C. M.
  Fans of Japan.
  Japanese Monographs. Asiatic Quarterly Review.

SARGENT, C. S.
  Forest Flora of Japan.

SATOW, Sir ERNEST.
  The Shintō Temples of Isé.
  The Revival of Pure Shintō.
  Ancient Japanese Rituals. See Vols. ii., iii., vii., and ix. of the *Transactions of the Asiatic Society of Japan.*

SMITH, R. GORDON.
  Ancient Tales and Folk-lore of Japan.

STRANGE, EDWARD F.
  Japanese Colour Prints.

TOMITA, K., and LEE, G. A.
  Japanese Treasure Tales.

TOMKINSON, M.
  A Japanese Collection.

WALSH, CLARA A.
  The Master-Singers of Japan.

WENCKSTERN, FR. VON.
  Bibliography of the Japanese Empire.

WESTON, REV. WALTER.
  Japanese Alps.

INDEX TO POETICAL QUOTATIONS

GLOSSARY AND INDEX

THE PRONUNCIATION OF JAPANESE NAMES

" Remember, in pronouncing Japanese, that the consonants are to be sounded approximately as in English, the vowels as in Spanish or Italian ; that is to say,

a as in	' father.'	*o* as in	' pony.'
e ,,	' pet.'	*u* ,,	' full.'
i ,,	' pin.'		

" There is scarcely any tonic accent ; in other words, all the syllables are pronounced equally, or nearly so. But particular care must be taken to distinguish long *ō* and *ū*. The short vowels are pronounced in a very light, staccato manner. Thus *O tori nasai* means ' Please take this ' ; but *O tōri nasai* means ' Please come [or go ; lit., pass] in.' Short *i* and *u* sometimes become almost inaudible. . . . In diphthongs each vowel retains its original force. Thus :

ai as in the English word	' sky.'
au ,, ,, ,,	' cow.'
ei ,, ,, ,,	' hay.'

" *g* is hard, as in ' give,' never soft, as in ' gin ' ; but in Tōkyō and Eastern Japan it sounds like *ng* when in the middle of a word, exactly as in the English words ' singer,' ' springy ' (*not* ' sing-ger,' ' spring-gy '). *s* is always sharp, as in ' mouse.' *w* is often omitted after *k* or *g*, as in *kashi*, ' cake,' for *kwashi*. Be very careful to pronounce double consonants really double, as in English words ' shot*tower*,' ' mean*ness*,' ' cock*c*row.' Thus *kite* with one *t* means ' coming ' ; but *kitte* with two *t*'s means ' a ticket ' ; *ama* is a nun, *amma* a shampooer."—*Murray's Handbook for Japan*, by B. H. Chamberlain and W. B. Mason.

GLOSSARY AND INDEX

GLOSSARY AND INDEX

216; Thunder God in, 250; thunder animal in, 251; tea-drinking in, 291, 292; Dragon of, 362

CHINU. Of Izumi, one of the Maiden of Unai's lovers, 313–316

CHINESE. Japan called Jih-pén by, xiv; banners, described, 162; myth, Kwannon known as Kwanjin in, 200

CHIYO. A beautiful woman slain by Shokuro, 254; restored to life by Raiden, 254; Shokuro makes peace with, 254; a poetess of the same name makes pathetic reference to a dragon-fly, 282; a touching *hokku* by, 385

CHIYODŌ. Child of Heitaro and Higo (Willow), 180

CHOKORO. Depicted releasing his magic horse from a gigantic gourd, 357

CHŌMEI. Twelfth-century Buddhist recluse; reference to his *Hō-jō-ki*, 160, 385

CHŌMEIJI. Place in Ōmi; one of the thirty-three places sacred to Kwannon, 204

CHOSEN. Otherwise the Land of the Morning Calm, the old name for Korea, 328

CHOW DYNASTY. Kwanjin originally the daughter of the King of the, 200

CHRONICLES OF JAPAN (" NI-HONGI "). Reference to, xv

CHRYSANTHEMUM. The Japanese flag and the, 161–163; Japan's national flower, the, 162; poetical naming of the, 163; Lady White and Lady Yellow, story of, 163–165; Kikuo (" Chrysanthemum - Old - Man "), retainer of Tsugaru, story of, 165–167

CHŪJŌ HIME. A Buddhist nun, the greatest early Japanese artist of embroidery, an incarnation of Kwannon, 201; retires to temple of Toemadera, 201

CONDER, JOSIAH. Tells of custom connected with pine trees at wedding feasts, 159

CONFUCIUS. Added fresh material to the *Yih-King* ("Book of Changes"), 344

CONTENTMENT, THE GOD OF. *See* Hotei, 211–213

CORPSE-EATER. *See* Musō Kokushi, 305–308; maiden who tested the love of her suitors as a, 311, 312

CRYSTAL, THE, of Buddha, 89–91

D

DAIBUTSU, THE. *See* Buddha (the Bronze), 82

DAIKOKU. One of the Seven Gods of Good Fortune, 115; associated with Ebisu (his son) and Hotei, the God of Laughter, 211; his wonderful Mallet, 211; a Rat the second attribute of, 211; old legend regarding jealousy of Buddhist Gods toward, 211, 212; the sixfold representation of, 212; usually pictured with his son, Ebisu, 212

DAI-MOKENREN. A great disciple of Buddha; sees soul of his mother in the Gakidō, 223

DAIMYŌ. Lady White reaches palace of, 164, 165

DAN-DOKU, MOUNT. The Lord Buddha's meditations upon, 80

DAN-NO-URA. The Taira clan finally driven into the sea by Benkei and Yoshitsune, 43, 44; Hōïchi receives stranger, who wishes to view scene of the battle of, 301–304

DARUMA. Son of a Hindu king, 297; tempted like St. Anthony, 297; Indian sage whose image was associated with the ritualistic drinking of tea by the Zen sect in Japan, 297–299; reference to, will be found in *Some Chinese Ghosts* and *A Japanese Miscellany*, by Lafcadio Hearn, 297, 299

DAVIS, F. HADLAND. Reference to *Land of the Yellow Spring* (page 113), by, 93, 149

GLOSSARY AND INDEX

GLOSSARY AND INDEX

GLOSSARY AND INDEX

411

GLOSSARY AND INDEX

GLOSSARY AND INDEX

GLOSSARY AND INDEX

GLOSSARY AND INDEX

GLOSSARY AND INDEX

GLOSSARY AND INDEX

GLOSSARY AND INDEX

GLOSSARY AND INDEX

GLOSSARY AND INDEX

GLOSSARY AND INDEX

GLOSSARY AND INDEX

GLOSSARY AND INDEX

GLOSSARY AND INDEX

GLOSSARY AND INDEX

GLOSSARY AND INDEX

GLOSSARY AND INDEX

GLOSSARY AND INDEX

A CATALOG OF SELECTED
DOVER BOOKS
IN ALL FIELDS OF INTEREST

A CATALOG OF SELECTED DOVER
BOOKS IN ALL FIELDS OF INTEREST

DRAWINGS OF REMBRANDT, edited by Seymour Slive. Updated Lippmann, Hofstede de Groot edition, with definitive scholarly apparatus. All portraits, biblical sketches, landscapes, nudes. Oriental figures, classical studies, together with selection of work by followers. 550 illustrations. Total of 630pp. 9⅛ × 12¼.
21485-0, 21486-9 Pa., Two-vol. set $29.90

GHOST AND HORROR STORIES OF AMBROSE BIERCE, Ambrose Bierce. 24 tales vividly imagined, strangely prophetic, and decades ahead of their time in technical skill: "The Damned Thing," "An Inhabitant of Carcosa," "The Eyes of the Panther," "Moxon's Master," and 20 more. 199pp. 5⅜ × 8½. 20767-6 Pa. $3.95

ETHICAL WRITINGS OF MAIMONIDES, Maimonides. Most significant ethical works of great medieval sage, newly translated for utmost precision, readability. Laws Concerning Character Traits, Eight Chapters, more. 192pp. 5⅜ × 8½.
24522-5 Pa. $4.50

THE EXPLORATION OF THE COLORADO RIVER AND ITS CANYONS, J. W. Powell. Full text of Powell's 1,000-mile expedition down the fabled Colorado in 1869. Superb account of terrain, geology, vegetation, Indians, famine, mutiny, treacherous rapids, mighty canyons, during exploration of last unknown part of continental U.S. 400pp. 5⅜ × 8½. 20094-9 Pa. $7.95

HISTORY OF PHILOSOPHY, Julián Marías. Clearest one-volume history on the market. Every major philosopher and dozens of others, to Existentialism and later. 505pp. 5⅜ × 8½. 21739-6 Pa. $9.95

ALL ABOUT LIGHTNING, Martin A. Uman. Highly readable non-technical survey of nature and causes of lightning, thunderstorms, ball lightning, St. Elmo's Fire, much more. Illustrated. 192pp. 5⅜ × 8½. 25237-X Pa. $5.95

SAILING ALONE AROUND THE WORLD, Captain Joshua Slocum. First man to sail around the world, alone, in small boat. One of great feats of seamanship told in delightful manner. 67 illustrations. 294pp. 5⅜ × 8½. 20326-3 Pa. $4.95

LETTERS AND NOTES ON THE MANNERS, CUSTOMS AND CONDITIONS OF THE NORTH AMERICAN INDIANS, George Catlin. Classic account of life among Plains Indians: ceremonies, hunt, warfare, etc. 312 plates. 572pp. of text. 6⅛ × 9¼. 22118-0, 22119-9, Pa. Two-vol. set $17.90

ALASKA: The Harriman Expedition, 1899, John Burroughs, John Muir, et al. Informative, engrossing accounts of two-month, 9,000-mile expedition. Native peoples, wildlife, forests, geography, salmon industry, glaciers, more. Profusely illustrated. 240 black-and-white line drawings. 124 black-and-white photographs. 3 maps. Index. 576pp. 5⅜ × 8½. 25109-8 Pa. $11.95

THE BOOK OF BEASTS: Being a Translation from a Latin Bestiary of the Twelfth Century, T. H. White. Wonderful catalog real and fanciful beasts: manticore, griffin, phoenix, amphivius, jaculus, many more. White's witty erudite commentary on scientific, historical aspects. Fascinating glimpse of medieval mind. Illustrated. 296pp. 5⅜ × 8¼. (Available in U.S. only) 24609-4 Pa. $6.95

FRANK LLOYD WRIGHT: ARCHITECTURE AND NATURE With 160 Illustrations, Donald Hoffmann. Profusely illustrated study of influence of nature—especially prairie—on Wright's designs for Fallingwater, Robie House, Guggenheim Museum, other masterpieces. 96pp. 9¼ × 10¾. 25098-9 Pa. $7.95

FRANK LLOYD WRIGHT'S FALLINGWATER, Donald Hoffmann. Wright's famous waterfall house: planning and construction of organic idea. History of site, owners, Wright's personal involvement. Photographs of various stages of building. Preface by Edgar Kaufmann, Jr. 100 illustrations. 112pp. 9¼ × 10. 23671-4 Pa. $8.95

YEARS WITH FRANK LLOYD WRIGHT: Apprentice to Genius, Edgar Tafel. Insightful memoir by a former apprentice presents a revealing portrait of Wright the man, the inspired teacher, the greatest American architect. 372 black-and-white illustrations. Preface. Index. vi + 228pp. 8¼ × 11. 24801-1 Pa. $10.95

THE STORY OF KING ARTHUR AND HIS KNIGHTS, Howard Pyle. Enchanting version of King Arthur fable has delighted generations with imaginative narratives of exciting adventures and unforgettable illustrations by the author. 41 illustrations. xviii + 313pp. 6⅛ × 9¼. 21445-1 Pa. $6.95

THE GODS OF THE EGYPTIANS, E. A. Wallis Budge. Thorough coverage of numerous gods of ancient Egypt by foremost Egyptologist. Information on evolution of cults, rites and gods; the cult of Osiris; the Book of the Dead and its rites; the sacred animals and birds; Heaven and Hell; and more. 956pp. 6⅛ × 9¼. 22055-9, 22056-7 Pa., Two-vol. set $21.90

A THEOLOGICO-POLITICAL TREATISE, Benedict Spinoza. Also contains unfinished *Political Treatise*. Great classic on religious liberty, theory of government on common consent. R. Elwes translation. Total of 421pp. 5⅜ × 8½. 20249-6 Pa. $6.95

INCIDENTS OF TRAVEL IN CENTRAL AMERICA, CHIAPAS, AND YUCATAN, John L. Stephens. Almost single-handed discovery of Maya culture; exploration of ruined cities, monuments, temples; customs of Indians. 115 drawings. 892pp. 5⅜ × 8½. 22404-X, 22405-8 Pa., Two-vol. set $15.90

LOS CAPRICHOS, Francisco Goya. 80 plates of wild, grotesque monsters and caricatures. Prado manuscript included. 183pp. 6⅝ × 9⅝. 22384-1 Pa. $5.95

AUTOBIOGRAPHY: The Story of My Experiments with Truth, Mohandas K. Gandhi. Not hagiography, but Gandhi in his own words. Boyhood, legal studies, purification, the growth of the Satyagraha (nonviolent protest) movement. Critical, inspiring work of the man who freed India. 480pp. 5⅜ × 8½. (Available in U.S. only) 24593-4 Pa. $6.95

ILLUSTRATED DICTIONARY OF HISTORIC ARCHITECTURE, edited by Cyril M. Harris. Extraordinary compendium of clear, concise definitions for over 5,000 important architectural terms complemented by over 2,000 line drawings. Covers full spectrum of architecture from ancient ruins to 20th-century Modernism. Preface. 592pp. 7½ × 9⅝. 24444-X Pa. $15.95

THE NIGHT BEFORE CHRISTMAS, Clement Moore. Full text, and woodcuts from original 1848 book. Also critical, historical material. 19 illustrations. 40pp. 4⅝ × 6. 22797-9 Pa. $2.50

THE LESSON OF JAPANESE ARCHITECTURE: 165 Photographs, Jiro Harada. Memorable gallery of 165 photographs taken in the 1930's of exquisite Japanese homes of the well-to-do and historic buildings. 13 line diagrams. 192pp. 8⅜ × 11¼. 24778-3 Pa. $10.95

THE AUTOBIOGRAPHY OF CHARLES DARWIN AND SELECTED LETTERS, edited by Francis Darwin. The fascinating life of eccentric genius composed of an intimate memoir by Darwin (intended for his children); commentary by his son, Francis; hundreds of fragments from notebooks, journals, papers; and letters to and from Lyell, Hooker, Huxley, Wallace and Henslow. xi + 365pp. 5⅜ × 8. 20479-0 Pa. $6.95

WONDERS OF THE SKY: Observing Rainbows, Comets, Eclipses, the Stars and Other Phenomena, Fred Schaaf. Charming, easy-to-read poetic guide to all manner of celestial events visible to the naked eye. Mock suns, glories, Belt of Venus, more. Illustrated. 299pp. 5¼ × 8¼. 24402-4 Pa. $7.95

BURNHAM'S CELESTIAL HANDBOOK, Robert Burnham, Jr. Thorough guide to the stars beyond our solar system. Exhaustive treatment. Alphabetical by constellation: Andromeda to Cetus in Vol. 1; Chamaeleon to Orion in Vol. 2; and Pavo to Vulpecula in Vol. 3. Hundreds of illustrations. Index in Vol. 3. 2,000pp. 6⅛ × 9¼. 23567-X, 23568-8, 23673-0 Pa., Three-vol. set $41.85

STAR NAMES: Their Lore and Meaning, Richard Hinckley Allen. Fascinating history of names various cultures have given to constellations and literary and folkloristic uses that have been made of stars. Indexes to subjects. Arabic and Greek names. Biblical references. Bibliography. 563pp. 5⅜ × 8½. 21079-0 Pa. $8.95

THIRTY YEARS THAT SHOOK PHYSICS: The Story of Quantum Theory, George Gamow. Lucid, accessible introduction to influential theory of energy and matter. Careful explanations of Dirac's anti-particles, Bohr's model of the atom, much more. 12 plates. Numerous drawings. 240pp. 5⅜ × 8½. 24895-X Pa. $5.95

CHINESE DOMESTIC FURNITURE IN PHOTOGRAPHS AND MEASURED DRAWINGS, Gustav Ecke. A rare volume, now affordably priced for antique collectors, furniture buffs and art historians. Detailed review of styles ranging from early Shang to late Ming. Unabridged republication. 161 black-and-white drawings, photos. Total of 224pp. 8⅜ × 11¼. (Available in U.S. only) 25171-3 Pa. $13.95

VINCENT VAN GOGH: A Biography, Julius Meier-Graefe. Dynamic, penetrating study of artist's life, relationship with brother, Theo, painting techniques, travels, more. Readable, engrossing. 160pp. 5⅜ × 8½. (Available in U.S. only) 25253-1 Pa. $4.95

HOW TO WRITE, Gertrude Stein. Gertrude Stein claimed anyone could understand her unconventional writing—here are clues to help. Fascinating improvisations, language experiments, explanations illuminate Stein's craft and the art of writing. Total of 414pp. 4⅝ × 6⅜. 23144-5 Pa. $6.95

ADVENTURES AT SEA IN THE GREAT AGE OF SAIL: Five Firsthand Narratives, edited by Elliot Snow. Rare true accounts of exploration, whaling, shipwreck, fierce natives, trade, shipboard life, more. 33 illustrations. Introduction. 353pp. 5⅜ × 8½. 25177-2 Pa. $8.95

THE HERBAL OR GENERAL HISTORY OF PLANTS, John Gerard. Classic descriptions of about 2,850 plants—with over 2,700 illustrations—includes Latin and English names, physical descriptions, varieties, time and place of growth, more. 2,706 illustrations. xlv + 1,678pp. 8½ × 12¼. 23147-X Cloth. $75.00

DOROTHY AND THE WIZARD IN OZ, L. Frank Baum. Dorothy and the Wizard visit the center of the Earth, where people are vegetables, glass houses grow and Oz characters reappear. Classic sequel to *Wizard of Oz.* 256pp. 5⅜ × 8. 24714-7 Pa. $5.95

SONGS OF EXPERIENCE: Facsimile Reproduction with 26 Plates in Full Color, William Blake. This facsimile of Blake's original "Illuminated Book" reproduces 26 full-color plates from a rare 1826 edition. Includes "The Tyger," "London," "Holy Thursday," and other immortal poems. 26 color plates. Printed text of poems. 48pp. 5¼ × 7. 24636-1 Pa. $3.50

SONGS OF INNOCENCE, William Blake. The first and most popular of Blake's famous "Illuminated Books," in a facsimile edition reproducing all 31 brightly colored plates. Additional printed text of each poem. 64pp. 5¼ × 7. 22764-2 Pa. $3.50

PRECIOUS STONES, Max Bauer. Classic, thorough study of diamonds, rubies, emeralds, garnets, etc.: physical character, occurrence, properties, use, similar topics. 20 plates, 8 in color. 94 figures. 659pp. 6⅛ × 9¼. 21910-0, 21911-9 Pa., Two-vol. set $15.90

ENCYCLOPEDIA OF VICTORIAN NEEDLEWORK, S. F. A. Caulfeild and Blanche Saward. Full, precise descriptions of stitches, techniques for dozens of needlecrafts—most exhaustive reference of its kind. Over 800 figures. Total of 679pp. 8⅛ × 11. Two volumes. Vol. 1 22800-2 Pa. $11.95
Vol. 2 22801-0 Pa. $11.95

THE MARVELOUS LAND OF OZ, L. Frank Baum. Second Oz book, the Scarecrow and Tin Woodman are back with hero named Tip, Oz magic. 136 illustrations. 287pp. 5⅜ × 8½. 20692-0 Pa. $5.95

WILD FOWL DECOYS, Joel Barber. Basic book on the subject, by foremost authority and collector. Reveals history of decoy making and rigging, place in American culture, different kinds of decoys, how to make them, and how to use them. 140 plates. 156pp. 7⅞ × 10¾. 20011-6 Pa. $8.95

HISTORY OF LACE, Mrs. Bury Palliser. Definitive, profusely illustrated chronicle of lace from earliest times to late 19th century. Laces of Italy, Greece, England, France, Belgium, etc. Landmark of needlework scholarship. 266 illustrations. 672pp. 6⅛ × 9¼. 24742-2 Pa. $14.95

CATALOG OF DOVER BOOKS

ILLUSTRATED GUIDE TO SHAKER FURNITURE, Robert Meader. All furniture and appurtenances, with much on unknown local styles. 235 photos. 146pp. 9 × 12. 22819-3 Pa. $8.95

WHALE SHIPS AND WHALING: A Pictorial Survey, George Francis Dow. Over 200 vintage engravings, drawings, photographs of barks, brigs, cutters, other vessels. Also harpoons, lances, whaling guns, many other artifacts. Comprehensive text by foremost authority. 207 black-and-white illustrations. 288pp. 6 × 9. 24808-9 Pa. $8.95

THE BERTRAMS, Anthony Trollope. Powerful portrayal of blind self-will and thwarted ambition includes one of Trollope's most heartrending love stories. 497pp. 5⅜ × 8½. 25119-5 Pa. $9.95

ADVENTURES WITH A HAND LENS, Richard Headstrom. Clearly written guide to observing and studying flowers and grasses, fish scales, moth and insect wings, egg cases, buds, feathers, seeds, leaf scars, moss, molds, ferns, common crystals, etc.—all with an ordinary, inexpensive magnifying glass. 209 exact line drawings aid in your discoveries. 220pp. 5⅜ × 8½. 23330-8 Pa. $4.95

RODIN ON ART AND ARTISTS, Auguste Rodin. Great sculptor's candid, wide-ranging comments on meaning of art; great artists; relation of sculpture to poetry, painting, music; philosophy of life, more. 76 superb black-and-white illustrations of Rodin's sculpture, drawings and prints. 119pp. 8⅜ × 11¼. 24487-3 Pa. $7.95

FIFTY CLASSIC FRENCH FILMS, 1912–1982: A Pictorial Record, Anthony Slide. Memorable stills from Grand Illusion, Beauty and the Beast, Hiroshima, Mon Amour, many more. Credits, plot synopses, reviews, etc. 160pp. 8¼ × 11. 25256-6 Pa. $11.95

THE PRINCIPLES OF PSYCHOLOGY, William James. Famous long course complete, unabridged. Stream of thought, time perception, memory, experimental methods; great work decades ahead of its time. 94 figures. 1,391pp. 5⅜ × 8½. 20381-6, 20382-4 Pa., Two-vol. set $23.90

BODIES IN A BOOKSHOP, R. T. Campbell. Challenging mystery of blackmail and murder with ingenious plot and superbly drawn characters. In the best tradition of British suspense fiction. 192pp. 5⅜ × 8½. 24720-1 Pa. $3.95

CALLAS: PORTRAIT OF A PRIMA DONNA, George Jellinek. Renowned commentator on the musical scene chronicles incredible career and life of the most controversial, fascinating, influential operatic personality of our time. 64 black-and-white photographs. 416pp. 5⅜ × 8¼. 25047-4 Pa. $8.95

GEOMETRY, RELATIVITY AND THE FOURTH DIMENSION, Rudolph Rucker. Exposition of fourth dimension, concepts of relativity as Flatland characters continue adventures. Popular, easily followed yet accurate, profound. 141 illustrations. 133pp. 5⅜ × 8½. 23400-2 Pa. $4.95

HOUSEHOLD STORIES BY THE BROTHERS GRIMM, with pictures by Walter Crane. 53 classic stories—Rumpelstiltskin, Rapunzel, Hansel and Gretel, the Fisherman and his Wife, Snow White, Tom Thumb, Sleeping Beauty, Cinderella, and so much more—lavishly illustrated with original 19th century drawings. 114 illustrations. x + 269pp. 5⅜ × 8½. 21080-4 Pa. $4.95

SUNDIALS, Albert Waugh. Far and away the best, most thorough coverage of ideas, mathematics concerned, types, construction, adjusting anywhere. Over 100 illustrations. 230pp. 5⅜ × 8½. 22947-5 Pa. $4.95

PICTURE HISTORY OF THE NORMANDIE: With 190 Illustrations, Frank O. Braynard. Full story of legendary French ocean liner: Art Deco interiors, design innovations, furnishings, celebrities, maiden voyage, tragic fire, much more. Extensive text. 144pp. 8⅜ × 11¾. 25257-4 Pa. $10.95

THE FIRST AMERICAN COOKBOOK: A Facsimile of "American Cookery," 1796, Amelia Simmons. Facsimile of the first American-written cookbook published in the United States contains authentic recipes for colonial favorites—pumpkin pudding, winter squash pudding, spruce beer, Indian slapjacks, and more. Introductory Essay and Glossary of colonial cooking terms. 80pp. 5⅜ × 8½. 24710-4 Pa. $3.50

101 PUZZLES IN THOUGHT AND LOGIC, C. R. Wylie, Jr. Solve murders and robberies, find out which fishermen are liars, how a blind man could possibly identify a color—purely by your own reasoning! 107pp. 5⅜ × 8½. 20367-0 Pa. $2.50

THE BOOK OF WORLD-FAMOUS MUSIC—CLASSICAL, POPULAR AND FOLK, James J. Fuld. Revised and enlarged republication of landmark work in musico-bibliography. Full information about nearly 1,000 songs and compositions including first lines of music and lyrics. New supplement. Index. 800pp. 5⅜ × 8¼. 24857-7 Pa. $15.95

ANTHROPOLOGY AND MODERN LIFE, Franz Boas. Great anthropologist's classic treatise on race and culture. Introduction by Ruth Bunzel. Only inexpensive paperback edition. 255pp. 5⅜ × 8½. 25245-0 Pa. $6.95

THE TALE OF PETER RABBIT, Beatrix Potter. The inimitable Peter's terrifying adventure in Mr. McGregor's garden, with all 27 wonderful, full-color Potter illustrations. 55pp. 4¼ × 5½. (Available in U.S. only) 22827-4 Pa. $1.75

THREE PROPHETIC SCIENCE FICTION NOVELS, H. G. Wells. *When the Sleeper Wakes, A Story of the Days to Come* and *The Time Machine* (full version). 335pp. 5⅜ × 8½. (Available in U.S. only) 20605-X Pa. $6.95

APICIUS COOKERY AND DINING IN IMPERIAL ROME, edited and translated by Joseph Dommers Vehling. Oldest known cookbook in existence offers readers a clear picture of what foods Romans ate, how they prepared them, etc. 49 illustrations. 301pp. 6⅛ × 9¼. 23563-7 Pa. $7.95

SHAKESPEARE LEXICON AND QUOTATION DICTIONARY, Alexander Schmidt. Full definitions, locations, shades of meaning of every word in plays and poems. More than 50,000 exact quotations. 1,485pp. 6½ × 9¼. 22726-X, 22727-8 Pa., Two-vol. set $29.90

THE WORLD'S GREAT SPEECHES, edited by Lewis Copeland and Lawrence W. Lamm. Vast collection of 278 speeches from Greeks to 1970. Powerful and effective models; unique look at history. 842pp. 5⅜ × 8½. 20468-5 Pa. $11.95

THE BLUE FAIRY BOOK, Andrew Lang. The first, most famous collection, with many familiar tales: Little Red Riding Hood, Aladdin and the Wonderful Lamp, Puss in Boots, Sleeping Beauty, Hansel and Gretel, Rumpelstiltskin; 37 in all. 138 illustrations. 390pp. 5⅜ × 8½.   21437-0 Pa. $6.95

THE STORY OF THE CHAMPIONS OF THE ROUND TABLE, Howard Pyle. Sir Launcelot, Sir Tristram and Sir Percival in spirited adventures of love and triumph retold in Pyle's inimitable style. 50 drawings, 31 full-page. xviii + 329pp. 6½ × 9¼.   21883-X Pa. $7.95

AUDUBON AND HIS JOURNALS, Maria Audubon. Unmatched two-volume portrait of the great artist, naturalist and author contains his journals, an excellent biography by his granddaughter, expert annotations by the noted ornithologist, Dr. Elliott Coues, and 37 superb illustrations. Total of 1,200pp. 5⅜ × 8.

Vol. I 25143-8 Pa. $8.95
Vol. II 25144-6 Pa. $8.95

GREAT DINOSAUR HUNTERS AND THEIR DISCOVERIES, Edwin H. Colbert. Fascinating, lavishly illustrated chronicle of dinosaur research, 1820's to 1960. Achievements of Cope, Marsh, Brown, Buckland, Mantell, Huxley, many others. 384pp. 5¼ × 8¼.   24701-5 Pa. $7.95

THE TASTEMAKERS, Russell Lynes. Informal, illustrated social history of American taste 1850's-1950's. First popularized categories Highbrow, Lowbrow, Middlebrow. 129 illustrations. New (1979) afterword. 384pp. 6 × 9.

23993-4 Pa. $8.95

DOUBLE CROSS PURPOSES, Ronald A. Knox. A treasure hunt in the Scottish Highlands, an old map, unidentified corpse, surprise discoveries keep reader guessing in this cleverly intricate tale of financial skullduggery. 2 black-and-white maps. 320pp. 5⅜ × 8½. (Available in U.S. only)   25032-6 Pa. $6.95

AUTHENTIC VICTORIAN DECORATION AND ORNAMENTATION IN FULL COLOR: 46 Plates from "Studies in Design," Christopher Dresser. Superb full-color lithographs reproduced from rare original portfolio of a major Victorian designer. 48pp. 9¼ × 12¼.   25083-0 Pa. $7.95

PRIMITIVE ART, Franz Boas. Remains the best text ever prepared on subject, thoroughly discussing Indian, African, Asian, Australian, and, especially, Northern American primitive art. Over 950 illustrations show ceramics, masks, totem poles, weapons, textiles, paintings, much more. 376pp. 5⅜ × 8.   20025-6 Pa. $7.95

SIDELIGHTS ON RELATIVITY, Albert Einstein. Unabridged republication of two lectures delivered by the great physicist in 1920-21. *Ether and Relativity* and *Geometry and Experience*. Elegant ideas in non-mathematical form, accessible to intelligent layman. vi + 56pp. 5⅜ × 8½.   24511-X Pa. $2.95

THE WIT AND HUMOR OF OSCAR WILDE, edited by Alvin Redman. More than 1,000 ripostes, paradoxes, wisecracks: Work is the curse of the drinking classes, I can resist everything except temptation, etc. 258pp. 5⅜ × 8½.   20602-5 Pa. $4.95

ADVENTURES WITH A MICROSCOPE, Richard Headstrom. 59 adventures with clothing fibers, protozoa, ferns and lichens, roots and leaves, much more. 142 illustrations. 232pp. 5⅜ × 8½.   23471-1 Pa. $3.95

CATALOG OF DOVER BOOKS

PLANTS OF THE BIBLE, Harold N. Moldenke and Alma L. Moldenke. Standard reference to all 230 plants mentioned in Scriptures. Latin name, biblical reference, uses, modern identity, much more. Unsurpassed encyclopedic resource for scholars, botanists, nature lovers, students of Bible. Bibliography. Indexes. 123 black-and-white illustrations. 384pp. 6 × 9. 25069-5 Pa. $8.95

FAMOUS AMERICAN WOMEN: A Biographical Dictionary from Colonial Times to the Present, Robert McHenry, ed. From Pocahontas to Rosa Parks, 1,035 distinguished American women documented in separate biographical entries. Accurate, up-to-date data, numerous categories, spans 400 years. Indices. 493pp. 6½ × 9¼. 24523-3 Pa. $10.95

THE FABULOUS INTERIORS OF THE GREAT OCEAN LINERS IN HISTORIC PHOTOGRAPHS, William H. Miller, Jr. Some 200 superb photographs capture exquisite interiors of world's great "floating palaces"—1890's to 1980's: *Titanic, Ile de France, Queen Elizabeth, United States, Europa,* more. Approx. 200 black-and-white photographs. Captions. Text. Introduction. 160pp. 8⅜ × 11¼. 24756-2 Pa. $9.95

THE GREAT LUXURY LINERS, 1927–1954: A Photographic Record, William H. Miller, Jr. Nostalgic tribute to heyday of ocean liners. 186 photos of Ile de France, Normandie, Leviathan, Queen Elizabeth, United States, many others. Interior and exterior views. Introduction. Captions. 160pp. 9 × 12. 24056-8 Pa. $10.95

A NATURAL HISTORY OF THE DUCKS, John Charles Phillips. Great landmark of ornithology offers complete detailed coverage of nearly 200 species and subspecies of ducks: gadwall, sheldrake, merganser, pintail, many more. 74 full-color plates, 102 black-and-white. Bibliography. Total of 1,920pp. 8⅜ × 11¼. 25141-1, 25142-X Cloth. Two-vol. set $100.00

THE SEAWEED HANDBOOK: An Illustrated Guide to Seaweeds from North Carolina to Canada, Thomas F. Lee. Concise reference covers 78 species. Scientific and common names, habitat, distribution, more. Finding keys for easy identification. 224pp. 5⅜ × 8½. 25215-9 Pa. $6.95

THE TEN BOOKS OF ARCHITECTURE: The 1755 Leoni Edition, Leon Battista Alberti. Rare classic helped introduce the glories of ancient architecture to the Renaissance. 68 black-and-white plates. 336pp. 8⅜ × 11¼. 25239-6 Pa. $14.95

MISS MACKENZIE, Anthony Trollope. Minor masterpieces by Victorian master unmasks many truths about life in 19th-century England. First inexpensive edition in years. 392pp. 5⅜ × 8½. 25201-9 Pa. $8.95

THE RIME OF THE ANCIENT MARINER, Gustave Doré, Samuel Taylor Coleridge. Dramatic engravings considered by many to be his greatest work. The terrifying space of the open sea, the storms and whirlpools of an unknown ocean, the ice of Antarctica, more—all rendered in a powerful, chilling manner. Full text. 38 plates. 77pp. 9¼ × 12. 22305-1 Pa. $4.95

THE EXPEDITIONS OF ZEBULON MONTGOMERY PIKE, Zebulon Montgomery Pike. Fascinating first-hand accounts (1805-6) of exploration of Mississippi River, Indian wars, capture by Spanish dragoons, much more. 1,088pp. 5⅜ × 8½. 25254-X, 25255-8 Pa. Two-vol. set $25.90

A CONCISE HISTORY OF PHOTOGRAPHY: Third Revised Edition, Helmut Gernsheim. Best one-volume history—camera obscura, photochemistry, daguerreotypes, evolution of cameras, film, more. Also artistic aspects—landscape, portraits, fine art, etc. 281 black-and-white photographs. 26 in color. 176pp. 8⅜ × 11¼. 25128-4 Pa. $13.95

THE DORÉ BIBLE ILLUSTRATIONS, Gustave Doré. 241 detailed plates from the Bible: the Creation scenes, Adam and Eve, Flood, Babylon, battle sequences, life of Jesus, etc. Each plate is accompanied by the verses from the King James version of the Bible. 241pp. 9 × 12. 23004-X Pa. $9.95

HUGGER-MUGGER IN THE LOUVRE, Elliot Paul. Second Homer Evans mystery-comedy. Theft at the Louvre involves sleuth in hilarious, madcap caper. "A knockout."—Books. 336pp. 5⅜ × 8½. 25185-3 Pa. $5.95

FLATLAND, E. A. Abbott. Intriguing and enormously popular science-fiction classic explores the complexities of trying to survive as a two-dimensional being in a three-dimensional world. Amusingly illustrated by the author. 16 illustrations. 103pp. 5⅜ × 8½. 20001-9 Pa. $2.50

THE HISTORY OF THE LEWIS AND CLARK EXPEDITION, Meriwether Lewis and William Clark, edited by Elliott Coues. Classic edition of Lewis and Clark's day-by-day journals that later became the basis for U.S. claims to Oregon and the West. Accurate and invaluable geographical, botanical, biological, meteorological and anthropological material. Total of 1,508pp. 5⅜ × 8½.
21268-8, 21269-6, 21270-X Pa. Three-vol. set $26.85

LANGUAGE, TRUTH AND LOGIC, Alfred J. Ayer. Famous, clear introduction to Vienna, Cambridge schools of Logical Positivism. Role of philosophy, elimination of metaphysics, nature of analysis, etc. 160pp. 5⅜ × 8½. (Available in U.S. and Canada only) 20010-8 Pa. $3.95

MATHEMATICS FOR THE NONMATHEMATICIAN, Morris Kline. Detailed, college-level treatment of mathematics in cultural and historical context, with numerous exercises. For liberal arts students. Preface. Recommended Reading Lists. Tables. Index. Numerous black-and-white figures. xvi + 641pp. 5⅜ × 8½.
24823-2 Pa. $11.95

HANDBOOK OF PICTORIAL SYMBOLS, Rudolph Modley. 3,250 signs and symbols, many systems in full; official or heavy commercial use. Arranged by subject. Most in Pictorial Archive series. 143pp. 8⅛ × 11. 23357-X Pa. $6.95

INCIDENTS OF TRAVEL IN YUCATAN, John L. Stephens. Classic (1843) exploration of jungles of Yucatan, looking for evidences of Maya civilization. Travel adventures, Mexican and Indian culture, etc. Total of 669pp. 5⅜ × 8½.
20926-1, 20927-X Pa., Two-vol. set $11.90

DEGAS: An Intimate Portrait, Ambroise Vollard. Charming, anecdotal memoir by famous art dealer of one of the greatest 19th-century French painters. 14 black-and-white illustrations. Introduction by Harold L. Van Doren. 96pp. 5⅜ × 8½.
25131-4 Pa. $4.95

PERSONAL NARRATIVE OF A PILGRIMAGE TO ALMANDINAH AND MECCAH, Richard Burton. Great travel classic by remarkably colorful personality. Burton, disguised as a Moroccan, visited sacred shrines of Islam, narrowly escaping death. 47 illustrations. 959pp. 5⅜ × 8½. 21217-3, 21218-1 Pa., Two-vol. set $19.90

PHRASE AND WORD ORIGINS, A. H. Holt. Entertaining, reliable, modern study of more than 1,200 colorful words, phrases, origins and histories. Much unexpected information. 254pp. 5⅜ × 8½. 20758-7 Pa. $5.95

THE RED THUMB MARK, R. Austin Freeman. In this first Dr. Thorndyke case, the great scientific detective draws fascinating conclusions from the nature of a single fingerprint. Exciting story, authentic science. 320pp. 5⅜ × 8½. (Available in U.S. only) 25210-8 Pa. $6.95

AN EGYPTIAN HIEROGLYPHIC DICTIONARY, E. A. Wallis Budge. Monumental work containing about 25,000 words or terms that occur in texts ranging from 3000 B.C. to 600 A.D. Each entry consists of a transliteration of the word, the word in hieroglyphs, and the meaning in English. 1,314pp. 6⅜ × 10.
23615-3, 23616-1 Pa., Two-vol. set $31.90

THE COMPLEAT STRATEGYST: Being a Primer on the Theory of Games of Strategy, J. D. Williams. Highly entertaining classic describes, with many illustrated examples, how to select best strategies in conflict situations. Prefaces. Appendices. xvi + 268pp. 5⅜ × 8½. 25101-2 Pa. $5.95

THE ROAD TO OZ, L. Frank Baum. Dorothy meets the Shaggy Man, little Button-Bright and the Rainbow's beautiful daughter in this delightful trip to the magical Land of Oz. 272pp. 5⅜ × 8. 25208-6 Pa. $5.95

POINT AND LINE TO PLANE, Wassily Kandinsky. Seminal exposition of role of point, line, other elements in non-objective painting. Essential to understanding 20th-century art. 127 illustrations. 192pp. 6½ × 9¼. 23808-3 Pa. $5.95

LADY ANNA, Anthony Trollope. Moving chronicle of Countess Lovel's bitter struggle to win for herself and daughter Anna their rightful rank and fortune—perhaps at cost of sanity itself. 384pp. 5⅜ × 8½. 24669-8 Pa. $8.95

EGYPTIAN MAGIC, E. A. Wallis Budge. Sums up all that is known about magic in Ancient Egypt: the role of magic in controlling the gods, powerful amulets that warded off evil spirits, scarabs of immortality, use of wax images, formulas and spells, the secret name, much more. 253pp. 5⅜ × 8½. 22681-6 Pa. $4.50

THE DANCE OF SIVA, Ananda Coomaraswamy. Preeminent authority unfolds the vast metaphysic of India: the revelation of her art, conception of the universe, social organization, etc. 27 reproductions of art masterpieces. 192pp. 5⅜ × 8½.
24817-8 Pa. $5.95

CHRISTMAS CUSTOMS AND TRADITIONS, Clement A. Miles. Origin, evolution, significance of religious, secular practices. Caroling, gifts, yule logs, much more. Full, scholarly yet fascinating; non-sectarian. 400pp. 5⅜ × 8½.
23354-5 Pa. $6.95

THE HUMAN FIGURE IN MOTION, Eadweard Muybridge. More than 4,500 stopped-action photos, in action series, showing undraped men, women, children jumping, lying down, throwing, sitting, wrestling, carrying, etc. 390pp. 7⅞ × 10⅝.
20204-6 Cloth. $21.95

THE MAN WHO WAS THURSDAY, Gilbert Keith Chesterton. Witty, fast-paced novel about a club of anarchists in turn-of-the-century London. Brilliant social, religious, philosophical speculations. 128pp. 5⅜ × 8½. 25121-7 Pa. $3.95

A CEZANNE SKETCHBOOK: Figures, Portraits, Landscapes and Still Lifes, Paul Cezanne. Great artist experiments with tonal effects, light, mass, other qualities in over 100 drawings. A revealing view of developing master painter, precursor of Cubism. 102 black-and-white illustrations. 144pp. 8¾ × 6⅜. 24790-2 Pa. $5.95

AN ENCYCLOPEDIA OF BATTLES: Accounts of Over 1,560 Battles from 1479 B.C. to the Present, David Eggenberger. Presents essential details of every major battle in recorded history, from the first battle of Megiddo in 1479 B.C. to Grenada in 1984. List of Battle Maps. New Appendix covering the years 1967–1984. Index. 99 illustrations. 544pp. 6½ × 9¼. 24913-1 Pa. $14.95

AN ETYMOLOGICAL DICTIONARY OF MODERN ENGLISH, Ernest Weekley. Richest, fullest work, by foremost British lexicographer. Detailed word histories. Inexhaustible. Total of 856pp. 6½ × 9¼.
21873-2, 21874-0 Pa., Two-vol. set $17.00

WEBSTER'S AMERICAN MILITARY BIOGRAPHIES, edited by Robert McHenry. Over 1,000 figures who shaped 3 centuries of American military history. Detailed biographies of Nathan Hale, Douglas MacArthur, Mary Hallaren, others. Chronologies of engagements, more. Introduction. Addenda. 1,033 entries in alphabetical order. xi + 548pp. 6½ × 9¼. (Available in U.S. only)
24758-9 Pa. $13.95

LIFE IN ANCIENT EGYPT, Adolf Erman. Detailed older account, with much not in more recent books: domestic life, religion, magic, medicine, commerce, and whatever else needed for complete picture. Many illustrations. 597pp. 5⅜ × 8½.
22632-8 Pa. $8.95

HISTORIC COSTUME IN PICTURES, Braun & Schneider. Over 1,450 costumed figures shown, covering a wide variety of peoples: kings, emperors, nobles, priests, servants, soldiers, scholars, townsfolk, peasants, merchants, courtiers, cavaliers, and more. 256pp. 8⅜ × 11¼. 23150-X Pa. $9.95

THE NOTEBOOKS OF LEONARDO DA VINCI, edited by J. P. Richter. Extracts from manuscripts reveal great genius; on painting, sculpture, anatomy, sciences, geography, etc. Both Italian and English. 186 ms. pages reproduced, plus 500 additional drawings, including studies for *Last Supper, Sforza* monument, etc. 860pp. 7⅞ × 10¾. (Available in U.S. only) 22572-0, 22573-9 Pa., Two-vol. set $31.90

THE ART NOUVEAU STYLE BOOK OF ALPHONSE MUCHA: All 72 Plates from "Documents Decoratifs" in Original Color, Alphonse Mucha. Rare copyright-free design portfolio by high priest of Art Nouveau. Jewelry, wallpaper, stained glass, furniture, figure studies, plant and animal motifs, etc. Only complete one-volume edition. 80pp. 9⅜ × 12¼. 24044-4 Pa. $9.95

ANIMALS: 1,419 COPYRIGHT-FREE ILLUSTRATIONS OF MAMMALS, BIRDS, FISH, INSECTS, ETC., edited by Jim Harter. Clear wood engravings present, in extremely lifelike poses, over 1,000 species of animals. One of the most extensive pictorial sourcebooks of its kind. Captions. Index. 284pp. 9 × 12.
23766-4 Pa. $9.95

OBELISTS FLY HIGH, C. Daly King. Masterpiece of American detective fiction, long out of print, involves murder on a 1935 transcontinental flight—"a very thrilling story"—NY Times. Unabridged and unaltered republication of the edition published by William Collins Sons & Co. Ltd., London, 1935. 288pp. 5⅜ × 8½. (Available in U.S. only) 25036-9 Pa. $5.95

VICTORIAN AND EDWARDIAN FASHION: A Photographic Survey, Alison Gernsheim. First fashion history completely illustrated by contemporary photographs. Full text plus 235 photos, 1840–1914, in which many celebrities appear. 240pp. 6½ × 9¼. 24205-6 Pa. $6.95

THE ART OF THE FRENCH ILLUSTRATED BOOK, 1700–1914, Gordon N. Ray. Over 630 superb book illustrations by Fragonard, Delacroix, Daumier, Doré, Grandville, Manet, Mucha, Steinlen, Toulouse-Lautrec and many others. Preface. Introduction. 633 halftones. Indices of artists, authors & titles, binders and provenances. Appendices. Bibliography. 608pp. 8⅜ × 11¼. 25086-5 Pa. $24.95

THE WONDERFUL WIZARD OF OZ, L. Frank Baum. Facsimile in full color of America's finest children's classic. 143 illustrations by W. W. Denslow. 267pp. 5⅜ × 8½. 20691-2 Pa. $7.95

FRONTIERS OF MODERN PHYSICS: New Perspectives on Cosmology, Relativity, Black Holes and Extraterrestrial Intelligence, Tony Rothman, et al. For the intelligent layman. Subjects include: cosmological models of the universe; black holes; the neutrino; the search for extraterrestrial intelligence. Introduction. 46 black-and-white illustrations. 192pp. 5⅜ × 8½. 24587-X Pa. $7.95

THE FRIENDLY STARS, Martha Evans Martin & Donald Howard Menzel. Classic text marshalls the stars together in an engaging, non-technical survey, presenting them as sources of beauty in night sky. 23 illustrations. Foreword. 2 star charts. Index. 147pp. 5⅜ × 8½. 21099-5 Pa. $3.95

FADS AND FALLACIES IN THE NAME OF SCIENCE, Martin Gardner. Fair, witty appraisal of cranks, quacks, and quackeries of science and pseudoscience: hollow earth, Velikovsky, orgone energy, Dianetics, flying saucers, Bridey Murphy, food and medical fads, etc. Revised, expanded In the Name of Science. "A very able and even-tempered presentation."—The New Yorker. 363pp. 5⅜ × 8.
20394-8 Pa. $6.95

ANCIENT EGYPT: ITS CULTURE AND HISTORY, J. E Manchip White. From pre-dynastics through Ptolemies: society, history, political structure, religion, daily life, literature, cultural heritage. 48 plates. 217pp. 5⅜ × 8½. 22548-8 Pa. $5.95

SIR HARRY HOTSPUR OF HUMBLETHWAITE, Anthony Trollope. Incisive, unconventional psychological study of a conflict between a wealthy baronet, his idealistic daughter, and their scapegrace cousin. The 1870 novel in its first inexpensive edition in years. 250pp. 5⅜ × 8½. 24953-0 Pa. $5.95

LASERS AND HOLOGRAPHY, Winston E. Kock. Sound introduction to burgeoning field, expanded (1981) for second edition. Wave patterns, coherence, lasers, diffraction, zone plates, properties of holograms, recent advances. 84 illustrations. 160pp. 5⅜ × 8¼. (Except in United Kingdom) 24041-X Pa. $3.95

INTRODUCTION TO ARTIFICIAL INTELLIGENCE: SECOND, EN-LARGED EDITION, Philip C. Jackson, Jr. Comprehensive survey of artificial intelligence—the study of how machines (computers) can be made to act intelligently. Includes introductory and advanced material. Extensive notes updating the main text. 132 black-and-white illustrations. 512pp. 5⅜ × 8½. 24864-X Pa. $8.95

HISTORY OF INDIAN AND INDONESIAN ART, Ananda K. Coomaraswamy. Over 400 illustrations illuminate classic study of Indian art from earliest Harappa finds to early 20th century. Provides philosophical, religious and social insights. 304pp. 6⅜ × 9⅜. 25005-9 Pa. $9.95

THE GOLEM, Gustav Meyrink. Most famous supernatural novel in modern European literature, set in Ghetto of Old Prague around 1890. Compelling story of mystical experiences, strange transformations, profound terror. 13 black-and-white illustrations. 224pp. 5⅜ × 8½. (Available in U.S. only) 25025-3 Pa. $6.95

PICTORIAL ENCYCLOPEDIA OF HISTORIC ARCHITECTURAL PLANS, DETAILS AND ELEMENTS: With 1,880 Line Drawings of Arches, Domes, Doorways, Facades, Gables, Windows, etc., John Theodore Haneman. Sourcebook of inspiration for architects, designers, others. Bibliography. Captions. 141pp. 9 × 12. 24605-1 Pa. $7.95

BENCHLEY LOST AND FOUND, Robert Benchley. Finest humor from early 30's, about pet peeves, child psychologists, post office and others. Mostly unavailable elsewhere. 73 illustrations by Peter Arno and others. 183pp. 5⅜ × 8½. 22410-4 Pa. $4.95

ERTÉ GRAPHICS, Erté. Collection of striking color graphics: *Seasons, Alphabet, Numerals, Aces* and *Precious Stones.* 50 plates, including 4 on covers. 48pp. 9⅜ × 12¼. 23580-7 Pa. $7.95

THE JOURNAL OF HENRY D. THOREAU, edited by Bradford Torrey, F. H. Allen. Complete reprinting of 14 volumes, 1837–61, over two million words; the sourcebooks for *Walden,* etc. Definitive. All original sketches, plus 75 photographs. 1,804pp. 8½ × 12¼. 20312-3, 20313-1 Cloth., Two-vol. set $120.00

CASTLES: THEIR CONSTRUCTION AND HISTORY, Sidney Toy. Traces castle development from ancient roots. Nearly 200 photographs and drawings illustrate moats, keeps, baileys, many other features. Caernarvon, Dover Castles, Hadrian's Wall, Tower of London, dozens more. 256pp. 5⅜ × 8¼. 24898-4 Pa. $6.95

AMERICAN CLIPPER SHIPS: 1833–1858, Octavius T. Howe & Frederick C. Matthews. Fully-illustrated, encyclopedic review of 352 clipper ships from the period of America's greatest maritime supremacy. Introduction. 109 halftones. 5 black-and-white line illustrations. Index. Total of 928pp. 5⅜ × 8½.
25115-2, 25116-0 Pa., Two-vol. set $17.90

TOWARDS A NEW ARCHITECTURE, Le Corbusier. Pioneering manifesto by great architect, near legendary founder of "International School." Technical and aesthetic theories, views on industry, economics, relation of form to function, "mass-production spirit," much more. Profusely illustrated. Unabridged translation of 13th French edition. Introduction by Frederick Etchells. 320pp. 6⅛ × 9¼. (Available in U.S. only)
25023-7 Pa. $8.95

THE BOOK OF KELLS, edited by Blanche Cirker. Inexpensive collection of 32 full-color, full-page plates from the greatest illuminated manuscript of the Middle Ages, painstakingly reproduced from rare facsimile edition. Publisher's Note. Captions. 32pp. 9⅜ × 12¼.
24345-1 Pa. $4.95

BEST SCIENCE FICTION STORIES OF H. G. WELLS, H. G. Wells. Full novel *The Invisible Man,* plus 17 short stories: "The Crystal Egg," "Aepyornis Island," "The Strange Orchid," etc. 303pp. 5⅜ × 8½. (Available in U.S. only)
21531-8 Pa. $6.95

AMERICAN SAILING SHIPS: Their Plans and History, Charles G. Davis. Photos, construction details of schooners, frigates, clippers, other sailcraft of 18th to early 20th centuries—plus entertaining discourse on design, rigging, nautical lore, much more. 137 black-and-white illustrations. 240pp. 6⅛ × 9¼.
24658-2 Pa. $6.95

ENTERTAINING MATHEMATICAL PUZZLES, Martin Gardner. Selection of author's favorite conundrums involving arithmetic, money, speed, etc., with lively commentary. Complete solutions. 112pp. 5⅜ × 8½.
25211-6 Pa. $2.95

THE WILL TO BELIEVE, HUMAN IMMORTALITY, William James. Two books bound together. Effect of irrational on logical, and arguments for human immortality. 402pp. 5⅜ × 8½.
20291-7 Pa. $7.95

THE HAUNTED MONASTERY and THE CHINESE MAZE MURDERS, Robert Van Gulik. 2 full novels by Van Gulik continue adventures of Judge Dee and his companions. An evil Taoist monastery, seemingly supernatural events; overgrown topiary maze that hides strange crimes. Set in 7th-century China. 27 illustrations. 328pp. 5⅜ × 8½.
23502-5 Pa. $6.95

CELEBRATED CASES OF JUDGE DEE (DEE GOONG AN), translated by Robert Van Gulik. Authentic 18th-century Chinese detective novel; Dee and associates solve three interlocked cases. Led to Van Gulik's own stories with same characters. Extensive introduction. 9 illustrations. 237pp. 5⅜ × 8½.
23337-5 Pa. $4.95

Prices subject to change without notice.

Available at your book dealer or write for free catalog to Dept. GI, Dover Publications, Inc., 31 East 2nd St., Mineola, N.Y. 11501. Dover publishes more than 175 books each year on science, elementary and advanced mathematics, biology, music, art, literary history, social sciences and other areas.